Shepherds

Shepherds

The Believer's Outline of Theology

DANIEL C. FREDERICKS

WIPF & STOCK · Eugene, Oregon

SHEPHERDS
The Believer's Outline of Theology

Copyright © 2017 Daniel C. Fredericks,. All rights reserved. Except for brief quotations in critical publications or reviews, no part of this book may be reproduced in any manner without prior written permission from the publisher. Write: Permissions, Wipf and Stock Publishers, 199 W. 8th Ave., Suite 3, Eugene, OR 97401.

Wipf & Stock
An Imprint of Wipf and Stock Publishers
199 W. 8th Ave., Suite 3
Eugene, OR 97401

www.wipfandstock.com

PAPERBACK ISBN: 978-1-5326-0603-8
HARDCOVER ISBN: 978-1-5326-0605-2
EBOOK ISBN: 978-1-5326-0604-5

Manufactured in the U.S.A.   JUNE 7, 2017

Dedicated to my children, Autumn, Ryan, Justin, and Sean, for whom I want to improve as a shepherd.

Contents

Preface | ix
Acknowledgments | xi

1 God's Eternal Design | 1
2 God Is Our Shepherd | 24
3 God's Shepherding Commission | 34
4 Providing the Shepherds | 47
5 Christ's Shepherding Commission | 66
6 Shepherding Spirits | 81
7 Shepherding Nature | 98
8 Shepherding Humanity | 113
9 Shepherding the Lord's People | 150
10 Shepherding the Believer | 184
11 Shepherding Essentials | 224
12 God's Commandments for Shepherding | 243
13 God's Wisdom for Shepherding | 287
14 Conclusion | 326

Preface

SHEPHERDS IS WRITTEN TO be an example of a theology that is pervasive in its explanation of how God has created reality to operate according to a single eternal design. *Shepherds* shows specifically how that eternal design includes each part of God's creation: each believer, each family, each church, each community, each people, humanity at large, as well as nature and the spirits.

However, this theology would not be owned by the systematic, biblical, or practical theological guilds for a number of reasons. Those valuable theological disciplines have been helpful in framing this theology, but in the end, they cannot contain it within their conventional frameworks. Instead, a new paradigm is offered here that traverses systematic, biblical and practical theology while providing a theology of history.

I have published before in typical academic style, providing copious footnotes and pointed comments about competing positions. But that is not the nature of this study. So, one will not find multiple discussions of various views on a single subject with opposing or confirming voices footnoted. Instead, *Shepherds* is written so believers can evaluate the broadest theological truths on the basis of their own ability to read the Scriptures for themselves first, then interpret them.

This study highly trusts in the clarity of God's revelation to us. By and large his Word is easy to read and understand. So I let the Testaments speak for themselves to their basic and recurrent themes. This study also trusts highly in the continuity of the Testaments. Sure, some discontinuities exist between them, but this study accentuates the consistency of the Testaments, both of which reveal how God shepherds his creation and how creation has worked with (or against) him in his eternal design.

Admittedly, such an ordinary word as 'shepherd' is a jarring contrast to the grand theological words of the academic and theological dictionaries; so it is understandable if one questions the word's adequacy. But please be patient as we develop the possibilities which lay behind this metaphor. After all, it is no different than other terms and analogies on which all theologies are built.

Preface

This book is only an outline which leaves much of the commentary for you and the footnotes to supply between the lines. In this sense, the footnotes become the most important part of this theology since Scripture alone carries the final and precise truth. My hundreds of pages of comments are modest footnotes to the authoritative Word which is referenced at the bottom of these following pages.

Acknowledgments

WHAT BETTER CO-WORKERS ARE there than friends, scholars and students? I am indebted to Dr. John Song and Dr. Gary Cockerill for their close reading of the manuscript and many recommendations necessary for its conceptual improvements. They have blessed and corrected me toward a more precise approach to the subject. My friend and colleague, Rose Mary Foncree has made my thoughts more intelligible, always disciplining me in my syntax and phrasing. I am grateful to my brilliant student, Corina Cater, for helpful recommendations on phrasing and perfecting the footnotes to support the main thoughts of this Believer's Outline of Theology.

1

God's Eternal Design

WE ARE BUSY PEOPLE. We move from one realm of life to another quickly and frequently each day. Some realms engage our thoughts and actions simultaneously.

> We participate in spiritual wars in *heavenly* places;
> We look into the limitless *cosmos* with awe;
> We watch the *global* news with serious concern;
> We support missionaries around the *world*;
> We vote for leaders who direct our *nation*;
> We serve and guide our local *communities*;
> We give our Spiritual gifts to our *church*;
> We work productively in the *marketplace*;
> We shepherd our *families*, near and far;
> We manage our private *thoughts* and *emotions*.

What is it that gives these apparent unrelated fragments in life any unified purpose and meaning? Speaking for myself, I often forget that God's eternal design gives the fullest meaning and direction to my each and every experience within these realms of life. His design unifies every one of my many daily activities into one explanation of who I am and what my purpose is.

Our experiences, privileges, challenges and responsibilities as citizens of God's kingdom only make sense when they are understood and are performed from within the Lord's unified perspective, that is, his "eternal design." What value and what meaning do all of our successes and challenges have? What meaning and value do the successes and challenges of every individual across the world have? Are they merely unrelated activities from here and there, now and then? Should we be satisfied with living lives made up of mere fragments of thoughts and efforts, too many to count, much less to analyze? Or do they all contribute to a single *eternal design* created by God?

While writing these two paragraphs on a plane from Atlanta to Minneapolis, the lady in the seat next to me asked to read what I was writing. After reading it she said,

"I'll tell you what I think unifies all parts of my life." I said, "Oh, what is that?" And she said, "God." We celebrated our agreement and then went a step further to discuss *how* God unifies all of our thoughts and activities in our life. That is what this book is about. What is it in God's nature and in his relationship with us that makes sense out of each and everything we do?

God could have let us muddle through our life without seeing our activities and experiences as an integrated whole; but graciously, the Lord's design includes our daily events and our activities: all of our trials, joys, failures, and successes. God has built into creation an eternal design, and our success in living a faithful life depends on our understanding that design and living in harmony with it.

WE ALWAYS DESIGN

We design every moment we live because we want our lives to be the least chaotic as possible. And we are happy when our designs work and our life is less hectic and less tragic. Designing can lead to success and peace. We design incessantly, and we will continue to design throughout eternity.

> We design philosophies and theologies about reality and how to manage it.
> We design dreams while asleep with plots, persons, landscapes and dialogue.
> We design our homes—what goes where and for what purpose.
> We design art with color and shapes to communicate creatively.
> We design machines for easier living and for battling enemies.
> We design the sentences we speak and write to others.
> We design our daily schedules, activities and priorities.
> We design our daily wardrobe so our clothes "go together."
> We design sounds into music.

Every culture designs these things and countless others. We design because we were created with the instinct and ability to design and to act on those designs. The diversity with which societies and civilizations develop these designs is a testament to human creativity, wisdom, and adaptability to the climate, geography and surrounding flora and fauna. The development of civilizations is possible because of the human ability to design ideas, visions, plans and systems and then to build infrastructures and superstructures consistent with those designs. The beauty of each civilization is unique because its designs are diverse for its attire, architecture, music, language, cuisine, polity, currency, occupations, and pastimes. There are countless cultural customs around the world that contribute to a civilization's overall cultural design which sustains adequate stability and security.

The opposite of design is chaos, and individuals and societies are destroyed by it. If our sentences are not designed our communication is incoherent. If our daily schedules are not designed our priorities are squelched, and our time is squandered. If homes are not designed they sag and collapse. If music is not designed, it is simply noise. If mechanisms are not designed we have to work harder and longer. If government is not designed a society is subjected to anarchy or a capricious ruler. If the cosmos had not been designed it would have no physical laws to sustain it.

God created an orderly creation, perfect in harmony and beauty. But from the start, Satan has sought to destroy the Lord's perfect creation by undermining its order and causing dissension and ugly turmoil. It is Satan's own kingdom design. Satan does not wait for destruction to happen; he does everything he can to accelerate and intensify it. If he can make the spirits to be the focus of a culture's worldview, he will draw its society into an openly demonic realm. If he can make nature the focus of a culture's worldview, he will drive a society to worship creation and idols rather than the Creator. If he can make the society the focus of a culture's worldview he will create a fascist state. If he can make the individual the focus of a culture's worldview, he will dissolve that society by selfishness and incivility.

GOD DESIGNS HIS EVERLASTING CREATION

Speaking more positively, the reason we have such a drive to design is that we are created to be like God, and he is the Grand Designer. He is the Creator who makes and sustains everything according to his design. And once he has set his mind on something, he pursues it in an infinite way.

> No purpose of yours can be stopped. Job 42:2
>
> The Lord's plan stands firmly forever . . . to all generations. Ps 33:11
>
> Your works are wonderful, faithful, true and according to your ancient plans. Isa 25:1
>
> From the beginning I announced the end, and I announced from antiquity what has not happened yet. My purpose will be accomplished since I do whatever I wish. Isa 46:9–10[1]

And the Lord's plans are wonderfully *personal* for each of us. Wonderful in the glorious responsibilities we each have only begun to fulfill in this life. Personal in that each individual has a unique kingdom role to play in God's eternal design.

> Inherit the Kingdom which my Father has prepared for you from creation. Matt. 25:34
>
> He chose us before creation to be holy and blameless in Christ. Eph. 1:3–4

---

1. Also, Jer 4:28; 23:20; 30:24; Lam 2:17

God has created an eternal creation, so his design for his creation is eternal too. But it is far more personal for him than that. One of his own personal attributes is his eternality, so his eternal nature gives both creation and its design his attribute of eternality. God is eternal, back into the past, and forward into the endless future.

eternity past ◄──────────── God ────────────► eternity

But his creation and its design is eternal only into the future.

God's Eternal Design

Creation ●──── God shepherds shepherding creation by his blessings ────► eternity

SO, WHAT IS GOD'S ETERNAL DESIGN?

So what is this eternal design? I will try to state the eternal design in the simplest and fewest terms to make a statement that is adequate to such a large idea. First, God has built his own attributes into his creation so that it will reflect who he is in his nature and his deeds. One of those attributes is his *shepherding* character, and this single characteristic of God employs all of his other attributes for the purpose of shepherding. So, a foundational truth is that *God Shepherds*. This is the source of the eternal design, but it is not all of it. Because creation expresses the Creator's nature and his deeds, it is not surprising that creation shepherds too. So God created a *Shepherding Creation*. The eternal design then, simply put is, *God Shepherds Shepherding Creation*.

There may be several reasons why this statement of an eternal design would sound inadequate. Perhaps we would be more comfortable with words of greater grandeur with more syllables and at least one of the words ending in "–ological." Good questions might be . . .

> God is far more than a shepherd, isn't he?
> Who shepherds these days anyway?
> Shepherds are too meek and lowly, are they not?
> Only humans have been shepherds, not creation, right?

However, please indulge me for the next several pages to see if shepherding does not begin to summarize everything God has done and what creation has been designed to do under his powerful, loving care.

One might suggest other words and phrases to describe an eternal design by God. There are many highly important ideas about God and his relationship with his creation that are often offered as the best description of the totality of God's design: Salvation, Sovereignty, Promises, Covenants, God's Glory, Christ's Kingdom, etc. All of these, and more, are foundational truths about God and his relationship with reality. But none are able to describe God's eternal nature and actions, and his creation's nature and actions most completely and as accurately as "Shepherding" in all its depth of meaning. At the risk of waiting too long, the topic of God's kingdom will be discussed at some length in chapter 5, though we will refer to the Kingdom a few times before then.

The eternal design is not based on abstract *intentions* of God alone; it is based more basically on his *nature* than anything else. And his nature is not simply to *be*, or simply to design. His nature is to *act* consistently with his intentions and design, to aggressively shepherd his creation in powerful and gracious ways. Since the Lord created reality to reflect his nature, his creation will reflect his eternal shepherding nature *and activity*. In the case of the natural world, he has designed it to shepherd by building into nature its physical laws. In the case of humanity, he has designed and revealed the moral standards by which we act as shepherds in his eternal design. He expects us to act in the same ways that he does himself—we are to be like God in every feasible way. He himself exemplifies these moral standards by how he graciously and patiently shepherds us. We in turn are expected to reflect God's shepherding attributes in our loving actions and service to the rest of his creation.

The purpose for this eternal design is not simply to "glorify" himself; God's purpose for the eternal design is to bless something else with the glory he has. Creation's glory is not infinite like God's, nor is it perfect like God's, but it reflects his glory in wonderful ways. So, reality was created to receive his eternal blessings and reflect his nature by blessing others. Yes, we certainly want to recognize and extol his glory, but he does not need that. His design is that we conform to his image in ever greater ways by pursuing His glory which he wants and created us to share.

In almost every way possible, the Lord wants to share his shepherding nature, his revelation, his kingdom and his glory with us. Then he wants us to pass these on to his creation through his numerous and various shepherding *chains*. Yes, even his glory he shares with us to share with others. True, he says, "I will not give my glory to another, or my praise to idols" (Isa 42:8), but he is referring to other gods whom the nations, and even Israel at times worshipped. But he will share his glory with us, his privileged sons and daughters, as Paul promised and as Peter agreed.

> We share in his sufferings so that we will also share in his glory. Rom 8:17

> When the High Shepherd appears, you will receive the unfading crown of glory. 1 Pet 5:4[2]

God's eternal design includes a shepherding sequence, a shepherding "chain" that starts with him as the shepherd of all creation. We start then with "God shepherds . . . creation." But then we have to move on to how creation shepherds too—"God shepherds *shepherding* creation." God shepherds his creation and then, in turn, creation

---

2. Also, 1 Thess 2:12; 2 Thess 2:14; 1 Pet 5:1

shepherds itself. Not that creation shepherds apart from God; on the contrary, creation can only shepherd itself by the Lord's example, by his laws and by his power.

The few pages that follow begin to explain the eternal shepherding chain where God shepherds his creation and then expects creation to shepherd too. We will appreciate increasingly how God shepherds (1) the world of the spirits, (2) nature, (3) the peoples, (4) his people, and (5) the individual believer. And, we will see how these five realms, angels, nature, the peoples, his people and the individual believer are to shepherd one another as God shepherds them.

The Biblical View of Shepherding

"Shepherding" is the Old and New Testament objective of God and his people and is discussed in literal terms of "shepherds," "sheep," "flock" and "pasture" throughout both Testaments. His and our shepherding is the precise subject of many passages in the Bible, not just the couple that are so precious in our memories like Psalm 23 and John 10. We will look at some of these in detail in our next chapter, and we will see the importance of God's and humanity's shepherding in his biblical message about his eternal design. But even beyond the literal references to shepherding, the methods and results of shepherding are explicit throughout the Testaments.

The word and concept of God as a "shepherd" is used often in the Bible because it best describes God's authority, actions and *heart* in his relationship with his creation. He is certainly the "king," the "sovereign Lord" of all reality. Innumerable books, theologies and sermons over the past twenty centuries are available to explain the Lord's glorious role as king and sovereign. So it could be correct to state the eternal design as "Sovereign God rules sovereign creation" or "God rules ruling creation" as long as we understand a couple of things: first, that creation's sovereignty is dwarfed infinitely by the Lord's sovereignty. Even then, phrasing the Lord's eternal design in terms of "kingship" or "sovereignty" does not reflect the *heart* of God and the richness of how he rules as creation's Shepherd.

Both "king" and "shepherd" refer to God's sovereignty. But the practical, caring functions of a shepherd who perfectly blesses, delivers and disciplines are not readily associated with ruling kings. They should be, but very unfortunately for creation, they are not. Good kings would shepherd their kingdom lovingly and with a balance of strength, compassion and justice; it is just that they seldom do. So when referring to the Lord's eternal design, "to shepherd" is preferred rather than "to rule" or "to be sovereign." If we rule like God rules we will be shepherds, unlike the seen and unseen rulers of this world whose practice is to rule selfishly through oppression and abuse.

Shepherding is not a warm and cozy profession. It is not a quiet and sleepy job. It is not all harps under fig trees with a lamb nearby to pet. Shepherding takes intense concentration and persistent management of all that is among and around the sheep. Shepherding can be misunderstood and limited to sentimental portrayals of an effeminate Jesus holding a cute lamb. This stereotype of a shepherd misrepresents the demanding and sobering responsibilities of a good shepherd. Strong discipline and judgment is an important part of what it means to be a shepherd. The greatest Old Testament shepherd was of course David, the shepherd who killed Goliath to defend God's sheep of Israel, just as he had killed the bear and lion to protect his father's sheep. David judged the giant for his arrogant insults against the Lord with the same slingshot he used to ward off the beasts of prey from his father's flock.

The Shepherding Roles: Bless, Deliver, and Discipline

Shepherds *bless* their flock by leading it for pleasant and productive purposes, providing food, water and resting places. But the shepherd also *delivers* the sheep when they wander. Yet, even if sheep stay put within the fold, the shepherd delivers the lamb from wild predators and violent thieves. One more thing the shepherd does: he *disciplines*. There is the discipline that the sheep need; it prods them to obey the shepherd so they will remain safe and calm. But the other side of discipline brings judgment against the enemies of the sheep who intimidate, injure, steal and kill them. Shepherding then, includes blessing, delivering and disciplining. It is not a placid job of finding faces in the clouds while the sheep bleat and bah. It is a demanding vocation that requires courage, sacrifice, strength, persistence and loving, intelligent care.

So we should not be confused nor try to protect the Lord from his fullest shepherding reputation in the Bible. We need to be teachable enough to accept the following ominous truth about our true Shepherd:

> Consider the kindness and severity of God;
> to the fallen, severity,
> but to you, God's kindness! Rom. 11:22

The New Testament highlights Jesus' intense shepherding: "The male child was born to *shepherd*[3] the nations with a rod of iron." Shepherding involves subduing what surrounds the sheep for their blessing, deliverance and discipline while judging forcefully anything that threatens them.

As we have said, the three basic elements of God's shepherding are blessing, deliverance and discipline. Isaiah 33:22 rolls these three into one verse:

> The Lord is our judge;
> the Lord is our lawgiver;
> the Lord is our king; he will save us.

It is a *blessing* that the Lord instructs us through his laws and wisdom instructions in the Testaments. He is our delivering *savior,* and he is our disciplining *judge.* The Lord

---

3. Rev 12:5; this Greek word means "shepherd," though Bible versions imprecisely translate the word as "rule."

tells the Israelites in just a few words in Exodus 34:6–7 what his vast shepherding heart is like:

> I, the Lord God am compassionate and gracious, slow to anger,
>> full of love, care and faithfulness for thousands,
>>> forgiving iniquity, rebellion and sin,
>>>> but not letting the guilty go unpunished.

He *blesses* through his compassion, grace, patience, love, care, and faithfulness. He *delivers* from physical and emotional dangers as well as from sin. He will patiently *discipline* his sheep so they will be more obedient and successful. But he will also apply the other side of discipline—he will *judge* the unforgiven, the wicked person.

Just a word about "blessing" and how I will use it. In one sense all that God does is a blessing since it is done from his loving and just heart. It is a blessing to be delivered, even to be disciplined. However, when he says the following to you and me, it is a blessing:

> Good job, good and faithful servant. You have been faithful with a few things so I will put you in charge of much more. Experience your master's joy over you. Matt. 25:23

This is not a statement of deliverance or discipline. It is God's kind act of promotion within his kingdom. Another example of blessing, as we will use the word, is that the Lord always intended to keep us fed and secure from the very beginning. That is his blessing to us. He delivers and disciplines us only now because we are prone to wander and sin since the Fall in Eden. God will bless us forever, but he will no longer deliver or discipline us throughout eternity since there will be no adversity, sin or need for judgment or discipline in the age to come.

We too can bless others: a smile or compliment does not deliver them from anything nor does it discipline them for any wrongdoing. A mother nourishes her infant, blessing the child with caresses and sustenance. She does not deliver the child from anything but a natural hunger. It is not an urgent, saving intervention. It obviously is not disciplinary either. Works of art are examples of blessing too. They may not deliver or discipline, but they bless in their beauty or there nudging us to see things from a different perspective. So I will use the term "blessing" for any act of kindness which is not deliverance or discipline, like a gift, a song, an affirming nod, a gesture that brings further joy, humor, satisfaction, or encouragement.

Another word, but this time about "discipline" and "judgement." I do not use these terms synonymously, assuming they are one and the same. Discipline is the more general term and judgment refers to a type of discipline. For our purposes in this study, "discipline" intends to redeem the one disciplined. On the other hand, "judgment" is a more final and penalizing act of discipline. For instance, I want the Lord's discipline to prod me toward reflecting his perfect image more faithfully. I do not

God's Eternal Design

want his judgment against me where the wages of sin is everlasting death. Or consider this: we want the Lord to discipline the wicked so they might redirect their steps toward conversion. But we also want God's judgment against the wicked who persecute, torture, and martyr our brothers and sisters. At least this is the prayer of the martyrs in Revelation.[4]

Combined, these shepherding functions of blessing, deliverance, and discipline are what constitute God's relationship with his whole creation: spirits, nature, and humanity. But further, these shepherding functions are the appropriate way for the spirits, nature, and humanity to shepherd in every era of history, on every area on the globe, and by every size of human social units. What I mean by "social unit" is any level of human authority, like national governments, community authorities, workplace administrators, religious leaders, family heads and the individual person. Every social unit is to shepherd as the Lord shepherds. To simply say they are all to "rule" is inadequate in our fallen world. Ruling has not been a problem for humanity in any era or area. All have been created with God's sovereign nature and so we all rule. But as a race, we do not rule as the Shepherd rules, with a heart for blessing, delivering and disciplining in loving and edifying ways. On the contrary, humanity has shepherded poorly: neglecting, abusing and acting unjustly.

As believers, we trust the Testaments when they honor the Lord's thorough and flawless shepherding: "God has made everything beautiful in its time" (Eccl 3:11), and "God works everything together for good" (Rom 8:28). So, these three shepherding roles will help us understand his perfect and beautiful ways—how they are beautiful and good, and how they serve as standards for us so we will beautify our lives and the lives of others.

Each of these shepherding roles is related to the other, as this simple diagram below illustrates. They rarely stand alone and often all three are done simultaneously though they are not the same thing. Blessing, deliverance and discipline are nearly always combined in some way by the Lord and by his creation which shepherds like him—ways which God designs and ways which we design. However, we will not fully know these complexities and their results until New Earth when the Lord will reveal all that we accomplished with him in restoring the world as his shepherds. The Lord combines his blessings, deliverances and discipline by his unfathomable wisdom, and he often folds them mysteriously into his perfect strategies in his eternal design.

---

4. Rev 6:9–11; 18:20–24

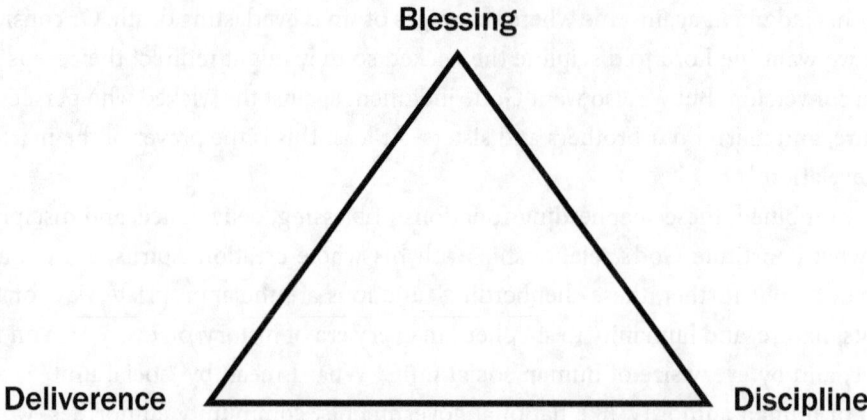

Everything God does is good and perfect, so every act toward his creation is a blessing. His deliverances and discipline are blessings as well. Though his discipline may not be considered a blessing by those who deserve discipline or judgment, it is a blessing to those who are no longer afflicted and are avenged by the Lord's judgment against sin and sinners. Also, believers appreciate that God's discipline of them is a blessing that steers us toward righteousness, putting us back on track toward wise and productive management of our lives. "Discipline at the time is painful, not pleasant; but those trained by discipline reap the fruit of peace and righteousness" (Heb. 12:11).[5]

The Lord may choose to measure his blessings, deliverances or discipline in any way he pleases. He may forgive and deliver up to a point but allow a portion of discipline still to remain and be felt. He may judge but then relax the judgment short of what pure justice would demand. Both of these situations show his wise grace.

Christ's Role in the Eternal Design

We have introduced the eternal design as having a shepherding "chain" of responsibility. A profound shepherding sequence is outlined in the New Testament . . .

> The Father shepherds his Son,
> > then the Son shepherd his disciples,
> > > then the disciples shepherd church leaders,
> > > > then the church leaders shepherd their sheep in their church,
> > > > > then parents in the church are to shepherd their children,
> > > > > > and employers are to shepherd their employees.

This chain shows a depth to the shepherding responsibilities within the church as a social unit. But there are many more shepherding sequences that show God's eternal design. That's why it's *the* design: it serves to frame every action of creation and humanity—in all eras and areas of history.

5. Pss 66:10–12; 89:30–34; Heb. 12:5–10

God arrived in human form to epitomize his own image within a human person. We carry that image too, but when Jesus Christ came as a human he modeled how a true image of God shepherds in a way never seen before.

What we mean by God's image within us will be discussed more in chapter 11, but to be short until then, these are the attributes of God that all humans carry. God's *emotions* are a standard for ours. For example, God is love, and he so loved the world that he gave us his Son! God's perfect *righteousness* is an attribute he expects humanity to copy as well. It is the standard by which he blesses, delivers and judges his creation. Human *creativity* also mirrors the nature of God. His invention and maintenance of the world started and continues as a protracted series of creative acts. Though the Lord is *all*-powerful, we are expected to apply our all of our limited power to his eternal design. *Transcending space and time* is not an attribute we share with God in a way similar to his other attributes. Yet the Lord has put the sense of eternity within us (Eccl 3:11) and we do have eternal life. The Lord's *complexity* is shown by his knowledge of absolutely everything. His complexity is not due to his knowledge alone however. He *acts* wisely, responding to everything he knows, which again, is everything. We are responsible to be as knowledgeable as possible so we can pray and act effectively as God's shepherding partners. The *sovereignty* of God is his attribute that combines and applies all his other attributes when shepherding his creation. So, our sovereignty as shepherds also depends on perfecting our godly attributes. Finally, God's *holiness* and *glory* are the summation of all of his attributes—together, his attributes compose the total nature of God which is overwhelming in its infiniteness.

Adam and Eve were told that their role in creation was to subdue, or shepherd, creation. That obviously did not work out well. That required Christ to come as the human who could begin to shepherd the earth as it should have been shepherded from the start. Christ, as human, yet the exact image of God, was commissioned by the Father to conquer, recapture and shepherd the world as the Trinity had designed it to be shepherded. Though we are God's sons and daughters with only a broken image of our Father within us, we still must shepherd as God's unbroken, perfect Son shepherds. That's the eternal design.

The eternal design is based on God's love and respect for his creation. The shepherding chain is motivated by love: Father loves Jesus => Jesus loves and died for us => We love and shepherd others. The perfect Son and Shepherd describes this critical shepherding chain:

> Just as the Father has loved Me, I have also loved you, so live in my love. If you keep my commandments you will live in my love just like I have kept my Father's commandments and live in his love . . . This is my commandment; love each other just like I have loved you. John 15:9-10, 12

This is the eternal design—God shepherds shepherding creation, including humanity.

Our Role in the Eternal Design

When the Kingdom was passed from the Father to the Son and then to us, another shepherding chain was formed within the eternal design. Jesus told his twelve disciples, "Just as my Father has given me a kingdom, I give you one . . . you will sit on thrones judging the twelve tribes."[6] But not only will the disciples inherit and rule the Kingdom, you and I will too. Jesus said he will give us authority over the nations, the authority his Father gave to him: "I will give authority over the nations to anyone who does my will until the end, like I have received authority from My Father" (Rev 2:26–27). Jesus repeated this shepherding chain in Revelation: "I will allow anyone who conquers to sit with me on my throne, since I also conquered and sat on my Father's throne with him" (Rev 3:21). God the Father graces the Son to sit on the Father's throne, and Jesus invites us to sit there too! God allows us, out of his shepherding love, to reign with him as his under-shepherds. Paul confirms this fact: "Everything is yours, you are Christ's and Christ is God's" (1 Cor 3:22–23).

Since we are partners in God's eternal design, and since we are made in his image and are filled with his Spirit, we can now shepherd according to his heart and priorities. It is not because God is incapable of doing anything and everything himself; it is because his eternal design includes us as partners. We bless, deliver and discipline in our own shepherding of creation within God's, and now our kingdom, using his biblical and spiritual wisdom. For instance, Proverbs 10:21 teaches that "The mouth of the righteous tends to many others." The Hebrew word used here is *rāyāh*, literally, "to tend," a word associated with a shepherd tending the sheep. Wisdom that comes from our mouths is just one way we shepherd others toward truth, righteousness and success; it is also a way we wisely discipline others in timely ways.

Several other shepherding chains are found in Scripture. Here are just a few examples:

> The Father will forgive us as we have forgiven others.[7]
>
> The Father sends Jesus so Jesus sends his apostles into the world.[8] John 17:18
>
> The Father gives life to the Son so the Son gives us life. John 6:57
>
> Jesus washes the disciples feet so they are to wash each other's feet. John 13:14–15
>
> Jesus feeds the disciples fish so they are to feed Jesus' sheep. John 21:12–13, 15–17
>
> The Father comforts us so we can comfort others. 2 Cor 1:3–4

---

6. Luke 22:29–30; also, Matt 25:34
7. Matt 6:12; Luke 11:4
8. Matt 28:19–20 // Mark 16:15; John 20:21

Another example of God's shepherding chain is found in Revelation 1:1. The whole book of Revelation is the result of at least five links of communication which the Lord designed to reveal his glorious Word to the world:

> God gives the revelation to Jesus who
> > then gives the revelation to an angel who
> > > then gives the revelation to John who
> > > > then writes the revelation to others who
> > > > > then tell the revelation to the world.

GOD'S PARENTHETICAL DESIGN

Though the Lord shepherds creation faithfully, humanity has turned its back and pursued its own selfish and self-destructive direction. It is not just that Adam and Eve did this; we each do it every day. Rather than shepherding and reflecting God's attributes, we often reflect the anti-shepherding attributes of the Enemy. This destructive alliance of humanity and Satan is the current state of our fallen world and fallen human nature. But this diabolical condition is only a relatively short *parenthesis* in human history. The perfectly created world of Adam and Eve will be re-perfected when the Lord creates the *eternal* New Earth. For us as believers this means something distinctive; we will return to humanity's original moral perfection and glory based on the perfect image of God within us: both in nature and in deed.

It is a marvelous fact that Jesus came to save sinners, nothing can diminish that. But we are not saved by his blood just to be saved from sin. We are saved for a further purpose, for nothing less than the eternal design—to shepherd God's kingdom wherever we are, forever. For example, the Israelites were not saved from Egypt just to be saved. They were saved to shepherd God's kingdom in Canaan. The Lord reminded the Israelites how he shepherded them while they were alien slaves in Egypt; so once in the Promised Land, the Israelites were to shepherd kindly the aliens who came into their land. "You must not oppress an alien, since you know their feelings since you also were aliens in the land of Egypt" (Ex 23:9).[9] That is another chain in the eternal design—to be kind to others as God has been kind to us.

Our salvation from sin is for a higher purpose than that salvation alone. Other deliverances than sin show that we are saved *for* something not just *from* something. I will give a couple of examples. I go to the doctor for my health to be restored, so I can then get back to doing those productive things the Lord has called me to do for my family and others. I am saved from sickness for a higher purpose. Or, I restore my house from fire or weather damage so my family can live in a safe shelter from which we can live our lives for kingdom purposes. The reason for restoring bodies and

---

9. Also, Deut. 24:18; Lev. 19:34

homes is not the restoration itself; the reason is *so that* we can continue on with our previous activities of productive kingdom work.

In the Old Testament, people were delivered from adversity *so that* they could get on with what God called them to do. Israel was saved from bondage in Egypt *so that* they could be free to conquer and shepherd Canaan along with the Lord. Samson was revived from having his eyes gouged out *so that* he could deliver the Israelites from the Philistines. David was forgiven for his adultery *so that* he could carry on as Israel's humbled but greatest spiritual leader. Jonah was rescued *so that* he could go on to give his message of salvation to the Ninevites. These deliverances were not for the sake of salvation alone, but *so that* the saved could continue accomplishing their kingdom responsibilities. Salvation, restoration or deliverance are not the eternal design alone, but they are critical if it is going to be accomplished during this parenthetical age.

Deliverance is only a *parenthesis* in creation's eternal history. Deliverance is a temporary process like recovering from an illness, like restoring a house, like exiting slavery. The Lord's redemption of creation is God's *parenthetical design*; it is his saving design within the context of his much grander eternal design. This timeline diagrams what the basic and eternal design is—when we are to shepherd perfectly and eternally as God does.

God's Eternal Design

Creation ●━━━God shepherds shepherding creation by his blessings━━━▶ eternity

This next timeline shows how things have become more complex and traumatic because of our sin in Eden and our sin in our own daily lives. Added to the delight of perpetual blessings is the necessity for shepherding deliverances and judgments that make up our lives in this fallen world as we respond to the results of sin.

The Parenthetical Design within the Eternal Design

Creation ●━ (fall, blessing, deliverance, discipline, cross, millennium) New Earth ━▶ eternity

A parenthesis in a sentence puts important words in their place. A parenthesis in a sentence helps prioritize the comments in that sentence, making those words in the parenthesis only secondary to the rest of the thought in the sentence, yet still significant. The parenthesis is part of the sentence, but it is not the main point. So, a parenthetical statement is found in the following sentence: "The woman drove to work (traffic was awful) and arrived ready to lead her department." A sentence with a parenthesis which contains a much more profound thought would be, "God designed us to shepherd with him (though we sin) so we will shepherd for eternity." This sentence has a critical parenthesis for sure, but the parenthetical phrase is still secondary to the main point of the sentence. It is an important part of the sentence, but it does not distract from the main point of the sentence. That parenthesis about sin is an agonizing one and cannot be ignored. But it must be appreciated within the total sentence about the Lord's eternal design.

The Testaments explain God's redemptive design during the parenthetical age, but within the context of his eternal design. In other words, the biblical redemptive message is a magnificent and specific application of God's eternal design. But the eternal design preceded the need for any redemption, it guided the parenthetical process of redemption, and it will continue on to New Earth again, without the need for redemptive acts of deliverance and discipline.

So, it would be inadequate to interpret the Bible message to be about redemption, or God's forgiveness, or "salvation," or, yes, even about Jesus' death on the cross without a thorough understanding of how God manages his creation. Such an interpretation of the Bible is not broad enough to explain and appreciate God's more complete and loving plan for us and the rest of creation. That plan includes, but it is not consumed by teachings on salvation from sin alone. Such a view often leads to fantasy interpretations of the Old Testament. For example, clearly narrated Old Testament events, actions or stories which teach profound truths and had profound implications for the Israelites in their day, are often exploited by imaginative interpreters who contort these passages into unintended illustrations about Jesus and the cross. This method of interpreting the Old Testament disrespects God's Word by foisting human imagination over the clear teaching intended by the Lord for the Israelites and for us.

The eternal design is not on hold during this parenthetical age, however. Rather, it designs what our shepherding responsibilities are to be during this tragic age as well. God's eternal design determines our actions into eternity, including this part of eternity now, this parenthetical age. We are living the first phase of eternity now. So God's eternal design applies as much to this moment as it will forever. Granted, we are living in a torturous time of eternity, but God's eternal design is the only way forward now as it always will be. He shepherds us through this challenging parenthesis in history as we shepherd others through it as well. We shepherd creation now by love and faith and by following the Lord's revealed moral standards and by the Spirit's power to strengthen us for our war against the flesh.

The struggle for salvation within this parenthetical age resonates in our ears on a regular basis, as it should. We refer to these goals and struggles by various terms and doctrines. Key words of the Christian faith reflect an understanding that we must get back to where we were before this horrendous parenthesis started in Eden. In other words, they imply that the eternal design is the context within which deliverance comes. We must *re-turn* to the perfection at creation. So, there are many "Re-" words in our Christian vocabulary that we take for granted. For example,

Regenerate—to generate us again toward perfection

Reconcile—to unite us again to God and creation

Redeem—to return us to his believing kingdom

Restore—to fix our destroyed world and souls

Repent—to return us to righteous behavior

Renew—to create and empower us as new

These "Re-" words remind us what God's parenthetical design is—to reclaim and reroute creation and humanity back into line with his eternal design. Only then can God and humanity continue, without resistance, the glorious pursuit of managing, enhancing, blessing, ruling, enjoying and sharing this awe-inspiring creation of the Lord.

God's parenthetical design *after* the Fall and *before* New Earth is a time of sustained shepherding by God and humanity. Before the Fall we were only expected to bless creation by tending it, caring for it. But *now* our shepherding role includes deliverance and discipline. Now, sin requires God, creation, and humanity to not only bless but also to deliver creation and humanity from evil and to judge against the wicked and their wickedness. Now God's shepherding has become a *redemptive* combination of blessing, deliverance and discipline.

Redemption and the Cross are necessary now because they mend humanity so we can carry on with God's kingdom work forever. However, this parenthesis in human history is a mere millisecond within the everlasting eon when we will never again have such struggles.

THE EVERLASTING JOURNEY

Creation's forward motion toward a re-perfected cosmos should be a great inspiration for us now. It charts the personal victory in our own brief life when we remain faithful. Our personal life is a shorter story of God's design on the great cosmic level of the eternal design—the Re-words apply to our journey with the Lord as he restores you and me and all of creation. Our daily experiences are the tiny but profound benchmarks toward our own perfect future, and they parallel the progress of all creation's perfect future. Of course our journey toward perfection is not a seamless evolution. We will still have fallen far short even after our gradual moral transformation—praise the Lord that there will be a definite event in God's grace that will take me from far-from-perfect to perfect after Judgment Day on New Earth.

But even then, God has designed our relationship with him as a sustained, eternal *journey* where we shepherd with him along the way. Fortunately our journey with him never ends, our shepherding responsibilities will never be over, or we would have no use for God's loving, caring, creative, strong, wise image within us. In other words, we will never finally "arrive." We will never be allowed to retire, nor would we want to, because ahead of us are an infinite number of rewarding, exciting goals, destinations and assignments as we reign with the Lord forever! The increase of his government will never end. We can only imagine the wonders we will be involved with in New Earth. Playing harps on clouds sounds like an eternal bore (except to a harpist,

I suppose). Loitering on streets of gold found within pearly gates will be terrific for a couple weeks . . . only. No, we will do no less than "reign *on the earth*" (Rev 5:10).

The shepherding roles of deliverance and discipline/judgement will no longer be necessary. They were not necessary before the Fall nor will they be in New Earth. That may take a lot of what we think is the interesting drama out of the world, but actually it only takes the devastating trauma from the world. Life will not get dull, it will only be more exhilarating.

Blessing will be the remaining shepherding function by God and his creation. I believe blessings will come every day in many ways in New Earth.

- We will gain a deeper and deeper knowledge of the Trinity, but God's infinite fathomlessness will never be fully comprehended.
- We will receive new responsibilities, new commissioned projects from which we will enjoy the greater and more diverse fruits from our labors.
- We will work together with the fruits of the Spirit, sharing responsibilities, sharing wisdom, and continuing to share our Spiritual gifts.
- We will create new architecture, theatre, sculpture, music, poetry, and dance.
- We will conceive and construct innovations for every purpose under heaven.
- We will study nature and progressively understand mysteries of science which were previously unsolvable.
- We will care for nature, its flora, fauna, waters, soil, and air.
- We will teach each other what we have learned about reality from our delegated assignments from the Lord.
- We will fellowship, play, worship, cook and eat with each other.
- We will travel, hike, stargaze, or anything that will make us more aware of the Lord's grandeur.
- We will explore areas of creation currently inaccessible or unknown.
- We will meditate and reflect on the most significant truths as God clarifies them for us.
- We will continue to commune with the Trinity as God's children, friends, servants, and fellow shepherds.

In other words, we will continue doing in New Earth what our callings and enjoyments have been during this parenthetical design. And they will be complete blessings since we will pursue all things without a fallen, easily distracted, and self-centered mind and heart.

We look forward to New Earth when we will understand more fully how God's brief message in the sixty-six books of the Bible fit within this grandest scheme of the eternal design. Until then our wisdom and discernment depend on revelation that is less complete, though completely adequate. However, we understand biblical history best only when we put the Testaments' various messages into the much larger context of God's shepherding design. Otherwise, the Testaments are understood only through parenthetical structures which emphasize incomplete interpretations of the Bible. These interpretations may focus only on getting saved and receiving God's grace rather than honoring God for his salvation and grace by obedience and responsible shepherding of others.

Until New Earth, I am confident the church will continue its robust pursuit of the gospel of the Kingdom and the cross by shepherding the lost and underprivileged through its international mission clinics and schools, through relief and development aid, in shelters for refugees and trafficked women and children. The church will continue to promote peace, to offer alternatives to abortion for desperate mothers, to provide food and clothing to the impoverished, to comfort heaven's citizens as they reel under grotesque and vicious persecution around the globe. The church has proven it is aware of the vast global needs and of its responsibility to meet bravely as many needs as it can. The Lord's bride, the church, is a valiant woman who shepherds with her Spouse, expanding the Kingdom of God to reach the victims of a devastated and cursed world.

WHAT DOES THE ETERNAL DESIGN LOOK LIKE?

The eternal design applies thoroughly to all of God's creation. This chart shows the structure of the Lord's shepherding—he shepherds everything he has created! He shepherds spirits, nature, all humanity, his people and the individual believer. Our task in this study is to appreciate exactly how the Lord blesses, delivers and disciplines all that he shepherds. One exception, however; evidently his holy angels do not need to be delivered and the fallen spirits never will be. Otherwise, this chart shows that his shepherding heart affects all reality, even in this parenthetical age.

		God Shepherds Each Part of Creation				
		Spirits	Nature	Humanity	Israel/Church	Individual
God	Blesses					
	Delivers					
	Disciplines					

The eternal design has another part to it though . . . God shepherds *shepherding creation*. The next chart obviously is more complex, but the eternal design's consistency helps us see that the design is repeated in all of relationships among creation's components. This chart shows on every level how extensive the eternal design is. It is woven throughout with the shepherding threads of blessing, deliverance and discipline.

God's Eternal Design

> God shepherds creation
> Angels shepherd creation
> Nature shepherds creation
> Humanity shepherds creation
> God's people shepherd creation
> The believer shepherds creation

All of creation shepherds each of the other parts of creation as God's instruments in his eternal design. Whether angels, nature, humanity, Israel or the church or the individual believer, none of the shepherds are independent of God's plans and all are used by him.

You might find a few places that are not shaded but you think should be. Maybe your thoughts will be answered by the rest of the pages in this study. On the other hand, there are a few realms where blessing, deliverance and discipline do not completely apply and they are indicated by the shaded areas. By the end of our study, we will have discussed each of these parts of the two charts, so just get a good feel for them now.

Each Part of Creation Shepherds the Others						
		Spirits	Nature	Humanity	Israel/Church	Individual
God	Blesses					
	Delivers					
	Disciplines					
Spirits	Bless					
	Deliver					
	Disciplines					
Nature	Blesses					
	Delivers					
	Disciplines					
Humanity	Bless					
	Deliver					
	Disciplines					
Israel/Church	Blesses					
	Delivers					
	Disciplines					
Individual	Blesses					
	Delivers					
	Disciplines					

A word about the spirits in this chart since much of the "Spirits" column is shaded. This is because there is little biblical comment on how the angels bless or deliver each other or nature. However, we do know that the holy angels do judge the fallen angels as they war against them and finally prevail at Armageddon. The spirit, Satan, does use natural disasters against Job's property, servants, and family. God does bless his angels by creating them and placing them so close to his glory, and they are used by him for his shepherding humanity. Humanity blesses the angels with joy when believers are obedient, and believers will judge the fallen angels in the final day.

If we were to show the eternal design as a graph rather than a chart, the basic shepherding realms and their relationships with one another would look like the following design. This graph reflects the eternal design in the simplest of ways, showing that there is a shepherding relationship with God and within creation.

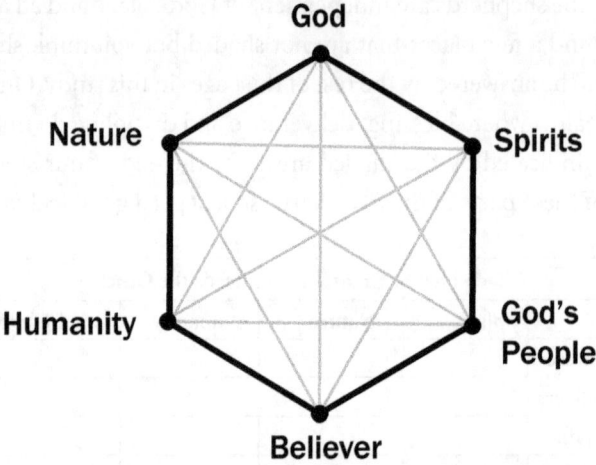

Basic Shepherding Realms

God's eternal design has each realm shepherding each of the others in a wonderfully complex network of blessing, deliverance, and discipline. Most of the single lines shown between the realms in the graph are made up of at least one or two strands of the shepherding tasks of blessing, deliverance and discipline, if not all three. So, to start with, we see each single line between the shepherds could consist of three lanes of shepherding. Shepherding relationships usually are not only one-way. In most cases shepherds bless, deliver, and discipline, but they are shepherded in the same ways as well. Here is one example.

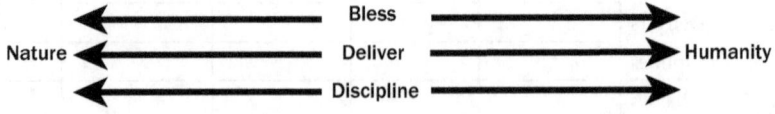

Nature and humanity shepherd each other by all three shepherding functions, from aiding each other's success to checking each other's excesses since the Fall. Nature blesses us with its beauty and its resources. It delivers by its white blood cells fighting our infections and by its eventual rains that end droughts. Nature also disciplines by sickening us when we over-indulge and by flooding our lands which have been deforested.

Humanity blesses nature by pruning its trees, making them more fruitful, yet also by leaving parts of the forest alone to flourish as God intended. We deliver nature by containing its excesses in wildfires and protecting its endangered species. Humanity also disciplines nature by defeating its diseases and thwarting attacks from its pests and other dangers.

Another example: God's people and the believer also mutually shepherd one another.

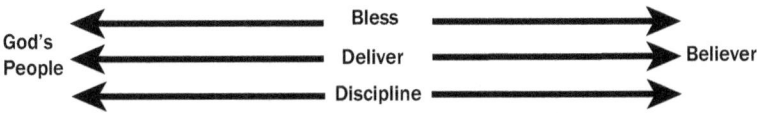

God's people bless the believer with loving fellowship and nurturing toward greater holiness. They deliver the believer from discouragement and even physical healing through prayers and the elders' anointing oil. God's people discipline the believer by holding one accountable by warnings and correction, and they serve as judges between believers in conflicts and legal disputes.

The believer, in turn, blesses the believing community by using one's Spiritual gifts for its edification and by contributing financial resources. One can deliver the believing community by offering one's wisdom and efforts in solving problems. The believer can also discipline the believing community by one's rebuke of its leaders when they are errant in their teaching or are arrogant and distant from those with needs.

Of course, in this parenthetical phase of human history, shepherding is not always characterized by blessing, deliverance or fair discipline. No one shepherds as they should, but too many shepherd in complete alliance with the Enemy. But even the capacity to shepherd wickedly implies that one is able to shepherd at all, even in opposite ways than righteous ways. Humanity and individuals frequently behave as anti-shepherds and ignore rather than bless, abuse rather than deliver, or act unjustly rather than discipline fairly.

Shepherding is done mutually between the spirits, nature, and humanity, and it is simple (but disappointing) to add anti-shepherding conduct to our illustration. So, we add "Ignore," "Abuse," and "Injustice" to our chart of relationships between shepherds. Fortunately, the Lord's return will remove these negative elements. Lord, come quickly!

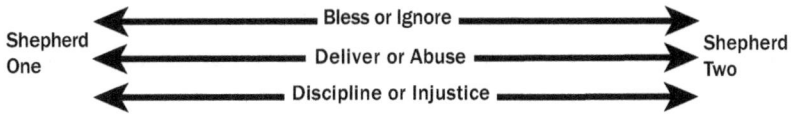

People often intentionally ignore humanity and nature when they should intentionally look for ways to bless. Abuse of people or nature creates the need for deliverance when a person should be looking for opportunities to deliver any aspect of God's fallen creation. Injustice is pervasive in personal relationships and in legal proceedings around the world. Though the holy angels are incapable of being anti-shepherds, the fallen angels are incapable of being anything else.

We will look at all of these realms and their interactions at different places in this study. We will see that this fairly simple graph above becomes much more complicated as we look deeper into the eternal design. But for now, understanding this basic pattern in the shepherding relationship between God and his created realms is an adequate start.

OUR STUDY

I close our first chapter with a few notes. First, the title of this study is *Shepherds* since that word can be used as a noun or a verb. As a plural *noun*, "Shepherds" describes the Trinity's *position* over us. It also describes our position as shepherds in creation. We *are* shepherds. But "shepherds" is also a *verb* that expresses our primary *action* as shepherds—God shepherds, and we shepherd. Why stress this obvious distinction? Because often we prefer only to *be* a shepherd, not *act* like one. Our God is a Shepherd and *does* shepherding. He not only *has* the authority of a shepherd, he *uses* it. And we do too. However, many want the privileges or recognition of being a shepherd without providing their bodies as living sacrifices.

Second, our footnotes are almost exclusively Bible references. I rely on Scripture to convince the reader of the thousands of biblical passages that speak to the eternal design. If the Word alone does not prove the eternal design to be the true and overarching thought of God about his creation, then this study fails, period. But please consider these important points when reading and using the footnotes.

- The topics in this study are so many and broad that most sentences could introduce their own paragraph or paragraphs of deeper comment. This is why the subtitle of this book is, *The Believer's Outline for Theology*; this is an outline, not a thorough explanation. So, the footnotes should be studied as extensions of these sentences. They provide a resource for a single day's devotional, a small group discussion, or a sermon's outline.

- The footnotes are not intended to be a complete listing of relevant passages, but enough are given to show there is adequate biblical evidence for the point being made.

- A single reference may not be convincing to you, though care is given not to cite unclear or heavily disputed passages. So read each reference in the footnotes within the context of the others next to it. The Bible interprets itself very well.

- The references in the footnotes are nearly always listed in the order they are found in the Bible to ease the reader's page-turning. Please work patiently through all the verses so the total footnote is considered. You might not find the first passage listed to be the most convincing, but the rest which follow will certainly help.

- There are times especially when the Gospels are referenced, when two parallel lines (//) are used to show the Gospels are probably recounting the same moment in Christ's ministry. This is also used at times when referencing passages in Samuel, Kings and Chronicles.
- Biblical quotations are usually my translations and will differ with other translations just as all translations do with one another, so use several translations to test a passage's meaning and relevance.

Third, I polled university students in my classes and asked on a scale of one to ten how important the following question was to each of them: "How important is it for you to know your purpose for your existence?" The average answer was a six! The average! Six! The point being, this book is not for everyone—only for those who enjoy thinking profoundly about the deepest and broadest questions that frame our view of God, his creation and the design of it all.

> God's eternal design is
> exciting yet consistent,
> complex yet beautiful,
> physical yet spiritual,
> everywhere yet here,
> caring yet powerful,
> known yet infinite,
> eternal yet now.

2

God Is Our Shepherd

GOD SHEPHERDS SHEPHERDING CREATION—THIS has been the Lord's design from creation's very start, and it will continue to be his design for the infinite future. I explained in the first chapter why the term "shepherd" is preferred in expressing the eternal design over "king, ruler, lord, sovereign" or any other terms for an authority. These terms for high authority are certainly accurate in describing God's and our role in the eternal design, but "shepherd" conveys a more personal authority. God's and our sovereignty is more than a political *position*; it is a series of loving, patient, and just *actions* from a determined but caring heart toward creation and humanity. The name "Shepherd" is used throughout the Testaments, connecting more graphically and emotionally an authoritative position with routine nurturing, protection, and discipline of one's subjects.

Surprising as it might be to some, the first instances of the word "gospel," or "good news" in the Bible are found in the Old Testament, not the New. The New Testament uses the Greek word *euangelion* for gospel. The Old Testament uses the Hebrew word *bāśar* for "gospel" over 20 times. As in the New Testament, there are various messages referred to as gospel in the Old Testament. One of the gospel messages in the Old Testament is proclaimed by Isaiah, namely, that the Lord was Israel's ruling shepherd.

> Bring the *good news* . . . Jerusalem, bring the *good news* . . . Like a *shepherd* He will care for His flock; He will gather the *lambs* in his arms. He will carry them tightly and gently lead them as little *lambs*. Isa 40:9, 11

So, one of the gospels given to the Israelites was that God was their shepherd. We will look at other gospels in the Old Testament in later sections of our study.

Both Testaments convince us that shepherding is the nature of God's relationship with us. What Christian does not find comfort in David's words, "The Lord is my *shepherd*" (Ps 23:1)? However, this is just one instance of over sixty passages in the Bible that describe the Lord literally as our shepherd and us as his sheep. And far beyond these passages, his shepherding heart is seen in his every word and act even if the exact words "shepherd, sheep, flock, pasture" are not used.

This chapter will focus on many biblical passages where God and Christ Jesus are referred to literally as shepherds. For instance, Micah prays that the Lord would be Israel's ruling shepherd: "*Shepherd* your people with your scepter, *shepherd* your *flock* and your possession" (Mic 7:14) Eventually I will flesh out the specific ways the Lord shepherds all of creation, but especially his shepherding of humanity. This chapter looks at passages where the Lord is called *literally* a "shepherd" who blesses, delivers, and disciplines us in that role, or where we are called his "sheep" or "flock." David praises the Lord for performing all three roles of a shepherd in Psalm 23. The Lord *blessed* him with kindness and eternal life (6). His Shepherd *delivered* him from exhaustion, death, and his enemies (3–5). His Shepherd also disciplines with his *rod and staff* (4) and judges the sheep's enemies with these implements.

GOD SHEPHERDS BY HIS BLESSING

David prayed that his personal Shepherd of Psalm 23 would also be the Shepherd of all Israel who would bless, deliver, and carry his people in his powerful arms into eternity.

> Deliver your people and bless your inheritance.
> Be their *shepherd* and carry them forever. Ps 28:9

Other psalms announce the same gospel that Isaiah and Micah announce,

> The Lord our creator is our God.
> We are the people in *His pasture, the sheep* in His hand. Ps 95:7

> The Lord is God, he is the one who created us—not us.
> We are his people and *the sheep in his pasture*. Ps 100:3

Ezekiel quotes the Lord's own words about his role as Israel's shepherd,

> You are *my sheep, the sheep in my pasture.* Ezek 34:31

The Lord designed creation so he could work with human shepherds who would also care for his creation. But more often than not throughout human history, including Israel's history, shepherds have not reflected well the Lord's shepherding heart. His shepherding ways were not often imitated by Israel's "shepherds." Ezekiel denounced them for ignoring the common people and letting them "scatter, *without a shepherd*" (34:5–6, 8). It is discouraging to read about the many evil shepherds who led the Israelites. An excerpt from Ezekiel's extended rebuke of Israel's shepherds highlights the severe lack of shepherding leadership.

> Should not *shepherds* take care of the *flock*? . . . You have not strengthened the weak or healed the sick or bound the injured. You have not brought back the strays or searched for the lost . . . They were scattered because there was no

> *shepherd*, and they became food for all the wild animals ... My *shepherds* have not searched for my *sheep*. Ezek 34:2, 4–5, 8

Other prophets rebuked Israel's shepherds for the same reasons.

> They are *shepherds* with no understanding, doing only what they want to do. Every one of them is unjust. Isa 56:11

> The *shepherds*[1] sin against me. Jer 2:8

> The *shepherds* are stupid ... and their whole flock is scattered. Jer 10:21

> Many *shepherds* have destroyed my vineyard. Jer 12:10

> Woe to the *shepherds* who destroy and scatter the *sheep* in my *pasture*. Jer 23:1

> My people are lost *sheep* because their *shepherds* have led them astray. Jer 50:6

> The people wander like *sheep* and are afflicted since there is no *shepherd*. Zech 10:2

> Their *shepherds* have no compassion for them. Zech 11:5

We will find that the hearts and priorities of the New Testament leaders, namely the Pharisees, Sadducees, and lawyer/scribes were no better in Christ's estimation.

The Lord promised in the Old Testament that he would deliver his sheep from these awful shepherds and someday place his David-like shepherd over them. Ezekiel gave Israel hope when he prophesized that "David" would come by way of one of his descendants to shepherd his people; of course, this prophecy was about Jesus:

> I will place one *Shepherd* over them, my servant "David." He will feed and *shepherd* them. 34:23

> My servant "David" will be their king so they will have one *Shepherd*. I will establish them and multiply them. 37:24, 26

Micah also prophesied that an effective shepherd would be born in Bethlehem even though he had always existed before.

> From you [Bethlehem], a ruler in Israel will come forward for me; he comes forward from the old, eternal days. ... He will stand and *shepherd* his *flock* in the strength of the Lord. 5:2–4

This is referring to the Messiah, the Christ, the eternal shepherd (Matt. 2:6).

So when Jesus Christ came, he renewed the Old Testament gospel of God as the shepherd of his people. In fact, John tells us that Christ was born not only to shepherd his people, but he was "born to shepherd the nations" (Rev 12:5). Unfortunately, many Bible translations err in rendering this passage "born to *rule* the nations," contrary to

---

1. The Hebrew here often translated "rulers" in Hebrew is literally "shepherds."

the clear meaning of the Greek word *poimainō*, "to shepherd." We should translate the word according to its literal meaning, to shepherd. After all, there were other words meaning "to rule" which John could have used.

Jesus confronted Israel's religious leaders for their lack of compassionate leadership, and he then installed new shepherds in his church. But Christ humbly and intentionally understated his perfection; he says he was merely the "good" shepherd. When New Testament Jews heard that Christ was the *good* shepherd, that meant far more than he was just a kind and good person (John 10:11, 14). The Jews had been victims for centuries under irresponsible and self-seeking shepherds like those in the Old Testament and at the hands of the overbearing religious leaders of the New Testament. So it was a great relief for Jews to hear from Christ that finally a "good shepherd" was among them. "All who came before me were thieves and robbers but the sheep have not listened to them . . . I am the good shepherd." (John 10:8, 11, 14).

Christ spoke at length about his role as the shepherd of God's sheep. He explained the difference between his godly shepherding and the selfish shepherding of the past and present shepherds in his extended discourse in John 10:1–29. As John says in Revelation 12:5, Christ knew he had come to shepherd all people, Jews and Gentiles. Jesus told the pompous Pharisees, "I have other *sheep* that I must lead too that are not of this fold. They too will listen to my voice making *one flock and one shepherd*" (John 10:16).

But with all the hope within the Old Testament gospel about the Lord as Israel's shepherd, there was also the tragic message about the coming Shepherd. Christ refers to himself as the prophesied Old Testament shepherd whom Zechariah says would be abused so badly that this his sheep would be scattered. By quoting Zechariah, Christ told his disciples what their reaction would be to his arrest and trial:

> All of you will fall back tonight because of me because it is written,
>
> "I will strike the *shepherd* and the *sheep* of the *flock* will be scattered."[2]

Christ was the promised Good Shepherd, but he was also the slaughtered sacrificial Lamb.

GOD SHEPHERDS BY HIS DELIVERANCE

The second function of shepherding is to deliver the sheep. Deliverance flows from God's love and kindness.[3] Deliverance of any kind would not be necessary if the Couple had not sinned in Eden and somehow humanity had avoided sin altogether in all eras and areas of the world since. Yet we need deliverance for many reasons because of deliberate sin or moral mistakes. We need salvation because—

We are suffering from God's curses on humanity and the rest of creation.

---

2. Matt 26:31 // Mark 14:27; Zech 13:7
3. Pss 13:5; 18:50; 40:11; 136:10–24

We are guilty by association with Adam and need forgiveness by association with Jesus.

Our sin or folly led us into harmful predicaments from which we need God's deliverance.

The sins of others have put us into situations from which we need deliverance.

None of these negative conditions will apply in New Earth, so there will be no need for salvation from anything then. But now in God's parenthetical design, we need him as our shepherd to deliver us frequently and dramatically.

Old Testament believers lived in an agricultural culture where the relationship between a sheep and a saving shepherd was well known. So it was a natural image for them to use. Jacob praised God as his personal shepherd.

> God has been my *shepherd* my whole life—the "angel" who has delivered me from every evil. Gen 48:15–16

> The hands of the Mighty One of Jacob, from the *Shepherd*, the Stone of Israel. Gen 49:24

We are very familiar with David's comfort in Psalm 23:4 because his Shepherd wielded implements for deliverance: "I fear no evil since you are with me; your rod and staff comfort me." But other psalmists also praise the Lord for his delivering care of common people.

> The Lord raises the afflicted above reach and treats their families as a *flock*. Ps 107:41

> I have strayed like a lost *sheep*. Search for me, your servant, since I do not neglect your commandments. Ps 119:176

David and Asaph saw the Lord as the delivering shepherd not only of the individual believer, but of all Israel. David appealed to God,

> Deliver your people . . . Be their *shepherd* and carry them forever. Ps 28:9

Asaph also begged for deliverance for God's people,

> Preserve those condemned to die . . . So we your people and *sheep* of your *pasture* will thank you forever. Ps 79:11, 13

> Please listen, *Shepherd* of Israel, who leads Joseph like a *flock* . . . come and deliver us, O God; restore us by your shining face that saves us. Ps 80:1–3

Twice the Lord delivered Israel out of oppressive foreign lands. First, they were led out of the Egyptian empire in their great Exodus:

> You led your people like a *flock* by the hand of Moses and Aaron. Ps 77:20

> He led his own people like *sheep*, guiding them through the wilderness like a *flock*. Ps 78:52

> He brought them through the sea along with the *shepherds* of his flock. Isa 63:11

Then, hundreds of years later, the Lord needed to deliver the Israelites again when they were exiles in the Assyrian and Babylonian empires. He brought them back to Israel, to their own pasture where the Shepherd wanted to bless them all along. When Jeremiah gave his message to the Israelites, it was a familiar announcement since their Shepherd had delivered them from Egypt already, centuries before.

> I will gather the remnant of my *flock* from every country where I have driven them, and bring them back to their *pasture* where they will be fruitful and multiply. 23:3

> He who scattered Israel will gather and watch over his *flock* like a *shepherd*. 31:10

> Israel is a scattered *flock* that lions have chased away. 50:17, 19

> But I will bring Israel back to their own *pasture* to graze. What *shepherd* can stand against me? 50:44

Ezekiel and Micah predict the same shepherding salvation from God.

> I will search and look after my *sheep*. As a *shepherd* looks after his scattered *flock* when with them, I look after my *sheep* . . . I will tend my *sheep* and have them lie down . . . I will mend the crippled and strengthen the sick . . . I will *shepherd* the flock with justice. Ezek 34:11–16

> I will gather them like *sheep* in the fold, a *flock* in its *pasture*. Mic 2:12

There will be a third deliverance of God's people before the creation of New Earth. That age will begin by the Lord delivering his community of believers, his precious flock:

> On that day, the Lord their God will deliver his people as a *shepherd* delivers his *sheep*. Zech 9:16

> O Jerusalem, tower of the *flock*, hill of Zion's daughter, your past dominion will surely come back to you. Mic 4:8

The New Testament quotes the Old Testament about God's compassionate heart as the shepherd of his people. In the Old Testament, Moses requested that Israel be given a human shepherd so they would not be hopeless and lost, "like *sheep* without a *shepherd*." So the Lord appointed Joshua to be that shepherd (Num 27:16–18). The same Old Testament phrase is used for Jesus when he saw the plight of the Jews of his day: "He looked on the crowds compassionately because they were distressed and helpless, like *sheep* without a *shepherd*."[4] Joshua's Hebrew name means "the Lord delivers," and Jesus' Greek name means "savior/deliverer," so how poetic it is that Jesus and Joshua's role were to be the shepherds God's people needed.

As the Good Shepherd, Jesus brought to God's flock his salvation from spiritual and physical sicknesses. Consistent with his name "Jesus," he saved individuals by healings, exorcisms, resurrections, and forgiveness because they were distressed, helpless, shepherd-less sheep. Jesus says he was sent to the "lost *sheep*" of Israel (Matt 15:24) to save the nation and even to rescue the one individual sheep.

> If a man owns a hundred *sheep* and he loses one of them, will he not leave the ninety-nine in the open pasture and search for the lost one? . . . He then gathers his friends and neighbors to announce, "Rejoice with me, I have found my lost *sheep*!"[5]

Jesus denounced the irresponsible religious shepherds who criticized him for delivering individuals from distress on the Sabbath: "Which of you whose *sheep* falls into a pit on the Sabbath, will not grab it and lift it out?" (Matt 12:11).

A strand of verses about the Lord's deliverances threads itself through the Testaments with specific reference to his shepherding role. The books of Isaiah, Zechariah, John, Matthew, and Hebrews connect our moral straying as sheep to the death and resurrection of the Good Shepherd.

> Like *sheep* we have all gone astray . . . But the Lord has put the sin of all of us to on him. Isa 53:6

> Wake up, sword! Go against my *Shepherd*, against my Associate . . . Strike the *Shepherd* so the *sheep* are scattered. Zech 13:7

> I am the good *shepherd* who lays down his life for the *sheep*. John 10:11

> You all will dissert me tonight because it is written, "I will strike the *Shepherd* and the *sheep* of the *flock* will be scattered. Matt 26:31[6]

> The God of peace raised from the dead our Lord Jesus, the Great *Shepherd* of the sheep. Heb 13:20

Jesus, applied the Old Testament prediction about a future shepherd's life and death for the sheep who had strayed in sin. Though the flock may be scattered and stray again, he will gather it again as the great shepherd whose blood saved the flock eternally!

---

4. Matt. 9:36 // Mark 6:34
5. Luke 15:4–7 // Matt 18:12–14
6. Also, Mark 14:27

GOD SHEPHERDS BY HIS DISCIPLINE

God disciplines extensively through all eras and areas of his world *because* he is a good shepherd. He is not a good shepherd only because he is gracious to those who are undeserving of grace; he is also a good shepherd because he disciplines those who are deserving of discipline. God has every right to judge us endlessly for our rampant and repetitive sin, but an unappreciative human race criticizes him even though his grace is so prevalent. His grace and blessings come to all persons when all deserve nothing but judgment. He restrains his justice with his perfectly balanced grace by his own Spiritual fruits of love, patience, kindness, goodness, faithfulness, gentleness, and self-control. This balance is illustrated by his impaled arms on the cross—one arm pointed in judgment to the perishing cursing thief, the other pointed in grace to the humble thief who that very day would share Paradise with his Lord.

When the Lord does judge and discipline it is most often an act of deliverance at the same time. Shepherding functions often overlap: *blessings* can be *deliverance*; *deliverances* can come by God *disciplining* others; and our *discipline* can be a *blessing* that leads us to greater moral maturity. Asaph says it clearly, "God rose to *judge*, and to *save* the humble of the earth" (Ps. 76:9). The enemies of God's people will be judged as his means of saving his people.

God has different purposes for his discipline and judgment. Those of us who love and honor the Lord and his instructions actually *desire* his discipline because we know that his judgments serve us graciously by motivating us to be wiser in our obedience. Proverbs 3:12 comforts us in the midst of discipline: "Whoever the Lord loves, he disciplines."[7] Hebrews quotes this proverb and adds, "He disciplines us for our own good so we might share in his holiness" (Heb. 12:10). What can easily be mistaken at first for our "unlucky" circumstances or injustices against us might well be God's blessing of corrective judgment. We should want his discipline to deter us from continuing down any path of folly as his stray lambs. Remembering the Lord's perfect prerogative to judge and sentence one to death for any sin, the psalmist is relieved to say, "The Lord has severely punished me, but at least not to death" (Ps. 118:18).

Ecclesiastes values God's disciplining tools just as David does in Psalm 23:4. David had mentioned the rod and staff, the shepherd's goading and grabbing tools. Ecclesiastes 12:11 mentions the shepherd's goading rod: "The words of the wise are like goads . . . they are given by one Shepherd." God's wisdom instructions that we find in Ecclesiastes, Proverbs, and Job are like the wood or metal rods used to keep animals moving along in the correct path. They prick the flesh, annoying and moving us in the directions where we might not want to go morally.

God's judgment is felt by all humanity. Throughout history past and until the Last Day's judgment, the Lord shepherds all peoples dramatically.

---

7. Also, Pss 94:12; 107:10–13, 17–19; 119:21; Eccl 7:5

> I will punish the world for its evil and the wicked for their sin. I will end the arrogance of the proud and humble the pride of the ruthless. Isa 13:11

> Pay back our neighbors seven times for the scorn they have thrown at you, Lord. Then we your people, the *sheep of your pasture*, will praise you forever. Ps 79:12–13

> O God, rise and judge the earth since you own all the nations. Ps 82:8[8]

Jeremiah refers to all kings of the earth as national "shepherds." In fact, Israel's surrounding nations used the shepherd metaphor for their kings too. They will all be judged as the shepherds who were supposed to pasture their own people generously. The Lord will hold national shepherds accountable for their treatment of their sheep.

> A commotion is heard to the ends of the earth for the Lord has an indictment against the nations . . . Weep and moan, you evil *shepherds*! Roll in the ashes, leaders of the *flock*! Your time to be slaughtered has come. Jer 25:31, 34

So, the kings of all the nations will be judged, including the Assyrian and Babylonian kings who scattered God's flock of Israel (Jer 50:17–19).

God's indictment in the Testaments was especially against her leaders who were supposed to be good and caring shepherds of his flock.[9] Yes, the sheep were guilty of wandering and straying from God's laws and wisdom, but these shepherds, themselves part of the flock of Israel, are portrayed as the bullying sheep who were only looking out only for their own hunger and thirst.

> I will judge between the fat and the lean *sheep* because you shove them with your side and shoulders, and butt the weak ones with your horns and scatter them abroad. Ezek 34:20–21

Zechariah reports God's execution of three such evil shepherd leaders (11:8–9) and there was a threat that the Lord would fatally wound another (11:17).

> Just wait, worthless *shepherd* who abandons the *flock*!
> A sword will slash his arm and pierce his right eye.

Judging the awful shepherds, even all peoples is one of the Messiah's responsibilities. Christ accepted this duty publicly, in front of all the Jewish leaders and the people. He says about himself,

> When the Son of Man comes in his glory with all the angels, he will sit on his glorious throne. All nations will be gathered to him, and he will separate the people as a *shepherd* separates the *sheep* from the goats . . . He will say to those on his left, 'Leave me, you cursed; go into the eternal fire prepared for the devil

---

8. Also, Ex 15:6–7; Pss 21:8–10; 68:1–2; 92:7–9
9. Jer 22:22; 23:2

and his demons . . . These will go into eternal punishment, but the righteous
into eternal life. Matt 25:31–32, 41, 46

Christ's shepherding actions certainly include his blessings and deliverances, but they also include his discipline in the strongest ways. Whether he condemns the Pharisees, assails the sacrilegious opportunists in the temple, or withers the unproductive fig tree, as the Good Shepherd, he will discipline his creation as extremely as he delivers it.

Christ's mission is not primarily to save and just do some disciplining along the way. He is appointed by the Father to be the judge of the peoples in addition to be our deliverer. In Psalm 2:9, God the Father announces that his Son will inherit and judge as the shepherd of the peoples:

> You are my Son. I am the Father who has begotten you. Just ask, and I will give you the nations as your inheritance, the *whole earth* as your possession. You will *shepherd*[10] them with an iron rod and dash them as pottery.

John quoted this psalm three times when he emphasized that Christ would shepherd the peoples: "He will *shepherd* them with a rod of iron." Usually, and unfortunately, the Greek word which is literally "shepherd" (*poimainō*) is changed by translators to read "rule." This is not helpful for honoring Christ for who he is; it obscures his true character and his compassionate but violently protective shepherd's heart.

> He will *shepherd* them with a rod of iron, like when pottery is dashed. Rev 2:27

> She gave birth to a son . . . who will *shepherd* all nations with a rod of iron. Rev 12:5

> From his mouth came a sharp sword to strike down the nations. He will *shepherd* them with an iron rod. Rev 19:15

Christ's role as the shepherding Judge is confirmed to be just as strong as prophesied in the Old Testament.

Fortunately however, New Earth will never need deliverance or discipline. It was the horrific global disaster of Adam and Eve's fall in Eden, and it has been humanity's regular practice of sinning since then, that now requires God's shepherding deliverance and judgment in his parenthetical design. It was the greatest of blessings to live in the perfect pre-Fall condition of creation when daily deliverance and discipline were unnecessary. And it is the utmost relief for us now to know New Earth will be void of deliverance and judgment as well; the effects of the Fall and any dangers it brought will be eternally absent. Glory to God for his persistence with his design, and praise him for his patience with us!

---

10. Less accurate translations render this word "rule" or "break."

3

God's Shepherding Commission

WE ARE GOD'S SHEPHERDS

THE LORD IS OUR shepherd and the Testaments throughout make it perfectly clear that he blesses, delivers, and disciplines as the Good Shepherd. Further, we are the Shepherd's under-shepherds who are expected to bless, deliver, and discipline as well. That is his eternal design: he shepherds his shepherds. Some are great and famous shepherds, like Moses, Joshua, David, Jeremiah, Zechariah and Christ, Paul and Peter; others are not so famous, like you perhaps, and certainly me. All of creation blesses, delivers and disciplines, including the spirits and nature and eventually we will look at how the spirits and nature shepherd. But now we will look at the biblical teachings that reveal the fact that believers are shepherds who are to bless, deliver, and discipline others.

Throughout the Old Testament, God is the Shepherd who worked with and through the efforts of his individual "shepherds." Joseph was the Shepherd's partner in defeating their enemies; Joseph was strengthened with divine power:

> Joseph's bow stayed steady, his arms and hands strengthened by the hands of the Mighty One of Jacob, by the *Shepherd*, the Stone of Israel. Gen 49:24

The Lord delivered his flock together with his shepherds Moses and Aaron. God shepherds his shepherds.

> Where is He who brought Israel out of the sea with their *shepherd* of His *flock* . . . and raised his glorious arm next to Moses' right hand? Isa 63:11–12

> You led your people like a *flock* by the hand of Moses and Aaron. Ps 77:20

Joshua was appointed to lead Israel as a shepherd so the Israelites would "not be like *sheep* without a *shepherd*" (Num 27:17). David was a shepherd of literal sheep when young, but then he became a shepherd of God's people as their king. The Lord took him from the sheep pens and made him the shepherd of his people, "Jacob":

God's Shepherding Commission

> He brought him from caring for *ewes* and their *lambs* to *shepherd* [the sons of] Jacob... So he *shepherded* them with his upright heart. Ps 78:71-72

> The judges of Israel, I commanded to shepherd my people.[1]

> The Lord said to David: You will *shepherd* my people Israel, and you will rule them.[2]

> I took you from tending the *flock* of the pasture and made you ruler over my people Israel.[3]

The Lord considered Israel's in each tribal locale to be his shepherds. Many others were responsible for godly "shepherding" of Israel and their success and failures define most of the Old Testament narrative.[4] Even a pagan king, Cyrus, was the Lord's "shepherd" of Israel and several other nations in his Persian empire. The Lord announced, "Cyrus is my *shepherd* who will fulfill all I desire" (Isa 44:28).

After the golden age of David and Solomon however, awful shepherds ruled Israel more often than not. The Old Testament laments their frequent and flagrant failures. They were destructive and abandoned and scattered the sheep.[5] But the Lord in his faithfulness promised that someday there would be "good shepherds." This included Jeremiah and Zechariah who accepted and performed their shepherding roles well. Jeremiah prays for personal deliverance by God, claiming he had been a faithful shepherd.

> Heal me... deliver me... I have not run away from being your *shepherd*. Jer 17:14, 16

And Zechariah also shepherded Israel faithfully.

> The Lord said: "*Shepherd* the *flock* that is to be slaughtered"... So I *shepherded* the flock that was marked for slaughter, especially the oppressed. Then I took two staffs which I called Favor and Union, and I *shepherded* the *flock*. Zech 11:4, 7

The Lord promised that future shepherds would bless and deliver God's people, and these effective shepherds started to appear in the New Testament times. Of course this included the Good Shepherd, but also the apostles and millions since the New Testament who have faithfully served with godly hearts:

---

1. 2 Chr 17:6 // 1 Sam 7:7
2. 2 Sam 5:2 // 1 Chr 11:2; also, 2 Sam 24:17 // 1 Chr 21:17
3. 2 Sam 7:8 // 1 Chr 17:7
4. 1 Kgs 22:17; 2 Chr 18:16; Isa 44:28; 56:11; Jer 3:14-15; 10:21; 12:10; 23:1-4; 50:6; Ezek 34:1-10; Zech 10:2-3; 11:4-17; 13:7
5. 1 Kgs 22:17; 2 Chr 18:16; Isa 56:11; Jer 10:21; 12:10; 23:1-4; 50:6; Ezek 34:1-10; Zech 10:2-3; 11:4-17

> I will give you *shepherds* with hearts like mine who will feed you with knowledge and understanding. Jer 3:15

> I will appoint *shepherds* over them who will care for them, and they will not be afraid again or be dismayed or lost. Jer 23:4

So as soon as the Good Shepherd preached God's gospel that "the Kingdom of God is at hand," he started recruiting disciples to be his kingdom shepherds (Mark 1:14–15).

One morning after his resurrection, Jesus prepared and fed these disciples breakfast (John 21:15–17). Peter felt so bad about having denied Jesus three times. Yet the Good Shepherd told Peter that there were profound ways he could still prove his love for his Lord. Jesus asked Peter three times about the disciple's love so that he could tell Peter three times what love for Christ meant:

> Do you love me?   Yes I do.   Then feed my *lambs*.
> Do you love me?   Yes I do.   Then shepherd my *sheep*.
> Do you love me?   Yes I do.   Then feed my *sheep*.

The love between John and Jesus is a perfect example of the eternal design—active, productive shepherding based on their loving relationship. As in every loving relationship, there are responsibilities, so after Peter insists three times that he loves the Lord, Jesus says, "Then feed my sheep," not, "Love me more." This conversation is not only about the love between John and Jesus; it is ultimately about John and Jesus' sheep.

In Numbers 27, Moses asked the Lord who would be his successor because he was concerned for Israel's well-being. So the Lord appointed Joshua to follow to lead Israel as their shepherd. The exact phrase that described God's concern at that time and throughout Israel's history is repeated when describing the empathy the Good Shepherd had for the New Testament Jews.

The Old Testament concern for shepherdless sheep:

> Who will lead them . . . so they will not be like *sheep* without a *shepherd*? Num 27:17

> I saw all Israel scattered on the mountains like *sheep* without a *shepherd*. 1 Kgs 22:17[6]

> Like *sheep* without a *shepherd*, all will return to their people. Isa 13:14

> The people wander like oppressed *sheep* without a *shepherd*. Zech 10:2–3

Jesus' concern for shepherdless sheep:

> Jesus felt sorry for them because they were like *sheep* without a *shepherd*.[7] Mark 6:34

---

6. Also, 2 Chr 18:16; Ezek 34:5;
7. Also, Matt 9:36

God's Shepherding Commission

The Father sent his Son to be the delivering Shepherd, and following the shepherding "chain" of the eternal design, Christ in turn sent his disciples to shepherd and deliver others:

> Go to the lost *sheep* of Israel preaching this message—"The Kingdom of heaven is near." Heal the sick, raise the dead, cure leprosy, cast out demons. Give others as freely as you have received.[8]

This chain stems from the Father who sent the Son, who sent the disciples, who discipled others, who were then sent to shepherd still others.

Christ Jesus came to seek the lost and wandering sheep and expected his disciples to go into all the world to do the same: healing, raising the dead, exorcizing demons, seeking other obedient disciples, and protecting them against false teachers. In the same language used to indict Old Testament leaders, Christ says, "Whoever does not gather [sheep] with me scatters" (Matt 12:30). So Paul challenged the Ephesian elders to guard the flock and shepherd against wolves with this shepherding heart:

> Keep watch over yourselves and all the *flock* . . . Be *shepherds* of the church of God . . . savage wolves will come in among you and will not spare the *flock*. Acts 20:28–29

Peter also instructed the church leaders to care for their flock. His instructions would apply to any leader of any flock, including one's family or business.

> *Shepherd* God's *flock* among you, overseeing them willingly . . . not for dishonest gain, but eagerly; not domineering them, but as examples to the *flock*. So when the chief *Shepherd* appears, you will receive the crown of glory that never fades. 1 Pet 5:2–4

Christ sent his disciples into the world with these shepherding responsibilities under his shepherding lordship.

Paul does not list "pastors" in his examples of Spiritual gifts, contrary to most translations (Eph 4:11). Whatever one might think being a pastor means, it should equal the word Paul uses. That literal word is "shepherd." So Paul's list is, literally, "apostles, prophets, evangelists, *shepherds* and teachers." If one is honored as a great "pastor," then the Lord expects that they are doing routine shepherding in the church. There is often a confusion between a good speaker or one with the gift of teaching and having the gift of shepherding. Performing as the lead shepherd in a church cannot be done primarily from the pulpit. Paul did not think of himself, nor did he have a reputation as a good speaker, but he was the best of shepherds.[9] Leadership leads by working hard to exemplify shepherding to the followers who are also shepherds to those closest to them in the family or community (2 Thess 3:7–10).

---

8. Matt 10:6–8 // Luke 9:1–2, 6
9. 1 Cor 1:17; 2:1, 4; 2 Cor 10:10; 11:6

THE PRIMARY COMMISSION

We are very familiar with the "great commission," that official assignment from Jesus Christ to his disciples. He commissioned them to multiply other disciples, in fact, to fill the earth with other disciples so they would obey his teachings (Matt. 28:18–20). Christ gave many other assignments as well, but the great commission is referred to frequently by the church because it is an impetus to fill the earth with obedient followers of the gospel of the Kingdom.

However, there is another historic commission that God assigned to us at the very start of all human history, and it is even more basic. It is found in the first chapter of the Bible and remains a thread throughout Scripture and will remain one throughout eternity. It defines our human dignity, purpose, and direction. It defines our realm over which we are to shepherd in godly ways. It defines our elevated role within the rest of creation. It defines our most basic privileges and pleasures. It even defines the context and the content of Christ's great commission.

> God blessed Adam and Eve by saying to them, "Be fruitful and multiply, fill the earth and subdue it. Rule over the fish of the sea, over the birds in the sky and over everything living and moving on the earth." Gen 1:28

At first, this may seem too remote a passage to be the foundation of the great commission, but when considered a bit longer, it becomes clear that Christ was intentionally building on this primary commission which empowers humanity to rule under the Shepherd's authority.

Let us consider the primary commission more deeply for a moment. This primary commission states why we were created. It may sound limited in its scope, referring only to the animal realm, but what else was there for the Lord to point to as Adam and Eve's realm at that point in human history? He says we are to control the whole earth (fill the earth and subdue it) and he gave examples of what that included. The animals are mentioned first and vegetation is added within the next two verses. The Couple were responsible to shepherd the earth and its contents. Psalm 115:16 reveals our authority very plainly: "The Lord has given the earth to the sons of men."

I will use the words "primary commission" for this eternal assignment given in Genesis. When someone is "commissioned" by an authority, they are given the authority to act on behalf of that authority. In this primary commission, the divine Authority gave authority to humanity to act on his behalf. Further, the word "primary" accentuates that it is the first, most basic and important commission that God has ever given, or will ever give. It is the foundational commission to all other commissions.

The primary commission has been confirmed by Scripture to be our "primary" commission throughout biblical and human history. God rules, but he shares that responsibility with us as well. God's reign becomes our reign. Genesis 1:28 first declared it, and Psalms, Isaiah, Daniel, Matthew, Paul, Hebrews, and Revelation reaffirm it for eternity. The Bible's first and last chapters highlight our reign over the earth. Examples are . . .

> Subdue the earth and rule. Gen 1:28

> You have created humanity to rule over your works. Ps 8:6

> The Most High's saints will receive the Kingdom and possess it forever, yes, for the eternal future. Dan 7:18

> The time arrived when the holy ones took possession of the Kingdom. Dan 7:22

> The sovereignty, power, and greatness of all the kingdoms will be handed over to the saints of the Most High. Dan 7:27

> The meek will inherit the earth. Matt 5:5

> If we endure, we will also reign with God. 2 Tim 2:12

> You have created humanity to rule over your works. Heb 2:8

> I will give authority over the nations to whoever is victorious and does my will to the end. Rev 2:26

> I will allow the victorious one to sit with me on my throne just as I was victorious and sat with my Father on his throne. Rev 3:21

> You have made them to be a kingdom and priests to our God; and they will reign on the earth. Rev 5:10

> They will reign forever and ever. Rev 22:5

What a pleasant New Earth it will be when it is shepherded by believers who are completely godly in character, morality, and effectiveness. We were created for this, but in this parenthetical age we are floundering in our righteous performance of it. Along the way we will be disciplined for our ineffectiveness in shepherding of the world, but the Lord's grace will finally commend us in his glorious courts in front of all creation.

How God created the universe is a model of how we are to shepherd in his image. We know that he spoke it into existence—he spoke; it happened. But we are told more: that the world was formless and without any design, just covered by water and darkness. The Trinity then went on to refine this undefined mass of matter with infinite creativity and power. God took the clump of the planet and like a potter, subjected it to his wisdom and might and crafted a reality that became the reflection of his glorious self. Though we do nothing close to the magnitude of these creative feats, still, we are to exert every wise effort to plan, design, communicate, form, refine, and maintain shepherding care and productivity of everything for which we are responsible in his creation. God's creation was more than just getting things started. It was the most magnificent illustration of how God wants you and me to creatively take assertive yet caring control of his creation.

The primary commission says that women and men "will rule" and that they must "subdue and rule" (Gen. 1:26, 28). Reigning can be done through an authority's selfish and horrific imposition of perverted, sadistic impulses, or an authority can rule by godly and beneficent shepherding of one's subjects. One can subdue the innocents by persecuting them for their righteousness' sake, or one can subdue the treacherous persecutor, defeating the one who sets oneself against God and persecutes his favored ones.[10] One can subdue enemy nations by massacre, genocide, and with little concern for collateral damage, or one can win by diplomacy or just wars.[11] Admittedly, the primary commission is stated in very strong terms which leave no doubt about its ultimate significance and required rigor. More modest words than "subdue" would have implied that compromises are expected when extreme force at times is necessary. A "softer" statement would have conveyed the expectation that the measures taken were to be mediocre and that the priorities may be negotiable. Notice it does not say we are simply to "try" shepherding our environment or try to fit the primary commission into the several other priorities we have. The severity of the primary commission's description of human shepherding makes it clear that we are not merely to hold the world at bay until Jesus Christ returns.

The strength of the primary commission's wording motivates us to subdue the earth now by whatever godly means are available. This is far from an oppressive, abusive tyranny that thwarts human dignity, creativity, and happiness. It does not condone exploiting the rest of creation. Rather it encourages us to lovingly direct all creation, humanity, and nature toward a more perfect reflection of God's glorious character and attributes.

The bigger picture in Genesis 2–4 explains humanity's reign over all physical creation by "serving," "shepherding," "keeping/guarding," not just "subduing."[12] The controlling relationship is to be edifying and purposeful; our reign helps the land and its vegetation, animals, and the human population to meet their potential fruitfulness. Just as God does, we are to manage creation by serving it, not abusing it for personal gain.

The Old Testament uses the word "shamar" when one gives responsible attention to something. God uses this word when he explains to the Couple what their subduing responsibilities were in Eden. Jacob used the word when he explained to Laban that he would be responsible for caring for Laban's sheep. In other words, subduing and shepherding is not a careless, self-centered role; it is a serving, edifying role.

> The Lord God put the man in the garden of Eden to tend and *care* for it. Gen 2:15

> Jacob replied, "Again I will shepherd your flock and care for it. Gen 30:31

---

10. Lev 25:43, 46, 53; 26:17; Neh 5:5; Ps 49:14; Isa 14:2, 6; 41:2; Jer 5:31; 34:11, 16; Ezek 34:4
11. 1 Kgs 4:24; Neh 9:28; Pss 72:8; 110:2; 144:2; Isa 45:1
12. Gen 2:5, 15; 3:23; 4:2, 9, 12; e.g., Prov 12:10

Nurturing creation is the goal, not exhausting it or exploiting it. The art of sovereignty wisely balances and blends forcing and encouraging, demanding and instructing, expecting and enduring, ruling and serving, correcting and forgiving, regulating and allowing, punishing and protecting. That is how our Lord lords us, and that is how we are to lord creation.

So, the primary commission and the eternal design are based on a primary attribute of God—God is love. Love is the basis for the Trinity's own unity; it is the basis for the Trinity's relationship with its creation, and it is the basis of our relationship with God and others. The Lord wants creation managed in a godly way because he loves it. We too will shepherd creation because we love it and its Creator.

The significance of the primary commission is appreciated further when we listen to the very few conversations among the Trinity that are revealed to us. These conversations always reveal the Trinity's unity in thought, and these conversations most often pertain to God's eternal design and the primary commission. For example,

> The Trinity plans the creation and the role of ruling humanity. Gen 1:26–28
>
> The Trinity responds to human subjection to the Serpent's rule. Gen 3:22
>
> The Trinity causes humanity to fill the earth. Gen 11:5–7
>
> The Father commissions the Son to rule all the earth's nations. Ps 2:7–9
>
> The Father seats the Son at his right hand to rule his enemies. Ps 110:1–2
>
> The Father gives the Son rule over all humanity. John 17:1–2

One might ask why anything would need subduing if God created a perfect world. But Adam and Eve were to *maintain* the perfect order that God had created. God chose in his wisdom to create a world where his energy and that of humans needed to be constantly and deliberately injected to keep the earth as a perfect reflection of its Creator.

Our role in godly management of the earth continued after the Fall and after the curses on creation. But it became even more strenuous since it was no longer just a *maintenance* task—it became an enormous task of *restoring* our fallen world. God has privileged us to be vital participants in delivering creation, including humanity, back to that 'good'ness it had when first created. Whereas humanity was first expected to manage a perfect planet, after Eden we are now expected to manage the restoration of a cursed and wayward planet.

"Multiplying" and "filling" are also included in the primary commission. They are not important only as steps to subduing and shepherding. They are also important because they themselves are acts of moral shepherding. Humanity is not to multiply and fill the earth in any possible way. For instance, multiplying, or procreation is restricted to married couples alone, and this for the sake of their own relationship and the stability of the family and community. And "fill the earth" does not mean by every possible way; the command does not justify stealing the earth from nature while all its species struggle to survive. It does not mean to spread and fill the earth by stealing the wealth, and natural and human resources from current residents and societies who are more vulnerable.

SHEPHERDING WITH GOD

So, the plan did not change. It never does with God. Because God gave the primary commission to humanity, we are still responsible for shepherding this earth. So Paul reminds us in Romans 16:20 of the crushing blow to Satan's head that was mentioned way back in Genesis 3:15, where humanity is prophesied to bring an end to the Serpent's influence. Paul encourages us that our victory is certain, but reminds us of our partnership with God in this victory: "The *God* of peace soon will crush Satan under *your* feet" (Rom 16:20). If there was any concern about the forcefulness of the word "subdue" and whether it is too strong of a word to describe our responsibilities under the primary commission, Paul dispels that concern by describing the massive forces we are up against.

The partnership between God and humanity is introduced in the primary commission to the Couple, and then again to Noah. First, there is no doubt about the preeminence of the Lord's authority in terms of the primary commission according to Ezekiel; using the same words of the primary commission he accentuates creation's inferiority:

> The fish of the water, birds of the skies, beasts of the field and all creeping things and all humanity on the face of the earth will shake at my presence. Ezek 38:20

But the separation between humanity and nature is also made very clear again to Noah after the Flood.

> All animals of the earth, all birds of the sky, all small animals that creep on the ground, and all fish in the sea will dread and fear you. They are placed under your authority. Gen 9:2

God condescends to partner with humanity, showing his respect and trust in us since we bear his image, and promising he will always persist with us in his eternal design. So we are not independent in how we administer God's world. Our sovereignty is a limited sovereignty, highly significant, but always subject to his purposes and strategies. At the same time, we must not conveniently underestimate our sovereign *responsibilities* to serve everything around us with him.

David explained God's willingness to work with each of us in subduing that part of the world the Lord has given us to shepherd. David acknowledged our need to fight our battles personally and to trust the Lord for his support as our helper.

God's Shepherding Commission

> Blessed be the Lord; he is my rock.
>
> He trains my hands for war, and my fingers for battle;
>
> He loves me as my fortress, my stronghold and my deliverer,
>
> He is my shield and in him I take refuge; he subdues the peoples under me.
>
> O Lord, who is man that you even consider him, or the son of man, that you think of him?
>
> Man is like a breath—his days as a passing shadow.[13]

On the military front, though Israel's land was a gift from God, she was expected to take possession of it. "Taking possession" of the land was possible only through the united effort of God and soldiers.[14] Again, it is not because God is incapable of doing anything and everything himself; it is because his eternal design includes us as partners. God's power is the ultimate reason for victory, but God's people are the instruments.[15]

Rather than partnering with God in Israel's management of its nation, Israel struggled with God in a couple ways: her preference for a monarchy rather than a confederation of tribes, and in forming alliances with other nations. In respect to preferring a monarchy, the collaboration with God was now more indirect—less intimate. Having a king now added another layer of management above the local-regional elders. This was irresponsible because it discouraged personal or community initiative to seek God's specific will in their own tribal localities. The original plan was more practical, where God ruled directly through the tribal elders who were closest to the issues. It was also irresponsible to concentrate so much authority in a monarchy where abusive power was magnified, affecting the whole nation.

Second, Israel struggled with God when compromising her strength by forging military and political alliances with foreign peoples. By doing so, Israel not only compromised their trust in the Lord as their partner and protector, but they now shared their sovereignty over their land and God's people with another sovereign king from another land. This led to the corruption of the standards of the perfect theocracy prescribed in the Mosaic law and wisdom instructions by adding a third, unwelcome and often contrary partner into the equation, marginalizing Israel's sovereign God.

Apart from human pride, there is no reason for opposition to the Lord since he has revealed clearly how we are to shepherd our world, his creation. We learn how to shepherd through his commands, covenants, wisdom instructions and promises in the Testaments. He gives instructions that carry penalties for disobedience. He designs covenants which are not negotiated but are far fairer than if we drew them up. He also makes promises that are gloriously gracious to the believer but horrifically punitive to the non-believer. Nonetheless, his preference is to move the eternal

---

13. Ps 144:1–4; also. Gen 49:22–25; Pss 18:29, 31–50

14. Num 32:22, 29; Deut 3:18; 5:31; 9:3; 12:29; 15:4; 25:19; Josh 18:1; Judg 3:30; 4:23; 8:28; 11:33; 1 Sam 7:13; 2 Sam 8:11; ? Chr 17:10; Neh 9:24; Pss 44:2–10; 47:3; 60:9–12; 68:21–23; 81:14; 118:10–14

15. Josh 6:7–16, 20; 2 Chr 20:20–23

design to its perfect continuance under his joint management with us as believers and members in his kingdom.

When Israel was exiled and had no land nor authority with which to shepherd, the Lord was still faithful to his eternal design by appointing the Babylonian king, Nebuchadnezzar, to be the primary commission's shepherd and ruler. Hear the words of the primary commission given even to Nebuchadnezzar, a pagan king.

> You, O king, are the king of kings, to whom the God of heaven has given the Kingdom, the power, the strength and the glory. He has given into your hand to rule over all humanity, the beasts of the field and the birds of the sky, wherever they dwell. Dan 2:37–38

God is persistent in his plans and eternal design. Though he forced the embarrassing Israelites into exile for their intentional disregard for his design for the land of Israel, he returns them from exile to that same land to try again. The precise reason the Lord called the humiliated Israelites back to fill their land is not surprising since Jeremiah had encouraged them with the primary commission: now multiply again, fill the land, but this time be better shepherds in the land of Israel.

> I will gather the remnant of my flock from all the countries where I have driven them. I will bring them back to their sheepfold, and they will be *fruitful and multiply*. I will set *shepherds* over them to *shepherd* them. Jer 23:3–4

> I will give you *shepherds* after my own heart who will feed you on knowledge and understanding. When you are *multiplied and increased in the land*, people will never say, "The ark of the covenant of the Lord." It will never enter their minds, be remembered, be missed, nor be remade. Jer 3:15–16

God's primary commission is critical in every era of his eternal design.

The primary commission continues throughout the New Testament too, as we will see in detail the further we go in this study. But for now, we recognize one example of the New Testament's focus on the primary commission—Hebrews 2:6–9. This passage explains that since humanity failed at managing Eden and has continued to fail ever since, it was necessary for Jesus to come and be that ruling human being who would himself fulfill the primary commission perfectly. The passage begins by quoting David's wonder from Psalm 8:4–5 and continues to explain why Jesus came.

> It has been testified somewhere, "What is man that you even think of him, or the son of man that you care for him? You made him a little lower than the angels, but crowned him with glory and honor." By subjecting everything to humanity, God left nothing outside humanity's control. Right now we do not see everything in subjection to humanity. But we see Him, who for a short time was made lower than the angels, namely Jesus, who was crowned with glory and honor because of the suffering of death.

In his primary commission, God subjected the earth primarily to humanity, not to angels or any other part of creation. The commission will come to more complete fruition in New Earth, but right now during the parenthetical age the Lord requires a perfect Human to rule with the greatest authority. To be consistent with the primary commission and to guarantee it this time, now the Man, Jesus, would subject all reality under his authority. By that Human, humanity would not fail again. Jesus' great commission starts out with this: "All authority in heaven and earth has been given to me"—everything has been subjected under his feet (Matt 28:18).

Psalm 8:4–5 and Hebrews 2:6 tell us that it is God's care for humanity that motivated him to share his rule with us. The primary commission has always been a critical part of the eternal design and always will be. By pursuing this design we will be the shepherds and rulers God intended for us to be when he gave us his own image. We will be successful through a mutual, caring and wise partnership while we tend the whole of creation, including humanity itself.

SHEPHERDING AGAINST GOD

God has honored humanity by sharing his sovereignty with us, but human history shows how we turn our privileged share into foolish opposition to him, century after century, millennium after millennium. The struggle against the Trinity rather than our collaboration with the Trinity is the tragedy of human history. This opposition is so pervasive throughout humanity that the very name that God gave to his own people was "Israel," meaning, "he struggles with God" (Gen 32:28). Unfortunately, as a whole, humanity seldom reflects a partnership between God and humanity. Humanity is still largely in partnership with the Enemy. Rarely is there a sustained attempt to seek the Lord's principles for shepherding and to obey them for his purposes. Instead, a duped humanity continues to pursue what it believes is its own ways, when instead, they are Satan's ways. Human history has shown nearly no interest in consciously working with the Lord to shepherd as he shepherds. Only where the believing, faithful church is at work do we see any such collaboration.

History books and current news are anyone's window into how well humanity is shepherding as God shepherds. Human history in this parenthetical age shows humanity blessing, delivering and disciplining the rest of creation in deep and profound ways. But overall, humanity's shepherding has been deplorable. Rather than bless, deliver, and discipline, we ignore, abuse, and act unjustly.

Rather than *blessing* creation, humanity has habitually *ignored* it. Our race is well-practiced at not considering much about creation, including nature and other humans. We are so self-absorbed that we do not even see the world around us. We fantasize about our own success and pleasures while we do not even consider the success and joys of those around us. We intentionally ignore our surroundings rather than intentionally inform ourselves of them. We cannot bless nature or others when we are oblivious to them. The shepherd cannot bless the lamb if he does not know that it exists or where it is. It is the shepherd's job to know, to inquire, to question, to count, to look, to care.

The opposite of *delivering* creation is to *abuse* it. We *cause* the very scenarios where deliverance is now necessary. Abuse of others can deliberately trap them into difficulty. Neglectful inaction contributes to the abuse of others as well. Rather than looking for opportunities to save, we prefer to abuse by subjecting much around us to our foolish and selfish priorities. We exploit circumstances and people to meet our objectives rather than seeing where we can deliver them from the complications and realities of this parenthetical age. The shepherd does not deliver the lamb if he walks too fast or leads it through dangerous zones. It is a cruel shepherd who does not scare off the raven who pecks the eyes out of a helpless newborn lamb or who does not defend the flock with his own life against lions, bears or thieves. It is his job to deliver the sheep rather than to be lazy, careless, pitiless, or brutal. If he does not shepherd the sheep, he is an abusive leader.

The opposite of proper *discipline* is to *act unjustly*, to be unfair and partial against the innocent. We are responsible for injustice when we are the unjust one or when we are passive and do not insist on justice for others. We are called to discipline others, but if we neglect this responsibility, the wicked will continue to intimidate and abuse. Yes, "Judge not or you will be judged" is a command for those who need to be careful of hypocrisy.[16] But Christ, Paul, and James also warn that there is a time and duty to judge and discipline others.[17] Chaos and greater sin are the only results to a lack of responsible correction (Eccl 8:11).

Moral shepherds must deliver and discipline others during this negative parenthesis in God's eternal design. Ignoring and abusing creation, and being unjust in our dealings, will end in New Earth. Until then, Christians live and shepherd within this perilous parenthetical pattern. But praise God for supplying us with the wisdom, compassion, and fruits of the Spirit to aid us in shepherding in righteous ways until Christ's victorious second coming.

---

16. Luke 6:37; Matt 7:3
17. John 7:24; 1 Cor 5:12; Jas 2:4

4

Providing the Shepherds

THE PATTERN OF THE PRIMARY COMMISSION

God's own nature determines the nature of what he creates; who he is and what he does determines what his creation is and does. By his nature, he is a shepherd of his creation, so by his nature, his creation shepherds too. But even the Primary Commission mirrors the Creator who gave it. The Trinity, Christ, and humanity all multiply, fill the earth and subdue it by constructive shepherding.

GOD MULTIPLIES

The Trinity is the model for the plurality and variety in creation. Since God is more than one Person, naturally he is interested in plurality. The Trinity is three different Persons, equally God, united in their being as a single deity, but they are not identical Persons. To be absolutely clear, the Trinity is not three persons because they have multiplied themselves or produced themselves in some way. The quality of being more-than-one is a fundamental attribute of the one and only God. However, all attempts to explain this Trinitarian pattern with much greater precision using analogies and symbols have always fallen short because the Lord did not create us with the capacity to fully understand or explain his infinite nature. Being finite, we will fall infinitely short of his infiniteness, so mysteries about God are inevitable and some will surely remain eternal.

Everything exists because of the Trinity's desire to multiply itself. Creation is the result of God's nature to multiply. God's purposes for creating us in his image are mentioned in the Trinity's planning session recorded in Genesis 1:26–27. God is not speaking here to angels since we are not created in the angel's image. He is not speaking to other gods since they do not exist. And it is not necessary to assume God is talking to himself, using a "royal we," since the rest of the Old Testament refers often to the Holy Spirit and to the Son and the Messiah. Notice how these verses of the primary commission emphasize God's image as his design for us.

> Let *us* make humanity in *our* image, to be like *us* so they can rule over the fish ... birds ... cattle and over all creeping things.... So God created humanity in *his image* in God's image he created humanity; he created them *male and female*. Gen 1:26–27

The phrase, "he created them male and female" is not just an unrelated, romantic detail—it explains how God formed his Trinitarian image of variety into humanity. Just as God is not complete as one person, humanity is not complete as one gender; God said, "It is not good for the male to be alone, I will create for him a suitable helper" (Gen 2:18). The Trinity is not three cloned Persons, neither was Eve cloned from Adam. The Trinity is three different Persons and Adam and Eve were two different persons. They are equally human, but they are not identical.

However, two genders were created for more than variety; two genders were also the way of perpetual multiplication. We would multiply biologically, however, not by forming new life from the ground. The Trinity's multiplication of itself is also the model for the family for which Adam and Eve were created. The first Couple gave birth to their images as God "gave birth" to his images.

When Joseph's genealogy is reviewed in Luke, this divine multiplication is intentionally highlighted. Adam's origin in God is certainly a different sort of procreation than that of the fathers and sons listed by Luke, but the list has a purposeful development to affirm God's multiplication of his image in Adam and all subsequent people. Starting with Joseph's father, Eli, the genealogy is in the typical format, "Joseph, the son of Eli . . ." Joseph's lineage is recounted all the way back, through King David, and concludes, "Methuselah, the son of Enoch, the son of Jared, the son of Mahalaleel, the son of Cainan, the son of Enosh, the son of Seth, the son of Adam, *the son of God*" (Luke 3:37–38).

God wants us to understand how much we are in his divine image to the extent that he even calls us "gods." We are so much like him that we are "gods"—not my word, not my interpretation. It is stated in both Testaments.

> I have said you are gods—all children of the Most High. Ps 82:6–7

Jesus then reminds us,

> Is it not written in your Law, "I have said you are gods"? John 10:35

The Lord fills the earth with little "gods" that are enough like him to shepherd with him in many of the same ways he shepherds. Paul agreed with pagan poets who had written, "In God we live and move and exist . . . so we are the offspring of God" (Acts 17:28–29).

Humanity is God's offspring, but as believers this is especially true when we become a new creation in Christ.[1] Then we look even more like the children of our divine Parent.

We can determine from the Lord's creation and Word that he loves growth. Growth is a development that is built into life forms. Apparently, it is also the nature of our universe as it expands towards unknown "space." Growth in knowledge and awareness of God's world has resulted in an expansion of civilizations and brought improvements in how to deal with the Edenic curses and the curses humanity has earned ever since. Growth in human, animal, and plant populations expands their presence across the planet. The Lord prefers growth, and it is so central to his design that he has promised that we will be involved in his eternally growing kingdom. New Earth will not be in an eternal stagnant state; the Messiah's kingdom will only continue to grow and grow: "The growth of his peaceful government will never end" (Isa 9:7).

God's preference for progressive ordering of his creation is shown in the very first stage of creation. First, God created the skies and earth, but it was "formless and void," covered by only water and darkness. As the Holy Spirit moved over those waters, God *then* subdued the darkness by creating light, *then* he differentiated levels of moisture, *then* he separated the waters to expose dry land, *then* he populated the skies, waters and land with life of all kinds of celestial bodies and life, and *then* commissioned one of those life forms to rule significant parts of creation with the Trinity.[2]

This process of creation reveals his preference for progression through time. Time is built into creation, and the Lord follows his own timetable to move from a formless beginning by an eternal design unto a creation that will never be stagnant or complete. He continues to determine the ever-changing borders, power and effects of the sky, water and earth. He creates the beautiful variety of nature and ensures their sustainability through physical laws. Then he commissions spirits, nature, and humanity to shepherd his creation beyond the parenthetical age unto an eternal sequence of blessing, creativity, and intricate human management, bringing the world to an even greater reflection of the infinite glory of its Creator. There will be no end to this process of developing fuller reflections of God since he is infinite, yet even infinite time will not be enough for creation to show God's glory fully.

God's kingdom has always been; but it will always be developing and never will have "arrived." There is no "finish line." His plans and kingdom will never come to an end or to any full fruition because he prefers to perpetually and eternally enhance, expand, and add to what he has made and done. This same goal of enhancement is what God shares with humanity to accomplish—to further cultivate creation to make it more productive and more of what the Trinity wished it to become from Genesis 1:1 through the everlasting ages.

---

1. Matt 5:9; Rom 8:14, 19; 9:26; Gal 3:26; 4:6; Eph 2:10; 4:20–24; Heb 12:7
2. Gen 1:2; 8:1; Job 33:4; Isa 40:13–17

HUMANITY MULTIPLIES

The Trinity assigned to us their same creative process to multiply their image. In Genesis 5:1, 3, both God and Adam produce humans in their image.

> When God created human beings, he made them in his likeness. (5:1)

> Adam reproduced Seth in his likeness and image. (5:3)

So we have been produced to reflect God's image just as a son or daughter reflects their father and mother: "like father like son." Adam and Eve pass their divine-image to their children. God's design for reproduction is also built into the natural world; but animals and plants replicate physically only, generating images that do not resemble God in his character to the extent that humans do.

The entire Father-God motif in both Testaments is built on this childbearing image, including the Holy Spirit's role in the birth of Jesus![3] The reason Jesus is called "the Son of God," according to the angel who appeared to Mary, is that he was born by the Spirit. He became God's only begotten Son in a unique way.

Multiplying becomes an important theme in the Bible. Humanity has been very obedient to the primary commission's first command to multiply. Adam and Eve complied, and history shows such success in its obedience that overpopulation has endangered the world in many ways. It has not been a challenge for humanity to multiply. Though abortion, infanticide, genocide, epidemics, war, tsunamis, and other natural disasters have brought massive depletions of the earth's inhabitants, we have still glutted this world with people who are poorly distributed and poorly cared for on the planet.

The biblical message that reproduction is a blessing and a necessity permeates both Testaments and the message will continue at least until New Earth. The following chart shows how the blessing and responsibility to multiply extends throughout the history of Israel and the church. Eventually we will see how multiplication pervades God's Word extensively, but this chart gives a few examples to get us started for now.

	MULTIPLY
Adam & Eve	Commissioned to "Be fruitful" "Multiply" Gen 1:28
Pre-Flood	Humanity started multiplying on the earth Gen 6:1
Noah	Commissioned to "Be fruitful" "Multiply" Gen 9:1, 7
Babel	Humanity's multiplication listed in genealogies Gen 5, 10
Abraham	Abraham to be greatly "multiplied" Gen 13:16; 15:5; 17:2–6
Isaac	Isaac to be greatly "multiplied" Gen 26:4, 24
Jacob	Commissioned to "Be fruitful" "Multiply" Gen 28:3, 14; 35:11
Egyptian Bondage	Israel was "fruitful" and "multiplied" in Egypt Ex 1:7
Mosaic Law	Obeying the Law ensures multiplication Deut 7:12–14; 28:62; 30:15–16
Conquest	Israel retains its "multiplied" status only by the Lord's grace Deut 28:63

---

3. Matt 1:18; Luke 1:35; Gal 4:29

MULTIPLY	
David & Solomon	Israel and David's seed as many as grains of sand 1 Kgs 4:20; Jer 33:22
Exile	Israel's numbers to be reduced when she is exiled Deut 4:27
Return from Exile	Israel is "fruitful," and "multiplies" Jer 23:3; Ezek 37:26
Messiah	Messiah's disciples will multiply Isa 9:3, 7; Matt 28:19
NT Church	Multiplication of believers in the early church Acts 2:41; 4:4
100+ AD Church	Multiplication of the church through the millennia until New Earth

As early as Genesis 6:1, "when humanity started multiplying on the face of the earth . . . ," procreation introduced an ominous era in human history. Noah's commission and each of the patriarchs' commissions require multiplication explicitly, as does Israel's commission to multiply even when she was exiled to other empires (Jer 29:6).[4] The book of Exodus begins with the Israelites multiplying successfully, and God continued to encourage Israel about their increasing population.[5] Israel's multiplication or decline in numbers was a sign of God's faithfulness or judgment to the patriarchs and his people. Reproduction became a standard reason for praise, as well as a repeated promise or implied threat that reproduction would be thwarted.[6] Interest in Israel's population is seen elsewhere. The wandering multitude of Israel and its success in multiplying was estimated for each tribe to the nearest multiple of fifty.[7] Later, David's census numbered Israelite men alone at 1,300,000 (2 Sam 24:9).

The enormous number of descendants from the patriarchs, Abraham, Isaac, and Jacob, was described to be as many as the visible stars of the sky,[8] or the grains of sand[9] or dust particles of the earth.[10] Just the descendants of David and Levi alone would be as numerous as the visible stars (Jer 33:22). The Lord's blessing of descendants is not only in number, however. Each individual child is not lost in this huge population but is a blessing to be cherished by its mother and father, even grandparents.[11]

God's promise of procreation to the patriarchs was repeated to the Israelites as a nation: " . . . love the Lord your God, walking in his ways, keeping his commandments . . . so you will live *and multiply*" (Deut 30:16). When Israel eventually failed to love her Lord, her numbers declined. She was constantly reminded that there would be

---

4. Gen 9:1, 7, 27; 16:10; 17:2, 6, 20; 22:17; 24:60; 26:4, 22–24; 28:3; 30:24; 35:11; 41:52; 46:3; 48:4, 16, 19; Ezek 33:24;

5. Gen 47:27; 48:3–4, 15–19; Ex 1:7–12, 20; 23:26, 30; 32:13; Lev 26:9; Num 22:3–5, 11; 23:10; 24:7; Deut 28:11; Pss 105:23–24; 107:38

6. Deut 1:10; 6:3; 7:13; 8:1; 10:22; 13:17; 28:18, 62–63; 30:5, 16; 33:6, 17; Josh 24:3; Ruth 4:11–12; 1 Kgs 3:8; 4:20; 1 Chr 5:23; 8:40; 16:18–19; 27:23; 2 Chr 1:9; 13:8; Neh 9:23; Pss 105:11–12; 107:35–38; Isa 51:1–3; 54:1–3; Ezek 16:7; 36:10–11; 37:26; Hos 1:10; Zech 8:4–5; 10:8

7. Num 1:20–46; 2:3–34; 3:27–34; 26:7–50, 57, 62

8. Gen 15:5; 22:17; 26:4; Ex 32:13; Deut 1:10; 10:22; 28:62; 1 Chr 27:23

9. Gen 22:17; 32:12–13; 1 Kgs 4:20; Hos 1:10

10. Gen 13:16; 28:14; Num 23:10; 2 Chr 1:9; also, about Job, Job 5:25

11. Pss 127:3–5; 144:12; Prov 10:1; 17:6

only a "remnant" of their original multitudes because of national unfaithfulness.[12] But God promised them over and over that they would he multiplied again, regardless of how their exiles jeopardized their multiplication.[13] He promised there would always be at least a remnant if not a great number of Abraham's seed.[14]

One purpose for the lengthy genealogies in the Old Testament was to address which nation, peoples, and families should fill which land (Gen 5, 10, 11). These genealogies separated the Lord's people from the rest of the nations and parceled out which lands they were to fill. From Noah's three sons the earth was populated and the population was separated and dispersed to definitive territories.[15] Abraham's first born son by Hagar, Ishmael received his own covenant and commission because his descendants were not to fill any part of Abraham and Isaac's covenant land.[16] The genealogy of Keturah, another of Abraham's wives, is listed but those people were also sent out to the east of Canaan to fill another territory (Gen 25:1–6). Isaac's first born, Esau has an extensive genealogy recorded, but his descendants filled the land southeast of Israel (Gen 36:1–43). It was the descendants of Isaac's second born, Jacob, who were given the privilege to fill the land promised to the patriarchs.

The extensive genealogies in early Genesis prove the success of both the Lord and humanity in this first part of the primary commission by multiplying the seed of Adam and Noah. It continues successfully up to the jarring account of Sarah's barrenness in Genesis 11:30.[17] The drama of reproduction, fertility, and barrenness in the Old Testament played a large role in the patriarchal narratives and throughout Israel's history. It was a great threat to the patriarchs' commission if they could not multiply and even get the commission started. Yet each matriarch needed God's intervention to further the patriarchal commissions along since they were barren: Sarah, Rebekah, and Rachel.[18] Removing their barrenness was God's great blessing of deliverance experienced by each matriarch, and later by Manoah's wife, Hannah, and the Shunammite woman.[19] Genealogies are so important that it takes the first eight chapters of 1 Chronicles to repeat and expand them.

In the genealogies of 1 Chronicles, it is clear that the primary commission is still a focus since the names of those who *did* multiply sons were recorded,[20] but those

---

12. Ezra 9:8; Neh 1:3; Hag 1:12–14; Zech 8:12

13. Lev 26:38–39; Deut 4:27; 30:4–5, 8–9; Isa 9:3; 49:20–21; 60:22; Jer 3:16; 23:3; 30:19; 31:8; 33:22; Ezek 36:10–11; 36:37–38; 37:26; Zech 2:3–4; 10:8

14. Gen 45:7; 2 Kgs. 19:4, 30–31; 25:11; 2 Chr 30:6; 34:9; Is. 1:9; 10:21; 37:4; 46:3; Jer 6:9; 23:3; 31:7; 42:19; Ezek 5:10; 11:13; 12:16; Amos 5:15; Mic 5:7–8; Zeph 3:13

15. Gen 9:19; 10:5, 11, 18–32

16. Gen 16:10–13; 17:20; 21:13; 25:12–18

17. Gen 4:16–22, 26; 5:1—6:1, 9–10; 10:1–32; 11:10–30

18. Gen 11:30; 15:2; 16:1; 17:15–21; 25:21; 29:31; 30:1

19. Gen 11:30; 21:2; 25:21; 29:31; 30:22–24; 49:25; Ex 23:26; Judg 13:2–3, 24; 1 Sam 1:2, 5–6, 19–20; 2:5, 20–21; 2 Kgs 4:12–17; Ps 113:9

20. 1 Chr 5:23; 7:4; 8:40; 23:17

who for some reason were not as productive or were not productive at all were named too: Seled, Jether, and Rehabiah died without sons; Shemei's brothers had only a few.[21]

Abraham's faithful intention to sacrifice Isaac, his only son by Sarah, struck at the very core of his and Israel's primary commission. If Isaac had been sacrificed, Israel would have had no future. God had said Isaac had to mature into a man and multiply his own descendants if Israel was to fill the land of Canaan with his father's descendants. God had promised that (Gen 26:4, 24).

When God threatened to wipe out all the wandering Israelites in Sinai because of their idolatry, Moses rushes to deliver them by quoting God's own primary commission given to the patriarchs: "Remember Abraham, Isaac, and Israel, Your servants to whom you swore . . . 'I will multiply your descendants as the stars of the heavens'" (Ex 32:13). Moses used God's own words pertaining to multiplication against such a depleting and devastating judgment.

But eventually in Israel's history, all that God said would come as judgments upon Israel did come. Military battles, disease, drought and blight reduced her numbers. It even affected the multiplication of their cattle.[22] Israel's faithfulness would bring them growth and success; but the clear opposite awaited unfaithfulness: "In the same way the Lord was satisfied to prosper and multiply you, so he will be satisfied in making you perish" (Deut 28:63). When judges ruled in Israel before the monarchy, there were two morally contrasting examples of how the Israelites tried to keep up their numbers. A vicious solution was applied to the tribe of Benjamin after it had been decimated in war. The other tribes kidnapped 400 virgins from Jabesh-gilead and trafficked them to the Benjamite men.[23] On the other hand, Boaz and Ruth followed God's legal instructions in the court system to ensure tribal and family fruitfulness (Ruth 4:5).

Ezekiel's Song of the Delivered Mountains sings of God's grace to multiply Israel within her lands. Though these mountains had been abused and the cities desolated, eventually they would be extolled with lush vegetation and enlivened again by the multiplication of humanity and beasts (Ezek 36:1–15). The Shepherd in his sovereignty would multiply Abraham's seed again, "The devastated cities will be filled with flocks of people as numerous as the flocks of sacrificial sheep at Jerusalem's seasonal feasts" (Ezek 36:38).

CHRIST MULTIPLIES

God models the primary commission by producing humanity as his images and children. Jesus Christ was born of the Holy Spirit, and in a significantly different way, God continues to reproduce "children" as new creations by the same powerful Spirit. We are repeatedly called the "children of God."[24] God's design for multiplication in the

21. 1 Chr 2:30, 32; 4:27; 23:17
22. Deut 7:14; 28:20–26, 58–63; Josh 23:12–16
23. Judg 20:46–47; 21:12–14, 23
24. John 1:12; 11:52; Rom 8:16–17, 21; 9:8; Eph 5:1; Phil 2:15; 1 John 3:1–2; 3:10; 5:2

New Testament is by his adoption of individuals and families to be his new believing children. Now, multiplication of God's children includes his global strategy for evangelizing and discipling the peoples.

Jesus' great commission is based on the Trinity's primary commission in Genesis and the great commission extends the primary commission until today and into eternity. Jesus' commitment to the primary commission and eternal design is obvious as he affirms and applies the primary commission as his strategy for redeeming the world. His intentional parallel between his great commission and the Trinity's commission to Adam and Eve confirms his loyalty to the Trinity's intentions in Genesis 1. After telling his disciples that his Father had given him all authority, he commissions them to teach the peoples how they should obey the Human King, Jesus Christ.

Primary Commission: Gen 1:26–28	Great Commission: Matt 28:18–20
Be fruitful and multiply,	Make disciples
fill the earth and	of all nations . . .
subdue it	teaching them to obey

Christ multiplied himself several times over by choosing and teaching his commandments to his closest twelve disciples, and having another circle of seventy disciples plus uncounted others who trusted him as their Messiah. Though he did not procreate literally, he did mentor scores of people to be godly as he was godly. Since the harvest was huge, according to Christ, many more workers were needed to be sent into the world to teach its peoples to obey the King. He foresaw a remarkable number of saints who would respond to his rule as the Good Shepherd (Matt 9:37–38). This multiplication occurs today; thousands and thousands of Asians alone are becoming Christians, every day! Praise the Lord and his ever-increasing government: "There will be no end to the increase of his government" (Isa 9:7).

Paul celebrates this multiplication of believers in God's kingdom: "As God's grace is multiplied to more and more people, there will be tremendous thanksgiving, and God will receive more and more glory" (2 Cor 4:15). The numerical expanse of the Kingdom interested the New Testament writers. Numbers mattered not because of some program for artificial growth, but because every new Christian would now manage a new part of God's world in obedience to the Lord's loving, shepherding standards. Luke records the new believers to be around 3000 at one event and 4000 at another.[25]

---

25. Acts 2:41; 4:4

GOD FILLS THE EARTH

God fills all *spaces* in the skies and on the earth with his presence: "Can anyone hide in secret places so I cannot see him? ... Do I not fill the heavens and earth?" (Jer 23:24).[26] He also fills all *time* since he has always existed and will always continue to exist.[27] His presence fills the eternal timeline back into the eternal past and forward into the eternal future. These are powerful consolations to us who feel at *times* he has left us *alone,* that he has left us in our own space and time without a shepherd.

God fills space in another way—he fills all the earth with his image in each created person living on the planet. Humanity has always excelled at multiplying, but when humanity refused to fill the whole earth and preferred to settle *en masse* at only one place, the Trinity entered into human history in an especially forceful way. Filling the earth was not the inclination of humanity at Babel. The goal was not to fill the earth, but to form only one community centered at the one city they built with the infamous tower (Gen 11:1–9). The primary sin was not that they built a tower; the tower only represented their more basic stubbornness against filling the earth (Gen 11:4). The reaction of God was not to destroy the tower but to destroy the rebellion against his primary commission. So he spread them out over the whole earth just as he had intended them to do since Adam and Eve. The Lord wanted to fill the earth with people carrying his image everywhere, but when they refused to obey that part of the primary commission, God intervened. Again we hear the Three Persons conferring: "'Let *us* go down there to confuse them by their language'" ... So the Lord dispersed them from there to cover the face of the earth" (Gen 11:7–8). It was not so much that humanity looked upward with their tower at Babel as much as they did not look across the globe to journey to its ends. Because of the Lord's intervention, humans now inhabit most of the planet's territories, developing the wide varieties of world cultures.

The Lord also created nature with the ability to multiply and fill itself with enthralling networks of interdependence. The ground was created so that below, on, and above its surface it would be filled abundantly and made sumptuously productive. However, the land is cursed when it is not filled and productive (Isa 45:18). Examples of nature's fullness are given in the creation account. Animals and plants populate nature extensively; animal and plant life densely occupy the spaces under and on the waters, as well as under and on the soil, and in the sky.[28] There is a frequent phrase in the Old Testament for the earth's richness, for its abundance of life and good things: "The earth and its fullness."[29]

---

26. 1 Kgs 8:27; Pss 139:7–10; Isa 66:1–2; Amos 9:2–4

27. Ex 15:18; Job 36:26; Pss 29:10; 45:6; 66:7; 90:2–4; 93:2; 102:12, 27; 135:3; 145:13; 146:10; Isa 40:28; Jer 10:10; Lam 5.19; Dan 4:3, 34; 7:9

28. Gen 1:20–25; 8:17; Ps 104:24–25; Ezek 47:9–12

29. Deut 33:16; Pss 24:1; 50:12; Isa 34:1; Jer 47:2; Ezek 30:12; Mic 1:2

So we must take Jesus' words at face value: "Go into the whole world and preach the gospel to *all creation*" (Mark 16:15). And Paul confirms that this is exactly what happened: "The gospel was proclaimed to *all creation* under heaven" (Col 1:23). In other words, when the message of God is preached, it is not announced only to humanity. The message is not given just to save souls. The message also brings praise and thankfulness to God for his blessings, deliverance, and discipline as the shepherd king over *all* creation. This message has now gone out for centuries not only to humanity, but also to nature and the spirits, including the holy angels and the demonic kingdom. Though the holy angels do not need to be delivered, and demons apparently cannot be delivered, still, the truth about God and his plans and acts are heard by them and the rest of creation. After all, creation everywhere deserves to hear the good news of its deliverance since it too is "still groaning" under the Lord's curses in Eden (Rom 8:22).

HUMANITY FILLS THE EARTH

God designed the whole earth to be full of his living creatures—plants, animals, and humans alike. The waters swarm with fish, the sky is host to birds and insects, and humanity has certainly filled the earth.[30] Humanity's shepherding commission to control the world requires our procreation and territorial expansion everywhere on the globe. Paul referred to this divine allotment of territory to the peoples of all eras and areas when addressing the Athenian philosophers: "From one man God made every nation of humanity to live over all the face of the earth, determining their appointed times and boundaries where they lived" (Acts 17:26–27).

The following chart shows how deeply the expectation to fill the earth is embedded in the Testaments. It is a foundational pre-requisite for human shepherding of creation—creation is worldwide, so there needs to be shepherds worldwide.

	Multiply	Fill the Earth
Adam & Eve	Gen 1:28	Commissioned to "Fill" Gen 1:28
Noah	Gen 9:1, 7	Commissioned to "Fill" "Swarm" Gen 9:1, 7
Babel	Gen 5, 10	Humanity avoided filling the earth Gen 11:2, 8–9
Abraham	Gen 13:16	Abraham's seed will fill its part of the earth, Canaan Gen 13:14–17
Isaac	Gen 26:4, 24	Isaac's seed will fill its part of the earth, Canaan Gen 26:3–4
Jacob	Gen 28:3, 14	Jacob's seed will fill its part of the earth, Canaan Gen 28:4, 13; 35:12
Egyptian Bondage	Ex 1:7	Israel "filled" Egypt to a disturbing level Ex 1:7
Mosaic Law	Deut 7:12–14	Obeying the Law allows Israel to remain to fill the land Deut 28:63–64

---

30. Gen.1:20–22; 8:17; 9:1, 7

	Multiply	Fill the Earth
Conquest	Deut 28:63	Israel does not fill all of her part of the earth, Canaan Judg 1:19, 27–34
David & Solomon	1 Kgs 4:20	Israel filled her land "from Dan to Beersheba" 1 Kgs 4:25; Ps. 80:8–9
Exile	Deut 4:27	Israel is scattered so unable to fill her land 1 Kgs 14:15–16
Return from Exile	Jer 23:3	Israel returns to fill her reduced land Isa 49:20; Ezek 36:10–11, 37–38
Messiah	Matt 28:19	Messiah's realm will fill the earth completely Dan 2:35; Matt. 28:19
NT Church	Acts 2:41; 4:4	Start of the global expansion of the church Dan 2:35, 44; Matt. 24:14
100+ AD Church	Church Growth	The church has expanded over the entire globe

Each patriarchal commission includes this "filling" element as a substantive part of God's promise and expectations. Abraham was told that a great nation would descend from him, implying that a land would be full enough to be great (Gen 12:1–3). He was told his descendants would be as many as the stars, so a habitable land was needed (Gen 15:5–7). Abraham was told that he would not only produce *a* great nation but *many* nations (Gen 17:4–8, 15–16). He was told to walk Canaan's length and breadth: to the north, south, east, and west to see the size and boundaries of the land which his descendants would fill (Gen 13:14–17). Isaac and Jacob also were told that their large numbers of descendants would possess all the lands which Abraham had walked. Jacob was also promised that his descendants would spread out and fill the land to the north, south, east, and west.[31] Eventually, Joshua was promised that wherever his feet walked, the land was his and that of the Israelites (Josh 1:5).

It is critical for God's eternal design that people populate their God-granted land and then shepherd it well. Yet Israel often found herself doing the right thing but in the wrong place. When she first multiplied, she was so successful that "the land was full of them." The problem was that it was not the Promised Land that Israel had filled—it was Egypt instead (Ex 1:7, 12). After the exodus from Egypt, Israel's multitude was forced to reside and wander in the Sinai desert for refusing to conquer and fill Canaan, their proper and Promised Land. Later, Israel fills the wrong lands when they are exiled captives or when they fled to foreign lands as fugitives.

The wrong peoples had already filled Canaan before Israel left Egypt and pressed toward their God-given land. These residents had to be evicted one way or another so the land could be filled with Abraham's seed. When the Israelites finally entered Canaan, they were not thorough in their efforts or successes. Judges 1:1—3:5 recounts their serious failure in driving out all the inhabitants and settling only for whatever land was easy to acquire and keep. The tribe of Dan essentially gave up and settled in a land centered in Laish, far, far north of its God-assigned territory (Judg 18:1–2, 27–31).

---

31. Gen. 26:2–5; 28:3–4, 13–15; 35:11–12; 46:3–4

This meant of course that the wrong people were filling much of Israel. This led to an incomplete subduing of the land not only militarily, but also morally and culturally. This resulted in centuries of uncomfortable and distracting co-existence between Israel and the remaining peoples until the golden years during the united monarchies of David and Solomon. And even then, under these two strongest of Israelite kings, the Philistines were still bothersome residents in Israel's land. The "wrong" peoples were planted in Israel again to fill the land during Israel's Assyrian exile. While they were gone, their land was filled with foreign peoples and the Assyrian army.[32]

The psalmist speaks metaphorically of Israel filling her promised land:

> You removed a vine from Egypt . . . and it took deep root and filled the land. Its shadow covered the mountains; its boughs covered the cedars of God. It sent its branches out to the Mediterranean Sea, and its shoots to the Euphrates River (Ps 80:8–11).

Like an overwhelming covering by a gigantic vine-tree, Israel's people were supposed to overrun the land. Also, phrases like "live in the land," "possess the land" and "inherit the land" implied that the Israelites should fill their land.[33]

Israel's covenant territory had definite boundaries which are described generally in the patriarchal commissions. Eventually, the land grants were clarified, detailing the topography and cities that landmarked Israel's boundaries.[34] Exceptionally, Reuben, Gad, and a portion of Manasseh were given certain lands to fill that were unanticipated, even by the patriarchs. After kings Og and Sihon were defeated during the Canaan conquest (Josh 13:8–33), the land of these kings was given as a bonus to those three Israelite tribes.

Which lands the Israelites were assigned to fill when they finally conquered the land was symbolized when the Lord assigned each tribe a certain place around the tabernacle. When the Israelites were still in the wilderness they were positioned appropriately on all sides of the Tabernacle: north, south, east, and west, each tribe having the same position as they would in Canaan's geography when they eventually lived in it (Num 2:1–34).

The specific borders for each of Israel's tribes, and even specific families, were also defined.[35] However, the Levites were not given a single block of territory in Israel since their numbers were distributed and helped fill all the rest of the other tribes' lands (Num 35:1–8). This too was illustrated through the Levites' encampments around the tabernacle; they surrounded the tabernacle on all sides, not comprising a single area

---

32. Isa 8:7–8; Lam 5:2; Ezek 7:24; Joel 3:17

33. Lev 20:24; Num 33:53; 35:8; 36:8; Deut 4:14; Josh 22:9; Judg 11:24; 1 Chr 28:8; Neh 9:23; Pss 37:11, 22, 29; 69:35–36; Isa 57:13; 60:21; Ezek 45:8; Obad 1:17–20

34. Num 34:1–15; Deut 4:47–49; 11:24–25; 34:1–4; Josh 1:3–4; 12:1–8; 13:1–7; 1 Sam 7:12–14; 31:7; 1 Kgs 4:25

35. Num 26:53–56; 33:54; 35:1–8; 36:1–12; Josh 11:23; 14:2, 13–14; 15:1—21:43; 1 Chr 4:38–41; 5:7–11, 15–16, 23–24; 1 Chr 6:54–81; 7:28–29; 8:28–32; 9:2–3, 16; Pss 78:55; Ezek 45:7–8; 47:8—48:35

like the other tribes (Num. 1:52–54). So the Levites were an example of what it meant to fill the lands. They actually spread out into all the other Israelite lands.

The land of Israel is God's gift to Abraham and his seed,[36] and his shepherding grace assures their success in finally filling the land. Israel does finally multiply and fill its land at the pinnacle of her national righteousness under kings David and Solomon. The peace and prosperity which eventually came is described in terms of the broad, pervasive filling of the land from the south (Beersheba) to the far north (Dan): "Judah and Israel lived safely during the whole time of Solomon, each one under his vine and fig tree from Dan all the way to Beersheba" (1 Kgs 4:25). Though there were many discouraging centuries, there are some encouraging moments when many new cities were built under Solomon, Asa, and Uzziah.[37]

During Israel's "golden age," jurisdiction over some surrounding nations came under David and Solomon: Moab, Edom, Syria, Hamath, Zobah, and Ammon.[38] These peoples and their lands became part of David and Solomon's empires. This pointed back to God's commitment to Abraham that he would be the father of many nations and his descendants would rule as far as the Euphrates River. True, the Israelites were not given these additional countries to fill themselves, but the lands were covered under the patriarchal commission nonetheless (Gen 15:18). There was no expectation for the Israelites to fill any lands not promised to the patriarchs apart from what was gained by Joshua from the defeated kings, Og and Sihon. Ironically however, Israel's filling of other peoples' lands was an option for God even when he disciplined Israel; he could send them as exiles into Assyria and Babylon.

Instructions about intermarriage with the Canaanites even among other Israelite tribes were intended to avert another threat to filling, owning, and controlling one's land. Compromises were inevitable in these marriages when sovereignty over one's land was negotiated or lost to other tribes through complicated marriage and inheritance situations.[39]

Obedience was the condition for permission to continue filling God's land.[40] On a wide scale, because of human wickedness, humanity was no longer allowed to fill the land, so the Lord removed them in the Flood. Only Noah and his immediate family were delivered to give a fresh start to the filling of the land. More narrowly, obedience was required for the Israelites to fill their promised land. The first generation of refugees from Egypt, including Moses, were not allowed to fill the covenant land because they refused to follow the Lord's lead into that land. Other impediments

36. Gen 15:7, 18–21; 17:8; Deut 11:8–9, 20–21; Josh 24:12–13; 2 Sam 7:10; Neh. 9:22–25; Pss 44:2–3; 135:10–13; 136:17–22

37. 2 Chr 8:5–6; 2 Chr 14:7; 2 Chr 26:6–10

38. 2 Sam 8:2–14 // 1 Chr 18:2–13; 2 Sam 10:6, 19 // 1 Chr 19:6, 19; 2 Sam 10:6, 19; 12:29–30; 1 Kgs 4:21–25; 1 Chr 29:29–30; 2 Chr 8:3; 9:26; Pss 60:6–9; 105:44–45; Isa 26:15

39. Ex 34:15–16; Num 27:1–11; 36:1–12; Deut 7:3–4; Josh 23:12–13; Judg 3:5–6; Ezra 9:1—10:44; 10:28–30; Neh 13:23–30

40. Gen 6:5–7; Deut 4:1, 40; 6:1–3; 11:20–24; Prov 10:30

to Israel filling her land came from the Lord's judgments for failure to control the land according to his perfect standards and instruction. Plagues, natural disasters and military defeats killed them or drove them out of the land, reducing their numbers with which to fill the land.[41]

On the other hand, the Israelites were encouraged that their children would fill their land by "prolonging their days" so that they would "live long in the land" if they shepherded their nation according to God's standards. However, the ominous implication was that there was the possibility of them no longer filling their land if they did not continue to obey. The length of time when God's people could fill the land was a promise, and an incentive, but also a threat to Israel.[42] In other words, there were conditions to filling the land. Israel failed in those conditions and was disciplined through bondage and exile—the northern tribes into the Assyrian empire,[43] the tribe of Judah into the Babylonian empire.[44] The northern tribes were scattered completely from its land during these defeats to Assyria[45] and Babylon.[46] This was a long-predicted outcome but came only after many centuries that proved God's patience and faithfulness to Israel regardless of their persistent unfaithfulness.[47] A portion of unfaithful Israelites even returned to Egypt after hundreds of years,[48] while others went yet further to Greece (Joel 3:5-6).

This is the point of the patriarchal commissions—the land was to be filled so that godly kings could shepherd the people. If this covenant relationship between the Lord and Israel was not treasured by the nation, then there would be a very public and negative portrayal of God at this all important intersection of the continents called Canaan. It would not simply be a neutral portrayal of a failed nation to the unbelieving world; it would be a disgrace to her sovereign Deity to allow such ingratitude to be flaunted.

The privilege of partnering with the Lord in sovereign shepherding of the earth is lost when one no longer is a resident of the land. As the Couple's management of their primary commission in the Garden was disappointing, and they were expelled from Eden, so Israel's disappointing management of the Promised Land led to their expulsion to Assyria and Babylon. Faithful to his own promises, however, God predicts,

---

41. Deut 28:25-26; Josh 23:12-16; 2 Chr 20:10-12

42. Gen 13:15; 15:13; 17:8; 24:7; 26:3-4; 28:4, 13; 35:12; 48:4; Ex 20:12; 32:13; 33:1; Deut 1:8; 4:26; 5:16, 33; 11:9; 30:17-20; 32:47; 34:4; Josh 24:3; 2 Chr 20:7; Neh 9:8; Ps 25:13; Prov 2:20-22; Jer 22:26-28

43. 1 Kgs 14:15-16; 2 Kgs 17:5-23; 1 Chr 5:25-26

44. 2 Kgs 17:19; 20:16-18; 23:26-27; 24:12-16, 20; 25:1-7, 11, 21; 2 Chr 28:19-21; 33:10-12; 36:6-7, 15-21; Ezra 5:12; 9:7

45. 2 Kgs 15:29; 16:7; 17:10-11, 18-23; 18:11-12; 2 Chr 5:25-26; Jer 50:17; Hos 8:7-9; 9:3; Amos 5:27; 6:7; 7:17

46. 2 Kgs 20:18; 24:14-20; 25:11, 21; 1 Chr 9:1; 2 Chr 36:20-21; Jer 20:4-6; 22:11-12, 26-30; 24:1; 39:6-10; 50:17; 52:15; Dan 1:2-4

47. Lev 26:32-33; Deut 4:26-27; 28:36-37, 64; 29:27-28; 31:20-21; 1 Kgs 8:46-47 // 2 Chr 6:36-37; 1 Kgs 14:15-16; 7:19-21; Esth 2:5-6; 3:8-9; Pss 44:11; 137; Isa 5:13; 8:22; 27:8; Jer 7:3, 15; 9:11, 16, 19; 10:18, 21; 12:14; Lam 1:3; 4:16; Ezek 4:13; 6:8-9; 12:3-16; 20:23; Hos 9:16-17; Zech 1:19-21; 7:14

48. 2 Kgs 23:34; 25:12, 22, but 25-26; Jer 24:8; 42:13-19; 43:4—44:30; Hos 9:3, 6

designs and leads the Israelites to return and refill the land.[49] In fact, there are more biblical references to the return of Israel than to her exile. Though some prophetic passages are difficult to determine whether the promises are about Israel's return under Zerubbabel and Ezra[50] or far into the future times of New Earth,[51] they are some of the most glorious and beautiful parts of Scripture. Isaiah predicts great successes again in Israel's multiplying and filling the land.

> Enlarge your tent; spread its curtains broadly and lavishly, for you will spread to the right and to the left. Your descendants will occupy other nations, resettling the ruined cities.[52]

As beautiful as the Lord created the earth's topography to be, there is a certain preference for fertile and inhabited regions over widespread wild zones. If a people's land is predominantly untamed and wild, it could indicate a lack of human shepherding of the land and its resources, including people. Early biblical humanity is touted for its management of animals, plants, raw materials and even sounds for composing music. Cain, Abel, Jabal, Jubal, and Tubal-Cain all controlled and created the basics for economics and civilization: agriculture, art and industry (Gen 4:2, 20–22). So civilization is good for the land since human residence and influence brings order, management and restoration.[53] So even Solomon and Uzziah's remote settlements in the wilderness show how seriously "filling the land" was taken by these kings.[54]

A barren wilderness possibly indicates not only the simple *absence* of human service and ingenuity, but it also can reveal the effects of sin either by abuse of the land, neglect of duty in caring for it, or some desolation of it by God's judgment. The earth and nature suffer because of human rebellion. Humanity should follow legal codes governing the use of land and water to ensure there continues to be an inhabitable and fruitful land to supply the needs of flora, fauna, and people. Otherwise, God is justified to remove people from the land they were assigned to manage, leaving it desolate, fit only for the wild beasts to "govern" the land.[55] The barren wilderness can be a negative portrait because it may reflect a lack of care and prosperity. Adam, Eve, and Cain are exiled to the wilderness, though Cain is quick to build a city (Gen 4:17). Ishmael is sent into the wilderness to separate him from Abraham, Sarah, and

---

49. Deut 30:4–5, 8–9; Neh 1:8–9; 9:7–8; Isa 9:3; 10:21–22; 27:13; 51:11, 14; Jer 12:15; 24:5–6; 27:22; 29:10, 14; 30:10; 31:8–10; 32:14–15; 32:37, 41; 50:19–20; Ezek 11:17; 20:41–42; 34:11–16; 36:24; 37:12–22; Hos 11:10–11; Amos 9:14–15; Mic 2:12; 4:10; 7:11; Zech 2:4–7; 8:4–8; 10:8–10

50. Ezra 1:2–6; 2:1–67; 5:13; 7:6, 12–13; 9:8; Neh 2:4–9; 7:5–72; 12:1–29; Isa 48:20; 51:11, 14; 54:7; Jer 24:5–7; 29:11–14; 30:3

51. 1 Chr 17:9; Is. 9:1; 11:13–16; 19:23–25; Jer 23:5–8; 33:15–16; Ezek 37:1–28; Joel 3:1–2, 20; Amos 9:13–15; Mic 5:5–9; Nah 1:15; Zeph 3:15–20; Zech 8:7–8; 9:8—10:12; 14:2–4, 10–11

52. Isa 54:2–3; also, 49:19–21

53. Gen 47:19; Ex 23:29

54. 1 Kgs 9:17–18; 2 Chr 26:10

55. Lev 26:31–34; 2 Kgs 17:24–26; Pss 80:8–13; 107:33–38; Ezek 14:15

Isaac (Gen 21:14, 20–21). It is in the barren wilderness where the Israelites suffer their forty-year judgment. The sacrificial scapegoat from the Day of Atonement is doomed to be led into the wilderness, after Israel's sins were ceremonially laid upon it (Lev 16:8–10). Nebuchadnezzar is sent there for a while too as discipline (Dan 4:31–33). Babylon is still a desolate ruin.[56] Unfilled land is a curse.

This is not to say that appropriate and intentional designs for certain lands and regions to be left wild is irresponsible. We need these virgin territories to direct our hearts and minds to the incomprehensible creativity and power of God.

CHRIST FILLS THE EARTH

God's promise that the Messiah's kingdom will fill the entire earth is the greatest encouragement about filling the earth. Since the beginning of time, God designed the whole planet for filling—not just Israel. His design has always been global, and in his parenthetical design of deliverance and discipline, Israel and the church have become his models for the eventual deliverance of all the peoples who fill their own lands.

Daniel prophesied that the Messiah's "stone kingdom" will fill the entire earth. Speaking of Jesus Christ's kingdom, he predicts a expanding and demolishing Rock that will defeat the world's powers.

> The rock that knocked down the statue became a huge mountain that filled the whole earth . . . The God of heaven will set up a kingdom that will never be destroyed or conquered. Dan 2:35, 44

We are in this phase of God's eternal design now. When Christ came, the Spirit started filling the earth with those he and the Son would shepherd and who, in turn, would then shepherd others. The Gentiles have come to Christ from around the world in a profound way so the stone kingdom has surely filled the earth. Yes, Satan still has his sub-territories on earth where his influence is great, but Christians live and shepherd even within those dark places.

Christ's intention was that the whole earth would be populated with godly shepherds—not populated with just "saved" people, but saved people who shepherd and contribute to the Lord's eternal design from the time of their personal conversion until and through eternity. His promise is that "The gospel of the Kingdom will be announced throughout the whole world, to all nations, and then the end will come" (Matt 24:14). He did not say the end would come immediately after the whole planet had heard, just that the end would come sometime after the announcement had truly been global.

Those who had come to the Pentecost revival where Peter preached, returned to their lands to share the news of Jesus Christ's expanded kingdom. The New Testament letters list city upon city where new disciples are filling their "land," their personal territory where they shepherded as God shepherds. We know the numbers of those saved

---

56. Isa 13:19–22; Jer 50:39

soon after Christ's resurrection were in the thousands. We know the apostles and others were aggressive in their evangelism and discipling. Paul encouraged believers to pray for the apostles to assure the rapid filling of the earth with the kingdom gospel.[57] John's letters, including those dictated to the seven churches in Revelation, and the book of Acts describe the wonderful, rapid growth of the church to Ephesus, Smyrna, Pergamum, Thyatira, Sardis, Philadelphia, and Laodicea.

The centuries that have followed New Testament times have seen massive global evangelism and Christians abound among nearly every people, even to their own persecution, even martyrdom. This filling of the earth by the church is exhilarating, but it happens during a dark time for many of our brothers and sisters. It is truer now than any other time in human history, "The blood of the martyrs is the seed of the church."

THE PRIMARY COMMISSION IS PERVASIVE

The following chart shows the Trinity's pervasive primary commission and how it is assigned to humanity in biblical history and since biblical times. Fifteen historical periods are listed below. These are not the extent to which the Bible applies the primary commission, but they are examples of its most general and significant applications. The primary commission's three over-arching themes and activities make it easy for us to see how the Lord planned consistently to achieve his eternal design. By multiplying, filling, and then reigning responsibly at every level of human activity, humanity fulfills its primary commission and accomplishes our privilege of shepherding God's creation with him. The column titled "Rule/Shepherd" takes our study into the third and climactic area of the primary commission. We have not spent time so far to explain our shepherding responsibilities in detail, but the subject will be addressed throughout this study as one of the two most prominent concerns: (1) how God shepherds and (2) how humanity is to shepherd.

We will not explain the chart in detail since its content is the subject of much that follows in this study. Just absorb the patterns and notice how pervasive the primary commission's parts are.

---

57. 2 Thess 3:1; also, 3 John 5–8

	Multiply	Fill the Earth	Rule/Shepherd
Adam & Eve	Commissioned to "Be fruitful" "Multiply" Gen 1:28	Commissioned to "Fill" Gen 1:28	Commissioned to "Rule" "Subdue" Gen 1:26, 28
Noah	Commissioned to "Be fruitful" "Multiply" Gen 9:1, 7	Commissioned to "Fill" "Swarm" Gen 9:1, 7	Creatures are put in Noah's hand Gen 9:2; Noah to rule justly 9:5–6
Babel	Humanity's multiplication listed in genealogies Gen 5, 10	Humanity avoided filling the earth Gen 11:2, 8–9	Humanity ruled only one locale on the earth Gen 11:4–6
Abraham	Abraham greatly "multiplied" Gen 13:16; 15:5; 17:2–6	Abraham's seed will fill its part of the earth, Canaan Gen 13:14–17	Abraham and Sarah's seed will have "kings" to reign Gen 17:6, 16; Isa 51:2
Isaac	Isaac to be greatly "multiplied" Gen 26:4, 24	Isaac's seed will fill its part of the earth, Canaan Gen 26:3–4	—
Jacob	Commissioned to "Be fruitful" "Multiply" Gen 28:3, 14; 35:11	Jacob's seed will fill its part of the earth, Canaan Gen 28:4, 13; 35:12	Jacob's seed will have "kings" to reign Gen 35:11
Egyptian Bondage	Israel was "fruitful" and "multiplied" in Egypt Ex 1:7	Israel "filled" Egypt to a disturbing level Ex 1:7	Ironically, Israel was ruled abusively by Egypt Ex 1:11–12
Mosaic Law	Obeying Law brings multiplication Deut 7:12–14; 28:62; 30:15–16	Obeying Law allows Israel to remain in the land Deut 28:63–64	The Law defines proper reign over Israel Deut 17:18–20; Prov 20:8, 26
Conquest	Israel retains its "multiplied" status only by Lord's grace Deut 28:63	Israel does not fill all of her part of the earth, Canaan Judg 1:19, 27–34	Israel did not rule their land morally, so she is oppressed Judg 2:10–14
David & Solomon	Israel & David's seed as many as sand grains 1 Kgs 4:20; Jer 33:22	Israel filled her land "from Dan to Beersheba" 1 Kgs 4:25; Ps 80:8–9	Moral reigns of David and Solomon and wisdom instructions.
Exile	Israel's numbers to be reduced when she is exiled Deut 4:27	Israel scattered, not able to fill her land 1 Kgs 14:15–16	Israel conquered, ruled over by Assyria & Babylon 2 Kgs 17:5–23
Return	Israel is "fruitful," and "multiplies" Jer 23:3; Ezek 37:26	Israel returns to fill her reduced land Isa 49:20; Ezek 36:10–11, 37–38	Zerubbabel, Ezra, Nehemiah lead Israel back to limited sovereignty
Messiah	Messiah's kingdom subjects will multiply Isa 9:3, 7; Matt 28:19	Messiah's realm will start filling the earth Dan 2:35; Matt 28:19	Global reign will start under the Messiah Isa 2:2–4; Hab 2:14; Matt 28:19–20
NT Church	Multiplication of the early church Acts 2:41; 4:4	Start of the global expansion of the church Dan 2:35, 44; Matt 24:14	Elder-shepherds in each local church Jer 3:15; 23:4; 1 Pet 5:2–4
100+ AD Church	Multiplication of the church through the millennia	The church has expanded over the entire globe	Expanse of liberated civilizations based on our Christian worldview

As the chart shows, the eternal design and primary commission are intended for the whole world throughout all time! They are his design for all peoples for eternity. This is not to say that all peoples in all eras and areas are redeemed by Christ. But he is love; he is the model of love in his care even for those who disrespect, despise, even defy him. Humanity was created as the highest functioning order of creation, and his primary commission requires us, as God's partner in global management, to have the nature that mirrors God's nature in significant ways.

Though this chart lists some momentous landmarks through the Testaments and subsequent history, the same principles apply to our daily, routine responsibilities. We too multiply, fill and shepherd. We will see that biblical moral standards apply to us as believers when we shepherd the part of the earth God has given to each of us. God's creation will exist forever,[58] and that includes those of us who love him, serve him and rule with him within his eternal design: "His servants will worship him . . . and they will rule forever and ever."[59] Our shepherding will never cease!

---

58. Pss 78:69; 104:5; 148:1–6; Eccl 1:4; 3:14
59. Rev 22:3, 5; also, Pss 30:12; 41:12; 52:9; 61:8; 86:12; 89:1; 145:1–2

5

Christ's Shepherding Commission

GOD THE SAVIOR

BOTH TESTAMENTS PORTRAY GOD and Christ as the ultimate rulers and shepherds of their creation. Their authoritative position is described in other ways too—many times as "King." Believers are called both God's people[1] and the Messiah's people[2] because both the Father and Christ are kings of humanity. A few times God is also referred to as a "Father"[3] in the Old Testament but much more frequently in the New Testament, mostly by his Son. In this chapter, we will look closer at the *Kingdom* of God, while remembering he is the King who has a shepherd's heart.

One of God's shepherding roles is to deliver, so in his role as a deliverer he is called a "savior" in the Testaments. There were many troubles their compassionate Shepherd saved the Israelites from, so he is praised as Israel's savior,[4] her protective refuge,[5] shield,[6] fortress[7] and rock.[8] Certainly, one massive matter from which God delivers his people is from sin. But this is not the only meaning that the Testaments intend when referring to the Lord as a "savior." There is much that our Lord delivers us from beyond his marvelous grace of delivering us from sin.

---

1. Luke 1:68; Acts 15:14, 17; 1 Pet 2:9–10; Rev 21:3
2. Matt 1:21; Luke 1:77; Titus 2:14
3. Ex 4:22; Deut 1:31; 8:5; 14:1; 32:6, 18–20; Ps 103:13; Isa 1:2; 63:16; 64:8; Jer 3:4, 19; 31:9, 20; Hos 11:1–3; Mal 1:6
4. Deut 32:15; 1 Chr 16:35; Pss 43:5; 68:19; 79:9; 85:4; Isa 17:10; 43:3, 11; 45:15, 21; 49:26; 60:16; 62:11; 63:8; Jer 14:8; Hos 13:4
5. Deut 33:27; Joel 3:16
6. Deut 33:29; Pss 33:20; 115:9–11; Isa 31:5; Zech 9:15; 12:8
7. Pss 46:7, 11; 48:3; Isa 17:10
8. Gen 49:24; Deut 32:13–15, 18, 31; 1 Sam 2:2; 2 Sam 22:32, 47; 23:3; Isa 17:10; 26:4; 30:29; 44:8; Hab 1:12

In the Old Testament, God is referred to as a "savior" in the context of sin only in two passages. Psalm 79:9: "Help us, O God our Savior . . . deliver us and forgive our sins." Even here, "deliver" could refer to other adversities. And Psalm 85:4 does mention salvation from both adversity and from sin: "You restored the fortunes of Jacob. You forgave the iniquity of your people . . . Restore us again, God our Savior." God is the Savior who delivers us from innumerable adversities including sin.

Of course, the Old Testament believers praised God for deliverance from their sin as we will see in chapter 8. But the Lord told them he was their savior, and they worshipped him as their savior, from all sorts of other dilemmas as well.

> You are the hope of Israel, her savior in times of trouble. Jer 14:8

> I have been the Lord your God since you came from Egypt.
> You must acknowledge no God but me, no savior but me. Hos 13:4

> I am the Lord your God, the Holy One of Israel, your savior . . .
> I am the Lord, and there is no other savior. Isa 43:3, 11

> You are a God who hides himself, O God of Israel, savior!
> There is no other God but me, a righteous God and savior. Isa 45:15, 21[9]

This is the saving God who came in the flesh. This is the savior we meet in Christ Jesus. His mission as savior cannot be limited to any one application of his saving grace. Joseph was given the wonderful message that he should name the Child "Jesus" because he would save his people from their sins (Matt 1:21). Mary's was told to name the Child "Jesus" too, but the angel did not emphasize to her that Jesus would save from sin, but that he was the Son of God and would reign an eternal kingdom (Luke 1:31-33). In other words, Jesus would save from sin and he would save from the awful kings who had reigned, and were reigning over Israel. The New Testament Savior is more than a sacrificed lamb, he saves us by being our valiant defender King and destroyer of our enemies.

THE FATHER COMMISSIONED THE SON

How better for God and humanity to work together than if God himself became a human too? This became the perfect collaboration since there is no risk of human failure in this arrangement. The Father and Son have always worked in harmony within the Trinity, and the Incarnation brought a new note in that harmonious relationship. Christ, in himself, became the ultimate relationship of God and humanity—a God/human, as one person, whose every single act was at the same time and place a divine

---

9. Also, Deut. 32:15; 2 Sam 22:3; 1 Chr 16:35; Ps 68:19-20; Isa 17:10; 63:8

and human act.[10] Though that was not how God arranged his partnership with humanity in Eden, it became the required one in this parenthetical design.

Jesus Christ had to arrive in human form so it could be said that humanity truly reigns and shepherds just as the Trinity intended in Genesis 1:26–28. At long last, a human being would reign in the perfect way the rest of humanity has failed to reign. Hebrews explains this divine and human merger as the fulfillment of the primary commission.

> When putting everything under humanity, God made everything subject to them. Though we do not see everything subject to humanity right now, we do see Jesus, who was made lower than the angels for a while, crowned with glory and honor. Heb 2:8–9

This was the eternal design's solution to human failure in shepherding—the Father shepherds his shepherding *Son*. God the Father commissioned God the Son to shepherd: to bless, to deliver, and to discipline.

Christ has always owned all of creation since he is a Person of the Godhead and was a co-Creator and a participant in the Trinity's plan to "create humanity in our image." There has never been a time when the Son has not owned the cosmos with the Father and the Spirit. But when God came in the flesh, he introduced a new phase in the history of his kingdom and eternal design. In this new phase of the Kingdom, the Father blessed his Son with a new description of ownership. The difference between Christ's ownership of the world while a Person of the Trinity and the ownership he was now given by the Father, is that Christ now owns the earth as the *human* shepherding king. Christ inherited the whole world as the *human* and *divine* king, when before he simply owned it as God. The divine Son's nature had changed by including a human nature so there was a new aspect to creation ownership. And as any human owner does, Christ walked over his territory including the wilderness, hills, and cities of some other nations to show his ownership of them: Judea, Samaria, Galilee, and the lands of the modern day peoples of Lebanon, Syria, and Jordan.

All creation would be ruled by this Person known as both the "Son of God" and the "Son of Man." That is why he is born of both a woman and of God the Holy Spirit. The Old Testament tells us this precisely, before Jesus came.

> The *Lord* said to me, "You are my *Son*, today I have begotten you . . . I will give you the nations as your inheritance, the whole earth as your possession . . . "
>
> Show respect to [kiss] the Son. Ps 2:7–8, 12

In Psalm 2:8 the Father blessed his Son not only with an inheritance of all the peoples of the world, but of all the world's lands, something Israel's greatest king, David, did not come close to inheriting.

---

10. Ps 110; Isa 9:6; Jer 23:5–6; Mic 5:2–4; Zech 9:9–10

This intimate partnership of the Father and the Son is repeated in Psalm 110:1–2: one Lord (the Father) will make the enemies of the other Lord (the Son) to be his footstool. Further, the same Lord (the Father) will stretch out the scepter of the other Lord (the Son) to rule. No closer partnership in shepherding could be portrayed any clearer than this.

> The Lord said to my Lord: "Sit at my right hand while I make a footstool out of your enemies." The Lord will stretch your mighty scepter from Zion, and say, "Rule among your enemies!"

Jesus, the Son explained the meaning of Psalm 110 and made it clear that it refers to his Father commissioning him to rule the earth. He denounced any idea that Psalm 110 referred to David, and he ridiculed the scribes and Pharisees for such a simplistic interpretation of the psalm.[11]

In the book of Daniel, the Father announced again that Christ would rule the world and its peoples. Here, the coming Messiah is introduced as a "Son of Man."

> One like a *Son of Man* was coming . . . To Him was given dominion, glory and a kingdom so all peoples, nations and every language group would serve him. Dan 7:13–14

Jesus often called himself "the Son of Man" in the Gospels. And as this Son of Man, Jesus claimed his Father's commission to be the supreme human ruler of the world—everything is subject to him: spirts, nature and all humanity were given to him. I have paraphrased the following verses:

> All authority has been given to me over heaven and earth. Matt 28:18

> The Father loves the Son and gave him authority over everything. John 3:3

> Jesus knew that the Father had given him authority over everything. John 13:3

> You have given him [the Son] authority over all peoples. John 17:2

> He has subjected all things under [Christ's] feet. 1 Cor 15:27

> All is summed up in Christ, things in heaven and things on earth. Eph 1:10

> God subjected everything under Christ's authority. Eph 1:22

> Everything has been created through him and for him. Col 1:16

Satan foolishly tried to get in the middle of this change in world ownership. He believed that he was the one who could give the kingdoms of the world to Christ Jesus when he did not even own them in the first place.[12] Satan may rule kingdoms in horrific ways as the true Owner allows, but he owned nothing which he could give to

---

11. Matt 22:41–46 // Mark 12:35–37 // Luke 20:41–44
12. Matt 4:8–10 // Luke 4:5–8

Christ. Only God can give the world and all peoples to whomever he wishes. We know that the Father had not given it to spirits; he had given it to humanity, including now, to the Human King (Ps 115:16).

In the Father and Son's relationship we learn something about them that is so important for our own humility and walk with God. Obviously, the very words "Father" and "Son" imply that there is a difference in authority between them. It is the Father's authority to appoint and send his divine Son as the human Messiah. Both Testaments note that the Father assigned the Son to sit at the Father's right hand.[13] Micah 5:2 explains that the Son/shepherd would come to Israel on behalf of "another," who is the Father. And the authority of the Father is accepted humbly by the Son who personally would "delight in obeying the Lord."[14] Jesus proved that his divinity did not stand in humility's way, since he even referred to his Father as 'My God.'[15] I challenge us to have that same humility to God and his authority that even God the Son, our Savior, had.

The Son's submission to his Father has a dramatic climax at the end of this parenthetical age. God plans for his kingdom to continue growing until Christ's victorious second coming when Christ will give all creation back to his Father. He will raise it to the Father as a perfected, eternal creation:

> Then is the end when he delivers the Kingdom to God the Father having abolished all rule, authority and power. He must reign until he puts all his enemies under his feet. 1 Cor 15:24–25

Finally, a once perfect creation will regain its pristine goodness which it had when it was first created.

THE GOSPEL OF GOD

A profound way to show our respect and appreciation for the Son is by how we refer to him. Three other names of Jesus are Messiah, Christ, and the Anointed. These three names mean the same thing in three different languages. The English word is "Anointed." The Old Testament Hebrew word for that is "Messiah" and the New Testament Greek word is "Christ."

Old Testament Hebrew	Messiah
New Testament Greek	Christ
English	Anointed

---

13. Ps 110:1; Luke 22:69; Acts 7:55–56; Eph 1:20; Col 3:1; Heb 1:3, 13; 8:1; 10:12–13; 12:2; 1 Pet 3:21–22

14. Isa 11:2–3; also, 53:7, 10–11; Heb 12:2

15. Matt 27:46 // Mark 15:34; Rev 3:12

So, when Peter says to Jesus, "You are the Christ," he says that Jesus was the Messiah, the Anointed.[16]

Old Testament kings, priests, and prophets were also anointed as a ceremonial confirmation of their official position. So as the anointed ones, they were all "messiahs" too. When Christ came, he came as a king, priest, and prophet, so he is the Anointed three times over. However, most Old Testament passages that deal with the coming Messiah refer to him as the ruling king.[17] So, Christ, the Messiah did not come only to reign as king; he came also to be the new high priest who would sacrifice, teach, and judge as did the Old Testament priests and to be the ultimate prophet of God.[18] Zechariah identified the Messiah as one who will "rule as *king* from his throne and will serve as *priest* from his throne with harmony between the two roles" (6:12–13). David also prophesied that the Messiah would be a Priest (Ps 110:4).

It is just as important to know that the name "Jesus" means "Savior."[19] What a wonderful name by which we are saved from adversities including our sin! However, in the books after the Gospels and Acts, the Son is far less often referred to simply as "Jesus." The apostles almost always join the name "Jesus" with his titles of kingly authority, either "Christ" or "Lord." The following names are the most frequent.

Christ Jesus

Lord Jesus

Lord Jesus Christ

Christ Jesus our Lord

Jesus our Lord

Jesus Christ

Yes, Jesus is our Savior, but he is our Lord *and* Savior, our Christ (Anointed King). In his new titles, his kingly position is usually the first word of his name, "Christ" or "Lord," accenting the ruling nature of our Savior. Furthermore, whenever "Christ" and "Lord" are used in referring to Jesus, God's kingdom is emphasized in the strongest terms, because the Son is the Anointed King of God's kingdom.

So, in the New Testament letters, Jesus' position as King and Lord is the predominant emphasis. When the New Testament believers heard the name "Christ Jesus," in their language they heard "Anointed Savior" or "King Savior." The sober reality reflected in these names is that it is impossible to receive only "Jesus." We must receive Jesus *Christ and Lord*! This is Paul's and John's definition of a Christian:

---

16. Matt 16:16 // Mark 8:29
17. Pss 2:8–9; 45:6; 110:2; Dan 7:14; Mic 5:2–4; Zech 6:13
18. Ps 110:4; Jer 33:18; Zech 3:8; 6:12–13
19. Matt 1:21; Acts 13:23

> If you declare with your mouth, 'Jesus is Lord' and your heart believes that God raised him from the dead, you will be saved. Rom 10:9
>
> Who is a liar? Whoever denies that Jesus is the Christ. 1 John 2:22
>
> Everyone believing that Jesus is the Christ has been born of God. 1 John 5:1

"Jesus is Savior" is a true statement, but it is not enough. We need to be convinced and act in a way that acknowledges that "Jesus is Lord," that he is the divine king.

There can be a tendency for individual believers and the church at large to speak almost exclusively about "Jesus," but this does not honor him adequately. Certainly, it honors him to call him by his birth or "given" name, Jesus. But his kingly name, "Christ" must flow from our lips as frequently as "Jesus," just as it did for the apostles. It can be an innocent mistake to emphasize our *salvation* from adversities and sin through Jesus more than our *responsibilities* to Christ our Lord. But it is spiritually immature and dismissive of God's Son and his authority over creation. If we love Jesus, we will honor him by frequently referring to him as our "Christ," our King, "Lord."

Paul encouraged preaching "the gospel" or "good news" in Romans 10:15 by quoting Isaiah's Old Testament gospel. We mentioned in chapter 2 that the Old Testament Hebrew uses the word *bāśar* for "gospel" or "good news" over twenty times. Isaiah spoke about spreading the gospel and his message is the foundation for Jesus' gospel.

> The feet of those who bring the *good news* are beautiful on the mountains,
> those who proclaim peace, who bring the *good news*, who proclaim salvation,
> who say to Zion, "Your God reigns!" Isa 52:7

God's kingdom reign is an Old Testament gospel, and God's kingdom brings peace and salvation.

When Jesus began his ministry, he fulfilled Isaiah's prophetic words by announcing the same gospel.

> Jesus came into Galilee preaching the gospel of God, saying,
> "The time is fulfilled and the Kingdom of God has come near." Mark 1:14–15

In other words, he came preaching that "God reigns." John the Baptist had already paved the way for Jesus by preaching this same Old Testament gospel about the Kingdom of God: "Repent for the Kingdom of heaven has come near" (Matt 3:2).[20]

What point of reference was there for Jesus Christ and those who heard his gospel of the Kingdom? What did the Jews understand him to say? God's kingdom was not a new topic for them by any means since they knew his kingdom had always existed. God's kingdom plans were explained in very plain language so that the Old Testament common believer could understand them. So Christ preached the gospel of God's kingdom to a Jewish population steeped in the knowledge about God's kingdom. They

---

20. Matthew uses the phrases "kingdom of God" and "kingdom of heaven" to mean the same thing.

knew that God had a Kingdom and that he had eternal goals for that Kingdom which included a human Messiah. People were waiting for this Messiah, this "Christ," and awaited his gospel of God's kingdom.

During Christ's ministry, if anybody had missed the obvious and asked him when the new phase of God's kingdom was going to come, Christ responded that the Kingdom had *already* come, through him. The proof that it had already come was that Christ had started to destroy Satan's kingdom through exorcisms and other demonic destruction: "If I cast out demons by the Spirit of God, then the Kingdom of God has come to you."[21] Christ told the Pharisees they were asking the wrong question about when the Kingdom would be coming—it had already arrived: "The Kingdom of God is in your midst" (Luke 17:20–21).

Christ's preaching about God's kingdom gospel is mentioned in over eighty passages in the New Testament. Furthermore, he refers to this Kingdom as *his* kingdom[22] and as his *Father's* kingdom.[23] This is not a contradiction or confusion by any means. Instead, Christ's kingdom gospel applies the partnership that the eternal design has always intended. The Father assigned the Kingdom to a Human sub-king under his authority as the Father King. After all, Christ tells us we should pray, "*Our* Father . . . *your* kingdom come."[24]

Christ was quite aware of why he was sent to us by the Father. He summarized the reason he was sent to settle the dispute between the two contending kingdoms. First he affirms his own kingdom purpose:

> I must preach the gospel of the Kingdom of God because that is why I was sent. Luke 4:43

There was a second reason for his visit to earth. It was the other side of the coin. Christ also came to destroy the Enemy's kingdom:

> The Son of God appeared for the purpose of destroying the works of the Devil. John 3:8.[25]

Hebrews gives the same reason for the coming of the Messiah:

> The Son came as flesh and blood so by dying he could take away the Devil's power of death. Heb 2:14

Christ's sacrifice was part of the Kingdom plan to accomplish why he was sent—to defeat the dark kingdom.

Jesus' gospel message is summarized repeatedly to be about God's kingdom. In addition to Mark's introduction to Jesus' preaching in Mark 1:14–15, we hear . . .

21. Matt 12:28 // Luke 11:20
22. Matt 16:28; Luke 22:29–30; John 18:36
23. Matt 13:43; 26:29
24. Matt 6:9–10 // Luke 11:2
25. Also, Matt 12:28–29 // Mark 3:27 // Luke 11:22

> Jesus began to preach: Repent for the Kingdom of heaven is near. Matt 4:17
>
> Jesus was traveling ... proclaiming the gospel about the Kingdom. Matt 4:23
>
> Jesus was traveling ... proclaiming the gospel about the Kingdom. Matt 9:35
>
> This gospel about the Kingdom will be preached in all the world. Matt 24:14
>
> I must preach the Kingdom of God ... since that is why I was sent. Luke 4:43
>
> He traveled ... proclaiming and preaching the Kingdom of God. Luke 8:1
>
> He was speaking to them about the Kingdom of God. Luke 9:11
>
> Since then, the gospel about the Kingdom of God is preached. Luke 16:16
>
> Be aware that the Kingdom of God is near. Luke 21:31

This gospel of the Kingdom of God was what Jesus passed on to his disciples to preach too; it didn't matter whether they were one of the unique twelve disciples (Matt. 10:7) or one of his many other followers (Luke 9:57, 60).

> Preach "The Kingdom of heaven is near." Matt 10:7
>
> Preach the Kingdom of God. Luke 9:60
>
> Say, "The Kingdom of God is upon you." Luke 10:9–11
>
> They believed Philip preaching the gospel of the Kingdom of God. Acts 8:12
>
> Paul preached boldly ... about the Kingdom of God. Acts 19:8
>
> You, to whom I have preached the Kingdom, will not see me again. Acts 20:25
>
> Paul was ... testifying about the Kingdom of God. Acts 28:23
>
> Paul was preaching about the Kingdom of God. Acts 28:31

The Lord's followers were to preach God's gospel of the Kingdom and at the same time perform miracles by the Spirit's power, just as their Master had done. His commission from his Father was the commission he gave to his followers as well. Christ's reign was shown in his Spiritual power over demons, sickness, and death, and he commissioned and empowered his disciples to exorcize, heal, and resurrect as well.

> Jesus traveled ... announcing the gospel about the Kingdom. And he healed every sort of disease and illness. Matt 9:35
>
> Jesus said: "As you go, announce this message: 'The Kingdom of heaven has come near you.' So heal the sick, raise the dead, cleanse the lepers and cast out demons." Matt 10:7–8[26]

---

26. Also, Luke 9:1–2, 6; 10:8–9

So Jesus blessed his disciples, commissioning them to work with him in the power and success of the kingdom. Again, it is the same partnership God intended and extended to the Couple in Eden—to work with him in shepherding the earth—the eternal design.

Jesus Christ was still preaching the Kingdom gospel of God after his resurrection and up to the very point of his ascension to his Father. The book of Acts begins in its earliest verses with Christ still "speaking about the Kingdom of God" (1:3, 8), and Acts ends by its final two verses reporting that Paul was "preaching the Kingdom of God and teaching about the *Lord* Jesus *Christ*" (28:31). But it is even more impressive to look at Luke's two volumes as a set: Luke's "Gospel" and his "Acts of the Apostles." The first chapter of Luke's Gospel says, "The Kingdom of Jesus will have no end" (Luke 1:33), and his last chapter of Acts recounts Paul's kingdom gospel preaching. In other words, from beginning to end, Luke writes about God's kingdom gospel.

Jesus introduces his own great commission by claiming that the Father's kingdom was being shared with him: "All authority has been given to me over heaven and earth" (Matt 28:18). He was repeating his Father's commission to him to be the Human King who had commandments that must be observed. He announced his own application of the primary commission by assigning to his disciples the responsibilities to multiply, fill, and subdue/shepherd.

In chapter 4 we looked at the parallels Jesus drew between the primary and great commissions:

Primary Commission Gen 1:26–28	Great Commission Matt 28:18–20
Be fruitful and multiply,	Make disciples
fill the earth and	of all nations . . .
subdue it	teaching them to obey

Jesus' renewed primary commission is part of God's corrective link in his eternal chain of shepherding from the Father down through history, to you and me. Corrective, because in this parenthetical age Jesus was given human authority over all creation because humanity had failed.

> God multiplies, fills, and shepherds.
> > The Trinity commissioned humanity to multiply, fill, and shepherd.
> > > The Father commissioned Jesus to multiply, fill, and shepherd.
> > > > Jesus commissioned his apostles to multiply, fill, and shepherd.
> > > > > The apostles commission their disciples to multiply, fill, and shepherd.

THE KINGDOM AND THE ETERNAL DESIGN

God built creation and humanity according to his eternal design—he shepherds shepherding creation. There may be different phases of it, but it is the same design. So being God himself, Jesus Christ's eternal design had not changed when he came. He came to focus on what the Old Testament had focused on, which was God's kingdom and God's generous sharing of his shepherding sovereignty with humanity. The Old Testament had said the Shepherd would come to bless, deliver, and discipline. The Shepherd would *bless* his people as a wise counselor who leads them into his peaceful kingdom where they serve him freely.[27] He would *deliver* his people from danger.[28] He would also deliver them from their sin, serving as their substitute sacrifice when they were the ones who should be sacrificed for their own sins.[29] Finally, the Shepherd would judge the wicked, defending and supporting his people against their enemies.[30]

The eternal design's chain of authority was the pattern here again—God shepherds the shepherding Messiah who shepherded his apostles who will shepherd the church.

> Everything has been handed over to me by my Father. Luke 10:22

> All that the Father has given to me will come to me. John 6:37

> God appointed his Son to be heir of all things. Heb 1:2

And then, Christ grants his kingdom to his disciples to shepherd.

> I give you a kingdom, just as my Father gave to me . . . and you will judge the twelve tribes of Israel while sitting on thrones. Luke 22:29–30

When Jesus our Savior gave himself for us, it was to deliver us from the darkness of Satan's kingdom—to deliver the entire planet from this current age into his and his Father's kingdom.

> Grace and peace to you from God our Father and the Lord Jesus Christ who gave himself for our sins to deliver us from the present evil age, just as our God and Father wanted, to whom be the glory forever. Gal 1:3–4

The New Testament phase of God's eternal design included the growth of his believing kingdom far beyond the borders of Israel. This growth would be at the expense of the declining and eventual extinction of the Enemy's kingdom. The Kingdom would not only be preached to a few nearby peoples around the Middle East, but to all peoples over the whole planet.[31] Christ predicted this through his parables of the mustard seed and leavened bread. He compared his kingdom to the small mustard

---

27. Ps 110:3; Isa 9:6; 11:2, 6–10; Jer 23:6; Zech 6:13
28. Ps 2:12; Jer 23:6; 33:16
29. Isa 53:4–6, 8, 10–12
30. Pss 2:9–12; 110:5–6; Isa 11:4; Jer 23:5
31. Matt 24:14; 28:18–20; Acts 1:7–8

seed that grows into the large plant, and to the small lump of dough that expands into the full loaf of bread.[32] The archangel Gabriel told Mary about this kingdom growth before the Messiah was born: "He will rule Jacob's descendants forever; his kingdom will never end" (Luke 1:33).

WE INHERIT AND RULE THE KINGDOM

The expanse of Christ's kingdom would come through our co-ownership of the world with him. Christ came preaching the gospel of the Kingdom of God, and he calmed and exalted his followers as sheep who possess the Kingdom along with God and who rule over it with God: "Do not be afraid little *flock*, because your Father is glad to give you the Kingdom" (Luke 12:32). In other words, these sheep have become ruling shepherds themselves. Christ had come to rule and he shepherds us as ruling shepherds. Though God does not need us to serve him (Acts 17:24–25), still he employs us to achieve his eternal design with him.

Christ Jesus exemplified for us how to fulfill the eternal design. Jesus is the bridge between God and humanity in the eternal design because what the Father did for his Son he does for us too, but only through his Son.

> The Father gave life to the Son, so the Son gives us life. John 6:57
>
> The Father gave Jesus his words, so Jesus gave them to us. John 17:8
>
> The Father sent Jesus into the world, so Jesus sends us into the world. John 17:18[33]
>
> The Father gives Jesus glory, so Jesus gives us glory. John 17:22
>
> The Father is in Jesus, and Jesus is in us. John 17:23
>
> The Father is known by Jesus, and Jesus is known by us. John 17:25
>
> Jesus was given authority to heal, so he gives that authority to us. Matt. 9:8[34]
>
> The Father gave a kingdom to Jesus, so Jesus gives a kingdom to us. Luke 22:29
>
> Jesus is God's and we are Jesus'. 1 Cor 3:23
>
> The Father gave Jesus rule over the nations, so Jesus gives us that rule. Rev 2:26–27
>
> The Father has Jesus seated on his throne, so Jesus seats us on his throne. Rev 3:21

---

32. Matt 13:31–33 // Mark 4:30–32
33. Also, Matt 20:21
34. Matt 10:7–8 // Mark 6:7, 13 // Luke 9:2, 6; Matt 28:19–20 // Mark 16:15; Luke 10:8–9

The Father was not miserly when he gave us an inheritance through his Son. He gave us nothing less than the whole earth! Of course, he had already given us the world at creation in the primary commission: "The Lord has given the earth to the sons of men" (Ps 115:16). And he gave it to humanity again but by giving it to Jesus Christ this time in order to assure the eternal design's success. Christ came as a savior and a human inheritor of the entire world. Both Testaments attest to this. The Father encouraged his Son to take the inheritance: "Ask me, and I will give you the nations as your inheritance, the ends of the earth as your possession" (Ps 2:8). And Hebrews confirms that Christ accepted that offer: "In these final days God has spoken to us through his Son whom he appointed heir of everything" (Heb 1:2).

Though Christ is the heir of all things, God had also promised this same privilege to Abraham thousands of years earlier: "For the promise to Abraham and his offspring that he would be the heir of the world did not come through the Law" (Rom 4:13). Since all believers are Abraham's offspring, we inherit that promise too: "If you are Christ's, you are heirs to Abraham's promise as his offspring" (Gal 3:29).[35] Daniel promises the same thing:

> The saints of the Most High One will receive the Kingdom and possess it forever. 7:18

> The Ancient of Days came and judged in favor of the holy people . . . The time arrived when the saints took possession of the Kingdom. 7:22

Paul inspires the Corinthians by telling them, "Everything belongs to you!" (1 Cor 3:21–23). Over twenty passages in the gospels and letters bless us with the promise that the Kingdom will belong to us.[36] Every believer will inherit the world, without prejudice: woman, man, , Gentile, Jew, servant, the poor, and the gentle.[37] Our *full* inheritance of the whole world will come only during New Earth, only after the Judgement. Eternal life is also our inheritance[38] since to possess the world forever, we must live that long.

In New Earth, Christ Jesus will continue to rule over all.

> Your king is coming to you; and He will speak peace to the nations; and His dominion will span from sea to sea . . . and to the ends of the earth. The Lord will be king over all the earth. Zech 9:9–10; 14:9

But both Testaments promise that we will rule and shepherd with him, fulfilling his eternal design.

> I will allow the victorious one to sit with me on my throne just as I was victorious and sat with my Father on his throne. Rev 3:21

---

35. Also, Eph 3:6; Heb 6:17

36. Matt 5:3, 5, 10; 19.14; 25:34; Luke 6.20; 12:32, 42–44; Acts 20:32; 26:18; Rom 8:16–17; 1 Cor 6:9–10; 15:50; Gal 4:7; 5:21; Eph 1:11; 5:5; Col 1:12; 3:24; Jas 2:5; Heb 12:28; 1 Pet. 3:7

37. Matt 5:3, 5, 10; Luke 6:20; Gal 3:28; Jas 2:5; 1 Pet 3:7

38. Matt. 19:29 // Mark 10:17 // Luke 10:28; Luke 18:18; Titus 3:7

In chapter 3, we showed the Genesis-to-Revelation thread of God's message about our human rule. Psalms, Isaiah, Daniel, Matthew, Paul, Hebrews, and Revelation are very explicit about our privileges and responsibilities as governing shepherds, and the rest of the Bible is a thorough commentary on our role.[39] Paul contends that legal issues should be handled within the local church since, after all, "since you will judge the world, are you not able to judge trivial cases? Do you not know you will judge angels?" (1 Cor 6:2–3). Of course the holy angels need no judge, but we will participate in the condemnation of the demonic realm. More will be said about the spirits in our next chapter.

RULING BY LOVE

We are to rule by the fruits of the Spirit, not by the fruits of selfishness or oppression. Christ says this in no uncertain terms.

> Whoever wants to be great among you must be your servant. Whoever wants to be first must be your slave just as the Son of Man did not come to be served, but to serve, giving his life as a ransom for many.[40]

Our shepherding cannot be abusive authority. Any authority we have over others cannot overrule their personal responsibility to submit to what God's will is for them (Rom 14:1–4, 13). This sounds obvious, but in many churches, authoritarian pastors, elders, and teachers are exactly the shepherds which the prophets, Paul, and the other apostles rebuked. And in too many Christian families, men claim authority over their wives and children, but their hearts are plagued with a domineering demeanor that can be careless at best if not nearly sadistic.

God's eternal design has been very successful since God's believing community has had a significant impact on this world during this parenthetical age. God's Bride, the church, has brought Christ to the world in very meaningful and profound ways. The church's maturity into the body of Christ has led to centuries of sacrificial giving to a woeful and wayward world. Medical clinics and hospitals, schools, Bible translations, water wells, millions of tons of food supplies, shelters, counseling centers; these are only some examples of how the church has generously shepherded this world by its extension of Christ's kingdom and our primary commission. These acts of love to the world by God's bride have been her achievements in the eternal design.

These loving acts of salvation and mercy by the church also prove to the world, whether the world is open to the truth or not, that God's believing community is blessed far more than those outside it. There is no worldview, religious or otherwise, that compares in its positive and edifying contributions to the peoples of the globe.

---

39. Gen 1:26–28; Ps 8:6–7; Dan 7:18, 22, 27; Matt 5:5; 2 Tim 2:12; Heb 2:8; Rev 2:26–27; 3:21; 5:10; 20:4–6; 22:5

40. Matt 20:26–28 // Mark 10:43–45

No nation, religion, or philosophy has been nearly the blessing the church has been to the nations and their civilizations. The church, with all its warts and bruises, has been God's showcase culture to a world that has responded favorably. The Spirit's power of conviction and conversion, along with the Bride's faithfulness to her Groom has accomplished the Old Testament's promise that Christ's kingdom would expand endlessly through the centuries (Isa 9:7). The church has multiplied and filled the earth and has to some significant levels subdued the earth with biblical, moral principles that have enriched and prospered many peoples.

The Old Testament Israelites were supposed to prove by their national condition and status that a relationship with the only existing Deity was beneficial and satisfying. The nation's central geographical location in the Middle East was to be the showcase where the glory of God and his shepherding relationship with his sheep was viewed and marveled at by the peoples of the world. Christ explained the same strategy. He says that if believers loved one another, the world would know we were his disciples (John 13:35). Christ prayed for this unity among his believers, and for a unity between believers and the Trinity so that the world would know that the Father had sent his Son to deliver the world (John 17:20–23). Peter understands this strategy, urging believers to be victors over the flesh so that the world would glorify God when his perfect judgment is finally revealed when Christ returns (1 Pet 2:11–12).

We need to be dignified rulers who reflect the image of God before the world. After all, we are overwhelming conquerors (Rom 8:37); after all, we are seated with Christ on his throne (Eph 2:6); after all, we are a "royal" kingdom of priests;[41] after all, we will receive "crowns," eternal glory and honor.[42] But let us be cautious about our self-image. We are a motley group of disciples, drawn from every walk of life. God has recruited you and me to be his shepherd and "fellow-worker" from a cross-section of humanity. He recruits mostly the common person.[43] In fact, he came as one himself—but look at him now, if your eyes are not blinded by his glory.

---

41. 1 Pet 2:9; Rev 5:9–10

42. Rom 2:7, 10; 8:17, 18; 9:23; 1 Cor 2:7; 2 Cor 4:17; 2 Thess 2:14; 2 Tim 2:10; Heb 2:10; Jas 1:12; 1 Pet 1:7; 5:1, 4; Rev 2:10

43. Mark 16:20; 1 Cor 3:9

6

Shepherding Spirits

GOD SHEPHERDS THE SPIRITS

THERE IS A REALM that we seldom consider, yet it is very important for our role as God's partners in governing this earth. The eternal design includes this realm as well: God shepherds shepherding spirits. I mentioned in chapter 1 that the spirits have fewer shepherding relationships than the rest of creation. We know little about how the angels bless or deliver each other. Angels do not appear to bless or to be blessed by nature. God blesses his angels by creating them, placing them close to his glory, and assigning them shepherding tasks for humanity, his people, and individual believers. The holy angels judge the fallen angels now as they war against them, and they will finally prevail at Armageddon. The redeemed will also judge the fallen angels. And we have said already that the holy angels do not need to be delivered, and the fallen spirits never will be. It is encouraging that we can bless the angels with joy through our righteousness as the Lord's people and as his individual followers. It is gratifying to know that the angels are full of joy when a sinner repents and that they continue to serve us who are saved.[1]

To our own peril, we tend to dismiss this heavenly realm of life because it is an unseen realm. But it teems with significant and powerful beings: powerful holy angels and fallen angels, and living but powerless spirits of the dead. The Old Testament says there are at least tens of thousands of the holy angels alone.[2] We know the Lord's will is done in the heavenlies from where holy angels shepherd, and from where the antishepherds, Satan and his sub-kingdom do the opposite. Christ prayed to his Father, pointing to the heavenlies as the model for what should be done on earth: "Your will be done on earth as it is in heaven" (Matt 6:10).

The angels possess elements of God's image. For example, they are relational, intelligent, and emotional; they communicate with each other and with humanity. They can take on human form, as can God! Some are righteous, very powerful, and

---

1. Luke 15:7, 10; Heb 1:14
2. Deut 33:2; Neh 9:6; Ps 68:17; 148:2; Dan 7:10

can transcend time and space. They have a will that can turn against God and humanity, seeking to destroy all that the eternal design is about.

Apparently there is a hierarchy within the angelic host since Michael is referred to as "one of the chief princes."[3] This means that there are other chief princes, and Gabriel, the only other named angel in the Testaments, perhaps is one of those.[4] Other angels are referred to as cherubs and are most frequently mentioned when describing ornamentation of the tabernacle and temple, and in Ezekiel's visions. Seraphs are mentioned in only one passage where they lead in worship (Isa 6:2–7).

THE PARENTHETICAL WAR

It is from the heavenly place where the most important battles are being waged. The battles take place there and on earth, but the battle strategies and highest authorities are not of this world. Of course, God is in no way threatened. Rather, he oversees a battle where each blow struck by either side is calculated and measured by him in his eternal design to shepherd his beloved creation. His deliverances and judgments are conceived and framed on this unseen battleground. We should be glad we are not allowed to observe the heavenly battles. They are not polite debates. They are violent struggles that spill onto the planet's surface and regions, invading all nations and everyone's personal lives with the torturous results which we call so gently, the "human condition."

This battle, though seldom referred to in the older testament involves God's holy angels. We are given a short but intriguing look into this global war when Michael and another angel battled the "prince" of Persia and eventually, Greece. This prince of Persia was either Satan or one of his minions because there were several "kings of Persia" involved in this heaven and earth battle (Dan 10:12–13, 20–21). Either way, the "prince" over these kings would have been satanic.

The book of Job is an enormous encouragement to the believer; the story explains the Lord's ultimate control of spirits in the heavens. All angels, good and evil, are held accountable for their work in the universe, including Satan himself. This is shown dramatically in two conversations between God and Satan.[5]

> The angels came to present themselves before the Lord, and Satan came with them too. The Lord asked Satan, "Where have you come from?" Job 1:6

This conversation ends in the Lord telling Satan what he can and cannot do with Job.

> Everything of his is in your hands, but do not lay your hands on him physically. Job 1:12

> Job is in your hands, but spare his life. Job 2:6

---

3. Dan 10:13; 12:1
4. Dan 8:16; 9:21; Luke 1:19, 26
5. Job 1:6–8, 12; 2:1–3, 6

It is a comfort to know that even in the midst of Satan's torrents and torments against us and the rest of the world, they are limited by the Lord's perfect and wise restrictions.

Satan's limitations are also revealed in Ezekiel's preaching. There, Satan's position and power is perhaps alluded to in God's rebuke of the king of Tyre.[6] The king's fall from power is paralleled to the fall of an evil Angel—a guarding Cherub. The once-perfect, highly esteemed Cherub fell from grace in Eden because of his arrogance. The Cherub is said to be a beautiful product of God's craftsmanship who will be humiliated eventually in front of all peoples.

The New Testament says there are thousands of created angels; 70,000 would have come to save Christ, meaning that at least that many holy angels were available.[7] We have no idea how many angels are in the dark kingdom. We find out further that angels cannot die (so the demons will suffer eternally),[8] and they do not marry, so they do not multiply and progressively fill anything.[9] Humanity's commission certainly was not that of the angels.

Since the Father raised Christ to his right hand and gave *everything* to him to rule as his possession, both holy and fallen angels are under his authority.[10] Christ's exorcisms show Satan's kingdom is subject to Christ's authority. Yet the holy angels evidently do not have such authority over the demons since they do not exorcize them. Even archangels defer to God's authority in spiritual warfare. Whether taking on false teachers who have offended the angels or battling Satan himself, angels do not take matters into their own hands but remain submissive to God's authority.[11]

Satan does have a sub-kingdom within God's overall kingdom of creation. It is a very large and powerful kingdom, but it is just a part of God's kingdom which is doomed to defeat and destruction. In this limited sense, and only during this parenthetical age, Satan is the "king of the abyss" (hell)[12] and he is "the ruler of this *world*" or "the god of this *age*."[13] If Satan is the ruler of this world (place) and age (time), then what is left for Christ Jesus and for us to rule in the parenthetical design? Is that why Jesus did not argue with Satan about world ownership during Satan's temptation? Absolutely not! There was no argument because Satan's claim that he could give the nations to Christ was ludicrous. Only the Father could do that, and he did give the nations to Christ. We can overestimate the extent of Satan's rule. He does rule, but if he ruled absolutely, there would we nothing left since his goal is to pillage and destroy

---

6. Ezek 28:11–19; perhaps Isa 14:12–14
7. Matt 26:52–53; Col 1:16; also, Heb 12:22; Rev 5:11
8. Matt 25:41; Luke 20:34–36
9. Matt 22:30 // Mark 12:25 // Luke 20:34–35
10. Eph 1:20–22; Phil 2:9–10; Col 1:16; Heb 1:4–5; 1 Pet 3:21–22
11. 2 Pet 2:10–11; Jude 8–9
12. Rev 9:11; also, Matt 9:34; 12:42 // Mark 3:22 // Luke 11:15
13. John 12:31; 14:30; 16:11; 2 Cor 4:3–4; Eph 2:2; 1 John 5:19; Rev 9:11

God's created kingdom.[14] There are far too many blessings and deliverances in all eras and areas in this world for Satan's rule to have overwhelmed God's rule.

So there are two kingdoms: (1) God's overall and eternal kingdom where he rules as the ultimate sovereign power over all reality, and (2) Satan's temporary and inferior sub-kingdom which contends and even wins many battles fought in human history. The difference between these kingdoms is as extreme as any difference can be. One can belong to only one of two families. One is born of God or of Satan (1 John 3:7–12). John tells us that the kingdom of Satan even reproduces many anti-Christs.[15] One either worships God or the fallen angels because there are no other gods, really. Satan and his demons exist, but the false gods which the demons promote do not (1 Cor 10:19–21). A person's citizenship is in one of these kingdoms but never in both. "Our citizenship is in heaven," Paul assures us (Phil 3:15). Sometimes we might act as the citizens of Satan's kingdom act, but we are forgiven and assured that we will not lose our citizenship in the heavenly kingdom. Instead, "The Lord Jesus Christ gave himself for our sins to deliver us from this evil age,"[16] so we are not "friends of the world" nor do we "listen to the world"; instead, we overcome it[17] as overwhelming conquerors with the help of our valiant reigning and battling King.[18]

The difference in the two kingdoms is as great as darkness and light.

> What does light have in common with darkness? 2 Cor 6:14

> You are all children of the light and day . . . not of night or darkness. 1 Thess 5:5

> God is light, there is no darkness in him whatsoever. 1 John 1:5

This is why Satan comes as an angel of light—to deceive us from seeing the total darkness from where he comes (2 Cor 11:14). Jesus came as the light of this world, to turn us "from darkness to light, from the kingdom of Satan to God."[19] Paul explains the influence of Satan's kingdom on the thoughts and behavior of the world's peoples in Ephesians 4:17–19: "They walk mindlessly, with darkened understanding."[20] Satan disguises himself as an angel from God's kingdom of "light."[21]

Christ told Pilate that his kingdom is not *of* this world: "My kingdom is not from here."[22] Again, there are only two possible sources for kingdom authority. There are no neutral states or kingdoms in the cosmos. One either serves the Kingdom of Light,

---

14. Matt 13:19 // Mark 4:15 // Luke 8:12; John 10:10
15. 1 John 2:18, 22; 4:3; 2 John 1:7
16. Gal 1:3–4; also, Matt 13:39–40; Rom 12:2; 1 Cor 2:6–8; Eph 5:16, "these days"; 2 Tim 4:10
17. Jas 4:4; 1 John 4:3–6; 5:4–5
18. Rom 8:37–39; Phil 4:13
19. Acts 26:18; also, Luke 2:29–32; John 1:4–5; 3:19; 2 Cor 4:6; Col 1:12–13; 1 Pet 2:9; 1 John 2:8
20. Also, Matt 6:23; Rom 1:21; 5:11; 6:12; 2 Pet 1:19; 1 John 2:11
21. 2 Cor 11:14; Rev 9:11
22. John 8:23; 18:36

or one serves the inferior, subservient kingdom of the dark. This dark kingdom is not an equal kingdom, yet it is currently in a futile war with the ultimate Kingdom.[23] While Satan may convince some that they have a chance against God's kingdom, he knows himself that he is leading all of his kingdom to defeat. This is what makes an already dark kingdom that much darker and desperate (John 3:19–21). It is doomed from beginning to end. Because we are the focus of the Trinity's creation, and because God is so patient with us, Satan is maliciously jealous and ferociously vindictive.

The magnitude of the current war between these two kingdoms is unimaginable to us, because we have no idea of the power of the combatants. The book of Revelation gives us an idea of the enormity of the battles, but those are mostly future battles and cannot show the scale of waged warfare through the past millennia. Yet in the heavens, the defeat of Satan is a foregone conclusion. The battle has already been decided since we are told that after Christ defeats all his enemies, he will raise to his Father a perfected, no longer contested world.[24] Since we are confined to living in space and time, however, we experience the outworking of that war now, on a daily basis.

James tells us that the demons have an accurate theological understanding about the nature of God; that is why they tremble under his authority.[25] Demons even expected the Messiah to come and engage in their sub-kingdom while he was in the world. They recognized immediately and announced publicly that Jesus was the Son of God (Mark 3:11).

GOD SHEPHERDS THE ANGELS

The Lord blesses, delivers, and disciplines the holy angels, fallen angels, and spirits of the dead. As the ruler of the heavens and earth, as the shepherd of seen and unseen life, he pervasively applies the methods of his eternal design. This chart, taken from the form of the master chart in chapter 1, shows examples of how God shepherds the spirits by his eternal design. He shepherds spirits based on which kingdom they support.

The Eternal Design	Each Part of Creation is Shepherded by God	
	Holy angels, fallen angels and spirits of the dead	
God	Blesses	Holy angels are blessed to be alive and are chosen to be near God
	Delivers	Some spirits of the dead rise and are delivered to eternal life
	Disciplines	Fallen angels and some spirits of the dead are disciplined

---

23. Matt 12:25–29; Luke 10:18–20; 22:53; Acts 26:18; 2 Cor 10:3–4; Rev 12:5–10
24. 1 Cor 15:23–24; Rev 17:12–14
25. Jas 2:19; Luke 8:28

God's holy angels are blessed by being "chosen," and so they were not destined to be part of the heavenly rebellion that exiled the Devil and his demons (1 Tim 5:21). The holy angels are in God's direct presence[26] and desire to serve and worship the Trinity.[27]

> The Lord has established his throne in the heavens and his sovereignty rules everything. Bless the Lord, you his angels since you have mighty strength to perform his word, to obey the words in his voice. Bless the Lord all you hosts, you who serve him by doing his will. Ps 103:19–21

The holy angels' responsibilities include forceful, mighty battles to protect us in the current and fierce spiritual warfare that determines much of our personal lives.

Alliances against the Lord are formed between Satan's kingdom and a people group or an individual. Alliances against Satan kingdom are formed by God and his believing community and its individual believers. There are no neutral territories. Even those who are unaware of this spiritual battle are aligned with Satan by default. They are unwitting soldiers for his destructive purposes. But Genesis 3:15 makes it clear that Satan and his associates will suffer a crushing blow to the head while the wounds to humanity will be harmful, but not terminal. In this verse, speaking to the serpent, Satan, the Lord speaks of humanity's eventual victory; "He (humanity) will strike your head, but you will strike only his heal." That is a conviction and a relief to us when we keep fighting in our personal lives against evil's threats.

Christ and Paul pick up on the prediction in Genesis 3:15 of the head-crushing of Satan. The Lord says, "I have watched Satan fall from heaven like lightning. Look, I have given you authority to tread on serpents and scorpions and on all the Enemy's power" (Luke 10:18–19). Paul continues the picture of Satan's defeat by believers: "The God of peace will crush Satan under your feet soon" (Rom 16:20). This is one way in which we will be involved in judging these angels of rebellion (1 Cor 6:2–3). There are no shepherding blessings for Satan and his kingdom apart from God's patience in suspending their hellish final judgment until the indefinite future; otherwise, God's shepherding judgment is all that is in store for them. As we have seen, the reason Jesus Christ came in the first place, says John, was to destroy Satan's works and his kingdom.[28]

Daily, Jesus publicly defeated Satan and other unseen rulers and authorities during his ministry (Col 2:15). And the Holy Spirit was very involved in the battle between these two kingdoms. He empowered the Son in his exorcisms as well as in the other signs and wonders. This proved that even in the life and ministry of the Second Person, the Spirit within was greater than the demons in this world.[29]

---

26. Matt 18:10; Luke 1:19; John 1:51; 1 Tim 3:16; Rev 14:10
27. Luke 2:13–15; Heb 1:6; Rev 7:11
28. 1 John 3:8; also, Matt 12:28–29 // Mark 3:27 // Luke 11:22
29. 1 John 4:2–4; also, Matt 4:24; 12:28 // Luke 11:20

We see Jesus winning this war already when he dominated Satan's demons, casting them out while they obeyed his every word.[30] Sadly, since the Jewish religious leaders of Christ's day could not admit that Jesus was God, against all logic they were forced to conclude that it was Satan who empowered his exorcisms.[31] Often demonic influence carried serious disabilities such as muteness, deafness, blindness, and epilepsy.[32] It was not only the exorcisms by Jesus that defeated Satan's kingdom but the many other miracles of healing and resurrections (including his own) which defeated the ultimate weapon of the Enemy, Death (1 Cor 15:25–27).

Demons knew there would be a final judgment when they would be tormented eternally. So, anguished over their certain doom, they asked if Jesus was going to speed up the timetable by his appearance: "Have you come to torment us *prematurely*?" (Matt 8:29). Of course, the Lord does everything in his perfect timing; nothing he does is premature. So, for now, the demonic kingdom is only restrained until the final judgment, though obviously it is still dangerous and tragically destructive. God in his perfect wisdom has allowed the dark kingdom to keep oppressing humanity for the time being. One can only think of the utmost damage this vile kingdom could bring if not contained by God's sovereign and perfectly wise reign over all his creation.[33] Eventually however, to the relief of the holy angels and humanity, Christ Jesus will completely destroy any remaining power of the demonic kingdom, climaxing in the final battle over the "beast" and a "false prophet" who will be imprisoned eternally in the Abyss along with Satan.[34]

Jesus bound Satan to a great extent by destroying some of Satan's deeds and kingdom: "The Son of God came for this purpose—to destroy the works of the Devil."[35] Satan has been judged already, defeated by God through the miraculous ministry of Jesus and the apostles.[36] The judgment against Satan has already been read; he is condemned.[37] Though human history is still tortured by Satan's schemes, the promise of God's ultimate victory is our encouragement that the judgment of Satan is secure.

GOD SHEPHERDS THE SPIRITS OF THE DEAD

The condition and location of spirits of the dead is veiled in obscure and mysterious language in the Testaments. The Old Testament points to Sheol as the soul's destination, a place that is at least the physical grave if not far "deeper" and more of a residence for

---

30. Matt 4:24; 8:16; Mark 1:23–26, 34, 39; 3:15; Luke 4:35–36, 41; 6:18; 13:32
31. Matt 9:34; 12:24 // Mark 3:22 // Luke 11:15
32. Matt 9:32–33 // Luke 11:14; Matt. 12:22; 17:15, 18 // Mark 9:17, 25–27
33. 2 Thess 2:6–12; 2 Pet 2:4; Jude 6
34. John 12:31; 1 Cor 15:24–25; Rev 17:8; 19:20; 20:1–3, 9–10
35. 1 John 3:8; also, Matt 12:28–29 // Mark 3:27 // Luke 11:22
36. John 16:11; Acts 8:7; 16:18; Col 2:15
37. John 16:11; 1 Tim 3:6

the soul than a mere tomb for a body.[38] Presumably, for the unbeliever's soul, it is an existence inferior to life on earth, to say the least, but how much inferior is not revealed.[39]

One of the most revealing passages about the dead is seen in the ascension of Samuel's spirit from the dead. The risen Samuel asked Saul why he had "disturbed" him. Evidently there was peace for someone as righteous as Samuel (1 Sam 28:15). But this case alone proves that "The Lord kills and makes alive again. He brings one down to Sheol, but brings one up again" (1 Sam 2:6).

God's shepherding justice and deliverance include a bodily resurrection of the faithful. This ultimate deliverance from death is mentioned over 20 times in the Old Testament.[40] Since the Old Testament says that Enoch and Elijah never died, did the Israelites believe they were the only two resurrected humans in heaven? Even Israel's neighboring pagan nations believed in the afterlife. In the New Testament, Martha knew from her Old Testament scriptures that the dead would be resurrected (John 11:23–25). Hebrews confirms that at least Abraham believed in the resurrection from the dead (Heb 11:19).

The New Testament presents the situation of deceased believers somewhat clearer than the Old Testament does. The agony of the unrepentant soul is compared with the *peace* of the delivered soul in a story Jesus tells in Luke16:19–26. A selfish rich man is in agony, but a poor believer is safe and peaceful in Abraham's arms. Samuel said Saul had disturbed his peace when Saul had a witch call him from Sheol. We can understand Samuel's annoyance since Paul says that it is better to be in heaven in the Lord's presence than to live on earth: "We . . . prefer to be absent from the body and home with the Lord."[41] Jesus encouraged the believing thief with whom he was crucified, telling him that he would be in Paradise with him (Luke 23:43).

Hebrews assures us that there is an assembly of saints praising God with the angels in heaven (Heb. 12:22–23). The martyred believers ask the Lord in heaven when they will be avenged (Rev 6:9–11). Others were raised from the dead by Jesus and the apostles, but only temporarily until they died again. Many who were raised from the dead when Jesus was crucified must have surprised their relatives and friends when they walked through Jerusalem again (Matt 27:52–53).

HOLY ANGELS SHEPHERD

Along with the rest of creation, the angels share in the Lord's shepherding responsibilities and are actively involved in his eternal design. They are often portrayed as those at

---

38. Gen 37:35; Num 16:33; Job 11:8; 17:16; Ezek 31:17; 32:17–21

39. Job 26:5–6; Ps 115:17–18; Isa 14:9–11, 16; 38:10

40. 2 Kgs 2:11; Job 14:12; 19:25–27; Pss 16:9–11; 22:26; 41:12; 49:15; 61:4–8; 73:24–26; 75:9–10; 115:17–18; 145:1–2; Prov 10:25; 12:19; 14:32; 15:24; 21:28; Isa 25:8; 26:19; Dan 12:2, 13

41. 2 Cor 5:6–8; also Phil 1:23

the Lord's side worshipping[42] and ready to do his bidding, or they are routinely called before him to give an account of their activities.[43] Biblical sacred art, poetry and visual images depict angels at his side and within his temple as guarding servants.[44]

At no time does humanity either summon or command angels; angels are solely under God's control. They are influential and wield awesome power. Nonetheless, humanity is the Lord's primary partner on earth and the primary focus of his written revelation. So the role played by the holy angels is to serve God and his eternal design and to shepherd his people. The holy angels serve by the same methods that God and humanity shepherd: by blessing, deliverance, and judgment. In that sense angels are commissioned, as is humanity, with the administrative responsibility of shepherding the planet.

The angels' role is to shepherd humanity, so they are fellow-servants of God *with* us, but also *for* us. We are under angelic protection and at times under their disciplining power. Eventually, we will be judges over the angels, presumably the evil ones who are awaiting their eternal damnation at the Judgment Day.[45] But the holy angels serve the Lord and us, so we are not called to serve or worship them.[46]

The angels *bless* humanity in their role as messengers. The inseparable word of an angel and the word of God is expressed in God's direction to the Israelites, "Obey the angel's voice and do all that I say" (Ex 23:22). At times the Lord himself appeared and spoke to people, for instance to Adam and Eve, Abraham and Paul, but very often angels are his emissaries from the supernatural realm. Their words were encouraging to Hagar, the wandering Israelites, Gideon, and Samson's parents.[47] They are also sent as messengers to interpret the visions of Daniel and Zechariah.[48] Stephen, Paul, and the book of Hebrews tell us that angels were instrumental in giving the Old Testament laws to Moses.[49] The angels mediated God's messages to humanity in the New Testament too. In Revelation, the Father and Son give the book's message to an angel who then gives the message to John. This string of revelations, from God to an angel, then to John, then to the seven churches in Asia and then to us, was one way the Lord inspired his writers of the biblical books.[50]

Gabriel appeared and spoke to Zacharias, Mary, and the shepherds, encouraging them not to fear but to receive his great news for them.[51] Presumably, it is Gabriel

---

42. Neh 9:6; Job 38:6–7; Ps 89:5–7; 103:20; 148:1–2; Isa 6:3
43. 1 Kgs 22:19; 1 Chr 21:27; Job 1:6; 2:1; Ps 103:20; Dan 7:10
44. 2 Kgs 19:15; 1 Chr 13:6 // Isa 37:16; Ps 80:1; 99:1
45. 1 Cor 6:3; 2 Pet 2:4; Jude 6
46. Col 2:18; 2 Pet 2:11; Heb 2:5–8, 9; Rev 9:10; 22:8–9
47. Gen 16:7–13; 18:1–14; 21:17–18; Ex 23:20–23; 24:40; Judg 6:11–23; 13:2–21
48. Dan 7:16; 9:21–23; 10:5–21; Zech 1:9–11, 19; 6:7
49. Deut 33:2; Acts 7:35, 38, 53; Gal 3:19; Heb 2:2
50. Rev. 1:1; 22:6, 16
51. Luke 1:11–14, 19, 26–36; 2:9–12

who speaks to Joseph as well, but apparently in dreams.[52] At least two angels, perhaps including Gabriel, appear and encourage the women who came to embalm Jesus in the tomb not to fear.[53] And some anonymous angel appeared separately to Philip, Cornelius, and Peter to tell them where they should travel next.[54] An angel also assures Paul and the others on a severely endangered ship that they would survive the dangerous storm (Acts 27:23–25).

Angels also *deliver* and guard humanity. Cherubs are first assigned to protect the Garden from further evil (Gen. 3:24). Angels are commissioned to patrol the earth and watch its affairs, to be ready to obey the Lord, and help keep order and progress in his eternal design.[55] The angel Satan is still on his patrolling routine, roaming destructively about the earth (Job 1:7). God promises the Israelites that angels will lead, guard, and deliver them as a nation from harm and their enemies.[56] For instance, an angel saved Israel from their enemies by killing 185,000 Assyrian soldiers in one night.[57] But he also assigned angels to protect individuals in the Old Testament: Lot, Abraham and Isaac, Jacob, Daniel and his friends.[58] Fortunately, the holy angels guard and deliver all believers.

> The Lord's angel surrounds and rescues all those who fear him. Ps 34:7; also, 35:6

> He will command his angels to guard you in all your ways. Ps 91:11

Holy angels strengthen and encourage God's people in the New Testament too, including our Lord Jesus. Satan taunts Jesus saying that the angels would surely save the Savior from death if he jumped from the temple heights. After Jesus rebuffed Satan's insults, the angels really did minister to Jesus in his bodily fatigue after the wilderness fasting.[59] Jesus could have called at least 70,000 angels to come from his Father to deliver him while he and his disciples were in the garden of Gethsemane (Matt 26:52–53). Instead, only one angel was sent to encourage Jesus in his agony in the garden (Luke 22:43).

Powerful angels deliver the Lord's people in the New Testament. An angel delivers Christ from the tomb by moving the huge stone and clearing the opening for Christ to walk out of the tomb (Matt 28:2). And an angel easily broke the chains off Peter's wrists so he could escape prison (Acts 12:7, 10). In the end when Christ returns, the angels' power will gather all of the believers from around the world to meet him.[60]

52. Matt 1:20–21; 2:13, 19
53. Matt 28:5–7 // Mark 16:5–7 // Luke 24:4–7, 23; John 20:12
54. Acts 8:26; 10:3–4; 12:7–10
55. Dan 4:13, 17, 23; Zech 1:10–11; 6:7
56. Ex 14:19; 23:20–23; 32:34; Num 20:14–16; Josh 5:13–15; 2 Kgs 6:15–17; Dan 12:1
57. 2 Kgs 19:35 // 2 Chr 32:21; Ps 78:49
58. Gen 19:1, 15–22; 22:10–18; 24:5–7, 40; 32:1–2; 1 Kgs 19:4–8; Dan 3:28; 6:22
59. Matt 4:5–6 // Luke 4:9–10; Matt 4:11 // Mark 1:13
60. Matt 24:31 // Mark 13:27

However, God's powerful angels also discipline and judge humanity. Again, a single angel judged those 185,000 Assyrians soldiers which achieved Israel's deliverance. But God's judgment could come through an angel to discipline his own people as well. For instance, 70,000 Israelites were struck by a plague at the hand of an angel for David's sin of calling for a census.[61]

In the New Testament, Gabriel comes to Zacharias and tells him not to fear, bringing comfort to a perplexed man. But because Zacharias dared to question such a magnificent being on a mission of mercy, Gabriel's grace turned to judgment. The angel struck Zacharias dumb for his disbelief (Luke 1:13, 19–20). Later, an angel killed Herod when the king proudly accepted the accolades of a crowd who likened him to a god (Acts 12:21–23).

The angels will be involved in judgment on a much grander scale when Christ judges the righteous and unrighteous in the last days: by the battle at Armageddon and in his courts at his Judgment. The angels will accompany Christ to assist in judging everyone according to their acts.[62] They will be witnesses of the Lord's judgment, but they are the ones who will carry out whatever punishment the Lord determines.[63] On the other hand, the angels have been appointed witnesses to human behavior and involved in judgment throughout human history. They witness the treatment and care for their assigned human children; they witness the persecution of the apostles; they witness the humility of believers who are under authority; they witness the fairness with which elders make judgments in the local church.[64] They are God's court witnesses of everyone's moral behavior, whether we are righteous or unrighteous.[65]

FALLEN ANGELS ARE ANTI-SHEPHERDS

All human history to this point is the drama of God and humanity restoring this world. We journey and struggle through creation until it regains its perfection. This journey carries us through immense territories which have been temporarily stolen, destroyed, and made into warfare encampments from which Satan launches dangerous campaigns to overcome the divine kingdom.

The Serpent used our desire to be like God when he duped the Couple into believing there was even more of God's image that they should have beyond what the Lord had created them to have (Gen 3:4–6). The Couple were already like God, even more than Satan was, but his goal was to divide us from our God and destroy that image.

Satan is described in Job 1:6 and 2:1, as one of the "sons of God," a created being. So Satan is limited and finite, but he is horribly wise and powerful with no other evil

---

61. 2 Sam 24:13–15 // 1 Chr 21:11–14
62. Matt 16:27 // Mark 8:38 // Luke 9:26; Matt 25:31–32
63. Matt 13:37–42, 49–50; 2 Thess 1:7–9; Heb 1:7; Rev 14:14–20; 16:1–21
64. Matt 18:10; 1 Cor 4:9; 11:10; 1 Tim 5:21
65. Luke 12:8–9; Rev 3:5

competitor. Satan's name in Hebrew means "enemy," and he is the Trinity's fiercest and most successful adversary in heaven and earth. He is the chief destroyer of God's creation; his target is anything good. We hear in *Job* that when the Lord allowed Satan to exert his miraculous powers as a supernatural being, he is able to inflict disease (even death if not restrained). He is also allowed to determine the weather and to incite the human spirit to fatal violence. But Satan is constrained to do only the harm that God's wisdom and timing allows.

Satan's purpose is to *destroy* God's purposes, including any progress in God's *restoration* of his kingdom during this parenthetical age. He is the very anti-shepherd who has no interest or motivation to act in ways that bless, deliver, or judge fairly. He is all about abuse and unfairness, making him the arch enemy to the eternal design. Satan devotes his sovereignty only to shattering rather than to shepherding.

Satan's targets are not only the believing community and individual believers; he attacks and destroys unbelieving societies and persons also. He has oppressed cultures through false religions, shallow philosophies, selfish priorities and oppressive social structures. His destructive weapons include demonic temptations, illnesses, self-destructive behaviors and brutalities, some which can hardly be described, much less watched. These horrors are at inestimable levels every hour and in every nation. Demons are mentioned explicitly only twice in the Old Testament, but where they are referenced, they led people toward false gods and religious practices.[66] These unseen, vile deceivers entice the majority of humanity to worship "gods" in atrocious ways. They incite practices that disrespect common decency through human sacrifice, self-mutilation, and temple prostitution. Demons hide behind religions that worship "gods" who do not exist, so when there is any obedience, the demons are those who are obeyed.

In the meantime, until Satan is eternally contained in Hell, the Lord tolerates and exploits him. Though Satan was demoted, the Lord permitted him to gather a demonic kingdom around him. Satan has also been allowed to enlist a mostly complicit humanity to battle against God and his eternal design. So humanity bombards God's believers with perpetual threats, dangers and martyrdom.

Though Satan jumps at any chance to deceive and destroy, and though he means it for evil, God can turn it into good. For example, the Lord accommodates Saul's delving into the occult when the king asked a medium from Endor to "raise" Samuel's spirit. God tolerated this so that Samuel's earlier prophecy about Saul's calamity would be reaffirmed (1 Sam 28:8–19).

On two occasions God uses Satan's destructive priorities and powers for his own divine purposes, similar to when the Lord used Satan's evil intentions against Job to instruct us about wisdom. Second Samuel 24:1 says that David's motivation to count the Israelites in a census was driven by God's anger. On the other hand, 1 Chronicles 21:1 attributes David's motivation to Satan. As God manipulated Satan in the book of *Job*, God manipulates Satan to tempt David. In another instance, the prophet Micaiah's

---

66. Deut 32:17; Ps 106:37–39

vision describes a heavenly conversation between the Lord and a deceiving spirit. The Lord recruits this spirit to mislead King Ahab's prophets and Ahab to fight the Syrians, ending in the king's just death (2 Chr 18:18–22). Satan's name when translated means "Enemy." So when Jesus addresses the Devil during his temptation, he calls him literally, "Enemy,"—"Leave me, Enemy (Satan)!" (Matt 4:10). And when Jesus rebukes Peter for his careless lack of understanding about the Savior's death, he calls Peter his "enemy": "Get out of my way, satan . . . your thoughts are human, not godly" (Matt 16:23).

John says that Satan has another name, "the Destroyer." In Old Testament Hebrew, the name is "Abaddon," and in New Testament Greek, "Apollyon." Satan is a schemer bent on the destruction of God's rule including the destruction of Christ and his believers.[67] Jesus tells Peter that Satan had specifically asked to destroy him (as he had asked for a chance to destroy Job!) but Christ prayed to his Father for Peter's deliverance (Luke 22:31–32).

Satan is also called the Devil, or "Slanderer" over thirty times—about as often as his name "Satan" is used. This name fits with his overall strategy of deception by lying about others. His first slanderous comments were made in Eden about the Trinity when he called God a devious liar about sin's results, when it was the Devil who was the only one guilty of lying (Gen 3:4–5).

Satan's temptations and deceit are his most dangerous weapons. He made sure he distracted Adam and Eve from their primary commission over creation in Eden; and was sure to be present to try the same distraction at the beginning of Jesus' ministry.[68] Paul draws attention to Satan's continued attempts to destroy even marriages and to undermine the persevering faith of believers in the local church.[69]

The Deceiver does more than simply tempt us, however. He is a like a wolf in sheep's clothing, disguising himself to make his efforts look like they are coming from God's bright kingdom rather than from his dark abode in Hell's caverns. He is a schemer, the first and greatest of liars, a blinder of the unbelieving,[70] and a confuser of believers who are taken in by false doctrine.[71]

God's patience and wisdom still allow Satan's kingdom to govern parts of creation until God's definitive Judgment. In fact, the shepherding Lord uses Satan's destructive drive to carry out much of the disciplining curses after Eden. In the Old Testament, Satan was used for the Lord's shepherding purposes—to bring judgment or discipline. This same purpose is mentioned in the New Testament. As with Job, God allows Satan to send a painful curse, a "thorn of the flesh" to Paul to keep him humble (2 Cor 12:7). And Paul himself delivers one sexual deviant over to Satan to save his soul, and he delivers

---

67. Luke 22:3; John 13:2, 27; 2 Cor 2:11; Eph 6:11; 1 Pet 5:8; Rev 12:13–17
68. Matt 4:1–11 // Mark 1:13 // Luke 4:2–13
69. 1 Cor 7:5; 1 Thess 3:5
70. John 8:44; Acts 5:3–4; 13:10; 2 Cor 2:11; 4:4; 11:3; Rev 12:9
71. 2 Thess 2:1–4; 1 Tim 4:1; Jas 3:15; 1 John 4:2–3; Rev 2:24

two other men to Satan to discipline them for their blasphemy.[72] It is a peculiar partnership where Satan is glad to inflict pain when allowed to, even when he means it for evil but God means it for good. Even Satan serves God's sovereign purposes.

HUMANITY SHEPHERDS SPIRITS

Humanity has a very significant responsibility to be a part of the realignment of our broken world with the eternal design. By opting for Satan's wisdom over the Lord's, the first Couple buried us all under the Enemy's evil influence. But who will deliver us from this spiritual and physical death? Humanity will be a deliverer along with the Lord! Paul takes the promise of Genesis 3:15 seriously and encourages us with it. "The God of peace will crush Satan under your feet soon" (Rom 16:20).

As far as human shepherding of the holy angels, it is mostly a one-sided relationship at this point in the parenthetical design. There is nothing to deliver the holy angels from, and they certainly do not need our discipline. The fallen angels present a completely different situation. We would not want to bless them, and apparently the Lord has no plan to deliver them. However, we are in a constant contact with demons as they tempt us to help them dismantle God's kingdom.

We do not "discipline" the fallen angels since that would imply that we are hoping to improve their moral condition through our resistance. Instead, we judge them as the Lord's and our enemies, and we battle and hopefully defeat them on a regular basis. Judgment is the only relationship we can have with the citizens of the dark while we war against them now. But later, on that Final Day, we will be their judges (1 Cor 6:2–3).

Jesus Christ gave his twelve disciples authority over the demons: "Go and preach, saying 'The Kingdom of heaven is here . . . cast out demons.'"[73] He expanded this authority, giving it to his wider circle of 70 disciples. He said there would be many others who would have his power of exorcism, including a number of unknown but legitimate exorcists who were already active during his ministry.[74] God's eternal design of shepherding humanity is evident in this chain of merciful authority given to his followers to free people from Satan's dark kingdom.

So the disciples and the wider circle of Jesus' followers, including Peter, Philip, and Paul, contributed to the public demise of Satan's works and kingdom by commanding spirits to stop their awful abuse and afflictions.[75] Paul exorcized a fortuneteller and blinded a magician.[76] Philip's ministry led to the probable conversion of Simon the magician, and many other occultists were saved and burnt their books publicly.[77]

72. 1 Cor 5:5; 1 Tim 1:20
73. Matt 10:1, 7–8 // Mark 6:7, 13 // Luke 9:1; Mark 3:14–15
74. Mark 16:17; Luke 9:49; 10:17–20
75. Acts 5:16; 8:6–7; 16:18
76. Acts 13:6–11; 16:16–18
77. Acts 8:9–10, 13; 19:14–19

As believers, we all fight against the rulers, powers, and world forces of Satan's dark kingdom (Eph 6:11–12). "Our fight is not against flesh and blood, but against the dark rulers and powers over this world; our fight is against spiritual wickedness in the heavens" (Eph 6:12). We resist Satan, so he flees from us. In the end, we will be part of the Lord's defeat of Satan under our feet.[78]

We do not fight merely a defensive battle of resistance and deflection. The Lord expects us to take the initiative and take the Enemy and his kingdom head-on. Only God's power can do the crushing, but he does so under our active feet that are prepared for battle. The God of peace will conquer Satan under our *feet of peace* (Eph 6:15). That does not mean we are at peace. It means we fight and achieve peace as victors—it is not the same as inactivity. It is also a peace that comes from the confidence that we are on the right side and that we are guaranteed the victory.

We are soldiers in this spiritual war that takes place in heaven and on earth, and we were never designed to be its vanquished victims.[79] And we are not victorious in any small way. Paul says, "we *overwhelmingly* conquer through him" (Rom 8:37–39); and John says, "The one who *overcomes* the world believes Jesus is God's Son" (1 John 5:5). Even when martyrs are fatally wounded in this treacherous spiritual war, they win as surviving citizens of an eternal kingdom: "Death is swallowed up in victory. Death, where is your victory now? Death, where is your sting?" (1 Cor 15:54–55).

When we are struck by Satan, we must be wearing spiritual armor to minimize the hit: "Put on the armor of light!"[80] Taking his lead from Isaiah 59:17 where the breastplate of righteousness and the helmet of salvation are first mentioned, Paul lists the armor we should be wearing and the weapons we should be wielding: truth, righteousness, peace, faith, salvation, the Bible, and prayer (Eph 6:14–18). Our armor is a combination of gifts from God and our righteous efforts. God and we fight together. He provides the truth, peace, faith, and salvation; we pursue righteousness, apply our faith, read the Bible, and pray at all times.

Pursuing righteousness and living by faith must be based on biblical instruction and prayer for the Spirit's specific directions. Spiritual warfare requires that we prepare ourselves with the knowledge and understanding of the Testaments, and it requires our effort and time in prayer. Satan attacks the Christian at the most foundational level, using the Word against us as he did with Jesus Christ, contradicting the Word of God as he did with the Couple, or tempting us not to apply it in our own lives, or not to read the Word much at all.[81] Satan's scheme with the Couple in Eden and with Jesus in the wilderness was the same.[82] However, Jesus resisted, the Couple did not.

---

78. Rom 16:20; Jas 4:7; 1 Pet 5:8–9; 1 John 2:13–14
79. Phil 2:25; 1 Tim 1:18; 2 Tim 2:3–4; Philem 2
80. Rom 13:12; also, 2 Cor 6:7; 10:3–6
81. 1 Cor 7:5; 1 Thess 3:5; 1 Pet 5:8–9
82. Gen 3:2–5; Matt 4:6 // Luke 4:9–12; Matt 13:19 // Mark 4:15 // Luke 8:12

In fact, John tells us in Revelation, in dramatic terms, how Satan lurked even over the birth of Jesus! So be alert because the devil is stalking in order to devour. "The dragon stood in front of the woman who was giving birth so it could devour her child as soon as he was born" (Rev 12:4.) But at the end of Satan's temptation of this "child," the "child" commanded, "Leave me!" (Matt 4:10). And Satan did. Just as Jesus's resistance of Satan in the wilderness chased the tempter away, James and Peter say that we must resist Satan; he will flee from us too![83] "Give Satan no place" Paul says (Eph 4:27). Failing to resist temptation leads to the same defeat as in Eden.

The Old Testament spoke repeatedly of the sneaking and powerful lion[84] and the evasive and poisonous serpent.[85] Isaiah and Amos even mention these two predators together in the same sentence as treacherous "beasts" that surround the individual.[86] The hovering Satan who sought to devour Jesus at his birth lurks around us too, looking for an opportunity to devour us: "Your enemy the devil prowls around like a roaring lion, looking for someone to devour" (1 Pet 5:8). And reminding us of the Serpent in Eden, Paul is concerned about Satan's temptation of believers: "I fear that as the crafty serpent deceived Eve, your minds will be led astray too" (2 Cor 11:3).

Satan's power to deceive and keep deceiving are impressive, unfortunately. There are those who intentionally join Satan's occult religion and activities as full-fledged citizens of the dark. It is frightening that Satan's power and human hatred of God and Christ could be so strong for temptation and deception to prevail to this extent in so many people's lives. Primitive cultures without the Kingdom gospel might succumb because of their ignorance. But how do those who have had the light of the biblical message surround them in western civilization, how do those who have experienced the blessings that come to societies which apply biblical standards, how do they become foolish and evil enough to worship Satan or encourage the immoral standards of his kingdom? Yet we live with a multi-billion dollar industry of demonic entertainment, including literature, film, clothing, and games. And more profoundly, we shield our eyes from seeing the medical treasure trove garnered by the primitive practice of child sacrifice through abortion and infanticide.

Though Satan's powers are strong, both Testaments promise his defeat; from Genesis through Revelation, we are encouraged that we are on the crushing side.

> [Eve's seed] will strike your head, but you will strike his heel only. Gen 3:15

> You will trample the lion and the serpent. Ps 91:13

> The Lord will punish the fleeing serpent, Leviathan. Isa 27:1

---

83. Jas 4:7; 1 Pet 5:9
84. Job 4:10–11; Pss 7:2; 10:9; 17:12; 22:13; Prov 28:15; Isa 35:9; Jer 4:7; 5:6; Ezek 22:25; Joel 1:6
85. Num 21:6; Job 26:13; Pss 58:4; 140:3; Prov 23:32; Isa 65:25; Mic 7:17; also, 2 Cor 11:3
86. Isa 30:6; Amos 5:19

> I have given you authority to trample serpents, scorpions and all the enemies' power. Luke 10:19
>
> The God of peace will soon crush Satan under your feet. Rom 16:20
>
> Satan was thrown down to the earth, and his angels with him. Rev 12:9
>
> The angel laid hold of the dragon . . . and bound him for a thousand years. Rev 20:2

Notice that God, plus his holy angels, plus humanity are all involved in Satan's final defeat. That defeat is inevitable, though only in our Savior God's own, unknown, but perfect timing.

7

Shepherding Nature

GOD SHEPHERDS NATURE

ALL CREATION IS COMMANDED to honor its creator God, and nature has always obeyed His commands and stands as an example to the rest of creation. Nature obeyed God perfectly when formed merely at the sound of His voice,[1] and it continues to perfectly obey the Lord's physical laws. Nature will obey its physical laws relentlessly until it is told otherwise. When God calls nature to extraordinary action, outside those physical laws, nature complies instantaneously, producing God's marvelous miracles which bend the physical laws to his purposes: water turned into blood as a plague on Egypt or water turned into wine at a wedding; a sunken axe head lifted from the water, or a fish with a coin in its mouth lifted from the water. Yet God prefers nature's usual consistency in following the physical laws he has built into it.[2]

When we speak of nature responding to the Shepherd and also shepherding humanity, we are not projecting human emotions, self-awareness or ethical righteousness upon nature. On the other hand, if we ignored Biblical terminology and phrasing, we would merely talk about nature as a meaningless machine. To avoid extremes I simply use the biblical expressions that portray nature as obedient to God, praising God, revealing God, for example, as well as the message that nature blesses, delivers, and disciplines humanity. Yes, this is poetic; nonetheless, there is less distance between the poetic and the literal than one might think, at least as far as how the Testaments express nature's role in the eternal design.

The cosmos declares God's glory simply by its vast beauty. It reveals God's orderliness, creativity, wisdom, and power (Ps 19:1–6). Nature's loyal, consistent, and perfect obedience to God's physical laws creates a harmonious chorus of praise to God with a countless variety of voices.[3]

---

1. Gen 1:3, 6, 9, 11, 14, 20, 24
2. Eccl 1:9; 3:15
3. 1 Chr 16:30–34; Job 12:7–10; 38:6–7; Pss 19:1–4; 50:6; 69:34; 89:5–8; 93:3–4; 96:11–13; 97:1;

Shepherding Nature

> You heavens, be glad, and earth, rejoice! Tell the nations, "The Lord reigns." 1 Chr 16:31

> The wild beasts honor me, jackals and owls, because I give water in the desert and streams in the wasteland. Isa 43:20

Changes in the climate are in the Lord's hands, including condensation, evaporation, cloud formation, rain, snow, hail, thunder, and lightning. The land does his bidding, whether jutting or spouting the rock strata upward to make the mountains or splitting the rock by cavernous fault lines. The waters are at his disposal—seas, lakes, ponds, marshes, springs, and rivers. The Lord reaches out to the largest galaxies and smallest atomic particles and compels them to achieve his purposes. One can read of this deep relationship between God and nature in five chapters in the book of Job (37–41) when Elihu and the Lord humble Job's self-centered arrogance.

Whether any non-human species are self-conscious or not, they certainly are not theologically astute. Yet nature "speaks" and reveals God's glorious attributes in its routine and perfect obedience to his physical laws. When he uses nature as he pleases, he affirms to the world that he is the world's king. He uses nature for his three methods of shepherding. Nature is God's means of blessing, deliverance, and discipline: "He sends the cloud . . . for correction, or out of kindness to the earth" (Job 37:11, 13). The Lord uses nature to reveal that he is the only God—to prove his exclusive claim as creator, owner, and king of all reality, natural or spiritual.[4]

The Bible does not start with a description of the shepherding sovereignty of humanity. Rather, it starts with the shepherding sovereignty of *nature*! The Lord's revelation starts with nature's contribution to the eternal design. God shepherds shepherding nature. Because of the centrality of humanity in the eternal design, we usually focus on shepherding humanity. In this chapter, though, we will see (1) how nature is shepherded by God, (2) how nature shepherds itself and the wider creation, and (3) how humanity shepherds nature.

The New Testament affirms the Old Testament description of God as the creating king of everything: spirits, nature, and humanity.[5] The New Testament also affirms the Old Testament description of the Father giving all reality to Christ to own and rule as the human king in the new phase of the Trinity's kingdom.[6] Christ's divine authority over nature and his use of that authority throughout his ministry was one of the proofs to the world that he had come as the Messiah to begin this new phase of the Kingdom. His authority over nature was clear in his miracles of multiplying fish and

---

98:7–9; 103:22; 145:10, 21; 148:1–4; 150:1, 6; Isa 42:10–11; 44:23; 49:13; 55:12–13; Jer 5:22–23; 8:7; 51:48; Hab 3:3; Rom 1:20

4. Ex 9:14–16, 29; 34:10; Deut 4:32–40; Job 36:30–32; 38:22–23; Pss 18:7–15; 78:12–53

5. Mark 13:19; Acts 4:24; 14:14–15; 17:24; Rom 4:17; 11:36; Eph 3:9; 1 Tim 6:13; Heb 3:4; 8:2; 9:11, 24; 11:3; Jas 1:17–18; 1 Pet 4:19; 2 Pet 3:5; Rev 4:11; 10:6; 14:7

6. Matt 28:18; Luke 10:22; 6:37; 13:3; 17:2; 1 Cor 15:27; Eph 1:22; Col 1:16; Heb 1:2

bread and reversing the destruction of sickness and even death; "even the wind and sea obey him!" (Mark 4:41). His message as the Messiah came with compassionate acts of physical deliverance that nullified the natural processes of the laws of physics.[7] Jesus told John the Baptist's disciples and he told the people of his own hometown that his healings and resurrections proved that he was the Messiah.[8] As the anointed king of the Trinity's new kingdom phase, he was simultaneously "announcing the gospel of the Kingdom and healing every disease and sickness" (Matt 4:23).

Many of Jesus' physical deliverances were combined with deliverance from the power of the demonic kingdom as well.[9] These deliverances proved Jesus' authority over nature and spirits. Our spirit enemies do not make the convenient distinction between our physical and spiritual lives. The demons do not separate reality into two parallel universes that are sealed off from one another. Neither did the Lord Jesus. He proved he was the king of "spiritual" and "physical" realms, including the cross-over zone where the two realms intersect and cause awful ailments, demonic possessions, and other torments.

GOD BLESSES NATURE

The Trinity created nature to be more than simply a comfortable surrounding for humanity. It has its own purpose, apart from humanity: to glorify and express the intricate, beautiful, powerful, and intelligent character of God. It was not created simply to serve us to whatever extent we wanted to abuse it. In fact, God has protected nature with covenants he has made with it. At the time of God's promise to Noah and his descendants to never send a massive flood again, God made an everlasting covenant with nature too. Within the span of only nine verses, ten times God specifically mentions his eternal concern for the land and animal life, using the language of the primary commission (Gen. 9:9–17). For example,

> I make my covenant with you and your descendants and with every living creature that is with you: the birds, the livestock, and every beast of the earth with you, as many as came out of the ark. The covenant is for every beast of the earth. . . . I have set my bow in the cloud, and it shall be a sign of the covenant between me and the earth. Gen. 9:9–10, 13

Hosea 2:18 makes another covenant with nature that goes far beyond protection from simply a huge flood. The Lord pledges his eternal interest and care for the stability of nature in New Earth. Again, he covenants with nature by the words of the primary commission:

---

7. Matt 4:24; 9:35; 12:15 // Mark 3:9–10; Matt 14:14 // Luke 9:11; Matt 15:30 // Mark 7:37; Matt 19:2; Mark 1:34 // Luke 4:40

8. Luke 4:17–18; Matt 11:2–5 // Luke 7:20–22

9. Matt 9:32–33 // Luke 11:14; Matt 12:22; 15:22, 28; 17:15, 18 // Mark 9:17, 25–27

Shepherding Nature

> I will covenant with the beasts of the field,
> > with the birds of the sky and
> > with the crawling creatures.
> I will abolish the bow, the sword and war from the land
> > so all of them can lie down in safety.

Even until that pristine time of paradise regained, God continues to bless nature in spite of humanity's rebellion.[10]

> The world is full of the Lord's love and kindness. Ps 33:5

> The Lord is good to everything and merciful to all his creation . . . You satisfy the desire of everything that lives. Ps 145:9, 16

The Lord cares even for the massive and ominous sun. He provides a "tent" for it from where it rises in the morning to provide its comforting, shepherding warmth and nurture to the earth and its residents.[11] The Lord has choreographed the dance of the sun and earth to produce the night and day. He calls his arrangement with the day and night his "covenant" and likens his faithfulness to this covenant with nature as an example of his loyalty to David and the Levites.

> If you could break my covenants that I have with the day and night so that they do not come at their set time, then my covenants could be broken with my servant David and my Levites who serve before me. Jer 33:20

We say in our best moments, "I am blessed to be alive!" Life, in most cases, is better than not existing at all. It is true for nature as well—it prefers to exist, shown by its sustained struggle for survival. David gives mind and voice to nature, personifying it so it can express its joy for the blessing of being created beautiful and productive.

> You call for the dawn and sunset to shout joyfully.
> You care for the earth lavishly with water and enrich it.
> The streams of God are filled with water . . .
> You drench the land's furrows, settling its ridges with softening showers;
> You bless its growth.
> The grass of the wilderness drips with moisture.
> The hills gird themselves with rejoicing.
> The meadows cloth themselves with flocks.
> The valleys cover themselves with grain.
> They all shout and sing with joy. Ps 65:8–10, 12–13

---

10. Gen 27:27; Ps 104:10–30
11. Ps 19:4–6; Eccl 1:5

More specifically, Israel's own land produced "milk and honey" because of God's unique care: "It is a land that the Lord your God cares for; his eyes are always on it" (Deut 11:8–12).

God also gifts the animals with instinctive skill for their success and joy just as he does for humanity.[12] His shepherding care extends to lowly and ignored creatures. He challenges Job's wisdom and abilities by asking a question about food for birds: "Who provides food for the raven when its young cry out to God and wander about for lack of food?" (Job 38:41).

Christ posed a similar question about food for birds, and the answer is just as obvious: "Consider the birds of the air. They do not sow or reap or gather food into barns but your heavenly Father feeds them. Are you not more valuable than they?"[13] The Lord's care and provision for nature's birds are a visible promise to us that he will faithfully provide our necessities too. In other words, nature is blessed to carry the message of God's existence and his infinite attributes, including his power, kindness, and faithfulness. Christ and Paul point to nature as proof that God exists and that his kindness is shown to all humanity.[14]

GOD JUDGES NATURE

The Fall in Eden was not an issue just between God and humanity. The Fall separated every part of reality—God, humanity, the spirits, and nature. The Lord, Satan, the serpent, trees, and their fruit, two arrogant humans, and at least two holy angels were all involved in this worst and most devastating event in history. The results shattered the perfectly created world and separated all shepherding components, except God and the holy angels who now guarded against any invasion of the Garden.

God cursed Satan, the czar of destruction. God cursed humanity, his own image-bearer and primary shepherding partner. He also cursed nature so that it has *groaned* ever since for a reversal of the sinful ways of humanity and demons.

> Creation longs eagerly for the sons of God finally to be revealed . . . together, until now, all creation has groaned as if suffering the pains of childbirth. Rom 8:19, 22

No wonder Jesus said that if the crowds were not allowed to praise him as the King of Peace, then the stones would begin singing in their place (Luke 19:40). Of course they would, because as part of creation, the stones were waiting for the King of Peace too. "For God so loved the *world*, that he gave his only begotten Son;" this "world" includes nature (John 3:16).

But in what ways is nature groaning? Nature praises God for its status, yet it awaits the time when it will no longer suffer under the constant sin and rebellion of

12. Job 38:39—39:12; 39:19–30; 40:15–24
13. Matt 6:26; also, 10:29; Luke 12:6
14. Matt 5:45; Acts 14:16–17; Rom 1:20; 1 Tim 6:17

humanity and evil spirits. Nature groans and mourns because earth's surface suffers under humanity's heinous sins. The ground and rivers are flooded with human blood shed by vicious slaughterers. The Lord said to Cain the murderer, "Your brother's blood is crying out to me from the ground" (Gen 4:10). Nature groans as it is called to be a witness in God's justice against the brutalities of rape, abortion, torture, slavery, and all other disobedience.[15]

Nature's suffering is due to human sin; it is our fault. The Old Testament says nature has plenty to mourn. For example, Isaiah and Jeremiah blame Israel for God's judgment that nature experienced because of the nation's sins.

> The land is defiled by her inhabitants because they disobeyed the laws, violated the statutes and broke the eternal covenant. So a curse devours the land. Isa 24:5–6

> How long will the land mourn and the grass of every field wither?
> Beasts and birds are swept away because of the wickedness of its residents. . . .
> Many shepherds ruin my vineyard. . . .
> They have made it a desolation and while desolate, it mourns to me. Jer 12:4, 10–11

But damage to nature can come by very direct, violent, and intentional abuse from humanity. We wear the land out, bring species to extinction, and poison the waters, air, and soil. Humanity's continual sin brings further damage to nature at a regular and dreadful rate.[16] No wonder nature is in unceasing despair.

Nature has its own rogue forces in natural disasters which injure itself, killing flora and fauna. Nature becomes ugly, desolate, scorched, and abused. Its productivity has been stilted, and in the case of one unproductive fig tree, it was killed by Jesus.[17] Nature too is pained during child birth, literally. Science shows it is particularly more painful for human mothers to give birth than most other mammals; still, the pain is there for many other species as well.

But the worst judgment on nature is its future, but only temporary eradication. This is the future for our current skies and earth. As innocent as it might be, nature will eventually be totally destroyed. The Lord may have promised never to destroy the earth by a flood, but the world will be destroyed by other means.

> God's word has committed the current heavens and earth to fire. 2 Pet 3:7

> The heavens will pass away with a roar, nature will be destroyed by fire, the earth and its dealings will be exposed. 2 Pet 3:10

> The heavens will be destroyed by burning and nature will melt away. 2 Pet 3:12

> This world and all of its cravings are passing away. 1 John 2:17

---

15. Deut 4:26; 30:19–20; 31:28; 32:1; Ps 50:4–6; Isa 1:2; Jer 2:12; 6:18–19; Mic 6:1–2
16. Isa 24:3–7, 19–22; 51:6–8; Jer 7:20; 9:10; 14:5–6; Hos 4:3
17. Matt 21:18–19 // Mark 11:12–14

However, we have quoted God's covenant with nature from Hosea 2:18 in terms of the primary commission. New Earth will bring a newer covenant between God and nature so it will regain its original purity, harmony, innocence, and joy. Though this earth will be scorched from all its growth, there will be a renewed nature to sprout up again. Nature will be resurrected just as we will be.

GOD DELIVERS NATURE

Nature's devastation will be the final event of the parenthetical age before the initial event of the eternal New Earth. God's eternal design to shepherd his creation promises to deliver nature. Until then its welfare is bound to humanity's moral conduct. But nature's groaning will stop eventually, and the joy and praise we hear only in part now will be pervasive and endless in New Earth. Until then, both God and humanity can deliver nature from its curses during this parenthetical phase even if only partially. That deliverance comes in episodes and is not completed until New Earth. For instance, Jonah concludes that in addition to God's saving compassion for 20,000 Ninevites, he saved all the *animals* too (4:11). The Lord's salvation was even for them.

We deliver nature as well. For instance, the Lord's commission to Noah parallels the primary commission's core message and in each detail and it results in Noah's salvation of nature's animals. God shepherded Noah, and Noah shepherded nature. After disembarking from the ark, Noah and the animals were in the same ruling relationship as the Couple and the animals in the original primary commission. The Lord edits the primary commission to be specific to the new phase of the human race.

Primary Commission Genesis 1:28	Noah's Commission Genesis 9:1-2
God blessed Adam and Eve by saying,	God blessed Noah and his sons by saying,
"Be fruitful and multiply,	"Be fruitful and multiply,
fill the earth	fill the earth.
and subdue it. Rule over	Fear and terror of you will be from
the fish . . . the birds . . . everything living and moving on the earth."	every beast . . . bird . . . everything that moves . . . all the fish."

But there was an additional responsibility mentioned in Noah's commission—to protect and judge nature when it is destructive. For example, when an animal killed a human being, it was put to death (Gen 9;5). We will see in later chapters that there are many Old Testament laws and wisdom instructions that speak to the care and protection of wild and domesticated animals. For example, the sabbatical years were enforced to allow the ground to refurbish itself and to feed the wild and domesticated animals. So, during this parenthetical phase of history, humanity is required not only to refrain from harming nature but we are required to deliver nature from its Eden curses and human abusers. That salvation would include disciplining those guilty of irresponsible and immoral shepherding care of nature.

The New Earth is the Lord's proof of his faithful deliverance of nature. Like the Flood of old and regional forest fires today, nature's surface is marred or charred, but not so deeply that new growth will not garland the land again. Nature may groan and even be decimated in the end times, but in New Earth it will continue its role in God's eternal design. Listen to these verses as they develop the fuller idea.

> The wolf will dwell with the lamb, and the leopard with the young goat . . . And a little boy will lead them.
> The nursing child will play by the hole of the cobra, and the weaned child will put his hand on the viper's den.
> These animals will not hurt or destroy in all my holy mountain, for the earth will be full of the knowledge of the Lord. Isa 11:6, 8–9

> He will make Israel's wilderness like Eden, and her desert like the garden of the Lord. Isa 51:3

> Just as the new heavens and the new earth which I will make will endure with me, so your offspring and name will endure. Isa 66:22;

> I will multiply the fruit of the tree and produce of the field, so you will not be disgraced by famine among the nations. Ezek 36:30

> We are looking forward to new heavens and new earth. 2 Pet 3:13

> This world and all of its cravings are passing away. 1 John 2:17

> I saw new heavens and a new earth since the first ones had passed. Rev 21:1

The biblical predictions about New Earth describe it as a very physical place. This New Earth is the setting for our eternal life with the Lord, and it is the same earth he created to be good and perfect but which we have spoiled. God's eternal design included our shepherding *this* place, not another dimension created where we could escape our original responsibilities. Nature will be given a new surface where it will be shepherded by the Lord and humanity, and where nature will shepherd the rest of nature as well as a perfect human population.

God's eternal design includes nature; the eternal design implies that God shepherds shepherding nature. This chart, extracted from the master chart in chapter 1, gives examples of how he blesses, delivers, and disciplines nature.

The Eternal Design	Each Part of Creation is Shepherded by God	
	Nature	
God	Blesses	Beauty; physical laws; God's care and covenant; shows God's glory
	Delivers	Protected by God & humanity; animals protect their young; New Earth
	Disciplines	God curses nature; nature groans now during the parenthetical age

NATURE SHEPHERDS BY ITS PRIMARY COMMISSION

The eternal design defines the shepherding role for all parts of creation: spirits, nature, and humanity. Nature subdues and shepherds itself and humanity in very forceful ways. It restricts itself and human freedom from reaching beyond what God allows by the laws of nature which he has created and which he sustains. When the Lord humbles Job, he refers specifically to nature's rule over humanity: "Do you know the laws of the universe or can you establish their rule over the earth?" (Job 38:33).

Humanity and nature are inseparable in many ways since both hold each other in check. But this mutual dependence has both positive and negative implications—positive when humanity and nature cooperate in what is best for both, negative when either one operates without regard for the other. If humans over-consume, nature suffers. If nature becomes imbalanced and unstable, humanity feels the rumble and rage of the earth and its elements. But given the centrality and preeminence of humanity, and the leadership role we play on this planet, when humanity loses self-control, the results are more devastating than any that may come from nature's wildness. Our moral failures wreak far more damage to nature and the rest of humanity.

God's primary commission for humanity given to the Couple in Eden is, "Be fruitful and multiply, fill the earth and subdue it" (Gen 1:28). God also gave nature its own primary commission. To the living animals created on the fifth day, God says, "Be fruitful and *multiply, fill* the water in the sea and the birds will *multiply* on the earth" (1:22). God shares his generating and shepherding capacities with all life. So non-human life procreates and *multiplies* as God has multiplied himself through his image-bearing humanity. Nature then *fills* the waters and skies with great variety: "Let the waters swarm with throngs of living creatures" (Gen 1:20). Animals produce "abundantly" and provide beauty and food for the rest of nature and humanity. Plant ecosystems also multiply and fill the land and seas.

The "subdue" part of the primary commission is not explicit in the recorded animals' primary commission in Genesis, but we know from the rest of Scripture, from experience, and from science that animal life is very assertive in controlling much of what it fills. The animals have their domain over humanity whether they are the small mosquito or the huge Behemoth and Leviathan.[18] Unfortunately, the serpent which moved over the land and which humanity was commissioned to subdue turned the tables and subdued humanity instead at that humiliating and extremely damaging moment of the Fall!

Through the laws of nature, higher animals act with emotion, wisdom, instinctive morality, creativity, power and authority. I suppose I believe these traits are less metaphoric than others believe them to be. Adults of animal species bless by providing for their young. They deliver their young from danger and discipline their willfulness while judging their predators severely. For instance, the duck blesses her ducklings

---

18. Job 40:24; 41:1–34

with nurturing care, delivers them from their straggling waywardness, and fends off the muskrat and snapping turtle. Nature delivers itself by the species protecting "their own" and at times warning the rest of creation by their motions and sounds of alarm. We might explain these actions as purely instinctive, but nevertheless, they do reflect obedience to God's laws and provide shepherd-like benefits to their territories. These animal characteristics, by complying with the eternal design, reflect some attributes of the eternal shepherding Designer.

The Lord gives nature its various kingdoms and territories to rule once it has filled those territories. For instance, the sun rules its solar system, protecting it from disintegration with its gravitational bond over its planets, meteors and comets. It blesses us with warmth and nourishing rays for our food, it delivers us from cold and dark nights, and it disciplines those who excessively indulge in its searing brightness or burning heat. The commission for the "lights" is to govern the day, the night, and the seasons; in other words, they rule strictly over *time*, having filled the skies with their brightness or its absence.

> God made two great lights, the brightest light to *rule* the day and the duller light to *rule* the night, including the stars. God set them in the spacious sky to give light on earth to *rule* the day and the night. Gen 1:16–18

The Lord considers this arrangement as "my covenants that I have with the day and night"[19] (Jer 33:20). We experience the tyranny of time over our daily and annual routines. These lights relentlessly govern us by their laws over the tides, over the forms of precipitation, and when exactly the Morning Glory's petals open.[20] But this ruling by the lights is at God's sovereign discretion since at any appointed time he may miraculously alter their regularity and effects.[21]

This shepherding power which nature exerts over humanity is pervasive. Gravity demands that we not levitate. The mere enormity of the universe restricts our movement about the cosmos. Atoms defy careless dissection to our great peril. The boundaries of the watery realms are set by God to bless the habitations and realms of incalculable species of flora and fauna—an unknown number of which have yet to be discovered.[22] Between the surface waters and the watery clouds is found the swarming realm of innumerable kinds of aerial insects and birds. God in his infinite creativity assigned more than one realm for some. Reptiles, amphibians, and certain insects traverse the water, land, or aerial realms. Some birds even enter the realms of the water at various depths for their sustenance, including the versatile penguin.

---

19. Jer 33:20; also, Ps 136:9
20. Gen 1:14–18; Job 38:12–13, 19–24, 33; Pss 74:16–17; 104:19–23; 136:7–9; Jer 5:24; 31:35; 33:20–21, 25–26; Amos 5:8
21. Josh 10:12–13; Hab 3:11; Zech 14:6–7
22. Gen 1:6–8; Job 38:8–11, 25–30; Ps 104:10–13; Amos 5:8

Nature shepherds in the same ways as God, his holy angels, and humanity shepherd, by blessing, delivering, and disciplining. Nature *blesses* creation through its multiplying, swarming, and shepherding laws, bringing wonderful benefits and pleasures to the globe. Humanity invents objects from nature's resources and develops civilizations with those inventions. The sheer beauty and power of nature blesses us with the smallest flowers of the smallest meadow (Matt 6:28–29) and the ominous presence of the vast stellar constellations (Job 38:31–33).

The rising terrain from the depths of the sea made room for itself by dividing the waters. Then that new land provided vegetation, animal life, water, and minerals.[23] The soil of these land masses serves the various species differently and abundantly.[24] Within God's fashioning hands, the soil is the source of human life. The soil sustains all life by its fertility. The soil's vegetation has multiplied, filled the earth and the seas, lakes, rivers, marshes and ponds, serving all animal and human life.[25] The land produces and sustains delicious plants and animals which should not be shunned because of any self-righteous traditions.[26] Nature blesses itself and humanity by providing its food-chain to all. Whether ostrich, fox, scorpion, swan, snake, beetle, sparrow, worm, cricket, or frog, they sacrifice themselves for one another and for our benefit because of their vulnerability to their predators.

Nature blesses itself and humanity by providing rain, warmth, seasons, natural shelters, and raw materials. Because of nature's built-in sovereignty and the blessings it extends to itself, the psalmist leads us in praising nature's Creator:

> To him who made the skies with wisdom—His kindness is eternal.
>
> To him who spread the land above the seas—His kindness is eternal.
>
> To him who made the bright lights—His kindness is eternal.
>
> The sun to rule over the day—His kindness is eternal.
>
> The moon and stars to rule over the night—His kindness is eternal. Ps 136:5–9

Praise the Lord for his blessing *for* nature and *through* nature because of his everlasting love.

Nature also *delivers* itself and humanity. God's covenants with nature and enlists it in his kingdom administration of salvation. This is evident several times in Israel's history when nature is called on to assist in her salvation, most noticeably when Israel was delivered by the natural disasters God sent Egypt's way, including frogs, insects, and hail.[27] God's wilderness deliverances for Israel by manna, quail, and water were

---

23. Gen 1:11–12, 24; 2:6, 11–12, 19; 4:22
24. Ps 104:18, 25
25. Gen 1:11–12; Ps 104:14–17, 27–28
26. 1 Cor 10:25–31; 1 Tim 4:1–5
27. Ex 3:20; 7:20—12:30; Ps 105:26–36

supposed to motivate Israel to faithfulness.[28] Elijah was fed by ravens (1 Kgs 17:6). Jonah was saved miraculously by a large fish and a large shade plant.[29]

Nature would have been only a means of God's grace, but human rebellion turned it into a means of God's *discipline* as well. Animals, vegetation, humanity, angels, and God were all put in conflict with one another in Eden. Though the earth brings life, food, water and minerals, it was cursed by God to be less collaborative with the rest of nature and humanity. Now, it grudgingly cooperates with humanity, including Cain for whom the land produced nothing at all (Gen 4:12). The earth now devours the flesh it produced, absorbing the dead into its graves and soil.[30] Though the earth and humanity were to be friends, they are now in perpetual, obstinate, and annoying conflict (Gen 4:10–11). And when vegetation and animals are not multiplying and making themselves available for whatever blessings they were intended to provide, it is a curse to the rest of life, including ours.

But more directly, when used wrongly, nature might react to the abuser with physical consequences. Whether a child pokes at and irritates a hornet nest or citizens significantly pollute a community's environment, nature's judgment may not be imminent, but certainly, it is eventual. Fire, real and figurative, is one of the first tools of justice associated with the Lord's response against sinful humanity.[31]

The Old Testament's consistent awareness of the Lord's primary commission often refers to it in various terms when emphasizing his authority. Ezekiel described God's authority over nature in these terms: "The fish of the water, the birds of the skies, the beasts of the field, and all creeping things, and all humanity on the face of the earth will shake at my presence" (Ezek 38:20). Referring to nature again, he promises to drastically de-create the earth: "I will remove everything from the face of the earth. I will remove humanity and beast; I will remove the birds of the skies and the fish of the waters" (Zeph 1:2–3). Lesser judgments through God's use of nature are prevalent throughout the Old Testament, and God's kingdom people are cursed with most of the very plagues of judgment that Egypt suffered when the Israelites were released from bondage.

Though we should have great appreciation for nature's power, sovereignty, beauty, and wonder—and though we should respect how God and nature work with identical goals—and though there must be a humble attitude toward nature and its many sovereign laws—and though the skies, ground, mountains, and hills are appointed to be condemning witnesses against humanity,[32] still, nature is certainly never to be worshipped. Whether it be a celestial body, bird, human, land animal, or fish, it is the

---

28. Ex 16:4, 8, 13, 31, 35; 17:6; Num 11:6, 31–32; 20:8–11; Deut 8:3, 15–16; Josh 5:12; Neh 9:15, 20–21; Pss 78:15–16, 20, 24–27; 105:40–41; 114:8; Isa 48:21; Ezek 20:9–10; Hos 13:4–5; Mic 7:15

29. Jonah 1:17; 4:6

30. Gen 3:19; 4:11; Eccl 3:20; 12:7

31. Gen 19:24; Num 11:1–3; 16:35; Deut 32:22; 2 Kgs 1:10,12,14; 1 Chr 21:26; 2 Chr 7:1; Joel 2:30–31; Amos 1:4, 14; 7:4

32. Gen 4:10–11; Deut 4:26; 30:19–20; 31:28; 32:1; Ps 50:4–6; Isa 1:2; Jer 2:12; 6:18–19; Mic 6:1–2

ultimate offense to worship an idol or anything created by God or man. Such idolatry is a stench to God who created everything that fools might choose to worship.[33]

The folly of revering any creature is found in every era and area. The object of excessive adoration might be as crass as an idol made out of some raw material. Or it could be living flora or fauna, the stars or one's ancestors. It might be more conceptual by elevating anything above God. Sexuality, wealth, comfort, popularity or any self-centered substitute for the preeminence of our Lord is our personal act of idolatry. Humanity has "served the creature, not the Creator," and has worshipped "images of corruptible humans, birds, and walking or crawling animal creatures" (Rom 1:22–25).

We will look again and again at how God uses nature for his purposes when we discuss his sovereign shepherding of sovereign humanity. We will see how his blessings, deliverance, and discipline of humanity are the results of nature obeying his commands.

Just a note here about the Lord's miracles: they are not always done in life and death situations but in more mundane situations, sometimes more as his acts of courtesy or convenience. For instance, there was nothing particularly critical when Jesus fed one meal to thousands of people with miniscule amounts of food[34] or when he walked on water,[35] killed a fig tree,[36] precisely located large schools of fish to be netted,[37] arranged for the disciples to hook exactly the one fish that had swallowed a coin (Matt 17:27) and turned the wedding water into wine (John 2:7–10).

HUMANITY SHEPHERDS NATURE

It was a dramatic moment when humanity was told to subdue the earth. That included the land itself, not only what moves on, around, and above the earth: " . . . rule over all the earth. . . . fill the earth and subdue it" (Gen 1:26, 28). One way ownership and responsibility over an area is shown in the Testaments is by "walking the land." God walking Eden, Abraham walking Canaan, Satan walking the earth, God walking in Israel, Israel walking on her mountains, Christ walking among us—these are all symbolic acts of sovereignty.[38] Walking this earth stakes humanity's claim just as animals patrol the area they rule.

Adam's task to name the animals required him to separate, sort, and manage them. Later, Noah was commissioned to deliver the animals, and he used a dove and olive branch to his advantage. But Noah was also instructed to judge the dangerous

---

33. Ex 20:4; Deut 4:15–19; 5:8; 17:2–7; 2 Kgs 17:16; 18:4; 19:15–19; 23:5, 11; Job 31:26–28; Ps 96:5; Isa 40:25–26; 44:12–20; Jer 2:26–28; Ezek 8:10, 16–17; Amos 5:26; Zeph 1:5;

34. Matt 14:17–21 // Mark 6:38–44 // Luke 9:13–17 // John 6:8–13; Matt 15:34–38 // Mark 8:5–9

35. Matt 14:25 // Mark 6:48 // John 6:18–19

36. Matt 21:19 // Mark 11:13–14

37. Luke 5:4–7; John 21:6

38. Gen 3:8–10; 13:14–18; Job 1:7; 2:2; Ex 29:46; Lev 26:11–12; Deut 6:13–15; 23:14; 1 Kgs 20:28; Ps 76:1–2; Ezek 36:8, 11–12; Zeph 3:15; Zech 2:11–13; 8:3

animals by killing those which had killed someone. Killing animals and plants is also necessary for food, clothing, and sacrifices, but otherwise they are to be cared for and protected.[39] Yes, everything created was good, yet God's provision for parts of that creation to be eaten, worn, or sacrificed was also good.

Multiplying and filling the earth moves on to subduing it in Genesis 4:1–2, 19–22 and 10:6–14. These passages describe the specific ways that primitive cultures subdued the earth and its resources for productive purposes. Adam and Eve birthed Cain and Abel who managed crops and animals respectively. Lamech and his two wives, Adah and Zillah, birthed Jabal, Jubal, and Tubal-Cain. Jabal and his descendants managed animals. Jubal and his descendants manipulated sounds to compose music and used other natural materials to make his musical instruments. Tubal-Cain mined the ground's ores and forged from them the tools with which to further subdue the environment.

Eventually, success in applying the primary commission has produced inventions from the wheel to wifi. Genesis 10:6–14 recounts the multiplication of Ham's descendants which led to Nimrod, a real "subduer" who aggressively built his own kingdom and civilization of many cities and peoples.

So far, we have addressed primarily nature's land, but lakes, rivers, ponds, creeks, wetlands, seas, and oceans are all included in the primary commission's reference to any life that uses the *waters* for their well-being: mammals, fish, shellfish, even insects. That does not even consider the plant life that makes the waters its home and domain. The management of the earth includes managing its large and small bodies of water with dykes, dams, locks, levees, canals, and irrigation systems. Earth management includes constructing and using floating and submerged vessels to navigate the waters to deliver food, oil, even military weapons. Solomon had his own merchant ships which navigated the waters as far as India (1 Kgs 9:26–28).

Ancient human management of the *skies* was obviously very limited, amounting to eating its birds and insects. Managing the information the skies offer for determining the times, seasons, and weather is also useful. Not until very modern times does sky management become more technical and far-reaching, as in human flight, satellite communication and weapon launches (beyond spears, stones and arrows).

Subduing the earth blesses it since a land which is not filled and subdued will become desolate, wild, and dangerous. So nearly any civilization is better than none since a human presence brings order and preferably godly management, production, and restoration of nature and its resources. Godly shepherding serves the land by following civil laws that benefit the soil and by instituting precautions that retain natural order for the safety and prosperity of its inhabitants, human and otherwise. Biblical instructions reflect the Lord's expectation that we are responsible for nature. Examples of how to avoid regional extinction of wildlife included leaving the wild hen alone while taking her eggs so she could bear more eggs and chicks (Deut 22:6–7). Care for

---

39. Deut 25:4; Prov 12:10

nature refreshed the soil when left fallow, and those fallow fields fed the wild animals with whatever the fields yielded during those sabbatical years (Lev 25:7).

Biblical stewardship is far more profound than simply taking the earth and its physical environment seriously as a public policy stance. The politics of environmentalism is profound, but it is only a fraction of the whole eternal design of God. Those who make the earth and nature their god rather than the Creator only scratch the veneer of what controlling and shepherding nature really means and why it is important. Shepherding nature requires a comprehensive ethical system for why and how it should be done.

James gives us an idea of how successful humanity has been in accomplishing the primary commission. Using the commission's words, he reminds of us our responsibilities and relative success over nature. God told Eve and Adam,

> Rule over the fish of the sea, over the birds in the sky and over everything living and moving on the earth. Gen 1:28

James says we have done exactly that to some extent.

> All kinds of beast, bird, reptile and sea creature can be, and have been tamed by humanity. Jas 3:7

However, as a race we are still very far from the level of shepherding care for nature that God requires.

The Lord Jesus does say that our authority, accompanied with faith, could move mountains and that our mere words could throw trees into the sea.[40] Are these examples of the power God intended for us to have and use when we are unencumbered by sin and faithlessness in the next age? The apostles and elders of the local church were partners with God in overturning nature's power over physical human bodies. These healings and resurrections by Jesus' followers show humanity can have authority over nature when used and propelled by God's power, even still, today! Christ says: "anyone believing in me will do the same works I have done—even greater works!" (John 14:12). This is not a promise for only the apostles, but for all of us. Since all of us have not had the privilege to witness these powers, I am hoping to participate in such wonders in New Earth! There will be no need for healings, resurrections, and exorcisms in New Earth, but the same extraordinary power will be available to us for other tasks as we shepherd with and by our all-powerful Lord.

---

40. Matt 17:20; 21:19–22 // Mark 11:20–24; Luke 17:6

8

Shepherding Humanity

GOD'S PLAN FOR HUMANITY

ALL OF HUMANITY IS the Lord's central interest in both Testaments. The peoples of the world are not mere marginal footnotes or a remote idea in a story about God, Israel, and the church. The peoples are *the focus* of God's attention in his eternal design. That means that his believing community is only an example during this parenthetical age of how the Lord wants all nations to relate to him and shepherd his creation. The Testaments point directly to the destination for all of creation, revealing the Lord's much broader, more pervasive and everlasting global design for humanity, nature, and the spirits. His eternal design is for all parts of creation to be eternally blessed by God and to be blessed by each other. That's the biblical message. Any other theological focus is too short-sighted and narrow.

God's relationship and plans for all peoples are made clear repeatedly in the Old Testament: by his promises to Abraham, in the ministries of Elijah and Elisha, in Israel's connections with her surrounding peoples, in the Psalms, and in nearly all the Old Testament prophets. Jeremiah was commissioned to be God's "prophet to the nations" in the Old Testament just as Paul was commissioned to be the apostle to the Gentiles in the New Testament.[1] The Lord's reign over all peoples is the precise point of the books of Obadiah, Jonah, and Nahum—books in which Israel, if even mentioned at all, is certainly not the focus. The Lord ruled the other peoples through his righteous international shepherds; for example, Melchizedek, Joseph, David, Solomon, Nehemiah, Mordecai, Esther and Daniel. Psalm 2 pits the Father and his Son against the world's arrogant nations who do not recognize the Son for who he is—the owner and king of even those disrespectful nations. Daniel 7:13–14 describes how the Father gave all nations to Christ, the Son of Man, so that he could shepherd them by his authority.

We find the word "gospel" used several times in the Old Testament. This includes Isaiah 40:9–11 which says that the Lord is Israel's ruling shepherd: "Bring the *good*

---

1. Jer 1:5; Acts 26:17; Rom 11:13; Gal 1:16

news ... Like a shepherd He will care for His flock." There is another "gospel" in the Old Testament which Paul quotes. It is the "gospel" God promised to Abraham, namely that the patriarch would be the one in whom all peoples of the world would be blessed. Paul explains,

> Scripture, seeing that God would eventually justify the Gentiles by faith, proclaimed *the gospel* in advance to Abraham saying, "Every nation will be blessed in you." Gal 3:8

So, this is a gospel too—God will bless all peoples through Abraham and his descendants, including his preeminent descendant, the Messiah king, Christ Jesus.

Then in Revelation, John speaks of "an eternal gospel" which reminds us of Abraham's gospel. It is a gospel for all peoples, the good news for all nations, that they too will be blessed at the Judgment by the Creator along with Israel and the church.

> I saw another angel flying in the sky who had an *eternal gospel* to preach to those sitting on earth—to every nation, tribe, tongue and people. The angel said loudly, "Fear God and glorify him because the hour of his judgment has come. Worship him, the creator of the earth, sea and springs of water." 14:6–7

This is the only time John uses the word "gospel" in his five books,[2] using it to refer to this eternal message to all peoples about their future with the Lord of all creation.

Our Shepherd's patience and grace are remarkable throughout his restoration of creation during this parenthetical age. His blessings, deliverance, and discipline are for individuals, families, the Israelites, the church, and the entire globe, in spite of the disobedience by each of these populations.

> Praise the Lord all you nations, exalt him all peoples!
>
> For his kindness overwhelms us and his truth is eternal. Praise the Lord! Ps 117:1–2

His patience through the millennia is the testimony to his love for humanity and his commitment to his eternal design. God's faithfulness in spite of the unfaithfulness of all "peoples" can be traced through all epochs of history. There will be wonderful discussions in New Earth when we review all those glorious moments when God's patience was shown to each and every person, family, community, tribe, village and nation in every moment of human history. That will be the *true* history lesson.

I use the term "peoples" more often than "nations" because one ethnic group can span many national boundaries. This is one of the most common reasons for wars and massacres. A "people" often want to reunite and govern itself, separating from their current nation. However, that nation will not allow such a separation unless forced by violent and bloody rebellions. However, it is critical to distinguish "peoples" from "people." The Lord does not save "all people, everybody" from their sin though he will have saved some from each people group before New Earth. Clearly,

---

2. Gospel of John, 1 John, 2 John, 3 John, Revelation

a universalist theology is contradicted throughout the Testaments, but in the end he will have brought all peoples into his kingdom: the various nations, ethnic groups, and other groups separated by dialect, language, or culture. We will have an exciting and eternal fellowship with the peoples from all parts of the world and we will appreciate and be edified by the diversity in creativity, worship, and their unique cultural approaches to fulfilling the primary commission.

GOD'S KINGDOM

Needless to say, God's cosmic and earthly kingdom dates back to the first day of creation. His commands to all creation and its generations are absolute and have always carried the same authority as when he demanded, "Light! Exist!" and immediately the nothingness glowed (Gen 1:3). The Flood, Babel, the patriarchal promises and the prophetic pronouncements reaffirm God's pervasive kingdom through all global eras and areas. The Old Testament scoffs at those who deny or even defy his ultimate authority.

> Who would not fear you, O King of the nations? You deserve this; for in all the kingdoms of the wisest nations there is no one like you. So the Lord is the true God—the living God and eternal King. The earth quakes at his anger and the nations cannot survive his wrath. Jer 10:7, 10[3]

Genesis through Malachi is a perpetual description of God's plans for *all peoples* as he reveals the flow of history along his eternal design. But his kingdom is even more compassionate and patient than it is wrathful.[4]

God is king of every *individual* too, whether they are believers or not. Every person's relationship with God is an example of God's relationship with all families, all communities, all nations; indeed, with the whole world because the Lord blesses, delivers, and disciplines each of these sociological units. When we hear Hannah's prayer, we hear the voice of an excited woman overwhelmed with her newfound fruitfulness—barren no longer. We hear her wise perspective that her *personal individual blessing* is only an example of God's rule and judgment over *all people* regardless of a person's political authority, social, or economic status.

> The Lord makes one poor or rich; he humbles and he exalts.
> He lifts the poor from the dust and the needy from the ash heap,
> seating them with nobles to inherit a place of honor.
> For the earth's pillars are the Lord's; he set the world on them.
> He protects the feet of his godly ones, but the wicked are silenced by darkness.
> For not by might shall a man prevail.
> The Lord shatters his opponents; he will thunder in the skies against them.

---

3. Also, Ps 2:2–6
4. 1 Kgs 8.23; Pss 22:27–28; 86.8–10

> The Lord will judge the entire earth.
>
> But he will strengthen his king, and exalt the horn of his anointed. 1 Sam 2:7–10

Frequently we are reminded of the royalty of God over the vast creation and the powerful nations and then immediately reminded as well of his concern for the smallest and weakest among humanity.[5]

It is especially encouraging that the powerful and comprehensive expanse of God's kingdom over space and time does not distract him from his particular interest in the disadvantaged, the single soul like Hannah. Praise God for his love and kindness! On the other hand, our personal accountability to the Lord is also sobering. Fear God and live! Each individual will stand *alone* before the Judge, not as a member of any of the wider sociological circles—not as a family member, not as a community or national citizen—we will stand alone and be condemned, or we will stand with Christ Jesus and be delivered.

God foresees all human decisions and by his wisdom, discretion, and power may allow or change them. His authority and purposes grant or confiscate the very land that any people might call their own realms.[6] God determines the political and military plans and activities of peoples, primarily by the decisions and abilities he plants in their leader's hearts.[7] Any who are in power are there because of a decisive act of God as the sovereign king over all nations.[8]

Such a decisive act of God can be seen among the Egyptian Pharaohs who reigned at God's discretion and for his purposes. He showed his own power to the whole earth through them. He told one Pharaoh, "I have raised you up to reveal my power to you, so that my name will be proclaimed in all the earth."[9] Jeremiah told Edom, Moab, Ammon, Tyre, and Sidon that the Lord had appointed king Nebuchadnezzar of Babylon to be their king (Jer 27:1, 6–7). Nebuchadnezzar was personally assigned to shepherd the peoples in terms of the primary commission: "God has given into your hand the rule over all humanity, the beasts of the field and the birds of the sky, wherever they dwell" (Dan 2:37–38). Later, the Persian emperor Cyrus is told that he would be the Lord's shepherd of Israel and other nations: "Cyrus is my *shepherd* who will fulfill all I desire" (Isa 44:28).

God honored Israel by making it the people to exemplify what all peoples would finally be in New Earth. But Israel was an embarrassment at times until God corrected the situation. The Lord had Ezekiel tell Israel,

---

5. Deut 10.17–19; Pss 9.18; 11.17–18; 72:2–4, 12–14; 74:12, 21; 82; 84:3; 113:4–9; 145:14–16; Isa 11:4; 61.1, 2

6. Gen 11:8–9; 12:1–2, 6–7; Ex 3.7–8; Deut 2.5, 9, 12, 19–21; 32:8; Josh 1:2–4; 3:10; 2 Sam 7:10; Pss 60:6–8; 135:10–13; 136:17–22

7. Ex 4:21; 7:3; 1 Chr 14:17; 29:12; 2 Chr 36:22–23; Ezra 1:1–2; 5:12; 6:22; 7:27; Job 12.18, 23–25; Pss 33:10, 16–17; Prov 21:1; Isa 41:2

8. Isa 44:28; 45:1–3; Dan 2:20–21, 37–45; 5:18, 21; 7:12–22; Hag 2:21–23

9. Ex 9:16; Rom 9:17

> It is not for your sake, house of Israel, that I am about to act, but for my holy reputation, which you have profaned among the nations where you went . . . *The nations will know I am the Lord when I prove myself holy* among you in their sight.[10]

The point of the Old Testament is that the nations were watching Israel. Solomon prays,

> May these requests I have made before the Lord be close to the Lord our God day and night so that he will sustain the daily goals of his servant and the daily goals of the Lord's people Israel *so that all the peoples of the earth may know that the Lord is God*; there is no one else.[11]

And there were moments when Israel was worthy of being watched and admired by the peoples. For example, the Queen of Sheba and other nations' representatives came to Israel to observe its God-given wisdom.[12]

CHRIST'S KINGDOM

Christ Jesus started a new phase in God's kingdom when, as the Second Person of the Trinity he was given a more direct leadership role over the world as a human being. Even though the Kingdom was given to Jesus, it was still God's kingdom because Jesus is God. So, when Jesus preached about *God's gospel*, he preached about his own continuing kingdom reign as well.

> Jesus came into Galilee preaching the gospel of God, saying,
> "The time is fulfilled and the Kingdom of God has come near." Mark 1:14–15

God's kingdom did not come for the first time in Christ. That would contradict the whole Old Testament message. The Jews would not have jumped to the conclusion that Jesus was going to overthrow the Roman rule if they had not known that God was the king of all nations, including Rome. That God was king of the nations was their encouragement; but they were confused, even angry, when God's believing community continued to include the Gentiles as it had in the Old Testament, with its inclusion of Rahab, Ruth, and the Ninevites.

It was the Trinity's kingdom that had come afresh in the Messiah. Christ's message was that his kingdom, the Father's kingdom, and the Spirit's kingdom had come to the Jews and to all peoples in this new phase of the Trinity's engagement with humanity. The Father sent the Son and Spirit to begin and sustain a new chapter that included a massive, global expansion of God's believing kingdom, and at an accelerated pace. Now the Son and Spirit lead an ever-increasing realm of believers—a kingdom that

---

10. Ezek 36:22–23; also, Ex 32:12; Num 14:13–16; Deut 9:28; 29:24–25
11. 1 Kgs 8:59–60, Ex 7:20; Lev 26:45; Num 33:3; Deut 4:6; 28:9–10; 1 Kgs 8:41–43; Ezek 38:16, 23; 39:6–7, 21–23, 27–29
12. 1 Kgs 4:34; 10:1–13

now spans the planet and adds thousands of courageous believers every day, most in territories hostile to our brothers and sisters!

New Testament voices reaffirm Abraham's gospel that every nation would be blessed through the patriarch (Gal. 3:8). When Mary and Joseph brought Jesus as an infant to the Temple, Simeon amazed them by saying their baby would not only be the savior of Israel but "a light to the Gentiles" (Luke 2:32). An excerpt of John the Baptist's preaching concludes, "All humanity will see God's salvation" (Luke 3:3–6). Even the Pharisees could not help but cry with irritation and panic, "The *world* follows him" (John 12:19). Matthew lists those peoples who were the first to follow Jesus, "Large crowds followed him from Galilee, Decapolis, Jerusalem, Judea, and beyond the Jordan" (4:24). When Mary hears the wonderful news that she would conceive the Savior, her thoughts go straight to the words of another joyful mother, Hannah of the Old Testament. Hannah's song of praise put everything in context in just a few sentences (1 Sam 2:7–10). Mary, a new mother like Hannah, also voiced her profound understanding of her own small individuality within the global political power of God: "The Mighty One has done great things for me . . . He has caused rulers to fall from their thrones and he has exalted the lowly" (Luke 1:49, 52). Mary and Hannah understood God to be the king of all nations and, at the same time, caring for the individual.

Jesus Christ walked the land beyond the political and ethnic borders of Judea to shepherd those who were not considered a part of the Lord's people, to Samaria and the Decapolis. In Samaria Christ told a woman that he was the Messiah, the anointed divine king (John 4:3–5, 25–26). His parable of the Good Samaritan was particularly annoying because the Samaritan was praised for his compassion when callous Jewish religious officials avoided compassion. He healed a girl during his visits to Tyre and Sidon (Lebanon) and exorcized demons in the Decapolis, east of Lake Galilee (Syria).[13] And the blessings to various peoples were shared by those who sought him out. Officials came from the East to visit the Infant. A Roman centurion pled for his servant's healing. Greeks came to visit and converse with Jesus just as the Queen of Sheba had come to King Solomon.[14]

The Testaments reveal the Lord's royal discretion to appoint whomever he wished to be the rulers over the various peoples in his global kingdom. Christ said this to Pilate's face: "You would not have any authority over me if it had not been given to you from above" (John 19:11). Paul taught submission to the political leaders since, "There is no authority that has not been established by God . . . it is God's ordinance . . . for it is a minister of God" (Rom 13:2–4). God's pervasive strategy to accomplish his eternal design includes his assigning human leaders to implement his plans, whether they are believers or not. He puts it in the hearts of kings to war against whomever he pleases for his disciplinary reasons (Rev 17:16–18).

---

13. Matt. 15:21–22 // Mark 7:24–26; Matt. 8:28, 32 // Mark 5:2, 15 // Luke 8:27, 35
14. Matt. 2:1–2, 11; Matt. 8:5–7 // Luke 7:2–5; John 12:20–23; 1 Kgs. 10:1–10

Shepherding Humanity

John says Christ was "born to shepherd the nations" (Rev 12:5).[15] John's claim refers to Psalm 2:8–9 when God the Father announced that his Son would inherit and discipline the peoples:

> You are my Son. I am the Father who has begotten you.
>> Just ask, and I will give you the nations as your inheritance, the whole earth as your possession.
>> You will shepherd them with an iron rod and dash them as pottery.

Christ came to gather all peoples to himself with all the authority of their king: "I call all humanity to myself" (John 12:32). Abraham acknowledged that God is the Judge of all peoples and their kings; he is the "judge of the earth" (Gen 18:25).[16] Christ claimed the same responsibility for himself: "All nations will be gathered to the Son of Man, and he will separate the people as a shepherd separates the sheep from the goats" (Matt 25:32).

Daniel prophesied in the Old Testament that the coming Messiah was "like a son of a man"; that is, a human who would represent all humanity.

> One like a *Son of Man* was coming . . . To him was given dominion, glory and a kingdom so that all peoples and nations would serve him regardless of language. Dan 7:13–14

In other words, he would not just be a son of David, he would be the Son of Humanity at large. This was the reason for the incarnation: so that finally a human would be the successful savior and shepherd who would destroy Satan's kingdom and free the peoples. The first man, Adam, failed. Now Jesus, the man/God would come and certainly succeed. Whenever Jesus called himself this *Son of Man,* he emphasized his appointment by the Father to be the king of all the nations. It is recorded over eighty times in the Gospels when he used this name for himself!

Christ will also prepare a celebration banquet for those he judges to be his true believers from all peoples.

> The Lord of hosts will prepare a feast of rich food for all peoples, a banquet with aged wine—with the best meats and the finest wines. Isa 25:6

Christ repeats this Old Testament prediction that his kingdom people would come from everywhere to sit at Abraham's table:

> Many will come from the east and west, and will take their dinner places with Abraham, Isaac and Jacob in the kingdom of heaven.[17]

---

15. Again, the word "shepherd" in the Greek is repeatedly mistranslated as "rule." Also, 2:27; 19:15.

16. Gen. 15:13–16; 2 Kgs 19.27–28; Job 34:16–20, 29; Pss 67:4; 94:10; 149:7–8; Isa 23.8–9

17. Matt 8:11–12; Luke 13:29

One of the great symbols of the unity of God and his people is to share a meal, like the Last Supper and our communion table. Perhaps this is the meal Christ referred to when he said at his "last" supper with his disciples, "I will not drink this wine until that day when I drink it again with you in my Father's kingdom."[18] What a thrilling scene and experience it will be in New Earth to celebrate with our Lord and Savior with all his guests from all the nations who have turned to honor the Lord.[19]

GOD BLESSES HUMANITY

God's grace extends to all peoples, both believing and unbelieving communities, both believers and unbelievers. This is what is called God's "common grace"; it is common to all peoples. It is very different, eternally different, from God's saving grace that brings people into his eternal kingdom of believers and New Earth. His blessings for all peoples are not reserved only for the future when all the globe is restored to perfection again. Even in this very challenging parenthetical era, every nation, every tribe, every neighborhood, every family, every person experiences God's generosity now. Not that all peoples and nations in all eras and areas are redeemed by Christ; unfortunately most peoples have not been impacted in that marvelous way.

Every person, family, neighborhood, tribe, and nation experiences the torturous effects of the Fall in uneven amounts and degrees. These tragedies blind us from recognizing and appreciating God's liberal daily gifts. Even if we see them for the blessings they are, within a second we will again ignore the Source of our countless moments of satisfaction, pleasure, fulfillment, and joy. One reason for this is that we consider our positive experiences as *earnings*, not blessings—the results of our own assets and efforts rather than gifts from God. Yet, the Lord assures us that our pride is very misplaced.

> Let not the wise boast about their wisdom, the mighty about their might, the rich about their riches. Let them boast that they know and understand me as the Lord who brings love and kindness, justice and righteousness on earth since I delight in bringing these things.[20]

God manages his entire earth with love and justice and ethical perfection. In fact, he "makes everything *beautiful*" in its own time and way (Eccl 3:11). To understand this generous King is the only way to fully appreciate how all peoples enjoy life as much as they do. Otherwise, our foolish conclusion is that we have blessed ourselves and one another independently from the King.

18. Matt 26:29 // Mark 14:25 // Luke 22:18

19. Pss 2:10–11; 22:27–28; 46:10; 66:3–4; 68:30–32; 72:17; 86:8–10; 102:21–22; 117; 126:2–3; 145:21; 148:11–14; Isa 2:1–5; 12:4–5; 18:7; 19:20–25; 25:6–9; 42:1–4, 10–12; 45:6, 14, 22–25; 55:3–5; 56:6–7; 60:7; 61:5–7; 66:18–19; Jer 3:17; Ezek 38:23; Mic 4:1–5; Hab 2:14; Zeph 2:11; 3:9; Zech 8:20–22; 14:16; Mal 1:11

20. Jer 9:23–24; also, Pss 36:5–9; 145:8–13

Shepherding Humanity

This following chart's format is certainly familiar now. It is taken from the master chart in our first chapter and gives just a few examples of how God shepherds all humanity in his eternal design.

The Eternal Design	Each Part of Creation is Shepherded by God	
	Humanity	
God	Blesses	Life; God's image; communication; nature; the Law; conscience
	Delivers	Improved life conditions; freedom from oppression; wisdom in adversity
	Disciplines	Eden curses, illness, death; oppression; rebuke; Judgment Day

God's greatest gift to all humanity is life itself since it is only in having life that we can enjoy God and all his creation (Job 10:12). He has blessed the whole world with an enjoyment of his creation even though that enjoyment has led to a misdirected and perverse worship of it. Life is such a blessing that the Lord has made it available eternally as part of his eternal design for humanity. Eternal life was available in Eden through the Tree of Life, and eternal life was the hope of Old Testament believers.[21] Indeed, many cultures without the Scriptures have considered eternal life such a blessing that they have hoped it was true. Adam was formed from the earth, so he was a product and part of finite creation.[22] God formed the animals and birds from that same ground from which Adam was formed.[23] Both humanity and animals are infused with life directly from God.[24] Both humanity and animals have bodies that return to the ground and breaths that come to a halt.[25] Yet, and it is a marvelous "yet," God further blesses his followers with eternal breath and eternal bodies.

However, this life would not be such a blessing if we were not embedded with God's own image.[26] The greatest blessing of life is that we, though not divine ourselves, have godly attributes. This is why we can have a personal, profound, and productive relationship with God. The capacity for love, joy, peace, fulfillment, pleasure, excitement, and compassion—these start an endless list of human experiences and attributes which all people share with God, even those who do not worship him.

God has planted a lavish garden over nearly the entire surface of our planet, of which Eden was a minute model. Eden was planted by God to serve as the domain where Adam was to rule; it must have been a beautiful sight before the Fall. But the whole earth is a domain for all humanity to explore, enjoy, and shepherd. Clinging to such a limited part of this domain was humanity's foolishness at Babel. Humanity cheated themselves from all the blessings the rest of the planet had available to them

---

21. Gen 2:9; 3:22; Job 19:26–27; Pss 22:26; 41:12; 61:4–8; 73:26; 75:9–10; 115:17–18; 145:1–2; Prov 10:25; 12:19; 14:32; 15:24; 21:28; Isa 25:8; 26:19; Dan 12:2, 13

22. Gen 2:7; 3:19; Job 10:8–11; Pss 90:3; 103:13–14; 104:29; 139:13–16; 146:4; Isa 64:8

23. Gen 2:19; Ps. 104:29–30; Eccl 3.18–20

24. Gen 2:7; 7:22; Num 27.16; Job 33:4; 34:14–15; Ps 104:29

25. Ps 146:4; Eccl 12:7

26. Gen 1:27; 5:1; 9:6; Eccl 3:11

when they preferred to assemble and live in one tiny part of it. Fortunately, God's grace and kindness separated and scattered them into the reaches of the world to benefit from its luxurious provisions.

The blessings from *nature* are commonly experienced by all peoples. Simply the light of day, the sun itself, is pleasant for all humanity to see (Eccl 11:7). It blesses humanity with the warmth and light by which to work. Throughout the world the rains fall and springs rise, regardless of its inhabitants' theology or worldview.[27] The sea and other waters provide transportation to distant destinations and food from their hidden depths to all humanity who have access to them (Ps 104:25–26). The Psalms call the peoples to do something that as a whole they will refuse to do until the Judgment.

> Let the peoples praise you, O God; Let all the peoples praise you.
> The earth has yielded its produce; God, our God, blesses us. Ps 67:5–6

All peoples benefit from the seasons and fruits of nature; they are God's gracious blessing because humanity deserves *nothing*. Though humanity does not deserve even to exist, as long as we do exist we deserve only the worst darkness and draught.

The Song of Solomon enumerates these pleasures that God has built into nature's variety and voluptuous qualities. The undulating topography and the produce of the land are compared with the beauty of the male and female body. Both the human body and the geological terrain are the Creator's sculptured masterpieces: arms, legs, breasts, necks, hills, mountains, and valleys. The Song highlights nature's exotic gifts: apples, dates, nuts, pomegranates, raisins, grapes, flowers, trees, bushes, herbs, spices, perfume scents, oils, milk, and honey. Fox, deer, gazelles, sheep, purring turtle doves and glistening black ravens are a short list of animals to be admired for their colors, shape, or agility. The natural environment of the Song extols the pristine goodness of God's creation as enjoyed by the two lovers.

Every culture has some semblance of God's creation design for the *family*. The loving and productive relationship between husband and wife,[28] the exhilaration of naked intimacy,[29] the thrill of a new baby, the joy from growing children, and the support of the extended family are the benefits of strong families in every society. Admittedly, a family can be the source of the greatest hurt too. But without the support of a family, a person can be totally on one's own, physically and emotionally; life would be overwhelmingly brutal, chaotic, and unsustainable. As far as family morality, even pagan leaders like Pharaoh and Abimelech were guided by their God-given conscience in what was sexually moral and rebuked Abraham for his deceit about Sarah being his sister, not his wife.[30]

God blessed individuals and peoples when they connected with Israel whenever she was a righteous nation. When Israelites adopted the alien into their society, it

---

27. Ps 104:10, 13–16; Job 5:10
28. Gen 2:18–25; Prov 31:10–12, 28–29; Eccl 9:9
29. Prov 5:18–19; 18:22; Song 2:14; 4:5, 9; 5:1–6, 14–16; 7:1–3, 7–8; 8:10
30. Gen 12:15–20; 20:4–9

was a true blessing for the foreigner because they could now experience God's grace through his people. Individuals like Ruth were blessed in this way, but even entire neighboring nations were absorbed and blessed by the imperial rule of Ruth's great-grandson, David. Isaiah encourages all alien residents of Israel to keep the Lord's commandments because he would joyfully accept their sacrifices and return joy to them (56:3, 6–7). Solomon had prayed at the Temple's opening consecration that the alien in Israel's midst would be heard by the Lord in the temple.

> When the alien comes and prays at this house, hear him in your heavenly residence and do whatever he asks of you. Then all the peoples of the earth may know your name, and revere you as your people Israel do. 1 Kgs 8:42–43

Eventually, all peoples will be blessed in God's perfect future for New Earth. His plan is for the whole earth to be united and for all races to trust and worship him as their sovereign God. And those peoples will have sovereign responsibilities in his eternal design when they reign in perfect harmony and peace at each social level—family, work, worshipping community, and the various levels of government.[31] God calls all the nations to him, and they will come in peace and will be ready for work rather than war.[32]

Christ says our Father makes the sun rise and the rain to fall over everybody, whether they are wicked or good, righteous or unrighteous (Matt. 5:45). This is God's common grace to humanity. So he says we should be kind to our enemies because the "Most High" is himself kind to the wicked and unthankful (Luke 6:35). Paul and Barnabas told the Gentiles that the *true* God had allowed all the peoples to go astray, but he still blesses those peoples with sustenance and joy.

> He let all the nations go their own way, but he has not left them without witness about his character, revealing his kindness in giving you rain from the skies and predictable crops in their seasons; he provides you with plenty of food and fills your hearts with joy. Acts 14:16–17

Though the peoples have not honored him as God, his attributes, power and deity have always been obvious to humanity through his dependable provisions (Rom 1:20).

Paul told Timothy the same thing. God supplies us richly with all things to enjoy (1 Tim 6:17). Both Acts 14:16–17 and 1 Timothy 6:17 cite joy as a blessing that all humanity experiences; joy is experienced by everyone to some extent. So imagine that much more joy for the peoples when they live and work in New Earth! There will always be music since its silence is a curse (Rev 18:22). There will be no tears, curses, pains or death, no reason for deliverance and discipline—all peoples will only experience perfect satisfaction and blessing while they shepherd and bless all of the Lord's creation.

---

31. Isa 2:3; 19:23–25; 29:18–21; Zeph 3:9–10; Zech 2:11
32. Isa 45:20–24; Mic 4:3–4

Pentecost confirmed that the Kingdom and all its blessings were for all language groups and peoples. Pentecost was part of the fulfilment of God's promise in Isaiah 45:23: "To me every knee will bow, every tongue will swear loyalty." The perpetually growing government of Christ which the Lord had promised in Isaiah 9:7 will eventually result in a global response when "At the name of Jesus every knee should bow ... every tongue confess that Jesus Christ is Lord."[33] The call from the psalmists to all nations and their leaders to praise the only Lord and God will be finally realized!

> The Lord reigns, let the earth rejoice; let the many shores be glad. Ps 97:1

> Praise the Lord from the earth ... , kings of the earth and all peoples;
> princes and all judges of the earth. Ps 148:7, 11

The peoples are also blessed by revelation, the message of God, as it comes through his authors and is distributed by his apostles, ancient and modern. Cultures without Scripture have proven that nature and conscience have a convicting amount of knowledge about the Creator. But without the Testaments, humanity is left to guess, inevitably incorrectly, about how best to please God and enjoy his shepherding. Nonetheless, there are many moral principles which unbelieving humanity has been able to detect and implement from their conscience. Even the unbeliever loves those who love them; even the unbeliever respects authority and obeys civil authority; and even unbelievers know that bad company does not edify.[34]

GOD DELIVERS HUMANITY

God delivers the peoples at every social level, including the international, national, tribal, family, and personal levels. God delivers the unsaved on these levels from absolute evil and destruction, at a daily, even moment-to-moment frequency. By his intense and constant care, the Lord sustains, corrects, and readjusts the plans, priorities, decisions, and actions of the peoples and their leaders. He assesses everyone's moral performance at these levels and patiently tolerates or justly punishes according to his perfect will. The Shepherd shows his patience, mercy, discipline, and restoration regardless of whether the person or social unit is a part of his believing kingdom.

When one is delivered from anything at all, it is the Lord's grace to a sinner. James writes, "Every good and perfect gift is from above and comes from the Father of lights" (1:17). Any turn for the better for any society or individual is God's deliverance since no culture or person ever deserves to be delivered from any adversity. Nature is commissioned by our saving Lord to deliver many afflicted individuals and societies around the world. As God's instrument, nature's delivering strength in times of need is experienced by nature itself and by humanity. For example, nature delivers humanity

---

33. Rom 14:11; Phil 2:10–11
34. Matt. 5:46 // Luke 6:32–33; Matt 5:47; Rom 13:3–7; 1 Cor 15:33

from starvation and a dissolving economic scenario by becoming fruitful again, replenishing the land and its people.

When there is any deliverance from the effects of the Fall, they are gifts from God even though most of his creatures are unaware or unwilling to acknowledge much less worship him for his gifts. When an unbeliever experiences physical or mental healing of any kind or deliverance from any tragedy, God is shepherding that one by his saving grace. His deliverance of peoples from their enemies and from natural disasters is not reserved for believing peoples alone. What else should receive any credit for these deliverances? False gods? Angels? Demons? Ancestors? Chance? Fate? Resourcefulness? Karma? Mystery? Nothing else, no one else, can be credited with delivering anybody or anything from adversity other than the Trinity. No other conclusion can be drawn than that it is our God who delivers the peoples since God's sovereignty determines or allows any act and all results.

God's moral character is a built-in moral compass in all humanity. Yes, that conscience has been infected, seared, and overwhelmed by ethical systems contrived from scratch, but even the contaminated image of God in the pagan conscience is better than no conscience at all. Satan would have long since destroyed all non-believing peoples and whatever they rule if the human conscience and the compulsion to follow it were not as strong as God has made it. So the Lord's deliverance comes from one's normal consequences of following one's conscience. However, the rewards for obedience to one's conscience do not come close to real righteousness that comes through a new creature washed and revitalized by the Holy Spirit. Believers obey both their redeemed conscience and the Lord's revealed instructions as an act of their love and trust in him. Nonetheless, deliverance also abounds in this life for unbelieving peoples and persons who obey their conscience and, by doing so, unwittingly obey the Trinity as their sovereign shepherd.

God did not postpone Abraham's gospel about Gentiles until the New Testament. Gentiles were delivered in the Old Testament too on a national and individual level. They were promised by the Lord . . .

> When I pronounce a judgment to uproot, tear down and destroy any nation or kingdom and that nation turns from its evil, I will change my verdict against it. Jer 18:7–8

This is precisely what happened to Nineveh. At Jonah's demands, that large Assyrian city turned from its evil, and the Lord did change his standing verdict to destroy it.

> When God saw how the Ninevites turned from their evil ways, he relented and did not destroy them as he had threatened. Jonah 3:10

God's deliverance of specific *peoples* other than Israel is predicted several times in the Old Testament. However, these deliverances are not because of a conversion to the true God as apparently it was in Nineveh's case. Rather, these were the Lord's gracious rescues of these peoples from their oppressors or natural disasters. Moab, Damascus, Egypt and Assyria are examples of God's national salvation for peoples outside Abraham's covenant.[35] God also delivered Gentile peoples through the heroics of his own faithful shepherds. For example, Abraham delivered Sodom, Gomorrah, Admah and Zeboiim from Chedorlaomer; Joseph delivered Egypt from famine; Joshua exempted the Gibeonites from extinction; Elisha delivered the Syrians.[36]

God's shepherding deliverance also came to Old Testament Gentile *individuals*. A widow in Sidon was miraculously given a perpetual amount of flour by Elijah. Then Elijah raised her dead son (1 Kgs 17:1–24). Naaman, Syria's army general, was healed of leprosy through the ministry of Elijah's successor, Elisha (2 Kgs 5:1–14). God's love extended to the small and great even beyond his covenant community in very specific and personal ways.

God condescended to struggle with humanity throughout the Old Testament, he did not despise nor totally reject our human race. Rather, he repeatedly re-initiated his relationship with humanity and prepared us for his dramatic, history-changing incarnation. However, humanity has always been surprised, even unbelieving, that God himself would come to suffer with us, by us, and for us. Such tragic blindness!

Yet it is with loving interest in all peoples that the great God and savior, Jesus Christ, assigned his disciples and Paul to announce the good news of God's kingdom to the world.[37] Paul is the central apostle in the New Testament for several reasons, but especially because his ministry and writings focused on the Gentiles, not Israel. He began in the Jewish synagogues in several towns, but the point of Acts and the subsequent apostolic letters is that God's global kingdom would now have a growing number of Gentiles, just as the Old Testament predicted.[38] Paul told worshippers of Zeus and Hermes that the Creator was gracious to all the nations. He told philosophers in Athens that the Creator expected all peoples to repent before Christ came to judge the whole world.[39] Paul's evangelistic and discipleship journeys took him to large sections of the Roman Empire and to its many various peoples under Roman rule.

Peter also informed Jew and Gentile alike that the Kingdom gospel was for all peoples. He reminded them of their father Abraham's gospel about the nations, and that Jesus had come to save the nations.[40] Later, when addressing the Gentile, Cornelius, with his family and friends, Peter's opening words were, "God is not partial, so he welcomes anyone from any nation who reveres him and does what is right . . . he is

---

35. Isa 16:4–5, 13–14; 17:1; 19:19–25; Jer 48:47

36. Gen 14:14–17; 41:46–49; 47:23–25; Josh 9:22–27; 10:6–15; 2 Kgs 6:20–23

37. Matt 28:19; Mark 16:15, 20; Luke 24:45–47; Acts 8:12, 25; 9:8, 13–15, 22; 20:25; 28:23, 31; 1 Tim 3:16

38. Isa 49:6; Acts 9:15; 13:47

39. Acts 14:15–17; 17:24, 30–31

40. Acts 3:25; 4:12

the Lord of all" (Acts 10:34–36, 43). Peter told the Jewish believers in Jerusalem that Gentiles were being delivered and had received the Holy Spirit too (Acts 11:15–18).

The flourishing kingdom of God grew with Gentiles to the point that church leaders dismantled nearly the entire ceremonial code of the Old Testament Mosaic law! James proposed a historic paradigm shift in biblical ethics at the "Jerusalem council" with no recorded resistance from the new church leaders (all Jews). This made sense to the leaders because the older testament had prophesied that a new religious order would come that would include the Gentiles.[41] Of course, universal laws of the conscience were still assumed valid; for example murder, stealing, respect for authority, etc.

However, God's loving, shepherding care of the Gentiles was a major stumbling block to many Jews. Like Jonah's attitude in the Old Testament, the Jewish leadership was angry and selfish and resisted Abraham's gospel about the Gentiles. Jonah ran the other way when commissioned to share God's gospel with the Gentiles in Ninevah, and the New Testament religious establishment followed Jonah's example. The Old Testament was clear enough about the shepherding interests of God for all humanity, not just Israel (Rom 15:8–12). But human nature, regardless of race, is prone to claim senselessly that God is just for them. But God's eternal design has always included the Gentiles as equal citizens and fellowrulers of his kingdom.[42] And it is not only the barrier of ethnicity that God ignores but gender and socio-economic barriers were not to exist: "There is neither Jew nor Gentile, slave nor free male nor female—you are all one in Christ Jesus" (Gal 3:28).

The Jews' damning resistance to their father Abraham's gospel is dramatized in Christ's prophetic parable about the vineyard keepers.[43] The story portrays God sending prophets and even his own Son to Israel, only to see them beaten or killed. In the story, those who were responsible for managing the land and being productive in God's world violently rejected the Lord's call for accountability. Christ concluded his parable by telling the unproductive Jewish chief priests and elders, "The kingdom of God will be taken away from you and given to a nation that produces kingdom fruit" (Matt 21:43). Christ did not say that he would build another kingdom alongside the Jewish kingdom of God. He says that the Kingdom would be taken and given to the Gentile peoples, not to the exclusion of Jews, but to the inclusion of any human who repented.

Paul experienced personally this parable's real-time reenactment in the cities where he ministered. In going to the synagogues first, Paul was like the messengers in the parable who were beaten and stoned. Acts 13:16–48 tells the story of Paul in Antioch where the Jews wanted to hear more of his message, but when an enormous crowd of Gentiles showed up too, the Jews dug in their heels and were no longer teachable. So Paul told them exactly what Christ had said in the parable, "The word

---

41. Acts 15:13–20, 27–29; Amos 9:11–12

42. Eph 2:12–13; 19; also, Matt 24:14; Mark 13:10; Luke 2:29–32; John 1:7–8; 8:12; Acts 1:8; 2:4, 9–11, 21, 38–39; 1 Cor 15:24; Eph 3:6, 8–11

43. Matt 21:33–46 // Mark 12:1–12 // Luke 20 9–19; also, Matt 8:11–12; 21:43; Acts 13:26–30

of God needed to be spoken to you first. Since you repudiate it ... we now turn to the Gentiles" (46). Needless to say, the Gentiles were ecstatic (48).

It took a startling vision for Peter to get this point (Acts 10:9–17, 28). Peter's vision of the sheet full of forbidden meat was an illustration for Peter that he should not shun anything that God had made clean. The vision encouraged Christian Jews to embrace Gentiles into the fellowship as new brothers and sisters. So in the Lord's perfect timing, while Peter was recovering from his shock over the vision of inclusion, a delegation from Cornelius the Gentile arrives to invite Peter to bring God's message to the centurion's family and friends.

GOD DISCIPLINES HUMANITY

It is amazing how easily humanity can take God's grace and use it as a law against him. Whenever something appears unfair, the primary suspect of injustice is God. Yet, it is our presumption that God must be equally gracious to all that makes *us* the primary suspects. God's grace is just that—an act of goodness to those who do not deserve it. That means no one deserves any blessing because we are all deserving of judgment in the most drastic way. If someone receives more judgment than another in a comparable situation, that person has been dealt with according to God's perfect justice. If one does not receive as much grace as another, one has no basis for a grievance against God. Anyone who criticizes God and his justice had better depend on God's grace rather than his justice come Judgment Day. So if there appears to be an uneven distribution of justice or grace, rest assured that God will prove himself righteous and wise in his judgments regardless of any criticism.

Abraham's gospel blesses the nations, but it also warns of discipline and judgment. The "gospel to Abraham," as Paul refers to it, remains the standard, even for us today, against those peoples who presume to posture and fight against his people.

> I will bless those who bless you, but the one who curses you I will curse.
> But, all the peoples of the earth will be blessed in you. Gen 12:3[44]

This is the promise that Israel's leaders and psalmists cherished when they called on God to avenge their national and personal foes. For instance, Asaph wrote ...

> Listen to your enemies' uproar ... They are scheming against your people, conspiring against your precious ones. They say, "Come, let's wipe them out as a nation so Israel will never be remembered." Ps 83:2–5

In another psalm, Asaph asked for the Lord to "shepherd" Israel and to curse their oppressive neighboring countries.

> Pay back our neighbors seven times for the scorn they have thrown at you, Lord.

---

44. Gen 12:3; 27:29; Num 24:9; Deut 32:36, 43; 2 Sam 22:38–43; Ps 79:6–7, 10

> Then we your people, the sheep of your pasture, will praise you forever. Ps 79:12–13

Joshua recounts thirty one kings who hazarded conflict with God's people during their wilderness wanderings and later during the Canaan conquest (Josh 12:7–24). More specifically, the following nations suffered the imbalanced odds against them when battling Israel and her shepherd King: Egypt,[45] Amalek,[46] Midian,[47] Edom,[48] Ammon and Moab,[49] Philistia,[50] Syria,[51] Ethiopia,[52] Assyria,[53] Babylon,[54] and Persia.[55]

The Lord proved himself to be earth's king by both his grace and justice.[56] We use the word "discipline" even when it appears to be only justice because even God's most severe judgments are intended to correct and instruct all humanity about his grace. And God will nurture a specific people until he sees the need for their temporary or terminal judgment. That the complete wickedness of peoples and individuals is curtailed at all, and that there is any order and civility left in this world is only because of God's wise judgments on all peoples and in each person's life.[57] In the end, no dynasty, empire, nation, or people will have been left unjudged.

The Father told the Son in the first testament that he would give him the nations of the whole earth to shepherd: "You will *shepherd* the nations with an iron rod and dash them as pottery" (Ps 2:9). John refers to this in Revelation when he reveals Christ's role in the judgment of the peoples. He uses the term "shepherd" (*poimainō*) in two instances.

> He will *shepherd* them with a rod of iron, like when pottery is dashed. 2:27

> She gave birth to a son . . . who will *shepherd* all nations with a rod of iron. 12:5

Christ continues God's shepherding discipline of humanity, but the Father promises personally to assist the Son in his judgment. He says to the Son, "Sit at my right hand,

---

45. Gen 15:13–14; Ex 3:19–20; 4:22–23; 7:4—11:8; 12:27; 14:26–28; 15:4–12; Deut 11:2–4
46. Ex 17:8, 13–16; 1 Sam 14:48; 30:16–18; Ps 83:6–7
47. Num 25:16–18; 31:7–10, 15–18; Josh 13:22; Ps. 83:9
48. 1 Sam 14:47; 2 Chr 25:7–8, 11–13; Pss 83:6; 137:7–9; Isa 34:5–6; Jer 49:7–22; Lam 4:21; Ezek 25:12–14; 35:2–3; Amos 1:11
49. 1 Sam 14:47; 2 Sam 10:9–19; 2 Chr 20:22–23; Ps 83:6–7; Ezek 25:3–4, 6–11
50. 1 Sam 5:6–12; 6:5; 7:10–14; 14:47; 17:50–53; 2 Sam 3:17–18; 5:18–25 // 1 Chr 14:8–16; 2 Sam 19:9; 21:15–22; 23:9–12 // 1 Chr 11:13–14; Ps 83:7; Ezek 25:15–16
51. 2 Sam 10:9–19; 1 Kgs 20:13–30; 2 Kgs 6:8–12; 13:3–5, 22–25; Amos 1:3; Obad 10–14
52. 2 Chr 14:9–13; 16:8
53. 2 Kgs 19:6–7, 20, 34–37; 20:6 // 2 Chr 32:20–22 // Isa 37:6–7, 18–20, 33–37; also, Isa 30:30–31; 31:5–9; Jer 50:17–18; Nah 1:2, 9
54. Jer 50:11, 17–18; 51:34–35, 49
55. Esth 7:9–10; 8:3–8; 9:5–10, 15
56. Pss 59:13; 83:2–3a, 17–18; 83:16
57. Pss 9:4–8, 15–16; 46:6; 59:5; 96:10, 13; 98:9; Nah 1:8–10

until I make your enemies your footstool" (Ps 110:1). Paul told the Athenians that God will judge the world through the risen Christ (Acts 17:30–31). The Lord raises kingdoms, and he lowers them. But in his time, the historical sequence of all kingdoms will come to an abrupt end in the eternal, universal kingdom of the Messiah in New Earth.[58]

The Sins of the Peoples

The Lord's Mosaic laws applied to Gentiles in two scenarios. First, obedience or disobedience by aliens in the land to Mosaic and wisdom instructions resulted in either a blessing or curse because they were morally responsible as part of God's covenant community. Second, this was even the case when the Israelites were expelled from their land as exiles, and Gentiles were transplanted into Israelite territory. The immigrants were held to Israel's Mosaic standards while there, even though the Israelites themselves were banished to other lands. God was still the landlord of Israel's territory and his rules still applied. He maintained his moral standards by sending lions to kill some of these immigrants for not obeying the Law. Though they had not converted to become true believers while in the land, God still shepherded his land by enforcing his revealed Law there (2 Kgs 17:24–41).

Apart from these two circumstances, God held all peoples responsible for their offenses against him regardless of the Mosaic law. Relatively few peoples throughout all human history have had the Bible available to them, but there is a moral law written into the human soul that reflects God's righteousness. Ancient cultures show that without their awareness of Mosaic law and wisdom instruction, a substantial common ethical code is pervasive enough among them to hold all peoples accountable for their disobedience to the Trinity. So God indicts, judges, and penalizes the nations of the past, present, and future in perfect fairness and on the basis of the moral laws he has built into the conscience of any nation's people. For instance, humanity became so disobedient and worthy of judgment that the catastrophic flood was a just punishment (Gen 6:5–7). Humanity had willfully sinned against some moral code that is not described. In the book of Jonah, Ninevah is also held accountable for undescribed sins.[59] There is no reason to believe these people had substantive instructions from the Lord. Nonetheless, they were held responsible for their wicked thoughts and actions because they defied the common conscience of humanity.

Though humanity continues to disobey God, it has not, and cannot erase his moral nature within the human conscience. It is clear to most societies because of their view of "religious" and "spiritual" dimensions that their gods have moral expectations. David says twice, "The fool has said in his heart, 'There is no God.'"[60] So societies legitimize their moral codes by warnings about their god's or spirit's judgments.

---

58. Pss 2:2–7, 11; 110:1–2, 5–6; Dan 2:37–45; 7:13–14, 27
59. Gen 6:5, 13; Jonah 3:8–9
60. Pss 14:1; 53:1

Most cultures believe communication with their gods or spirits is essential. Prayer, sacrifice, symbols and holy objects are invented to impress the supernatural with the reverence of the individual and of society.

If it were not for the laws of conscience, Hell would be now. Life would not be merely hellish, it would be Hell. The laws of conscience have protected humanity from its mutual annihilation. In fact, God is so gracious to humanity that this life is far better than bearable for almost everyone on the planet.

Before Moses and the Mosaic law, peoples and individuals were held accountable for their moral actions. They were accountable to their imbedded moral compass for maintaining social and personal goodness and justice. Marriage, sexual purity, compassion, honesty, and loyalty are examples of what every culture knows to be basic moral standards to maintain a society's stability and individual safety. A study of the legal codes from the cultures before and during Israel's history would show innumerable moral standards that are consistent with the Mosaic laws. The wisdom literature of Egypt and Mesopotamia and far eastern philosophies show common laws of conscience throughout the cultures of Israel's neighboring empires.

Officials in every society around the world enforce the laws of conscience which have been codified into civil law. There are no societies that do not have "enforcers" of most of God's moral laws of conscience. Judicial systems are found in every society. This is not to say that the social and personal conscience has not been distorted, selectively marginalized, and highly compromised. However, enough goodness exists in enough places, in enough times, and in enough people to keep God's humanity from spinning into the total moral oblivion where Satan wishes it to go.

The sanctity of *marriage* is common in cultures and most have customs and ceremonies that affirm its sanctity. Though polygamy was a blind spot for many Old Testament men, at least polygamous relationships were sealed by a marriage arrangement. An Egyptian pharaoh shamed Abraham for his and Sarah's marital deceitfulness (Gen 12:11–19). Thick-headed Abraham repeated his same scheme with the same shame from Abimelech (Gen 20:1–16). Isaac was also rebuked by Abimelech for the same sin of deception and near infidelity (Gen 26:7–11). Even believing men can be embarrassed by the pagan's conscience.

Lot was a morally confused man, offering his daughters to an eroticized mob in exchange for the safety of his two male angelic guests (Gen 19:1–9). The story is infused with moral standards for sexual purity with clear indication of the wickedness of Sodom.[61] The moral contrast is vast between that treachery and the pristine process pursued by Abraham and his servant to match the virgin Rebekah with his son Isaac (Gen 24:13–21). Shechem's rape of Dinah is denounced as an obvious sin (Gen 34:1–2, 7, 31). Reuben is disqualified to be the favored son because of his fornication with Bilhah.[62] Deception and fornication continue in the story of Joseph and

---

61. Gen 13:13; 18:20
62. Gen 35:22; 49:4; 1 Chr 5:1

Potiphar's wife where he refuses to be seduced and lands in jail for his righteousness (Gen 39:7–20). These moral scruples all predate the Law.

Other behavior was immoral according to the conscience before the Mosaic law. Simeon and Levi's slaughtering *murder* of Shechem's family was severely criticized by their father Jacob. He cursed their violent anger and their cruelty to men and animals (Gen 49:5–7). *Stealing* was considered wrong before the Ten Commandments (Gen 26:18–22). Rebecca and Jacob *deceived* Isaac, and Laban deceived Jacob.[63] *Kindness* shown through hospitality was and still is a common Middle Eastern ethical principle (Gen 18:1–7). *Loyalty* and *truthfulness* in friendships and covenants were necessary assumptions to keep order in a contentious world.[64] One might write these off to a utilitarian ethic where there is no altruism in human nature, only self-seeking survival. Yet this is not the experience of most who find personal pleasure in doing the right thing toward others.

Three specific reasons are given most often in the Old Testament for God's discipline and judgment of the Gentiles: their arrogance,[65] brutality,[66] and idolatry.[67]

> Rise, O Lord! Do not let humanity win. Judge the nations before you.
>
> Terrify them, O Lord. Prove to them that they are only human. Ps 9:19

Our Lord indicts all who ignore him, all who contend with him or worship their own "divine" concoction. Since all peoples benefit from his gracious blessings and numerous deliverances, anything less than obedience and gratitude to him is condemned by the Lord.

Violent, torturous brutality against other peoples is the charge the Lord brings against ravaging oppressors who expand their boundaries. Nations who massacre or deport, and even those peoples who merely look on are held guilty. Murderous persecutions by the peoples against God's martyrs will be judged severely.[68]

Conscience in the New Testament

The New Testament agrees with the Old Testament that the conscience of unbelievers will lead to commendable moral behavior to some extent, but Christ's commands raised the ethical bar far beyond that. His point was that the laws of conscience are effective but they are only a start toward righteousness.

---

63. Gen 27:15–29; 29:21–25
64. Gen 14:13; 21:22–32; 26:27–31
65. Isa 10:12–15; 14:13–15; 16:6; 23:8–9; Jer 48:26, 29–30, 42; 49:16; 50:29–32; Obad 3–4
66. Isa 13:11; Amos 1:6–12
67. Jer 10:3–5; 50:2, 38; 51:17–18, 47, 52; Hab 2:18–19
68. Rev 6:9–11; 18:20–24

> What reward is there if you love only those who love you? Even tax collectors do that. How are you any different if you welcome only your friends? Even pagans do that. Matt 5:46–47

> Why should you get credit if you love only those who love you? Even sinners love those who love them. Why should you get credit if you are good only to those who are good to you? Even sinners do that. Luke 6:32–33

Laws of conscience motivate our righteousness as we pursue it through the power of the Spirit. It is when we act morally by the Spirit, out of love for God and trust in his love that our mere morality becomes true righteousness.

Paul also emphasizes the law of conscience and its serious implications for all humanity.

> Even Gentiles who have not had God's written Law prove that they know what his Law is when they obey it instinctively... They show that God's Law is written in their hearts when their conscience and thoughts accuse them of doing wrong or confirm them doing right. Rom 2:14–15

Paul was educated in the secular philosophies and literature of his age. He knew that moral truth is known and practiced by unbelievers. He quoted a pagan intellectual, Menander, on the danger of associating with immoral people: "Bad company corrupts good character" (1 Cor 15:33).

Paul's instruction to comply with Roman laws was based on the goodness and justice which those laws contained. Were they perfect like the Old Testament laws, wisdom instructions, and the moral commandments of Christ and his apostles? No. Were they still helpful? Yes.

> Do what is good, and you will receive a ruler's approval since he is God's servant for your good... an agent of God's wrath on law breakers. Rom 13:3–7

During the reign of the Caesars at that time, this was a hard message to deliver and hear. Of all governments, theirs have been some of the worst, including the assassination of God's own believing children. Nonetheless, laws of conscience are so effective that it restrains even these governments.

Humanity has been remarkably thorough in writing and enforcing laws that reflect the Creator's character and his design for human order. These laws are often compromised by authorities with oppressive motives. Offenders of laws are often brutalized with disproportionate sentences and punishments. Nonetheless, a concept of justice and fairness has permeated most societies because the human conscience reflects God's moral nature which all humans bear (Rom 2:14–16).

Job and David say that the Lord's glorious character is shown in creation. The following passages make it clear that not only is God's character revealed through creation, but that all peoples see his righteous attributes and works, understand them to be good, and even respond to what they have seen. Unfortunately, all peoples do not respond with saving faith, but the peoples react to the obvious message from creation about its Creator.

> God is exalted in his power . . . Everyone should exalt his works, for which men have sung in praise. *All humanity has seen it*, even if from afar. Job 36:22, 24–25

> You formed the mountains by your power;
> you stilled the roaring seas and waves, and stilled the turmoil of the nations.
> The heavens tell of God's glory and the skies declare it through his hands' work.
> Their message goes out to all the earth and their words to the world's end. Ps 19:1, 4

> *Those who live at the ends of the earth stand in awe of your signs.* Ps 65:6–8

> The heavens declare his righteousness and *all the peoples see his glory*. Ps 97:6

The Old Testament does not say that all who see the Lord's attributes in creation conclude that it is *Israel's* God who should be revered. For this, God's more detailed revelation of himself was needed through the Bible. But according to Paul, there is enough known about God without the Bible's witness to leave no one with an excuse for their sin.

Paul narrates in Romans 1 and 2 the moral decline of the human race in general and how that decline repeats itself in any degenerating culture. His description of humanity's regression of moral decline concludes by our race lowering itself to degrading idolatry and sensuality. This has included humans worshipping animals, and our fleshly lusts disgracing our souls. We will follow his reasoning in the next few paragraphs as he reconstructs this discouraging devolution of human dignity.

Humanity can see that God exists, but much more than that, all peoples can see his admirable, powerful and glorious qualities.

> Ever since the world was created, his invisible attributes, his eternal power and divine nature have been seen clearly and understood through what has been made, so that they are without any excuse. Rom 1:20

But every people suppresses truths about God's power and character. They speculate and devise their own various, foolish views of what human priorities, worship, wisdom, and morality should be. "Claiming to be wise, they became fools" (Rom 1:22). They have not honored God but preferred to trade his truth for their false and deceptive views (1:21, 25).

Yet humanity's response gets even worse! Our response has not been just an intellectual denial of God's existence or wonderful nature. We perpetually insult the Lord by not acknowledging his shepherding power and his moral guidance and not being thankful for his blessings and deliverances. So humanity has found other things to acknowledge, honor, and worship instead—ourselves, idols, and animals (1:21–23). Paul uses the primary commission's phrasing to describe what humanity prefers to worship as their authorities rather than the Creator.

> Birds and animals and crawling creatures. Rom 1:23
>
> Birds in the sky and over everything living and moving on the earth. Gen 1:28

Humanity has humiliated itself by subjecting itself to the very things we were created to subjugate. This includes the once creeping, crawling serpents (Gen 3:14). Not only has humanity worshipped these creations through idolatrous ceremonies, but they "*serve*" them as only the Creator should be served (Rom 1:25).

The hearts of these people are doubly darkened, by God and by themselves while "turning to their own speculations." The Lord "gave them over to . . ." the impure desires of their hearts (1:24), shameful passions (26), and a depraved mind (28). In other words, their foolish heart was darkened, and they became fools (22). As fools, they multiplied themselves by teaching others to be fools also (32).

For these reasons, Paul says that not only humanity as a whole, but individuals as well, are without excuse for not honoring God as the divine, sovereign king to whom all are accountable for their moral actions: "People have no excuse" (1:22) and "You are without excuse, anyone who judges another" (2:1). God's wrath is certainly justified since the standards of judgment, the existence of a judge, and the sins of humanity should be obvious to everyone (1:18–19). However, the blinding darkness has overwhelmed the world, having its way with a wooed and willing lover.

One way God disciplines humanity is by allowing it to wear its disgrace in public view. It does not matter whether those who should feel disgraced and humiliated actually feel degraded or not. If they do not, they not only are self-disgracing in their conduct, but they are even more foolish for not recognizing it. God's judgment is not deferred to the Day of Judgment since the peoples judge themselves to be moral fools now. If we are frustrated that God's judgment has apparently not come and is taking too long, we fail to see his judgment is in process already. So how is it that humanity and individuals dishonor themselves? By greed,, malice, envy, murder, strife, deceit, malice, gossip, slander, hatred of God, insolence, arrogance, disobedience to parents, untrustworthy, heartless, unmerciful, and nodding approval of others who commit the same sins (1:29–32). The one public disgrace which Paul dwells on in this passage that humiliates humanity is homosexuality (26–27).

Fallen human nature propels the human moral condition even deeper downward. Fortunately, the conscience convicts individuals and societies to an extent that prevents their perversity from reaching utter moral anarchy. At least there is some general, sustainable, and effective ethical equilibrium around the globe because the human conscience checks human depravity. That is, God allows no culture to plummet to complete moral chaos. That is his shepherd's heart for all humanity! That is his daily defeat of Satan.

Judgments on the Peoples

Some consider themselves wise to say in troubling times, "No one said this world was fair." But God's administration of his world is always fair in his perfect ways. He oversees the tragedies and afflictions that humanity suffers due to the Couple's sin and our own sins. I offer some cryptic comments here.

> Any good we experience is not "fair" since we do not deserve anything good.
>
> Experiencing God's grace is not fair because we only deserve condemnation.
>
> So, if God were "fair," nothing good would happen to us at all.
>
> So fortunately, God is not "fair"; if he were "fair" we would not experience any goodness.
>
> One is correct in saying that the world is not "fair" if one means there is too much *good* in the world.
>
> By admitting that this world is far *better* than "fair," we show we truly appreciate God's grace.

If this is what is meant when one says, "No one said this world was fair," then one is wise to say it. God's pervasive grace proves that this world is not fair; it is far better and more gracious than fair. "Anything good and every perfect gift is from above, coming down from the Father" (Jas 1:17).

Some also consider themselves wise to propose this argument against God's existence: "There is too much evil in the world. How could a good God exist who allows so much evil?" It is as shallow a question as fools believe it to be profound. A far better question is not how a good God could exist, but why does the questioner still exist? The foolish argument that a good person's existence depends on one's tolerance of great evil, is self-condemning. If one who tolerates evil should not exist, then of all who should not exist would be everyone but God. Such questioners not only tolerate great sin, they contribute greatly themselves to the sins of the world, something God does not do. The philosophers who feel they have a case against God have only made a case against their own right to existence. They should have been destroyed by God's perfect justice long ago. But even the Lord's accusers experience his grace for the time being.

Regardless of the community, discipline will come to the wicked.[69] The Psalms pray for judgment on the wicked; the psalmists cry out for freedom from any type of oppressor. The wicked hope foolishly that a powerful God does not exist, or if he does, that his goodness requires him to forgive everyone. But the Lord is not only good because he is gracious to the undeserving; he is also good because he punishes the deserving.

I am not minimizing the excruciating pains and tragedies that certain people and societies suffer at the hands of wicked people. After all, our brothers and sisters in Christ Jesus, even now, this decade, this year, this month, this day, this hour, this

---

69. 1 Sam 2:9–10; Job 27:7–23; 34:23–28; 36:6, 11–14; Pss 1:5–6; 3:7; 28:3–5; 31:17; 34:16; 36:12; 37:9–10, 13–15, 20–22; 73:18–20, 27; 104:35; 112:10; 119:118–119; 125:5; 128:4–7; 139:19–22; 140:9–11; Prov 3:33–34

moment, have been subject to unprecedented oppression including rapes, dismemberments, torture, hunger, imprisonments, literal crucifixions and other forms of heinous executions. As God's people, Christians are currently one of the most oppressed peoples. Do they question whether their God exists? No. Rather, they are looking forward to meeting him as his most courageous and faithful souls. God's people who trust him thoroughly are not the ones who conclude he could not exist. They are convinced that he does exist even though their greatest hopes are not fulfilled at the moment.

> Some were tortured . . . Others were mocked and whipped, chained and imprisoned. They were stoned, sawed in two, killed with the sword. They wore only sheepskins and goatskins, and were destitute, oppressed, and mistreated . . . They were all praised for their faith, even though they had not yet received what they had been promised. Heb 11:35–37, 39

The peoples of the world are disciplined in various ways for their disrespect of the Lord. They are punished by annoying plagues, by brutal subjection to other peoples, and even by extinction. Those who stand against the Lord will experience his discipline wherever they are:

> Those who fight against Yahweh will be shattered, from heaven he thunders against them. The Lord judges the whole earth. 1 Sam 2:1

God disciplines the peoples through his pervasive curses given ever since the Eden debacle. For instance, those who might have threatened Cain were warned they would be avenged by God himself (Gen 4:15). The rebellious, disobedient congregation in Shinar was judged for refusing to fill the earth (Gen 11:5–9), and the multiplication of their languages has been a serious communication impediment for humanity ever since. The Lord continues his judgments against intolerable nations which compromise his global moral balance, judging in ways largely unperceptible to us.

The Tree of Knowledge was the ominous test of the first two realms of human shepherding—one's self and one's marriage. It was the test of whether Adam and Eve would align with God and his sovereignty or insist on their own freedom and sovereignty. Their sin defied the primary commission since they did not subdue their surroundings. Instead vegetation (fruit) and an animal (snake) subdued them. Appropriately, God's judgments against the Couple, nature, spirits, and the rest of humanity were patterned after the primary commission itself: multiplying, filling the earth, and ruling. All of creation was targeted by God in his judgments, and the spirits, nature, and humanity have been pitted against each other ever since (Gen 3:14–19).

First, the serpent was cursed to the humiliating level of slithering in the dust, even in New Earth (Isa 65:25). Snakes are the quickest to infiltrate and thrive in a cursed desolate land, and they have always been one of the most repulsive and dangerous creatures for humanity (Eccl 10:8). There would be a battle between the serpent's seed, and the seed of Eve (humanity). The snake's threat to humanity comes from the nearly imperceptible point of attack from below. Its slow but deliberate approach, and its lethal bite, are an image of many deadly temptations. The snake's damaging access point is the heel since it slinks nearly always at foot level. But it is exactly at that location where the snake is most vulnerable to the heel of humanity which will crush its head easily. We are encouraged that the Serpent will be crushed under our feet (Rom 16:20).

Eve and all women are sentenced to reproductive curses for her part in the Eden rebellion. Pain would begin at puberty and continue through multiple child deliveries (Gen 3:16). Additionally, women would experience the same curses given to men. Though her attraction to her husband leads to conception and the eventual agonizing pain of childbirth, she will tolerate his authority even though that authority would be abused during this parenthetical age. Impediments to multiplication for Israel included outright barrenness, spontaneous abortion, and reductions in populations due to God's judgments on humanity for its disobedience.

The earth is also cursed, and its efficiency has been reduced, making it less productive than it was before the Fall and less productive than it will be in New Earth. In God's global discipline, nature has stopped multiplying generously, providing less for itself and humanity.[70] The land is broken and disfigured by earthquakes and other natural disasters.[71] It is deserted by its fleeing, evacuated, or destroyed residents. It is desolated by meteorological disasters like drought, mildew, hail, and wind.[72] In too many cases the land is laid waste and made most suitable for only the wild inhabitants of creation.[73] Thorns and weeds prevail and destructive flora and fauna invade productive plots and areas of the world.[74]

Several other unidentified but ruinous natural disasters are sent by the Lord for judgments against the foolish and disobedient;[75] for example, fire at Sodom and Gomorrah[76] and plagues like those in Egypt. The waters were created to shepherd the land, plants, animals, and human life, but they are also used by God to discipline humanity through floods or drought. God will even send bears, lions, birds or huge fish to devour the disobedient, dead or alive.[77] Infestations of insects seem to be some of

---

70. Lev 26:19–26; Deut 32:24; 2 Sam 21:1; 1 Kgs 8:35–40; 16:30—17:1; Isa 5:7–10; 7:19–25; 14:23; 32:10–13; 34:11–15; Jer 3:2–3, 9; 4:23–26; 14:18; Ezek 5:12, 16–17; Hos 2:8–9; Hag 1:6–11; Zech 14:18

71. Num 16:31–32; Hab 3:6, 10

72. Ex 10:19; 14:21; Num 11:31–33; Deut 28:22, 39; 1 Kgs 18:45; Job 38:22–24; Ps 46:8; Isa 19:5–10; 24:5–6; Jer 12:4, 10–11; Ezek 13:10–13; 29:12; Amos 4:9; Jonah 1:4, 15–16; 4:7–8; Nah 1:3–6; Hab 3:5

73. Isa 13:20–22; 14:23; 34:11

74. Hos 9:6; 10:8; Zeph 2:14–15

75. Gen 12:17; Num 11:33; 14:36–37; 16:46–49; 25:8–9; Ezek 5:16–17; Amos 4:10; Hab 3:5

76. Gen 19:24–28; 2 Pet 2:6

77. Lev 26:21–22; Deut 28:26; 32:24; 1 Kgs 13:24–26; 14:10–11; 16:1–4; 20:35–36; 2 Kgs 2:23–24; 17:24–25; Jer 12:9; 15:3; 34:20; Ezek 5:17; 39:4, 17–20; Jonah 1:17; 2:10

the Lord's favorite creatures for bringing justice to humanity: gnats, locusts, crickets, flies, bees, and larvae.[78]

God's curse of the land makes it rebuff human effort to cultivate it and make it more productive. While humanity serves and cultivates the land, the land fights back with stubborn and ruthless resistance to becoming any more fruitful. Men and women who manage this earth should be blessed by the pleasure of labor, but working with the earth became more strenuous and less successful. Creation's resistance to human management can be frustrating in many ways because the earth's thorny weeds puncture the flesh and choke the crops. Rather than simply pruning fruit trees, we now must cope with blight, pests, and various other curses.

A typical way for God to discipline a people is to transfer its sovereignty to another nation; all nations and empires have come and gone, or ultimately will. The Lord does not necessarily transfer power to more morally worthy nations; it is simply that in his sovereign discernment and appropriate timing that they become his instrument for discipline.[79] All of Israel's neighbors and oppressors were scheduled for devastation within Israel's history: Egypt, Edom, Moab, Ammon, Syria, Phoenicia, Assyria, and Babylon.[80] God's judgment of Egypt came by Babylon, and in turn, Babylon's judgment came by Persia.[81]

God does not simply discipline the peoples; sometimes he inverts their pride to humiliation. For instance, the book of Judges recounts the eventual humiliation of many of Israel's oppressors. Eglon's obesity is ridiculed in his assassination by Ehud; Shamgar killed six hundred Philistines with a simple farm tool; Sisera's death by a woman was his embarrassing dishonor; Gideon's mere three hundred men defeat the entire Midianite army; an unknown woman mortally wounds Abimelech with a piece of machinery; Samson killed one thousand Philistines with an animal bone and later, while blind, he killed three thousand more.[82] The arrogance of a people was the reason for the Lord's humiliation of them, including Tyre, Assyria, Babylon, Moab, and Egypt.[83]

The Lord used Israel frequently as an instrument of his justice against her enemies to keep his promise that those who bless her will be blessed and those who curse her will be cursed.[84] Israel was a showcase to the peoples of how the sovereign Shepherd loves, blesses, protects, even disciplines his believing community. But she was also an effective, often violent weapon of God's judgment on those same observing peoples.

---

78. Ex 8:17; Ex 10:4; Deut 28:38–42; Joel 1:4, 10–12; Amos 4:9; 7:1; Isa 7:17–19

79. Isa 19:4; 44:28—45:3; Jer 46:13, 25–26; 50:2, 9–10; Ezek 25:4–10; 29:19–20

80. Isa 14:23; 15:1, 6; 16:8–9, 14; 17:1–3; 19:5–10; 23:1, 13; Jer 48:1–4, 8; 49:17–18; 50:2–3, 9–13; 51:1–2; Ezek 25:4–7, 13–14; 26:3–4, 21; 29:8–12; 30:7, 11–14; 31:10–14; Zeph 2:4–13; Mal 1:2–5; 9:6

81. Ezek 30:10–11; Isa 13:17–19; 47:5–7

82. Judg 3:17, 21–22, 31; 4:9; 5:27; 7:7; 9:53–54; 15:15–16; 16:27–30

83. Isa 14:8; 23:8–9; Jer 46:24; 48:26–30; 50:11–12; Ezek 29:4–5, 14–15; 31:18; Nah 3:5–7

84. Gen 12:3; Num 23:23–24; 1 Sam 15:2; Ps 149:5–9; Jer 51:19–23; Ezek 25:13–14

This alliance of God and his believers is another way by which human shepherding and the Lord's ultimate sovereignty work together in God's eternal design.

Ever since the Couple's exile from the Garden, God uses expulsion or scattering the peoples as a judgment: "Rise, oh Lord, and scatter your enemies" (Num 10:35). So, the result of the sin at Babel in Shinar was the scattering of the peoples (Gen 11:7–9). The Israelites were supposed to expel the Canaanites from the Promised Land along with their ethically repulsive cultures.[85] Peoples were forced to leave their lands as fleeing fugitives[86] or as captives who were force-marched into exile. God's discipline-by-exile was applied to Moab, Ammon, Hazor, Elam, Syria, and even Egypt.[87] The Lord's military judgments inevitably ended in death for some or most of a nation's inhabitants by the swords, spears, and arrows of invaders.[88] If all inhabitants had not fled, entire populations were wiped out.[89]

God's death sentence which was first pronounced in Eden has been executed by many diverse methods. The Couple were banished and separated from the Tree of Eternal Life—so we all die. The brevity of life is the Lord's judgment on all humanity.[90] God might accelerate death's arrival for the wicked, short of a "natural death." Life ended catastrophically for humanity in the Flood, and Haman's wicked life ended by hanging (Esth 7:9–10). "This is the path of the foolish . . . ; as sheep they are laid in the grave; death will be their shepherd" (Ps 49:13–14). Some justice systems apply capital punishment for various crimes. Governments assist the Lord in maintaining order through discipline and judgments against their lawless citizens.[91] Finally, one can invite the curse of death upon oneself by personal carelessness of many sorts or by abusing one's body by unhealthy living.[92]

Perhaps one thinks that only the Trinity would be responsible for judgment and deliverance. One would be partially correct in ascribing that honor to God but incorrect in not accepting that honor for oneself too. Rather than being petrified at the prospect of going alone against this filthy opponent's power, we are assured by the Old Testament that a Human Being, who is God, would lead us in that battle. For God to keep his promise that humanity would succeed in this global war, he needed first to come himself in human form to bind Satan,[93] and then to return again to conclude the crushing of Satan. The Messiah will then present God's creation to the Father "when he delivers the Kingdom to the God and Father, having abolished all rule, author-

---

85. Lev 18:24–28; Josh 24:18
86. Isa 15:5; 16:2–4; Jer 48:6, 9; 49:5
87. Jer 46:19; 48:7; 49:3–5, 32, 36; Amos 1:5, 15; Ezek 29:12–13; 30:23, 26
88. Amos 2:2–3; Isa 15:9; 19:2; Jer 49:26; 51:3–4; Ezek 26:6–8; 30:4–5
89. Judg 5:31; Isa 13:15–18; 14:21–22, 30; Jer 47:4; Ezek 25:16–17; Amos 1:8;
90. Gen 6:3; Ps 90:3–12
91. Rom 13:1–7; 1 Pet 2:13–14
92. Eccl 7:17; 10:8–11
93. Matt 12:29 // Mark 3:27

ity and power" (1 Cor 15:24). He will have raised and lowered kingdoms, including Satan's. The sequence of kingdoms in all eras and areas will come to an abrupt end in the eternal, universal kingdom of the Messiah in New Earth.[94]

Christ said that he would return as the Judge and "shepherd" the nations, dealing out grace and judgment. He explained his authority to decide the eternal destination of people in terms of his shepherding role.

> All nations will be gathered before him [Christ]; and as the shepherd separates the sheep from the goats, he will separate them; and he will put the sheep on his right, and the goats on the left . . . then he will say to those on his left, "You who are cursed, leave me, go into the eternal fire!" . . . They will go into eternal punishment, but the righteous into eternal life. Matt 25:32–33, 41, 46

The book of Revelation tells us in more violent terms what Christ's role as judge will be.

> From his mouth came a sharp sword to strike down the nations. He will shepherd them with an iron rod. Rev 19:15

The Old Testament had already prophesied that the final judgment of the nations will come under the perfect but fierce military adjudication by the Messiah himself.[95] Christ is the shepherd of severe sentences on the nations and each citizen regardless of social, political, or economic level.

> The kings of the earth, rulers, generals, the rich and powerful, every slave and free person hid themselves . . . and called to the mountains and rocks, "Fall on us and hide us from the face of him sitting on the throne, and from the wrath of the Lamb, for the great day of their wrath has come, and who will survive it?"[96]

Jesus said he was not sent to judge the world but to save it, but that was true of only his "first coming."[97] When he returns he will save or judge every nation and person. He will judge those who do not obey the gospel of God and destroy those who have contributed to the destruction of the Creator's earth.[98] Jesus will lead God's army against the dark kingdom; he will strike the nations and shepherd them with an iron rod.[99]

And again, those who are foolish enough to abuse God's children will find God as their enemy. Like David's call for God's justice against his enemies, the New Testament's assures believers that will be avenged eventually.[100]

---

94. Pss 2:2–7, 11; 110:1–2, 5–6; Dan 2:37–45; 7:13–14, 27; 8:4–26; 9:25–27
95. Pss 2:2, 6–9, 12; 110:1–6
96. Rev 6:15–17; also, 14:14–16
97. John 3:17; 12:47
98. 1 Pet 4:17–18; Rev 11:18
99. Rev 19:11–21; 20:7–10
100. Luke 18:6–8; Phil 1:28; 2 Thess 1:6; 1 Pet 4:4–5

Nature will have its role to play in this final day too. Earthquake, famine, pestilence, fire, death, and wild beasts are said to be involved in the judgment on the nations[101] just as the Lord previously used nature for discipline in the Old Testament.

HUMANITY SHEPHERDS HUMANITY

The eternal design is not that only the Lord shepherds. It is "God shepherds *shepherding* creation." Creation shepherds, and humanity shepherds as parts of that creation, and God increased his circle of fellow-shepherds progressively through space and time. The most general new phases would be . . .

>Adam and Eve
>>=> Noah's descendants
>>>=> Israel as a nation
>>>>=> Church as a global kingdom
>>>>>=> All peoples perfected in New Earth

God's kingdom *regions* have also expanded from Eden to Babel to Canaan to the globe's western hemisphere, then to its eastern hemisphere, and finally to the all-encompassing New Earth. And the corresponding *eras* of this expansion have also grown through the never-ending growth of the Messiah's kingdom.

God exercised his right to separate and then name the parts of his creation. He named what only he can administrate, namely the "day, night, sky, seas" (Gen. 1:5–10). Then he shared authority with humanity over parts of creation and left Adam to separate and name the animals he ruled (Gen 2:19–23). Authority over people follows the same pattern of naming creation. Adam named "Eve"; Cain named his city "Enoch"; Eve named "Seth"; Seth in turn named "Enosh"; and Lamech named "Noah."[102] Naming something implies sovereignty over it.

Human control of the earth could only happen when it had filled the earth and developed the earth's many elements to form numerous cultures.[103] The Couple developed into numerous families, and then into entire peoples. Cities were built and rural herds were domesticated. Art and artisanship, mining and manufacturing, and human justice are examples of societies developing diverse civilizations and cultures. Human shepherding of their environment makes people and nature more productive. For example, inventing hand tools and the wheel, controlling fire, devising elaborate irrigation, forging metals and harnessing electricity, all bring health and comfort. Progress in legal systems protects individual property rights and protects the nature in and around that property.

---

101. Joel 2:30–31; Amos 1:4, 14; 7:4; 2 Pet 2:52 Pet 3:7, 10–12; Rev 6:1–8 // Jer 15:2–4; 24:10; 29:17–20; Rev 6:12—7:3; 8:7—9:19; 11:13, 19; 16:2–14, 18–21; 19:17–18

102. Gen 2:23; 4:17, 25; 5:3, 26, 29

103. Gen 2:11–12; 4:17–24

However, as commissioned shepherds, humanity has largely failed to edify the earth and its contents. Adam and Eve failed; Cain failed; we all have failed to follow the primary commission because we have failed at the start to subdue the temptation that pursues us and pounces on us when we open the door merely a crack. Temptation leads to an unconditional surrender, and nothing positive is received in return. Forcing our personal wishes on the world has led only to global, moral disorder. Though the peoples have created what appear to be orderly societies, each has its measure of injustice and oppression. The Lord's growing kingdom has meant a declining yet still highly destructive realm for Satan. Sadly, humanity has aligned itself with the Enemy not only in Eden but in every garden, desert, valley, mountain, village, and city in every era since then. Our authority granted by the primary commission has been exercised tragically and routinely to deface and dismember creation.

But fortunately, human rebellion is only momentary in God's eternal design. New Earth will realign humanity with the Lord who will bless us to continue reigning with him forever. In the meantime, God expects his people to counteract destruction and disorder as we subdue our surroundings by the Savior's example and the Spirit's strength. Yes, even believers can make things worse in this parenthetical age, but when we take the eternal design and primary commission seriously, we will restore our personal surroundings.

HUMAN REALMS WITHIN WHICH WE SHEPHERD

Humanity instinctively seeks community because we are made in the image of a divine Community of Persons. In the first chapter we introduced the six basic shepherding realms: Trinity, Spirits, Nature and the three human realms (humanity, the Lord's people, and the believer). Now we add marriage, family, the community, and any specific people group to those basic realms. These human realms range from one person to the total population of the earth, and each realm contains shepherding responsibilities.

These realms form concentric spheres where each human realm is surrounded by the next largest realm. However, these concentric realms are not so neatly unrelated as if they never intersect. Rather, each overlaps and combines with the others in nearly every possible combination. We start with ourselves as the smallest realm and move ever-outwards to our largest human context—the whole human race.

SHEPHERDS: THE BELIEVER'S OUTLINE OF THEOLOGY

Human Realms Within Which We Shepherd

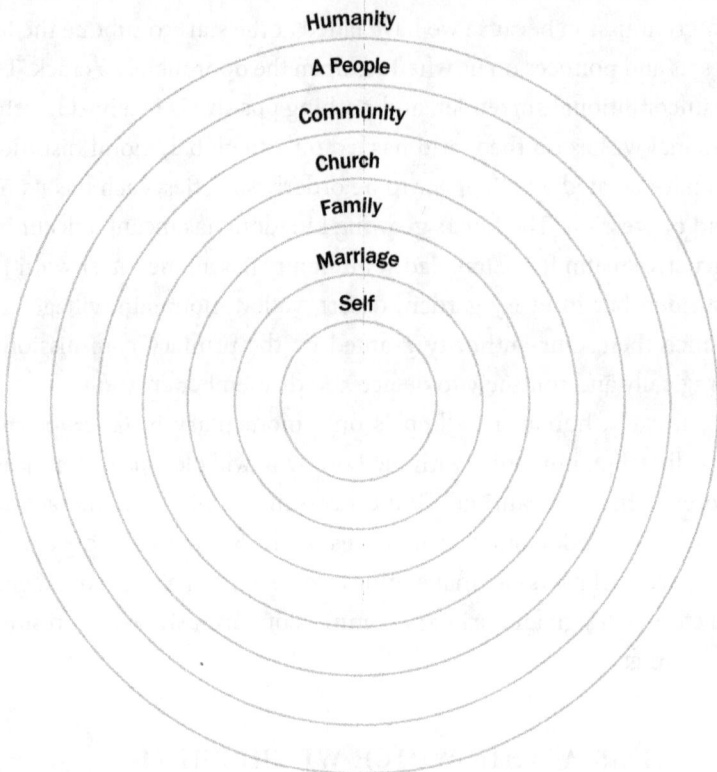

Each realm shepherds the others according to God's eternal design, weaving an intricate fabric of blessing, deliverance and discipline between them. Blessing, deliverance, and discipline form the routine web of interactions between the realms. Too often, however, these realms act as anti-shepherds, aligning with Satan to contradict the eternal design by neglect, abuse, and injustice. So the ideal lanes of shepherding as we saw in chapter 1 would only be the righteous ways to shepherd. But, as we know, anti-shepherding is too frequent in this parenthetical age.

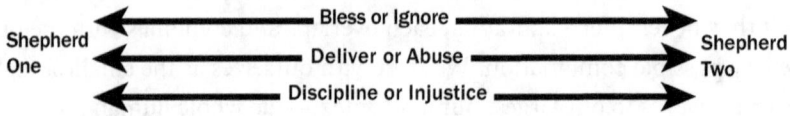

The next graph shows the shepherding relationships between all these human realms. Like the graph in chapter 1, the single lines in the graph between the realms each consists of at least one or two strands of the shepherding tasks of blessing, deliverance, and discipline, if not all three. For example, a married individual shepherds the family by blessing, deliverance, and discipline. But within the family each member shepherds the others by delivering from adversity and by godly discipline. Instruction can come even from the mouth of babes who convict their parents of insensitivity and carelessness.

The Human Realms Bless, Deliver, and Discipline One Another

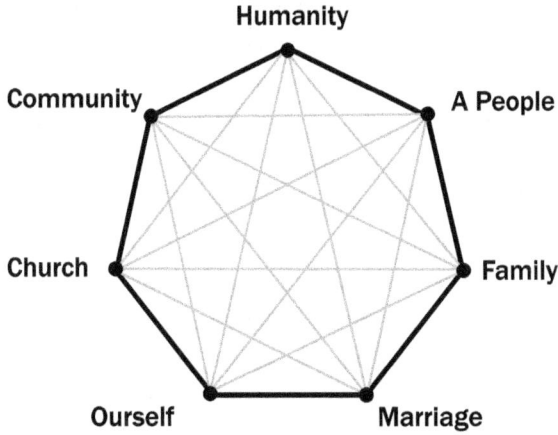

God's indwelling Spirit gives us the desire and strength to subdue *ourselves* and live obediently to the Lord's ethical standards. This allows us then to begin shepherding the other realms in godly ways—as God would: the realms of marriage, family, church, community, a people, and total humanity. The eternal design is the only ultimate guide for how all of our plans and actions contribute to God's kingdom. Rather than simple fragments of righteousness here and there, we understand that our righteousness toward any of the other realms results in godly shepherding of those realms.

The next most intimate shepherding relationship is within *marriage*. In love, the couple bless each other, they protect each other, and they confidently discipline each other by confronting the weaknesses and offenses of the other. Sexual relations are not always spousal, unfortunately. When they are outside marriage (in any way), they present enormous trials for those directly involved and for those family and friends who trusted the immoral person's commitment to sexual purity and faithfulness. This does not only pertain to physical acts of unmanaged sexual drive in fornication and adultery but to unconquered lustful thoughts (Job 31:1, 9–10) and the devastating and disabling power of pornography.

The primary commission presumes that the majority of adults will multiply themselves through children. The *family* presents many high and low points even for those who live together under God's laws and wisdom. Relationships within the family and relationships with other families compose dramatic storylines in the Bible where blessing, deliverance or judgment or their opposites are shown. These stories range from exhilarating to agonizing.

The *local believing community* is the next largest realm to shepherd the individuals and families who comprise it and to be shepherded by those same individuals and families. The Lord's believing community shepherds its broader community, the nation, and the world by living according to his instructions as a witness to his greatness. The Old Testament community that trusted the Lord and followed his ethical standards blessed its residents. Boaz delivered Ruth and Naomi from poverty; he used the judicial system to sort out his rights; Naomi shepherded Ruth with compassion and wisdom. The local church does the same in the New Testament and today. It cares for its sheep internally and is good to all humanity externally: "Do good to everyone, especially those belonging to the family of believers" (Gal 6:10).

The larger *civil community* is the context for the various religious, social, economic, and judicial activities in a society. In the Old Testament, the city walls were, for the most part, a fortress where the families of farmers and shepherds went for protection but also to carry on their legal and economic business.

Several families and their communities made up each of the twelve tribes of the *people* of God. However the *nation* of Israel, and for a brief time the *empire* of Israel, included other peoples within its borders too. Israel was an example of how a "nation" is different from a "people." By "nation" we mean the political and diplomatic borders of some governing body. "Peoples" can be any number of ethnic and cultural groups that are within a nation or that straddle a nation's border.

Believers and Humanity

Neither Testament tells us about every specific people in the vast stretch of the globe's seven continents. We hear only about the three continents which intersect at Israel: the corners of western Asia, northeastern Africa, and southeastern Europe. However, we are encouraged generally with biblical promises of all peoples from the ends of the earth worshipping the Lord. His believing individuals and his "people" are part of each of the remaining concentric realms.

The global church is a people whose residence and borders are not measured by acreage, counties, districts, or provinces. Members of the church reside in many of these locales across the planet, but they are not the only residents. Christians, the "royal priesthood" of believers, are like the Old Testament tribe of Levi who lived within every tribe as a minority population and served that locale as God's commissioned priests and religious workers. Christians also live as a minority population and serve their locale as God's commissioned "priests" and religious workers. We are the multiplied disciples in all the nations who obey what Jesus had commanded the disciples. The Great Commission is not centered on simply "converting" the peoples to Jesus; it is about nations having an internal Christian people publicly *obeying* Jesus with converted behavior—"teaching them to obey all that I commanded you" (Matt 28:20). The gospel of God's eternal kingdom is that all the peoples and nations, though currently and perpetually divided by geography, worldview and rancor, will be wonderfully united under the Messiah. The whole world is the endgame.

God holds all peoples and their leaders accountable for how well they shepherd their lands, whether they are believers or not. Jeremiah refers to all kings as the shepherds of their nation, and since their responsibilities are great, their accountability is great. They can lead their people along the lines of their Creator's character or lead drastically in the other direction. National, provincial, and local leaders are all judged as shepherds who are entrusted to effectively and compassionately pasture their people. But, as expected and shown throughout human history, too many national leaders are all the way from lazy to abusive.

> A commotion is heard to the ends of the earth, for the Lord has an indictment against the nations . . . Weep and moan, you evil *shepherds*! Roll in the ashes, leaders of the *flock*! Your time to be slaughtered has come. Jer 25:31, 34[104]

Nonetheless, governments are essential in God's eternal design since, even in this parenthetical era of sin and oppression, God's grace instills order and protection through the laws and morals of every culture. To a greater or lesser extent, governments generally follow the normal conscience. So, any government is better than none since government brings orderly management rather than anarchy and chaos. Yes, there have been and still are horrendous governments and shepherds as the Testaments acknowledge. Yet, even in the worst of oppressive governments, the Israelites are instructed to contribute to the national well-being of the countries where they lived as exiles. To do this, they were to pursue the primary commission as if they were in their own land. They were to multiply, and while filling the areas where they were sent, they were to manage their lives.

> Build houses to live in and plant gardens to eat from . . . Marry and become fathers of sons and daughters . . . Multiply there and not decrease. Seek the well-being of the city where I have sent you into exile, and pray to the Lord for it, since its well-being means your well-being. Jer 29:5-7

Christ and Paul affirm this same attitude toward governing authorities. Under one of the most decadent and oppressive regimes in human history, Paul writes in the strongest terms:

> Everyone must submit to the governing authorities because all authority comes from God since those in authority have been put there by God. So anyone rebelling against authority condemn themselves for rebelling against what God has ordained. Rom 13:1-2

Paul echoes the words of Christ:

> Christ says: "Give back to Caesar what is Caesar's, and to God what is God's."[105]

> Paul writes: Authorities are servants of God . . . Pay taxes to whom taxes are owed. Rom 13:6-7

---

104. Isa 13:11; 14:4-6, 9-11; Jer 50:17-19; Amos 1:6-12; Nah 3:18
105. Matt 22:21 // Mark 12:17 // Luke 20:25; also, Matt 17:25-27

Even more than simply to submit to the authorities, we are to pray for them as Jeremiah 29:7 says. Jeremiah instructed the exiled Israelites, "pray to the Lord for the city": And Paul echoes the same:

> [Pray] for kings and all who are in authority so that we can live peaceful and quiet lives marked by godliness and dignity. 1 Tim 2:2

Our prayers synergize with God's plans which, in his grace and timing, will ensure peace, security, and dignity in our lands. No one denies that this grace is not seen in all eras and areas because God's perfect and unquestionable wisdom allows for turmoil and torturous treatment of Christians. There has never been a worse time of persecution than our present day for Christians around the world. Still, the synergy between God and even the worst of governments shows the Lord's persistent pursuit of his eternal design despite the wickedness of the ungodly shepherds that he oversees with absolute sovereignty. He oversees Satan; he will certainly oversee dictators.

"Subdue" is an assertive term for "shepherd" and leads to the civilization of the earth and its societies. In New Earth, assertive shepherding will not involve brutal tribal, national, or international battles or wars; there will be no need nor inclination for them. Nonetheless, wars are necessary now in the parenthetical design.[106] Wars against God and his people are instigated by the Enemy. But wars are also used by God for deliverance and judgment. There is a time for war, but thankfully, a time for peace as well.

We offer one final version of an eternal design graph. Even this graph is by no means the extent of the mesh of shepherding relationships between God and creation. There are tens of thousands of individual spirits, and 7.5 billion people currently on our globe, and each have specific shepherding (or anti-shepherding) relationships with innumerable components of creation. So the following graph is still very simple compared with the incomprehensible complexity of God's eternal design. The graph has twelve points and nearly all of them are two-way streets of blessing, deliverance, and discipline. In other words, most points on the graph are both sources of shepherding and the objects of shepherding.

---

106. Judg 3:30; 8:28; 11:33; 1 Sam 7:13; 2 Sam. 8:1; 1 Chr 18:1; 20:4; 2 Chr 13:18

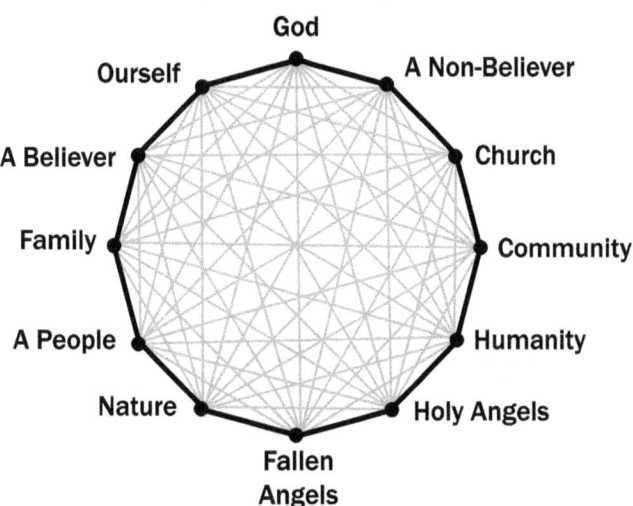

Again, like the graph in chapter 1, the single lines between the realms each consist of two to six strands of shepherding tasks of blessing, deliverance and discipline. Also, again, this graph assumes that the opposite and evil shepherding relationships that are so pervasive in these realms can be the connection rather than a connection of righteous shepherding. For instance, rather than blessing, there can be neglect; rather than deliverance, there can be abuse; rather than discipline, there can be injustice.

9

Shepherding the Lord's People

GOD BLESSES HIS PEOPLE

God's kingdom includes all reality, from the angelic realm and all galaxies, to our human race and each person within it. But during the parenthetical age he allows a dark sub-kingdom. So his kingdom includes the holy angels and the sub-kingdom of fallen angels; his kingdom includes his believing people and the sub-kingdom of unbelieving peoples. However, there is no part of his creation that is beyond his shepherding eye, no part that is not blessed, delivered, or disciplined. Yet, of course, he has an intense and positive interest in his own people, and how he shepherds them is our focus in this chapter.

God is Israel's specific king while he is the king of the rest of humanity too. Israel was created by the Lord to be a chosen people for whom he had planned a unique royal role. Again, that royal role is described in literal shepherding terms.

> The Lord our creator is our God.
> We are the people in *His pasture, the sheep* in His hand. Ps 95:7
>
> The Lord is God, the one who created us—we did not.
> We are his people and *the sheep in his pasture*. Ps 100:3
>
> You are *my sheep, the sheep in my pasture*. Ezek 34:31

But the extent of his sovereignty is also expressed without explicit shepherding terms.

> The Lord is our judge. The Lord is our lawgiver.
> The Lord is our king. He is our savior. Isa 33:22
>
> I am the Lord your Holy One, your king as creator of Israel. . . .
> The people I created for myself will declare my praise."[1] Isa 43:15, 21

---

1. 1 Chr 28:5; 2 Chr 9:8; 13:8; Pss 45:10–11; 98:6; 114:2; 147:19–20; 149:1–2; Isa 41:21; 46:3–4; Obad 21

The Lord makes it clear that he is not only the glorious God and Shepherd, but that he is the compassionate and caring "Father" as well—a common Middle Eastern image for a nation's king.[2] Though he is above all, he is still near all. Christ also confirms our right to call God our Father: "Our Father who is in heaven" (Matt 6:9).

Israel was blessed to work especially close with God in his eternal design but not because of her merits or strengths. God's continued love for Israel in spite of her constant rebellion was due to his love for the patriarchs. So Malachi reminded the Israelites that their privileged relationship with the Lord was based on his love for Jacob over Esau; it was his unexplained choice, not Israel's right or anything they had earned.[3]

The Israelites' were blessed to be the example to the world of what should have been true from Eden and throughout eternity. She was to be the model of the Lord's eternal design for all humanity to see. God crowned Israel and adorned her as a queen to be the example to the world of how wonderful he is to the simplest and weakest.[4] He elevated her to a reigning position, for him and with him:

> I also put . . . a beautiful crown on your head . . .
>
> You were exceedingly beautiful and proceeded to royalty. Ezek 16:12-13

Israel's successes in morality, economics, health, spirituality, politics, family, and military battles were to prove to the rest of the peoples in the world how wise God and his people were.

> So obey my statutes since that is your wisdom and understanding in the sight of the peoples who will hear all these statutes and say, "Absolutely, this great nation is wise and understanding." For what great nation has a god as close as the Lord our God is when we call on Him? Deut 4:6-7

Israel, in its glory was to prove that the God of Israel was not only the greatest God, but the *only* God.[5]

Israel would be an example to the world and through her the peoples would be blessed generously. Abraham's gospel was the foundation of Paul's personal ministry to the Gentiles.

> The Scripture, seeing that God would eventually justify the Gentiles by faith, proclaimed the gospel to Abraham saying, "Every nation will be blessed in you." Gal 3:8

---

2. Deut 32:6; Ps 89:26; Isa 63:16; Jer 3:19; also, "sons of God," Deut 14:1; Ps 82:6; Hos 1:10

3. Mal 1:2-3; also, Deut 7:6-9; 1 Chr 16:16-19

4. Gen 17:7-8; Ex 6:7; 29:45; Lev 11:45; Deut 7:6-9; 8:17-18; 9:4-6; 14:1-2; 1 Kgs 8:53; 1 Chr 17:20-24; Jer 2:2-3; 13:11

5. Deut 4:34-39; 26:16-19; Josh 4:23-24; 2 Sam 7:22-26; 1 Kgs 8:41-43; 9:6-9; 10:1, 9; 1 Chr 16:8, 24-28; 2 Chr 6:32-33; 32:23; Ps 67:1-3, 7; Prov 14:34; Isa 37:20; 42:4; 55:5; Dan 9:19; Zech 8:23

God promised the patriarchs that all the peoples of the globe would be blessed through them.[6] It would be from Israel that an eternal king would appear and reign as the global king who saves—the Son of Man, the Shepherd, the Servant, and the Messiah. God's persistent benediction of grace and peace begins with Israel, but eventually extends to all peoples as they find grace and peace in him (Num. 6:24–26).

The New Testament certainly identifies Jesus as the Good Shepherd, but Nathaniel and thousands of others recognized that Jesus was the Messiah, the Anointed King as well, "the Son of God and king of the Jews" (John 1:49). Jesus was *born* "King of the Jews" and *died* "King of the Jews." At the beginning of the account of Jesus' life, Matthew writes that the wise men from the East asked, "Where is the one who has been born king of the Jews?" Then, tragically and wonderfully, near the end of his Gospel, Matthew records the inscription posted above Christ's suffering body: "This is Jesus, King of the Jews."[7]

Israel was blessed with the same universal blessings given to all humanity, but as God's special people, they received additional blessings. Let us look at a few examples of God's blessings on Israel: territory, communication, Spiritual gifts, and rewards for obedience.

Territory

As king of the globe, God blessed Israel with a small territory, their "Eden," so to speak, which they were to fill, subdue, and cultivate agriculturally and culturally. He gave the Israelites a place to fulfill their national primary commission by multiplying and being fruitful: "He will love and bless you, Israel; he will multiply you, bless your womb's fruit and the fruit of the ground" (Deut 7:13).[8] The commissions given to Abraham, Isaac, and Jacob had promised Canaan to them and their descendants, and it eventually was distributed at each concentric circle of society: to the nation, tribes, and families. The Lord determined the very boundaries for Israel's twelve tribes (Josh 18:5–7), blessing Israel with even more lands not part of the original promise, including Heshbon, Bashan, and Midian.[9]

The patriarchs had not earned or paid for their land in any way.[10] The Lord was the one who owned the land, so only he could give the land as a "possession" to the Israelites. But there was no transfer of deed of ownership to Israel. Rather, God essentially *leased* the land to them: "The land is mine; you are only aliens and tenants living with me" (Lev 25:23). As he had given Eden to the Couple, he gave Canaan to Abraham and his descendants. As the landlord, just as he had the right to evict the Couple

---

6. Gen 12:3; 18:18; 22:18; 26:4; 28:14

7. Matt 2:2; 27:37

8. Gen 13:14–17; 15:18; 17:8; 24:7; Ex 6:4; Lev 25:23; Deut 1:8, 20–21; 3:19–20; 4:40; 6:10; 32:43; Josh 1:2–5; Ps 108:7–8

9. Num 21:21–35; 25:16–18; 31:1–12; Deut 2:30–37; 3:3–7; 11:24; Neh 9:22–25

10. Deut 9:4–6; Gen 15:7; 26:3; 28:4, 13; 48:4; Ps 105:43–45

from Eden, the Lord had the right to *evict* the Israelites if they violated the terms of the lease—something he had to do through the Assyrian and Babylonian exiles.

As the landowner, God expected his tenants to offer some of the land's produce back to him. This was done by bringing offerings from the fields to present to him through the priests, leaving some produce in the fields for fellow Israelites and for aliens in the land, and to provide for domestic and wild animals (Deut 26:1-5, 9-11). This land arrangement between God as the owner and his people as tenants forms the background of Christ's four vineyard parables.[11] The setting of these stories is that there is an Owner of the vineyard who employs whomever he wishes, pays them generously but expects the employees to respond appreciatively. Even the Owner's Son is included in these stories of a "Family business."

Israel's land was exceptionally fruitful and was placed strategically in the Middle East for her greatest success. It was not a difficult land to manage; it "flowed with milk and honey."[12] It was a pleasant land with water, forests, and ores. When they took possession of the land, it already had houses, wells, cisterns, crops, and vineyards.[13] Her placement bridged three continents (Asia, Europe, Africa), giving her the advantage of being the hub of lucrative international commerce. But her central location also placed her at the center of those continents' attention, forcing them to compare their god's meager blessings to those from Israel's true and only God. Israel was also a "communication bridge" between God and the world since the Lord used Israel as his voice to bless, deliver and discipline the nations.

When it came time for the conquest of Israel's territory, the Lord carefully sequenced Israel's succession of military victories, timing them so that the Israelites could gain control gradually rather than in a single event. God had even synchronized Israel's exodus with his judgment of the wicked Canaanites (Gen 15:16). In God's pragmatic wisdom, this cadenced march through Canaan allowed his people time to subdue the land in a methodical way, saving the Israelites from frantically defending all of the land's produce from wild animals at one time (Deut 7:22). In his kind timing then, the Lord gave the land and peace to his people.[14]

The Lord lived and walked among his kingdom people within the territory he gave them.[15] Moses pled with the Israelites to understand this privilege of God's closeness: "Which nation is there that has a god as near as the Lord our God who hears whenever we call on him?" (Deut 4:7, 33-36). The phrase "walking with" is a way to speak of God's close relationship with his people; it is the same description of

---

11. Matt 20:1-8; 21:28-32; Luke 13:6-9; Matt 21:33-41 // Mark 12:1-9 // Luke 20:9-16
12. Ex 33:3; Num 13:27; Deut 1:25; 8:7-10; 26:8-9, 15; Jer 32:21-22; Ezek 20:5-6
13. Num 24:5-7; Deut 6:10-11; 8:6-9; 11:10-15; Neh 9:25, 35; Isa 5:1-4; Jer 2:7; Ezek 19:10
14. Josh 21:43-45; Ex 23:31; 33:1-3; 34:11; Num 23:21-24; 24:8, 17-19; Deut 1:29-31; 4:37-39; 7:22-24; 1 Chr 17:21; 2 Chr 6:34-35; 20:7; Pss 20:5; 21:5; 44:1-3
15. Exod 17:7; 25:8; 29:46; Lev 26:11-12; Deut 6:13-15; 23:14; 1 Kgs 20:28; 1 Chr 23:25; 2 Chr 6:18; 7:15-16; Ps 76:1-2; Ezek 37:26-27; Zeph 3:15; Hag 1:13; 2:5; Zech 2:10-13; 8:3

God's intimate presence, ownership, and authority while he walked with the Couple in Eden and when God-Incarnate, Christ Jesus, lived and walked with us.[16]

The Testaments speak of the comfort from the ever-present Holy Spirit who was with the Israelites in their territory and was to be the comforter of believers within the church. In the Old Testament, the Lord's presence was not limited to simply the tabernacle or temple. "My Spirit abides among you, so do not be afraid."[17] During Israel's wandering, the pillar of fire and the cloud were visual guides for all of Israel to see God's presence.[18] Fire was a visual aid for Israel to prove God's presence and provision.[19] The Lord went before Israel to guide and protect her: in Egypt, from Egypt, from battle to battle and wherever thereafter; "The Lord shepherded them . . . and guided them with his skillful hands."[20]

When Christ Jesus came, there was a "new Israel" which is made up of the true children of Abraham, that is, any believer in Christ whether they are blood descendants of Abraham or not.[21] John the Baptist said true children of Abraham could even descend from rocks. One who is a Jew ethnically might not be one spiritually if one is hardened and does not accept Jesus as the Messiah (Rom 11:7). There is no "Jew" and "Gentile" any longer; any believer is one of "Abraham's children" (Gal 3:29). And all believers, regardless of ethnicity are brothers and sisters in the same "body." There is no other body since Jews and Gentiles worship and work together as the only body: "There is one body and one Spirit."[22] Christ "made both Jews and Gentiles into one and . . . reconciled them both in one body to God through the cross" (Eph 2:14, 16). The church continues Israel's Old Testament role now as "a chosen race, a royal priesthood, a holy nation and God's possession as a people."[23]

But, now there is no single geographical nation for God's people with a land mass as small as Israel's was. Now the geographical expanse of God's kingdom of believers is approaching what it will be in New Earth. Christians are found in virtually every nation and among most peoples, broadly defined. Of course, the density of believers in these regions is not as complete as it will be in New Earth. Then it will be populated only by Christians. But the general footprint for New Earth's pervasive believing population is nearly set, and that framework is filling in as more Christians swell the globe's believing population on the continents. Presently, concentrations of believers is skewing toward Asia, while the western church gorges itself into materialistic

---

16. Gen 3:8; 5:22, 24; 6:9; Mic 6:8; Mal 2:6; John 1:14; 6:66; 2 Cor 6:16; Gal 5:16; Rev 3:4

17. Hag 2:5; Isa 63:11

18. Ex 13:21–22; 33:9–10; 40:34–38; Num 9:15–22; 10:33–34; Neh 9:12; Pss 105:39

19. Ex 3:2–4; 13:21–22; Deut 4:36; Judg 6:21; 1Kgs 18:38; Joel 2:30–31

20. Ps 78:72; also, Ex 23:20–23; 33:2, 14–16; Num 23:21; Deut 23:14; 31:6–8; Josh 1:9; Pss 48:14; 77:20

21. Matt. 3:9 // Luke 3:8; John 8:39; Rom 9:7; 1 Pet 3:6

22. Eph 4:4; also, Rom 12:4–5; 1 Cor 10:17; 12:12–14, 18–20, 25

23. 1 Pet 2:9; also, Rev 1:6

obesity. However, eventually the property of all the nations will belong to the people of New Earth.[24]

God's ever-enlarging *believing* kingdom is the marvelous fulfillment of Abraham's gospel. The Lord's kingdom is in real time and space. His kingdom is not just his position and power of authority; his kingdom is as earthy and physical as any human nation. This is true in two ways: (1) the whole physical universe is in his kingdom, and (2) any place where one of his believers applies his laws and wisdom is a physical location of God's kingdom. The Lord's believing kingdom is geographical, wherever devoted believers influence their surroundings with righteousness. The provinces within the realm might not be vast spaces, but neither was tiny Israel.

Christ dwells with the church as he did with Israel as the Second Person of the Trinity. I have mentioned Matthew's bookend statements in his Gospel's first and closing chapters about Jesus as the king. He does the same when emphasizing the Lord's nearness. In Matthew's last chapter, Jesus Christ says, "I am with you always" (28:20), fulfilling what was promised in Matthew's first chapter that Jesus would be named "Immanuel," meaning "God with us." John confirms this promise in the last book of the Bible.

> I saw new skies and a new earth . . . And I heard a loud voice coming from the throne saying, "God's dwelling is with man. He will dwell with them, and they will be his people; God himself will be with them." Rev 21:3

This is God's greatest blessing for us, his people—he lives with us, and we live with him and for him.

Communication

In addition to his comforting *presence*, God repeatedly communicated with Israel's leaders and sometimes with an ordinary person. He compassionately shepherded his people with his words of love, affirmation, and encouragement, and with his promises, plans, instructions, and discipline: "Secret things belong to our Lord God, but his revealed things belong to us and our sons forever" (Deut. 29:29). He communicated promises and covenants to individual patriarchs and matriarchs. He even covenanted with the abused servant, Hagar, and her son, Ishmael (Gen. 16:8–13).

Isaiah revealed the Old Testament "gospel" or "good news" that the Lord was Israel's ruling, caring, and gentle shepherd.

> Zion, bring the good news . . . Jerusalem, bring the good news . . .
> Like a shepherd He will care for His flock;
> He will gather the lambs in his arms.
> He will carry them tightly and gently lead them as little lambs. Isa 40:9, 11

---

24. Matt 5:3, 5, 10 // Luke 6:20

It was good news for the Israelites that God would provide a national shepherd from Bethlehem who would "stand and shepherd his flock" (Mic 5:4). Ezekiel likens this coming shepherd to David: "I will place one shepherd over them, my servant "David." He will feed them and be their shepherd" (34:23).

At times God has communicated his global divine plans to individuals. He confided to Abraham what his plans were for Sodom and Gomorrah; to Joseph he explained his plans for Egypt; to Daniel he described his plans for the destructions of empires; and to the prophets he revealed his future blessings, deliverances, and discipline for Israel as well as for all nations.[25] The Lord or his angel was not only heard but was sometimes revealed in the flesh.[26]

God conveyed laws to Israel that described how he intended his people to be shepherded.[27] Keeping these laws ensured that Israel and her individual citizens would be able to "multiply" and subdue the land God shared with them: "Carefully follow every command I am giving you today, so you will live and multiply and then enter and possess the land" (Deut 8:1).[28]

In addition to the Law, instructions for righteousness are revealed in the wisdom literature which was delivered from the Lord himself, the "one Shepherd" (Eccl 12:11). There are hundreds of wisdom instructions, many more than there are laws. These principles found in Proverbs, Job and Ecclesiastes, carry the same authority as the Mosaic laws. They are not mere options for holy living, not just suggestions for the more advanced believer. We will look at these commandments and wisdom instructions in detail in chapters 12 and 13.

God's love for communication includes inviting his people to talk to him as well. Prayer is one of our greatest blessings. There is no stopping the impulse to speak to God once it is known that he understands human speech and appreciates other acts of worship. Prayers have been lifted to deities in virtually all eras and areas. But no pagan religion talks to their god as easily as believers are encouraged to talk to the Lord. Believers' prayers can be formal, informal, measured, emotional, lengthy, short, spoken, thought, personal, public, informed, confused, thankful, moaning, prepared, and impromptu—all forms and ways to communicate are demonstrated in the Bible. And the Lord promises to communicate back to the faithful, but in his own wisdom and timing.

God blesses the church with his same willingness to communicate in the New Testament. Christ is the Word—he was God's Revelation in the flesh (John 1:1). In Christ's words and by his actions he revealed to us who the Trinity is[29] and what shepherding expectations the Trinity has of us. The Lord gave the laws for his New Testa-

---

25. Gen 18:17-21; 41:15-32; Dan 2:28-45; 4:18-26

26. Gen 18:1-2; 32:24-30; Ex 3:2-6; 23:20-23; 32:34; 33:11; Num 22:21-35; Josh 5:13-15; Judg 6:11-23; 13:2-5, 9-23; Dan 10:10-21

27. Deut 17:18-20; 33:3-4, 7-11; Josh 1:7-8; Neh 8:1-3, 9-12; 9:13-14; Pss 119; 147:20; Hos 8:12

28. Deut 8:1; 30:16

29. John 5:19-21,30-31; 6:38-39; 8:29; 14:16, 26, 31; 15:10, 26; 16:7, 13-15; 17:4

ment church just as he had for Old Testament Israel. Old Testament commandments were given to Moses by God, and wisdom instruction came through the sages. Similarly, Christ gave his commandments[30] and the apostles wrote authoritative letters of wisdom that expand Jesus' ethical instructions for his believers. The New Testament gospels and letters follow Old Testament ethical and wisdom themes very closely as we will see when studying God's moral design in our final two chapters.

Old Testament mediators blessed Israel by speaking God's mind: prophets, angels, and human historians. The same type of mediators are found in the New Testament. In addition to the prophetic voice of our Savior, John the Baptist spoke God's mind. Luke mentions several other men and women who prophesied.[31] The archangel Gabriel spoke to Zacharias, Mary, and the Christmas shepherds.[32] Angels spoke to Joseph and Mary and the Easter women at the tomb.[33] An angel guides Philip, Cornelius, and Peter. An angel encourages Paul, telling him that he and others would be delivered from a storm at sea.[34] In the book of Revelation, John is hosted by an angel who escorts him through his visionary experience.[35] Though the New Testament had no poets, the testament did have its share of history writers who wrote the Gospels, including Luke's two volumes (Luke and Acts). Comparable to Old Testament sages, the apostles wrote wise sayings about righteous living.

Spiritual Gifts

The Spirit was very active in Old Testament times because his presence, power, and heart have always carried, and will always carry believers beyond their natural talents so they can shepherd Spiritually, not just naturally as non-believers shepherd. So, of course, Israel was blessed with Spiritual gifts, including prophecy, healing, miracles, artistry, courage, physical strength, administration, knowledge, and wisdom.

Yes, God's relationship with humanity through the Holy Spirit does intensify in the New Testament in two ways: he empowers Jesus specifically for his signs and wonders, and then after Christ's ascension he initiates a global outpouring of power and wisdom to propel God's eternal design even further over the globe. Old Testament prophets said the Messiah's anointing would repeat David's anointing by the Spirit,[36] and following the Messiah's ascension, the Holy Spirit would be poured out on Israel and, fortunately, on all mankind.[37]

30. Matt 28:20; John 13:34; 14:15, 21; 15:10–14, 17
31. Luke 1:67; 2:36–38; Acts 11:28; 13:1; 15:32; 21:9–10
32. Luke 1:11–14, 19, 26–36; 2:9–12
33. Matt 28:5–7 // Mark 16:5–7 // Luke 24:4–7, 23; John 20:12
34. Acts 8:26; 10:3–4; 12:7–10; 27:23–25
35. Rev 1:1; 22:6, 16
36. 1 Sam 16:13; Isa 11:2; 42:1; 61:1; then Luke 4:17–19
37. Isa 32:15–16; 44:3; Ezek 36:26–27; 39:29; Joel 2:28–30; Zech 12:10; then Acts 1:8; 2:4

In the New Testament, these Spiritual gifts are provided to both Jews and Gentiles (1 Cor 12:11, 13) and the purpose for these gifts is to edify others, not oneself (1 Cor 14:26). So after Paul urges us to pursue the greater gifts (1 Cor 12:31), he introduces immediately the gift of loving others (1 Corinthians 13). Of course the greatest gift is love since it is the greatest summation of the law—love God and love your neighbor.[38]

Spiritual gifts are used by various believers of both Testaments. Because of the new function of the "apostle," it appears to be a new Spiritual gift in the newer testament. Also, apparently new gifts of tongues and interpretation are mentioned in the New Testament lists of examples of Spiritual gifts. The rest are seen in the lives and the history of the Israelites: prophets, teachers, the wise, the knowledgeable, evangelists (proclaimers), exhorters, givers, servers, the celibate, the merciful, shepherds (pastors), miracle workers, healers, those with great faith, those who are hospitable and those with Spiritual discernment.[39]

Israel's National Blessings for Obedience

God blesses all creation because of his infinite goodness and shepherding heart. His nature is to create, empower, and care for everything he has enlisted in his eternal design. It does not matter whether the creature is inanimate, animate, degenerate, or regenerate. However, there are further and deeper blessings for those who obey his laws and instructions out of faith and love.

God's eternal love for Israel is a covenant he will never break; it was the hope of his unconditional love that kept Old Testament believers believing.[40] We will see, however, that there was a foundational difference between the Lord's *unconditional* love for his elect nation and his *conditional* provisions and protection for them. He would always love Israel, but he generously blessed, delivered, and severely judged them as well. God's commitment was clear—

> The Lord, the Lord God, is compassionate and gracious, patient, full of love, kindness and truth. For thousands he is loving and kind, forgiving sins of every kind. But he will surely punish the guilty. Ex 34:6–7

The Lord set the terms for his blessings when he connected the Israelites' success to their obedience. God assured the Israelites that his commandments were not too hard to understand or keep. Most of the moral law was in their hearts and mouths already, simply from the moral law of their conscience (Deut 30:11–14).

> Today I promise you either life and goodness, or death and disaster, by commanding you to love the Lord your God and to walk in his commandments so

---

38. Matt 22:40, 37–39; also, Mark 12:29–33; John 15:17; 1 Cor 13:1–13; 16:22; 1 John 4:21
39. Rom 12:6–8; 1 Cor 7:7; 12:8–10, 28–30; 13:1–3, 8–10; Eph 4:11; 1 Pet 4:9–10
40. 1Kgs 8:23; Pss 23:6; 40:5; 89:1–4, 14; 100:5; 103:8, 11–13; 118:1–4; 2 Chr 5:12–13; 20:21

> that you will live and multiply and so the Lord your God will bless you in your land. But if your heart turns to disobedience . . . you will certainly perish. You will not live long in your land. Deut 30:15–18

Israel's blessings and future were determined by her compliance with God's instructions. Yet, blessings still came by his continual patience and faithfulness in spite of her unfaithfulness.[41] There was a limit, though.

For God to shepherd Israel into life and goodness, Israel had to take its own shepherding responsibilities seriously. The Lord considered Israel serious when she loved the Lord, was appreciative, and obeyed his success-insuring instructions. The nation would then continue to be blessed and allowed to stay in the land.[42] It was not enough simply to accept the privileges of his goodness and promises. Nor was it enough to simply vocalize national commitment to God's laws. There had to be a heartfelt reverence for God leading to genuine, routine obedience (Deut 5:28–29).

A clear indication of God's conditional blessing, deliverance, or discipline was whether Israel's military was successful or defeated. They were promised military victory and security if they remained faithful to God's laws.[43] Joshua 7–8 explains that the battle for Ai was first loss because of Achan's *disobedience,* and then the battle was won after Joshua's *obedience.* Even mere sounds brought the most devastating destruction to Jericho's walls when God's instructions were followed precisely (Josh. 6:2, 20). Leviticus 26:3–8 combines God's promises of blessings of military success and of having ample food: "You will eat until you are full . . . your enemies will fall by your sword."

The productivity of her land also depended on Israel's obedience from a sincere heart. The fruitfulness of wild and domesticated animals and vegetation was affected by Israel's moral conduct.[44] Obedience would bring God's continuous provisions of rain, pure ground water, grain, oil, wine, orchards, trees, herds, and flocks.[45] The Lord's blessing included the fruitful womb so that the Israelites could multiply and fill the land.

Israel was successful only when the primary commission of multiplying, filling, and shepherding, was accomplished by Israel's sociological realms. Individuals, spouses, families, communities, cities, tribes, and the nation—all could expect his shepherding care when they shepherded by his standards. So, there were times and places where Israel's righteousness brought abundance and peace. In her golden age under Solomon, Israel was a multiplied people who filled her land.

---

41. Deut 32:4; 1 Sam 2:2; 2 Sam 22:2–3; Neh 9:17, 30–33; Pss 40:10; 89:1–2; 100:5; 145:8; Isa 58:13–14

42. Ex 19:5–6; 20:5–6; Deut 5:9–10; 7:9, 12; 12:28; 26:18–19; 28:3; 2 Chr 15:1–7; Pss 31:19; 111:4–6; 115:13–15

43. Ex 23:27–31; 34:23–24; Deut 1:42–44; 7:16, 22–24;11:22–25; 28:7; 33:27–28; Josh 1:5–7

44. Ex 23:25–26; Lev 26:3–5, 9–10; Deut 7:12–14; 11–14; 28:4–5, 11–12; 30:4–5, 8–10

45. Lev 25:18–22; 26:3–5; Deut 11:11–16; 28:8; Ps 144:13–14; also, in the new phase of his kingdom, Mal 3:10–12

> South and North Israel were as numerous as the sand on the seashore and were eating, drinking and rejoicing . . . Everyone lived in safety under his vine and fig tree from Dan to Beersheba. 1 Kgs. 4:20, 25

This picturesque description of Israel's success in her primary commission set the standard for the rest of her history prior to, and after the great reigns of David and Solomon.

Tranquility and fruitful living by the isolated but obedient communities are seen in Israel's less glorious eras too. The book of Ruth is set in a morally exemplary community within Israel's wider chaotic, idolatrous, and perverted age during the time of the judges. To an extent then, a community can insulate itself by its righteousness regardless of the wider wickedness that surrounds it. Also, when Solomon's son Rehoboam was humble and repentant at the beginning of his reign, life was good for South Israel (2 Chr 12:12). Proverbs is quite direct about a community's success: "The city rejoices when the righteous succeed, and there is glad shouting when the wicked die" (Prov 11:10).

We will discuss at the end of this study the specific laws and wisdom God gave to Israel by which she was to shepherd. However, we give a few examples here of critical instructions which, if obeyed, would be rewarded with God's blessings on the nation.

Israel's kings, elders, and other leaders had to lead by the Mosaic law and the wisdom instructions if the eternal design was to be visible within Israel and to the world around her. Her strength and peace as a nation depended on it. The stability of the monarchy was determined by the extent the *king* eliminated wickedness from his court and from his nation.[46] Rest and peace came from God's reward to the king and to his people for his obedient service.[47] Security was insured by fair, disciplining *elders* in their legal proceedings, including their judgments and sentences. Citizens without resources to defend themselves in court were not to be victimized. *Priests* were to teach God's revealed truth faithfully, to lead in national and personal confession, and to carry God's blessings and encouragements to the people. The *prophets* were to keep Israel apprised of God's thoughts and plans for his people and to do so faithfully regardless of the severity of the message.

Obedience to the land laws assured God's blessing on the territory of tribes and families, and graciously reunified families at least every 49 years when land was returned to the original owners. The land's fruit fed its owner primarily but was shared with the impoverished, including the widow, orphan, poor, alien, elderly, and handicapped. The Lord promised to bless "the work of *their* hands."[48] God blessed the hands that blessed his land.

Keeping the commandments ensured economic viability for each person and family. Debtors were not burdened with interest and their debt was forgiven every seven years at the latest. To avoid humiliation and dehumanization, servants were to

---

46. Prov 16:12; 20:28; 25:5; 29:4, 14; Eccl 5:8–9; 10:17
47. Num 6:23–27; 1 Chr 23:25; Ps 29:11
48. Deut 28:8, 12; 30:9

be treated as employees, and their community citizenship was not to be denied. Abusing these souls was grounds for suit or even death.

God's promise to keep Israel fertile and populated was his blessing to individual families. After all, children are a delight to their parents.[49] God guaranteed Israel's multiplication if she was faithful. This guarantee kept Israel fertile and made filling the land possible for an indefinite time if not for eternity.[50] The blessings for the families were protected by severe penalties for betraying the family and defiling the sanctity of marriage. Sexual infidelity through adultery, incest, homosexuality, bestiality, and temple prostitution were abhorrent and worthy of execution. Respect for parents and the elderly, and the social order which respect for authority and wisdom instilled, allowed the family to be the nurturing, loving, learning, and worshipping center in the community.

Obedience to God's laws determined a community's health and safety. Extensive precautions were prescribed to prevent contracting and spreading infectious diseases. There were enough delicious and legal foods to eat without resorting to meats that were prone to bacteria. Purification rites that may appear extreme to us served as insurance that the transmission of disease was kept to a minimum. Vitality was possible only with the Sabbath rest for humans and beasts of burden. Joy and relaxation were encouraged in the sabbatical events and festive celebrations.[51] Gluttony and drunkenness destroy the body and endanger others. Violent physical crimes including murder, human sacrifice, rape, and kidnapping were deterred by the death sentence. God promised he would protect the Israelites even from wild beasts if they would be faithful to him.[52] And beyond these precautionary health laws, the Lord promised health because of his direct involvement through protection and healing.[53]

GOD DELIVERS HIS PEOPLE

We will discuss Israel's salvation from sin in the next section, but now we focus on how God saved his people when they were in adverse situations. As we mentioned in chapter 5, there were a variety of difficulties from which the Shepherd saved the

---

49. Pss 127:3–5; 128:1–6
50. Ex 20:12; Deut 4:40; 5:33; 6:2; 11:8–9, 20–21; 22:6–7; 25:15; 30:19–20; 32:47; 1 Chr 28:8
51. Ex 31:17; Lev 23:7–8, 24–25, 34–36, 39–41; Deut 12:6–7, 12; 16:10–15
52. Lev 26:6; Ezek 34:25
53. Ex 23:25; Deut 7:15

Israelites. He is praised as Israel's savior,[54] redeemer,[55] her protective refuge,[56] shield,[57] fortress,[58] and rock.[59]

God Delivers His People from Adversity

David prayed that the Lord would deliver Israel just as the Lord had delivered him, personally. He and Asaph prayed that Israel's Shepherd would bless and deliver them eternally by his powerful arms.

> Deliver your people and bless your inheritance.
> Be their *shepherd* and carry them forever. Ps 28:9

> Preserve those condemned to die . . .
> So we your people and *sheep* of your *pasture* will thank you forever. Ps 79:11, 13

> Please listen, *Shepherd* of Israel, who leads Joseph like a flock . . .
> come and deliver us, oh God; restore us with your shining face and save us. Ps 80:1-3

Micah also pled with the Lord to keep his promise and deliver Israel who was alone in her tiny territory tucked away in the Middle East.

> *Shepherd* Your people with your staff, the *flock* of your inheritance who live alone in Mount Carmel's forests. Mic 7:14

The Lord shepherded Israel out of Egypt, delivering them from oppression and protecting them in their life-threatening wilderness march in Sinai:

> You led your people like a *flock* by the hand of Moses and Aaron. Ps 77:20

> He led his own people like *sheep,* guiding them through the wilderness like a *flock.* Ps 78:52

> He brought them through the sea along with the *shepherds* of his flock. Isa 63:11

God's care for Israel in their beleaguered condition in the wilderness started with Pharaoh's desperate release of the slaves. Then, the Egyptians lavished their good-riddance provisions on the departing Israelites. Yet Israel still grumbled much of the

---

54. Deut 32:15; 1 Chr 16:35; Pss 68:19; 79:9; 85:4; Isa 17:10; 43:3, 11; 45:15, 21; 49:26; 60:16; 62:11; 63:8; Jer 14:8; Hos 13:4

55. Pss 25:22; 78:35; Isa 41:14; 43:14; 44:6, 24; 47:4; 54:5, 8; 60:16; 63:16; Jer 50:34

56. Deut 33:27; Joel 3:16

57. Deut 33:29; Pss 33:20; 115:9-11; Isa 31:5; Zech 9:15; 12:8

58. Pss 46:7, 11; 48:3; Isa 17:10

59. Gen 49:24; Deut 32:13-15, 18, 31; 1 Sam 2:2; 2 Sam 22:32, 47; 23:3; Isa 17:10; 26:4; 30:29; 44:8; Hab 1:12

way while God miraculously supplied water, quail and manna. These gifts were hardly rewards for righteousness; they were undeserved gifts for unappreciative souls.[60]

This salvation from Egypt served other purposes. It eventually inspired a pervasive thread of praise for God throughout the Old Testament.[61] It encouraged Israel to continue trusting and obeying such a strong and faithful savior God. They were never lord-less; they were blessed to have such a gracious Lord rather than the abusive Egyptians.[62] The Exodus also showed the surrounding world exactly how faithful and all-powerful Israel's Lord was, which should have motivated the nations to respect Israel and her God.[63]

God saved Israel by choosing her from among the nations. He brought her from rags to riches, from death's door to the royal court, from a trashed infant to a mature queen.

> The day you were born you were dumped in a field to die. When I passed by you wallowing in your blood, I said to you, "Live!" I multiplied you as the buds of the field; you grew tall and were adorned perfectly. Your breasts were fully formed and your hair had grown long, yet you were naked and exposed. . . . You were at the time for love; so I covered your nakedness and entered into a covenant with you so that you became mine. . . . I clothed you with embroidered cloth. . . . I adorned you with ornaments, put bracelets on your hands and a necklace around your neck. I also put a ring in your nostril, earrings in your ears and a beautiful crown on your head. . . . You were exceedingly beautiful and proceeded to royalty. Ezek 16:5–8, 10–13

The Lord truly makes everything beautiful in the right season! Pictured as a victim of attempted infanticide, Israel was salvaged by God's grace to became a ruling nation.

God often accentuates his love for salvation by promoting the vulnerable to positions of victory and by subjugating their opponents. Isaiah and Jeremiah give examples of this rags-to-riches narrative.

> Everyone who is devouring you will be devoured. All your adversaries, each will be captured.
>
> Those plundering you will be plundered. Everyone preying on you I will make your prey.[64]

The prayers of his humble, believing community acknowledged their dependence on the Lord for his salvation. The Exodus was one of God's responses to his people's

---

60. Ex 16:4, 8, 13, 31, 35; 17:6; Num 11:6, 31–32; 20:8–11; Deut 8:3, 15–16; Josh 5:12; Neh 9:15, 20–21; Pss 78:20, 24–27; 105:37, 40–41; 114:8; Isa 48:20

61. Ex 18:8–10; 29:46; Deut 26:3–11; 2 Sam 7:23–24; 1 Chr 17:21; Neh 9:9–11; Pss 78:42–51; 81:5–7, 9–10; 105:26–36; 114:1–2; 136:10–12

62. Ex 19:3–4; 20:2; Lev 26:11–13; Deut 4:32–40; 5:6, 15; 6:21; 8:11–17; 11:1–9; 1 Sam 10:18

63. Num 23:21–22; 24:8–9

64. Jer 30:16; also, Isa 60:15–17

cry for deliverance.[65] Their prayers were an instrumental cry to God for redemption from their enemies.[66] Other national prayers included the Israelites' prayer for Esther's safety as she prepared to enter Ahaseurus' court illegally (Esth 4:16). Ezra led the Israelites in prayer for the Lord's protection and deliverance from ambush while on their journey back to Israel from their decades of exile (Ezra 8:21–23, 31).

Deliverance from Enemies

Within the parenthetical design are the innumerable cycles of blessing, discipline and deliverance which define the history of God's people. These shepherding cycles were routine for Israel. When the Lord saw his blessings taken for granted because the sheep went their own way, he disciplined his people and they repented; he responded with deliverance and blessed his people again.

> God blesses his people . . .
>   they are unfaithful
>   => they are disciplined
>   => they repent
>   => they are delivered
>   => they are blessed again

Several of these cycles are concentrated in the book of Judges where the frequency of Israel's unfaithfulness, oppression, repentance, and deliverance mark the repetitive military narratives. This rhythm is sustained by the succession of deliverers like Deborah, Gideon, and Samson. The psalmist summarized these cyclic deliverances recorded in Judges:

> He gave them into the hand of the Gentiles; those who hated them ruled over them.
> Their enemies oppressed them and powerfully subdued them.
> He delivered them many times but they rebelled intentionally and sank in sin.
> Yet he pitied them in their distress when they cried out. Ps 106:41–44

As disappointing as these cycles are, still, God's deliverance of his people was a testimony to all peoples of the globe: "The Lord reveals his holy arm in all the nations' sight so that the ends of the earth will see his salvation."[67] If not immediately, then eventually, God's grace and mercy will be acknowledged by everyone.

---

65. Ex 7:5; 14:4, 18, 25; Josh 4:23–24; 1 Sam 12:8; Ps. 81:6–7

66. Num 10:9; Judg 3:9, 15; 4:3, 23; 6:7–8; 10:10–16; 1 Sam 7:8–10; 12:10–11, 19–22; 1 Kgs 8:46–53; 2 Kgs 19:14–19; 2 Chr 13:13–15; 14:9–12; 20:9–13, 22–23; 32:20–22; Neh 9:27–28

67. Isa 52:10; also, Pss 67:1–2; 77:14–15; 98:2–3; 102:13–22; 106:7–8

God promised the Israelites material blessings and military deliverance. It was God's expectation however, that Israel fight hard, knowing the Lord's deliverance came through the partnership of God and soldiers.[68]

> You will eat until you are full . . . your enemies will fall by your sword. Lev 26:5-7

The Lord our God is with us to help us to fight our battles.[69]

> When they were very few and were strangers in Canaan, wandering from nation to nation, kingdom to kingdom, he allowed no one to oppress them, reproving kings on their behalf. 1 Chr 16:19-21

At times only portions of Israel were saved. The salvation of the clans of Joseph, Judah, Levi and Benjamin are mentioned in specific prophecies.[70] Military leaders in the book of Judges were victorious for specific tribes or regions within Israel.[71] David delivers the region of Keilah from the Philistines and Ziklag from the Amalekites.[72] And after the Promised Land is divided between a southern kingdom (Judah) and the northern kingdom (Israel), these separate kingdoms are delivered by God the Savior from multiple enemy peoples, and even from each other!

Before the split between North Israel and South Israel, the Lord's people were saved from thirty one kings in their wanderings and the conquest of Canaan (Josh 12:7-24). Conquered lands which the Lord delivered to Israel included Heshbon, Bashan and Midian.[73] Saul defeated the kings of Moab, Ammon, Edom, Zobah, Philistia, and the Amalikites (1 Sam 14:47-48). David's multiple battles with the Philisines, beginning with Goliath, assisted Saul's reign.[74] Through Esther's wisdom and courage, the Israelites were delivered from a holocaust at the hand of Haman.[75] And those remaining Israelites who ventured out of their exiles back to Israel were delivered from road ambushes and those who sought their wealth and lives along the way (Ezra 8:31).

The Lord often saved North Israel from their enemies even though that nation never had even one righteous king among their nineteen. It proved God was patient and faithful to his people even if their leaders were not. For instance, Ahab, the worst northern king, is victorious over the Syrians (1 Kgs 20:13-30). The north was again delivered from the Syrians by Elisha's wisdom (2 Kgs 6:8-12). The Lord delivered the

---

68. Deut 9:3; 12:29; 25:19; Neh 9:24; Pss 44:2-10; 47:3; 60:9-12; 68:21-23; 118:10-14

69. 2 Chr 32:8; also, Deut 33:26-29; Judg 10:11-12; Pss 44:4-8; 53:4-6; 60:11-12; 124:1-8; 136:24; Isa 41:10-14; Nah 1:12-13; Hab 3:12-13

70. Gen 49:22-24; Deut 33:7, 11-12

71. Judg 2:15-18; E.g. Deborah, Jael 4:9, 17-22; a certain heroine 9:52-54; Tola 10:1

72. 1 Sam 23:1-5; 30:1-2; 16-20

73. Num 21:21-35; 25:16-18; 31:1-12; Deut 2:30-37; 3:3-7; Neh 9:22-25

74. 1 Sam 17:50-53; 2 Sam 3:17-18; 5:18-25 // 1 Chr 14:8-16; 2 Sam 19:9; 21:15-22; 23:9-12 // 1 Chr 11:13-14; also, Syrians and Ammonites, 2 Sam 10:9-19

75. Esth 8:3-8; 9:2-16

northern kingdom yet again from the Syrians during the reigns of Jehoahaz and his son Jehoash (2 Kgs 13:3–5, 22–25).

South Israel was delivered in battle against her sibling North Israel several times. South Israel's king, Abijah was delivered from North Israel's king Jeroboam I; Ahaz defeated North Israel with the help of Assyria's king Tiglath-pileser.[76] When North Israel took 200,000 captives from South Israel, the captives were released because of Oded's warnings, and they were respectfully delivered back to Jericho (2 Chr 28:8–15). South Israel was saved from foreign nations too. King Asa was saved from the Ethiopians; king Jehoshaphat and South Israel were delivered from the Ammonites and Moabites.[77] South Israel, Jerusalem, and king Hezekiah were saved from the brutal Assyrians through Isaiah's intercession.[78]

Before the split into two separate kingdoms, Israel's military victories and deliverances from her enemies were primarily based on their faithfulness to God's laws and wisdom.[79] We mentioned the battles with Ai already, where Achan's *disobedience* led to defeat, but Joshua's eventual victory came from his *obedience* in purging Achan and his family from the community. By trusting God's unconventional strategy to defeat Jericho, Israel brought the walls of Jericho to rubble simply by shouting and trumpeting. Samuel promises that God will deliver the Israelites: "If you return to the Lord . . . and turn your hearts to serve him only, he will deliver you from the Philistines."[80]

During the exodus, God protected them when chased by the Egyptian army for the entire night before and during the march through the miraculously divided waters.[81] After the exodus, salvation in the wilderness was a reference point throughout Israel's history. God's wilderness deliverances by his provision of manna, quail, and water is leveraged to motivate Israel to faithfulness: "In the howling waste of a wilderness he shielded them with care, watching them in the center of his eye" (Deut 32:10).[82]

Israel was delivered from Egypt by the natural disasters God sent Egypt's way, including frogs, insects, and hail.[83] But these plagues that could have damaged the Egyptians and Hebrews and their property affected only the Egyptians.[84] Later,

---

76. 2 Kgs 16:7–9; 2 Chr 13:13–19; Isa 7:1–4, 10–16

77. 2 Chr 14:9–15; 20:22–23

78. 2 Kgs 19:20, 34–37; 20:6 // 2 Chr 32:20–22 // Isa 37:6–7, 18–20, 33–37; also, Isa 30:30–31; 31:5–9

79. Ex 23:27–31; 34:23–24; Lev 26:3, 6–9; Deut 7:16, 22–24;11:22–25; 28:7; 30:1–5; 33:28; Josh 1:5–7; 1 Sam 12:20–22; 2 Chr 15:1–6; Ps 81:13–16; also, in New Earth, Mal 4:1–3

80. 1 Sam 7:3–4, 11–14; 14:23; also, salvation from the Ammonites and Moabites, 1 Sam 11:11–13; 12:9

81. Ex 14:19–28; 15:1–12; Pss 66:6; 78:13, 53; 106:7–11; 136:13–15; Isa 43:16–17; 51:10

82. Ex 16:4, 8, 13, 31, 35; 17:6; Num 11:6, 31–32; 20:8–11; Deut 8:3, 15–16; Josh 5:12; Neh 9:15, 20–21; Pss 78:15–16, 20, 24–27; 105:40–41; 114:8; Isa 48:21; Ezek 20:9–10; Hos 11:1, 4; 13:4–5; Mic 6:4; 7:15

83. Ex 3:20; 7:20—12:30; Ps 105:26–36

84. Ex 8:22; 9:4–6, 26; 11:7

hornets, thunder, and hailstones are sent to pave the way for Israel's victories in Canaan.[85] God divided bodies of waters for dry passage not only when Israel left Egypt, but when they entered Canaan forty years later. Waters were parted yet again for Elijah and Elisha.[86] The Lord sprung water from rocks and the ground.[87] He sweetened and purified waters, and even raises a logger's axe from the water.[88] God controlled sicknesses and health for his people, delivering them from leprosy and boils, delivering the blind, deaf, dumb, and lame, and even raising the dead![89] Reproductive challenges were answered with deliverance from miscarriages and barrenness.[90] Finally, the Lord will reverse his curse on nature when he purifies all creation in New Earth, where humanity will enjoy the fullest of nature's provisions.[91]

Deliverance through Obedience

Israel's routine, daily salvation followed her when she followed God's prescriptions for a thriving society. By obeying the Lord's instructions, she delivered herself from the results of disobedience. In this sense, Israel delivered herself from the tragedies and severe disappointments that all peoples experience when they disobey the laws of conscience or are not privy to God's laws and wisdom teaching. Obedience is deliverance. Deliverance is experienced moment to moment by a society, family, or individual who benefits from the Lord's protective provisions for stability, justice, and health. So rest and peace came to Israel as God's reward for their service to him and to his people.[92]

God's moral architecture in the Law and the wisdom literature assured ways for the Israelites to save one another from harm. Israel was to protect and manage their society according to those plans. For instance, the Lord's salvation of Israel from slavery in Egypt was used as a model to motivate the Israelites to save their own poor who lived in their midst once in the Promised Land.[93] Phinehas was "reckoned to be righteous" when he delivered Israel from a plague by executing those who disobeyed God's marital laws.[94]

---

85. Ex 23:28; Josh 10:11; 24:12; 1 Sam 7:10
86. Ex 14:21–22; 15:8; Josh 3:13–17; 2 Kgs 2:8, 14; Ps 74:12–15
87. Ex 17:6; Num 20:8; Ps 105:41; Judg 15:18–19; 2 Kgs 3:20–23
88. Ex 15:25; 2 Kgs 2:20–22; 2 Kgs 6:5–6
89. Deut 7:15; 1 Kgs 17:21–22; 2 Kgs 4:34–35; 5:6,14; 20:5–7; Isa 35:5–6;
90. Ex 23:26; 1 Sam 1:5–6 19–20; 2 Kgs 4:14–17
91. Isa 30:23–26; 35:9; 41:17–20; Jer 31:11–12; Ezek 34:25–29; 36:29–30, 35; Joel 2:23–31; Zech 8:12
92. Num 6:23–27; 1 Chr 23:25; Pss 29:11; Isa 9:6–7; 26:3; 55:6–7, 12
93. Lev 25:35–38; Deut 15:12–18; 24:17–18
94. Num 25:6–9; Ps 106:28–31

Shepherds: The Believer's Outline of Theology

Deliverance from Exile

Moses prophesied that the Lord would punish Israel with captivity and exile into other far-reaching lands. But he also foresaw God's subsequent merciful and faithful deliverance of Israel (Deut. 30:1–5). Solomon followed up, requesting that the Lord save Israel if she was ever exiled.[95] The Lord's gathering and delivering his scattered flock is a constant refrain from Deuteronomy to the end of the older testament.[96] Though many prophetic passages are unclear about which of God's "gathering" deliverances may be in mind, many do clearly refer to the promises about Israel's return from exile under Zerubbabel, Ezra, and Nehemiah[97] or Israel's re-gathering to the Promised Land at the time of New Earth.[98]

The Shepherd returned Israel from exile to her own pasture where he wanted to bless her from the start. Jeremiah's message to the exiles echoed the shepherding words from the time of their exodus from Egypt. In words from the primary commission, Jeremiah conveyed the Lord's promise to Israel.

> I will gather the remnant of my *flock* from every country where I have driven them, and bring them back to their *pasture* where they will be fruitful and multiply. 23:3

> He who scattered Israel will gather and watch over his *flock* like a *shepherd*. 31:10

> Israel is a scattered *flock* that lions have chased away . . . 50:17, 19

> But I will bring Israel back to their own *pasture* to graze. What *shepherd* can stand against me? 50:44

Ezekiel and Micah prophesied this return to the original pasture in language that reflects Psalm 23 and anticipates Jesus' words as the Good Shepherd in John 10 and his parable of the Lost Sheep.[99]

> I will search and look after my *sheep*. As a *shepherd* looks after his scattered *flock* when with them, I look after my *sheep* . . . I will tend my *sheep* and have them lie down . . . I will mend the crippled and strengthen the sick . . . I will *shepherd* the flock with justice. Ezek 34:11–16

> I will gather them like *sheep* in the fold, a *flock* in its *pasture*. Mic 2:12

---

95. 1 Kgs 8:46–53 // 2 Chr 6:36–39

96. Pss 106:47; 107:2–3; 126:1–4; Isa 10:21–22; 11:11–16; 35:10; 43:5–7; 45:1, 13; 49:24–26; Jer 23:3, 7–8; 30:9–11; 46:27; Ezek 36:8–12; Hos 11:9–11

97. Ezra 1:2–5; 2:1–67; 7:12–13; 9:8; Neh 2:4–9; 7:5–72; 12:1–29; Ps 85:4–7, 12; Isa 48:20; 51:11, 14; 54:7; Jer 24:5–7; 29:11–14; 30:3

98. 1 Chr 17:9; Isa 9:1; 11:13–16; 19:23–25; Jer 23:5–8; 33:15–16; Ezek 34:25–31; 37:1–28; Joel 3:1–2, 20; Amos 9:13–15; Mic 5:5–9; Nah 1:15; Zeph 3:15–20; Zech 8:7–8, 11–13; 9:8—10:12; 14:2–4, 10–11

99. Matt 18:11–14 // Luke 15:4–7

God's eternal design to shepherd his shepherding people had its historical peaks and valleys. However, the steady drone of minimal success by Israel is the best that can be said for most of human history as well. The cycles of Israel's faithful and unfaithful behavior climaxed in her exiles. They had no land of their own to subdue for God's purposes while in exile, so they were banished from fulfilling their primary commission. But, fortunately, their deliverance and return to the Promised Land renewed their opportunity to manage their land according to God's principles.

Of course, the ultimate deliverance for Israel will come when the Messiah appears a second time and defeats all foes of the Trinity's eternal reign.[100] Not only will Israel be saved, but all of creation. New Earth will end the Lord's shepherding deliverance of his precious sheep since there will be none lost ever again:

> On that day the Lord their God will deliver his people as a *shepherd* delivers his *sheep*. They will sparkle in his land like gems set in a crown. Zech 9:16

This encouragement from God about a newer phase in his kingdom is an example of God's continual, unmerited encouragements to Israel's hopes: hopes for deliverance, hopes for restoration.

God Delivers His Church

Moses prayed for a strong and effective future leader who would give hope and direction to Israel so they would not be "like *sheep* without a *shepherd*" (Num 27:17). God chose Joshua to be that shepherd. As we noted in a previous chapter, Joshua's name means "the Lord saves," and Jesus, whose name also means "savior," resumes this saving passion during his daily ministry of saving people from illness, demon-possession, storms, even death when he resurrected some people. The same concern that Moses had was exactly Jesus' concern: "He looked on the crowds compassionately because they were distressed and helpless, like *sheep* without a *shepherd*."[101]

It would be hard to say that the plight of Israel and the church has vastly improved during our parenthetical age. The first century after the Resurrection saw further violence against Israel by the Romans. Israel saw little relief from persecution and its accompanying adversities. But, the ministry of Christ did give believing Jews and Gentiles a hope for the future deliverance of God's people from all oppression, sickness and sorrow in New Earth.

There is no doubt that the church is under global attack in this twenty-first century as well. Believers and their fellowships are the targets of nations which are officially atheist on the one hand and those who are officially religious on the other. But whether the nation is atheist or religious does not matter since the official ideology simply masks the sole core commitment which both governing systems have in common—dictatorship.

---

100. Pss 2:2–7, 11; 110:1–2, 5–6; Dan 2:37–45; 7:13–14, 27; 8:4–26; 9:25–27
101. Matt 9:36 // Mark 6:34

The millennia-long rivalry between the descendants of Abraham and Sarah and Abraham and Hagar is peaking again in our century to the extent of unprecedented persecution of Sarah's physical and spiritual children. There are many exciting accounts of the growth of God's kingdom in the Far East and his salvation of many thousands of people from sin *each day* around the world. But the accounts of inhumane and criminal persecution are startling and deeply saddening nonetheless.

We await the Lord's second coming to see the ultimate salvation of the church from its troubles. This salvation will include justification by the blood of Jesus, but the salvation we anticipate is broader still and will include the Shepherd's deliverance from hunger, thirst, heat, and sorrow.

> These came out of the great tribulation, and have washed their robes to be white by the blood of the Lamb . . . They will never be hungry or thirsty; nor will the sun or any scorching heat beat down on them for the Lamb in the center of the throne will be their *shepherd*, and will lead them to springs of living water; and God will wipe every tear from their eyes. Rev 7:14, 16–17

God Delivers His People from Sin

Troubles, trials, and adversity are caused by sin in this parenthetical era within God's eternal design. We would not have adversity if there had not been that moral collapse in Eden. God's Eden curses and our own sins require the Lord's deliverance, or total despair and chaos would reign. Sin is an adversity in itself. It seeks to rule us, destroy us. It plagues us by pernicious persistence in tempting us and driving us to do the very things we know we should not do. But God's unlimited patience with humanity, with his people, and with us as individuals shows him to be even more persistent than sin and will prove him and us as the victors.

Though he exiled Israel from their land and has allowed their persecution throughout history, his promises for them as a nation stand. His covenants with Israel were broken by them daily, but his faithfulness to his own plans and people is eternal. Humanity's Fall began a time of restoration that will continue until the new creation. Israel's many "falls" will end in its perfect restoration in a new Jerusalem. And our own personal "falls" will end in a perfect restoration of our body and soul in New Earth where we will reign with God forever.

Our gracious God does not always wait for the perfect repentance of his people before he keeps his promises. He does not require repentance in all cases before he will deliver his people. It was simply God's own faithful commitment to Israel that kept the nation in his favor. God delivers on his own initiative, in his own timing, and by his own integrity to his covenant promises without depending and waiting on the reluctant or unrepentant response of Israel. Israel's confession of its national sin was not always necessary for the Lord's deliverances and blessings.

On the other hand, God's deliverance of Israel and her believers was often based on their repentance and her intentionally asking for forgiveness. In many cases, this is simply implied when the older testament recounts that they "cried out" to the Lord.[102] There is no explicit request for forgiveness of sins in these cries. Yet, we understand they could not expect their Lord's deliverance unless they were sorry for their sins to the extent of committing themselves as a nation to refrain from sin. We surmise that what is not said in these cases is filled in by Asaph's observations:

> When God killed them, they began to seek him again, searching hard and returning to God. They remembered that their rock was God and their redeemer was the Most High God. Ps 78:34–35

At other times, intercessors call for God's mercy even though his people as a whole may have been unrepentant. Job reflects this on a family level when he mediated for his children to the Lord (Job 1:5). Moses interceded for Israel in her worst moments and God spared all the people or only part of them, depending on the situation.[103] Nehemiah and Daniel asked for God's forgiveness of their compatriots, and we do not know whether Israel as a nation was repentant at the time.[104] Asaph and the "sons of Korah" pray for forgiveness on their nation's behalf.[105]

The Lord's feasts and sacrificial system provided the context where Israel could request and be granted forgiveness of their sin as a nation. Their national confession of sin and true repentance brought God's promise of grace, deliverances, and blessings. The whole burnt offering was offered daily by the priest, a sacrifice to reconcile God and Israel.[106] The Day of Atonement was the annual remission of Israel's sin as a nation.[107] On that day, a slaughtered goat was killed for Israel's sin, and a live goat was spared and released into the wilderness, carrying Israel's sin with it. Other sacrifices were required when a past national infraction of the Law was either not known or dealt with in a timely way, or when culpability could not be accurately placed on anyone in the community for lack of evidence.[108] Regardless of how diligent the nation and priests were in hosting the feasts, performing the ceremonies, and offering the sacrifices, mere formalities were not enough—it took the genuine heart of a humble nation to maximize the blessings and deliverances of the Lord.[109]

---

102. Num 21:7–9; Judg 3:7–9, 12–15; 4:1–3; 10:10–15; 1 Sam 12:9–11; 1 Kgs 8:30, 33–40, 46–53 // 2 Chr 6:24–31, 36–39; 2 Chr 7:13–14; Isa 64:8–9; Jer 3:13–15, 25; Ezek 16:62–63; 36:33; Hos 14:1–7; Joel 2:12–19

103. Ex 32:9–14; 34:6–9; Num 14:11–21; Deut 10:10

104. Neh 1:4–11; 9:17; Dan 9:3–19; also, Amos 7:1–7

105. Pss 79:8–9; 85:2–7

106. Lev 1:3–17; 6:8–13; 7:8; 8:18–21; 16:24;1 Chr 6:49

107. Lev 16:3–34; 23:27–32; Num 29:7–11

108. Lev 4:13–21; Num 15:22–26; Deut 21:6–9; 2 Chr 29:6, 20–24; 30:16–20

109. 1 Sam 22:22–23; 40:6–8; 51:16–17; Pss 40:6; 51:16–19; 69:30–31; 141:1–2; Prov 15:8; 16:6; 21:3, 27; Jer 7:2–24; Isa 1:10–17; 58:5–7; Hos 6:6; Amos 5:21–27; Mic 6:4–8

Eventually, the prophesied sacrifice of the Servant of God was a key part in a new phase in God's kingdom. Isaiah's prophecy of the Suffering Servant who would die for the sins "of us all" showed the length to which God would go to save his people.

> Each of us has turned to our own way; but the Lord has caused the iniquity of us all to fall on him. My Servant, will justify the many, since he will bear their sins . . . He emptied himself to death, yet was numbered with the sinners; yet he himself bore the sins of many, and interceded for those transgressors. Isa 53:6, 11–12[110]

This is the most basic and exciting provision of this promise to Israel—he would forgive the sins of Israel, the sins of the Messiah's newer kingdom, including the Gentiles, and he would usher all his believers sinless into New Earth.[111]

GOD DISCIPLINES HIS PEOPLE

Israel's role was to model the Lord's eternal design to the rest of the world. They were to be the international billboard of how God shepherds his shepherding creation. They were to be the blessed and delivered people who attributed all of their success and well-being to the only God in existence who is as gracious as he is wholly sovereign. Israel's example was to be the Lord's call to all peoples to submit to Israel's gracious God so they might experience the same blessings and deliverances planned for Israel.

Israel's persistent disobedience made them no less a sign, however. Unfortunately, they were too often a sign to the world of what happens to a society that turns against God and experiences his fair judgment. God's discipline was a substantial part of his sovereign rule over a fallen, rebellious Israel. But his discipline was a blessing in its effect on his wayward nation. By motivating Israel to righteousness, they were again eligible for all the blessings that were dependent on obedience. His discipline was redemptive by driving his people back to proper, moral management of their land and of their people; it directed them away from their deserved destruction.

Sins of Israel's Leaders

God's shepherding by blessing, delivering, and disciplining is also the standard for successful human management of this world demanded by the primary commission. However, the primary commission is a two-edged sword that can either bless or curse. Many Old Testament leaders blessed, even delivered Israel and other peoples. Yet human history is a continuous line of leaders who have not led with grace but have ruled by their own standard of shepherding. Israel's leaders were no exception since their unique and privileged call to shepherd the Lord's people made their failures

---

110. Also, Pss 85:2; 130:3–4, 7–8; Isa 1:18–20; 40:1–2; 44:22–23; Mic 7:18–19; Zech 3:3–5, 9
111. Isa 4:3–5; 27:9; Jer 31:31–37; 33:5–9; 36:3; 50:17–20

particularly disappointing: "The shepherds have sinned against me" (Jer 2:8). Kings, princes, priests, and prophets were all rebuked for their poor shepherding and for leading God's sheep to sin and disaster.[112]

The overwhelming volume of rebukes of Israel's leadership was against their religious apostasy. This was not merely a failure to keep all the ceremonial laws on a routine basis. Rather, Old Testament historians, poets, sages, and prophets were primarily concerned about the dangerous dualism that plagues every culture: faithfulness to empty religiosity but unfaithfulness to the daily, moral conduct from a genuine love, trust, and devotion to the Lord. One's ethics are determined not only by what one believes but, obviously, by what one does. Israel's leaders are reprimanded repeatedly for their disobedience to laws and wisdom outside of the ceremonial laws, proving their lack of love and commitment to the Lord.

Israel insisted on having a monarch and conforming to human models of shepherding. It was not God's wisdom that drove them to opt for kings who would eventually abuse their power. Further fault was found in their poor choices of those kings; for instance when the ten tribes appoint Jeroboam I to be their leader (1 Kgs 12:20). For rejecting God as the King, Israel suffered the typical excesses of a monarch, including unnecessary military drafts, daughters forced into labor, commandeering of private property, and undue taxes.[113] If a monarch felt entitled to extravagance, they were defying Deuteronomy 17:14–20, where the clear instructions were for the king to be humble, not self-indulgent. For example, David's sin of taking a census of his lands and people revealed his pride in quantifying his greatness. A census can also lead to increased taxes and more unnecessary draftees into the army.[114]

An Israelite king's distrust in God was shown by his over-sized military, indicated by the number of horses the king had.[115] Beyond trusting one's own army and resources, was the fruitless dependence on foreign alliances which the Lord considered a direct affront to his own loyalty to his people and to his all-sufficient power. In these agreements, Israel's kings shared their authority over territory and people with another lord. The result was intrusive, misleading, and unholy standards that made God only a third party at the governing table. These alternative alliances were forged with Egypt, Syria, and Assyria. South Israel was also guilty when they aligned themselves with the apostate North Israel after the nation's split.[116]

The audacious independence of Israel's kings was most obvious in their self-enacted laws that substituted for the absolute Mosaic laws: "Woe to those who decree false laws and write oppressive edicts" (Isa 10:1). Whole legal codes and subsequent

112. Jer 2:8; 5:31; 32:32; Hos 5:1; 7:3–5; Zeph 3:4

113. 1 Sam 8:11–17; 12:17–18; 1 Kgs 12:2–4

114. 2 Sam 24:2, 10–12, 15; 1 Chr 21:2, 9–14

115. Deut 17:16; Pss 20:7; 33:16–17; 44:3–8; 147:10; Prov 21:3; Isa 2:7; 31:1; Ezek 33:26; Hos 10:13; 14:3

116. 1 Kgs 15:16–19 // 2 Chr 16:1–3; 2 Kgs 8:18; 2 Chr 18:1–3; 20:35–37; Isa 30:1–5; 31:1; Ezek 16:24–29; Hos 7:11; 8:8–10; 12:1; 14:3

court decisions would be affected when Israel's kings instituted new religious ceremonies and absorbed pagan cultural norms with false ethical standards. In his clean break with Rehoboam and South Israel, Jeroboam I redefined worship in all its facets: idols, places to worship, shrines, non-Levitic priests, and new feasts.[117] The prophets who reminded and warned North Israel and her kings of the Lord's judgments against such rebellion were habitually ignored by the kings,[118] endangering the king and his people even to the point of death.[119]

Because of the iron fist of a despotic monarch, people are forced to obey even the most unreasonable and oppressive laws. Israel's kings were held personally responsible for misleading God's sheep into new cultural corruptions. This is explicit in the history of North Israel and her litany of leaders whom the Lord judged because of the sin of each king, sin "which he committed and with which he made Israel sin" (1 Kgs 14:16). This started in North Israel with Jeroboam I and continued throughout the reign of the renegade nation's nineteen kings.[120]

But some kings of South Israel were equally culpable; for example, Rehoboam (2 Chr 12:1). Partial commendation is given when there may have been a *personal* faith of this king, yet his weak leadership of the people did not deter *them* from following false religion on their own or under other powerful regional leaders.[121]

Priests and *prophets* were chided for their lack of shepherding priorities. Israel's priests were guilty of poor shepherding, of misleading the people with idolatry,[122] of not teaching the holy standards,[123] of personal greed,[124] and of abusive treatment of good people.[125] The prophets were also abusive of the people in undefined ways.[126] But the prophet's greatest sin, of course, was not speaking God's mind truly and directly to the people. Rather than presenting the Lord's messages, they conveyed their own messages or those they knew a king wanted to hear.[127] And they took these messages from the ominous and illegal, occultic sources of divination and sorcery.[128]

---

117. 1Kgs 12:26–33, 14:9–10; 2 Chr 11:15

118. 2 Chr 36:15–16; Jer 5:12–13; 7:25–26; 18:18; 20:7–10; 25:4; 26:4–6; 35:15; 43:1–4; Ezek 33:30–33; Dan 9:6, 9–10

119. 2 Chr 16:7, 10; Isa 30:10–11; Jer 26:7–15

120. 1 Kgs 15:26; 16:12–13; 21:22; 22:51–52; 2 Kgs 3:3; 10:31; 2 Chr 21:12–13; 28:19, 23; 2 Kgs 21:9 // 2 Chr 33:9

121. 2 Kgs 14:3–4; 15:3–4 // 2 Chr 26:16–18; 2 Kgs 15:34–35 // 2 Chr 27:2, 6

122. Jer 2:26–28; 8:1–2; Zeph 1:4

123. Ezek 22:26; Zeph 3:4; Mal 2:8

124. Jer 6:13; 8:10; Mic 3:11

125. Lam 4:13; Hos 6:9; 10:5, 13

126. Ezek 13:17–23; 22:25

127. Is 9:15; Jer 2:8; 5:31; 6:13–14; 14:14–15; 23:13–27; 27:14–22; 28:1–4,15; 32:31–35; Lam 2:14; Ezek 12:22–24; 13:1–23; 22:28; Zech 10:2

128. Isa 2:6; 44:24–25; Jer 14:14; 27:9; 29:8–9; Ezek 12:23–24; 13:6; 22:28; Hos 4:12; Mic 3:6; 5:12; Zech 10:2

There were sins of the leaders not attributed to any one leadership position but were applied generally across the board for all leaders. False religious practice, including idolatry was frequent.[129] Greed and unjust ways of amassing wealth,[130] often connected to judicial injustice was prevalent in some eras.[131] Violence, neglecting the well-being of the disadvantaged,[132] and abusing the common people frequently brought God's strong words and discipline for Israel.[133]

Sins of Israel's People

On the other hand, the people themselves were guilty too, regardless of poor leadership. Second Kings 17:22–23 rebukes Israel's perpetual preference to *follow* the poor leadership of a king like Jeroboam I; it eventually led to the discipline of exile: "The sons of Israel walked in all the sins of Jeroboam . . . until the Lord had them leave his sight." So there were no distinguishable moral differences between them and the previous peoples of Canaan (17:7–8). Isaiah describes Israel's sins and the broken relationship with the Lord they caused.

> Your sins have cut you off from God, so he has turned his head not to listen.
> For your hands are defiled with blood, your fingers with sin.
> Your lips speak falsehood and your tongue mutters injustice. Isa 59:2–3

Israel broke all God's legal instructions; for example, business policy, family standards, health precautions, judicial protocol, protections for the disadvantaged, principles of truthfulness, curbs on violence, and of course the ceremonial laws. They also did not follow the hundreds of other moral guides in their wisdom literature, like Proverbs.

A fundamental sin was the people's failure to fill all of the land God had given them. Because they did not subdue it thoroughly and did not fill it exclusively with Israelites, it was impossible for them to shepherd all rural and urban areas by God's moral principles. Even under the great Joshua, Israel failed to fill its land, settling for the hill countries especially, leaving important lands in the hands of their predecessors. This included the Mediterranean Sea's main commercial route for all Middle Eastern commerce.[134] The whole tribe of Dan even emigrated from its assigned land on the Mediterranean coast to the northern extremity of the Promised Land.[135] Since the people made themselves culturally irrelevant in these neglected regions from the

---

129. 1 Sam 7:3–4; 8:8; 12:10; Isa 41:27–29; Jer 2:8, 26–28; Hos 10:5
130. 1 Kgs 21:7–10, 16; Isa 1:23; 56:10–11; Jer 6:13; 8:10; 22:17; Ezek 22:27; 45:8–12; Amos 2:8; Mic 3:11; 7:3
131. Isa 3:14–15; 5:23; 29:21; Jer 21:12; 22:3; Lam 3:35–36; Ezek 22:12; Amos 5:10–12; Mic 3:11; 7:3
132. Isa 3:14–15; 32:7
133. Jer 6:13; 22:17; 32:35; Lam 4:13; Ezek 11:6; 22:6, 12, 27; Zeph 3:4; Zech. 11:4–5
134. Judg 1:19–36; 2:20–23
135. Judg 1:34; 18:1–2, 27–31

outset, it was fitting that God would eventually make them irrelevant to all of Canaan by exiling them to the lands of the Assyrians and Babylonians.

One of the believer's greatest sins is deficient thankfulness and praise to our gracious, delivering Lord. Anything beyond our basic survival is luxury since we do not deserve even that. Yet grumbling ingratitude, and rebellion against God was Israel's well-developed habit from its very beginnings[136] including the early example of the greedy and unthankful hoarding of the quail which God sent them during their wilderness wandering.[137]

Israel's citizens were greedy in the marketplace, often a place of scamming, extortion, and human resource abuses. Personal greed was rampant in many communities.[138] Stealing took different forms since a fallen heart is not satisfied with fair commerce and hard work.[139] Lands that God intended to stay in the hands of families for perpetuity were acquired illegitimately.[140] Rigged scales and other commercial measurements cheated one's fellow citizen.[141] Unjust loans which charged interest[142] and delaying payments for services rendered took advantage of the poor or common laborer.[143] Zedekiah had once enforced the freedom earned by indentured servants after six years, then the people forced these servants back into subservience the first chance they had (Jer 34:8–16).

Sexual sins were as widespread as in any godless society. Reuben's fornication with his father's concubine, Bilhah, is the first recording of uncontrolled lust in Israel's patriarchal history,[144] but it was followed by fornication and adultery throughout Israel's history after that.[145] The residents of Gibeah intended to rape the male Levite who was traveling with his adulterous concubine, but they decided to violate the concubine instead (Judg 19:2, 22–25). Samson had no trouble finding a prostitute, and Solomon tolerated prostitution in his reign.[146] False religions effectively marketed themselves by offering illicit sex to Israel's citizens by temple prostitution.[147]

Simeon, Levi, and their descendants were dishonored for their violent cruelty to beast and human (Gen 49:5–7). They foreshadowed Israel's future physical abuse of its

---

136. Num 16:1–3, 31–35, 41–49; 21:5–6; 26:9–10; Ps 106:16–18
137. Num 11:31–34; Pss 78:27–31; 106:13–15
138. Isa 57:17; Jer 5:26–27; 17:11; Ezek 18:18; 22:12; Amos 8:4–6
139. Jer 7:9; 21:12; Ezek 18:7; 22:25, 29; 33:15; Hos 4:2; 7:1; Mic 2:8; Mal 1:13
140. Isa 5:8; Ezek 45:8; Mic 2:2
141. Ezek 45:10–12; Hos 12:7; Amos 8:5; Mic 6:10–11
142. Ezek 22:12; Amos 2:8
143. Jer 22:13; Mal 3:5
144. Gen 49:3–4; 1 Chr 5:1
145. Jer 5:7–8; 7:9; Ezek 22:10; 33:26; Hos 4:2, 11–13; Mal 3:5
146. Judg 16:1; 1 Kgs 3:16–27
147. 1 Kgs 14:24; 15:12; 2 Kgs 23:7; Hos 4:14; Amos 2:7–8

own innocent citizens.[148] The disadvantaged were frequently unprotected from abuse. The poor and afflicted,[149] the widow and orphan,[150] and the alien[151] were victimized repeatedly in Israel's history. Those citizens with the least strength and resources were ill-treated the most by the courts and their decisions.[152]

Other sins for which Israel was judged nationally included a disregard for truth and honesty,[153] disrespect for parents,[154] and unhealthy practices of drunkenness,[155] eating forbidden meat,[156] and sex during menstruation.[157] False religion, idolatry, and sorcery punctuated Israel's unfaithfulness.[158] Not paying their tithes and breaking their solemn oaths were sins judged as well.[159] The dangers of intermarriage and the resulting personal and societal moral compromises from imported religious worldviews came early in Israel's history, including Solomon's reign.[160] Responsible shepherding that is in line with the eternal design and the primary commission becomes harder and harder to find as one continues through the Old Testament.

Types of Discipline on Israel

God's curses in Eden were a pattern for his future judgments against his people, Israel, and against the nations too: the Couple were conquered by Satan, oppressed and humiliated (Israel was conquered, oppressed, and humiliated); the Garden was cursed (Israel's land was cursed); Adam and Eve were driven from shelter and comfort (the Israelites were exiled too). The Lord's discipline of *his people* is always intended to be redemptive discipline not punitive (Deut 8:3–6). Even the Eden curses are intended to drive us toward God's grace and back into pursuing his eternal design. So, Israel's forty years of wandering was not merely punishment for refusing to advance on Canaan when the Lord told them to; it was gracious instruction on the blessings of obeying the Lord in the first place.[161]

---

148. Isa 5:7; 33:15; 59:3, 6–7; Jer 2:34; 7:6, 9; 19:4; 22:3; Ezek 22:4, 9, 12; 33:25; Hos 4:2; 12:1; Amos 3:10; Mic 3:2–3; 6:12; 7:2; Hab 1:3; Zech 11:5

149. Isa 32:6–7; 58:6–7, 10; Jer 2:34; Ezek 16:49; 18:7; 22:7, 29; Amos 2:6–7; 4:1; 5:11; 8:6

150. Ezek 22:7; Mic 2:9; Zech 7:10; Mal 3:5

151. Jer 7:6; 22:3; Ezek 22:7, 29; Zech 7:10; Mal 3:5

152. Isa 10:1–2; Jer 5:28; Amos 5:12

153. Isa 32:6–7; 33:15; 59:3–4; 13, 15; Jer 8:8; 9:3–5; Ezek 22:9; Hos 4:2; 7:1; Mic 6:12; Zeph 3:13

154. Ezek 22:7; Mic. 7:6

155. Isa 5:22; 28:1–3; 56:10–12; Hos 4:11; 7:14; Amos 4:1; Mic. 2:11

156. 1 Sam 14:32; Isa 65:4; 66:17

157. Ezek 18:6; 22:10

158. Num 25:1–9; Josh 24:20; Judg 2:17; 1 Kgs 11:33; Ps 106:28–31; Isa 8:19; 57:3; 65:4; Jer 27:9–10; Mic 5:12; Mal 3:5

159. Jer 5:2, 7; 7:9; Hos 4:2, 15; 10:4; Mal 3:5, 8–9; Zeph 1:5

160. Num 25:6–9, 14–15; Josh 23:12–13; 1 Kgs 11:1–8; Neh 13:23–28; Ps 106:28–31

161. Num 14:22–23, 28–35; 26:63–65; Deut 1:34–36; Josh 5:6; Pss 95:8–11; 106:24–27

God had warned in general terms what would come of Israel's disobedience:

> In that day, my anger will be embroiled against them . . . and they will be devoured by the many evils and troubles that come at them. Deut 31:17

And he was also quite specific in what that discipline would be. In one passage alone he promised, plagues, illness, depopulation, exile, fear, despair, and humiliation (Deut 28:58–68).

The primary commission set the standard for freedom and responsibility for all humanity, including Israel, by assigning the responsibility to multiply, fill, and subdue the land. The Couple gave up that freedom by submitting rather than subduing. The Snake which was to be subdued became the subduer of the Couple by their submission to their own lust for taste and knowledge. An inversion of power comes when those commissioned to rule are instead ruled by those whom they were intended to rule. It was true in Eden, and it came true for Israel and her citizens.

The Lord warned Israel that they would be invaded and conquered because of their distrust and disobedience, and it did not take long for it to happen after the partial conquest of Canaan. Rather than thoroughly subduing and ruling their own land and affairs, Israel's Canaanite enemies became their subduers who restricted their freedom and well-being. So, Israel's subjugation came from within and outside their borders. From within, the Canaanites who were not fully driven out during Joshua's conquest became God's means of discipline for Israel.[162] The Philistines were the most persistent nemesis from within.[163] From without, before the massive and devastating invasions of Assyria and Babylon, other peoples invaded, ruled, and oppressed Israel. Powers from Mesopotamia, Moab, Midian, Ammon, Syria, Edom, and Egypt each came at least once to harass if not defeat and conquer God's people.[164] Egypt's Pharaoh imprisoned South Israel's Jehoahaz until the king died in Egypt (2 Kgs 23:33–35).

This inverted reign was predicted before the Israelites even set foot in Canaan: "You will be struck down by your enemies, and those who hate you will *rule over you*" (Lev 26:17). Isaiah lamented that it finally happened that way, "O Lord our God, other lords than you have *ruled over us*" (Isa 26:13). Habakkuk alluded to the primary commission when he mentions foreign rule over Israel because Israel had no faithful leader: "Why have you made us like the fish of the sea and crawling things that have no *ruler*?" (Hab 1:14).

The world was to watch how the supreme Shepherd shepherded his people who would then shepherd like him. The world was supposed to see how this wonderful, joyous, productive, partnership was a pilot for the universal and eternal godly

---

162. Lev 26:25, 32–33; Num 33:55–56; Deut 28:25–26, 29–33, 47–52; Judg 2:14–15, 21–23; 3:1–4; 4:2; Neh 9:26–30; Pss 78:58–64; 89:40–46; 106:40–43

163. Judg 13:1; 2 Chr 21:16–17; 28:18–19

164. Judg 3:8; 3:12–14; 6:1–6; 1 Kgs 11:14, 25, 31–33; 1Kgs 14:22–26 // 2 Chr 12:1, 5–6, 9; 2 Kgs 10:32–33; 24:1–2; 2 Chr 24:23–24; 28:5–6, 17

shepherding of humanity over all the earth. Instead, since the Israelites polluted the land with immorality and cavorted with other religions and idols, Israel revealed a contradictory picture of that partnership. Israel had to go, literally. So, finally both South and North Israel were not only conquered but were marched into exile into their conquering empire's land: North Israel into the Assyrian empire,[165] South Israel into the Babylonian empire.[166] This was prophesied very specifically, more than simply threatened in books of the Law.[167]

The Lord also uses nature for his shepherding objective to discipline: "God summons the skies above and the earth to judge his people" (Ps 50:4). We have noted God's discipline of humanity through geological, biological, and meteorological disasters, and we see the same actions against Israel. The curse of the ground in Eden to produce stubbornly and inefficiently was a part of the curse which humanity experiences in all eras and areas. For Israel, God would make it even more difficult to profit from the soil if they did not remain loving and faithful: "You will exert your strength uselessly since your land will not produce and your trees will not bear fruit."[168] This is a specific fulfillment of God's curse on the land in Genesis 3.

Other disciplinary acts of God included making domesticated animals as barren as the land (Deut 28:18). God's discipline could come by a devastating fire at the outskirts of a town (Num 11:1–3) or by a maritime disaster that mysteriously destroyed Jehoshaphat's ships (2 Chr 20:35–37). The Lord of nature and health also reserved the right to send diseases to discipline Israel, including human barrenness.[169]

God's discipline of Israel society came on a routine basis through the legal judgments prescribed by Israel's Law. The Law assumed that "the evil will bow before good judges and the wicked will bow in the courts of the righteous" (Prov 14:19). Otherwise, an unjust court *system* would inflict heavy judgments on the innocent, the poor, the weak or any who could not defend themselves against the deep pockets and schemes of the rich and powerful (Ex 23:6–8). Old Testament sentences were not supposed to prefer the rich over the poor or vice versa, placing everyone on the same legal level where divine law and truth prevailed, not privilege nor sentimentality. If witnesses were called to testify, the truth was to be obtained from more than one witness. And if the witness lied, the witness would suffer the penalty the accused would have suffered had the perjury been believed (Deut 19:15–21).

---

165. 1 Kgs 14:15–16; 2 Kgs 17:5–23; 1 Chr 5:25–26

166. 2 Kgs 17:19; 20:16–18; 23:26–27; 24:12–16, 20; 25:1–7, 11, 21; 2 Chr 28:19–21; 33:10–12; 36:6–7, 15–21; Ezra 5:12; 9:7; Ezek 36:17–19

167. Lev 18:26–28; 20:22; 26:25, 32–33; Num 33:55–56; Deut 4:25–27; 28:32, 37, 41, 64–65; 29:25–28; Josh 23:12–16; 1 Kgs 8:33–34, 46–48; 9:6–7; 14:15–16; 2 Chr 7:19–20; Ezek 36:17–19

168. Lev 26:20; also, Lev 26:26, 32; Deut 11:16–17; 28:17–18, 21, 24, 38–42; 29:22; 32:24; 1 Kgs 8:35–39

169. Ex 23:24–26; Lev 26:16; Deut 28:22, 27–28, 35, 58–62; 29:22; 2 Sam 24:15, 25; 2 Kgs 6:18–20; 2 Chr 21:12–15, 19

Judges, elders, priests, and kings were given some discretion in the application of the laws and their sentences. Fines and restitution might be considered the mildest of sentences. A fine was assessed for causing a premature birth during a brawl. An inattentive owner of a frequently injurious, violent animal was offered a fine as an alternative to his own execution.[170] When sacrifices were part of a legal sentence, they essentially became fines as well. The sacrificial meats or grains left with the priests were for their subsistence, and for all intents and purposes were "court fees."

Restitution was required at the monetary level of lost income for a victim now unable to work. For instance, the offender paid for any injuries from brawling, or for a death from one's violent domesticated animal (Ex 21:18–19, 32). Restitution came in the release of a servant's debt if the owner's abuse led to a servant's lost body part or a loss of its use (Ex 21:26–27). When one was responsible for the death of another's animal, he needed to pay for the lost animal. Restitution for losing someone else's property was also expected. Outright stealing of another's animals or property was subject to restitution of up to five times the value.[171] Indentured servitude was a form of restitution when one's debt was too much to pay, including when the debt was due because the debtor had actually stolen the other's property.[172]

Physical punishments would come in the form of public beating or amputation.[173] References to this punishment are sparse in the Mosaic law, but warnings about it are found in the wisdom instructions. The blows were not to exceed forty, saving the guilty one's life and dignity.[174] Admittedly this punishment was severe, but even in this shepherding act of public discipline, the image of God was not to be disrespected by humiliating the scourged and their families (Deut 25:1–3).

Apparently, because of its severity as the ultimate punishment, execution was prescribed in much more depth and breadth than were fines, restitution, and physical punishments. Execution was designed to be fair in its application as well as a deterrent to strong violence (Deut 17:12–13). Execution was by stoning, primarily, followed by burial or in some instances, cremation of the body or hanging it on a tree before burial.[175] There were only two cases when the guilty were to be burned, but it is not clear if burning was the means of death or the subsequent disposal of the body.[176] Punishment of families or communities was by mass execution by the sword (Deut 13:12–15). Murder, rape, perpetual disobedience to parents, kidnapping, child sacrifice, and fornication of all sorts, adultery, incest, homosexuality, bestiality, prostitution, including

---

170. Ex 21:22, 29–32
171. Ex 22:1–5; Lev 6:2–5; Prov 6:31
172. Ex 22:1–4; 2 Kgs 4:1; Neh 5:5
173. Ex 21:22–25; Lev 24:19–20; Deut 19:21
174. Deut 25:3; Prov 10:13; 14:3; 19:25–26, 29; 20:30; 21:11; 26:3
175. Deut 21:22–23; Josh 7:25
176. Lev 20:14; 21:9

temple prostitution, were all capital crimes. Death was the ultimate judgment for these extreme sins:[177]

> The one who wanders away from understanding will rest together with the dead. Prov 21:16

> The waywardness of the simple will kill them. Prov 1:32

Death sentences came to those who committed certain crimes. But the Lord's judgment of death also comes as the natural consequence of dangerous living. Fatal results from drunkenness or associating with violent fools should not have come as a surprise. Disobedience to certain Mosaic health laws endangered the individual with infections of all sorts.

On the other hand, the older testament records many cases when the Lord's immediate judgment comes without trial or without waiting for sin's natural and destructive consequences to take effect. God's discipline is always perfect, though it can be perplexing in its apparent disproportionality to the crime. However, since any sin deserves death in God's pristine moral order, anything less than a death sentence is grace. So, if at times God does what is purely just, rather than gracious, there can be no wise questioning of his strong reaction to what might appear to be even a small offense. The Lord killed Er and Onan himself for their wickedness, and he killed a prophet for his disobedience.[178] Uzzah's seemingly alert attempt to stabilize the Ark of the Covenant ended in his summary execution directly by the Lord.[179] God was behind the fatal judgments of forty-two young people who were killed by bears for mocking Elisha (2 Kgs 2:23–24). Eli's thieving sons, Hophni and Phinehas, eventually died in an unrelated massacre.[180]

On a national level, the ultimate judgment of *death* was unfortunately a recurrent tragedy for significant numbers of Israel's population by military, medical, or seemingly random means. The defeat at the hands of Israel's military foes implied death for its soldiers, of course, but it also implied rapacious invasions with violent pillaging, looting, and the massacre of women and children. If Israel was not fair with her resident aliens, they were warned that they would be killed themselves by invading swords (Ex 22:21–24). Grumbling, disobedience, and idolatry brought plagues that killed tens of thousands of Israelites at one time.[181] An earth fissure and fire killed many others who questioned the authority of God's commissioned shepherds, Moses and Aaron.[182]

As I have explained before, this severity of God's judgment could be seen as unfair and disproportionate, involving so many "innocent" victims of God's anger.

---

177. Ps 34:21; Prov 10:21, 25, 27; 11:19; 12:7; 13:9; 15:24; 16:25; 24:19–20

178. Gen 38:6–10; 1 Chr 2:3; 1 Kgs 13:24–26

179. 2 Sam 6:6–7 // 1 Chr 13:9–10

180. 1 Sam 2:31–34; 3:12–14

181. Num 11:31–34; 14:36–37; 16:41–49; 21:5–6; 25:6–9, 14–15; 2 Sam 24:2, 10–12, 15; 1 Chr 21:2, 9–14; Pss 78:27–31; 106:13–15, 28–31

182. Num 16:1–3, 31–35; 26:9–10; Deut 11:3, 6; Ps 106:16–18

It is hard to reason with this position since it stems from a simplistic, even idolatrous view of God that carves an image of him as one who must always be gracious, without exception. But simply put, any moment of life is grace, not justice. No one deserves to be alive. Any moment that grace is suspended or life is ended can be seen as God's perfect justice. Our study speaks of God's grace throughout. It is the evidence of God's wonderful tolerance and patience with humanity, his believing community, and the believer. But, as we have said, we cannot use his grace as a law against him, a law which commands him to always be gracious. And when he is not gracious, and he is just instead, some dismiss that as an Old Testament teaching, as if God somehow became more sanctified sometime between the books of Malachi and Mathew. I have a one-word answer for those who make this insipid divide between the Testaments—Armageddon.

GOD DISCIPLINES THE CHURCH

Jesus Christ echoed the Old Testament evaluation of Israel and its leaders. Nothing had changed by his time; no moral improvements evolved between Malachi and Matthew. Jeremiah had said, "The shepherds have sinned against me" and "Shepherds scattered the flock and destroyed them."[183] Christ picked up on these words with those of his own: "Whoever does not gather with me, scatters" (Matt 12:30). He says Israel's leaders were "the blind leading the blind" (Matt 15:13–14). So when Christ had breakfast with his disciples on the beach, he makes sure that the disciples understood that loving him meant shepherding his sheep: "Do you love me? . . . Then tend my *lambs*" (John 21:16).

Christ's rebuke of the religious leaders was straight out of the Old Testament. Quoting from Isaiah 29:13, he reminded the leaders that they had fulfilled the prophecy:

> Isaiah was right when he prophesied about you hypocrites, "These people honor me with their lips, but their hearts are far from me. They worship me in vain; their teachings are merely human rules." . . . You are experts at setting aside the commandment of God in order to keep your tradition."[184]

The Lord announced a number of his own woes against the leaders: for their lack of humility but no lack of showiness;[185] dishonoring their parents;[186] for their abuse of widows and robbery;[187] for physical violence and killing.[188] Herod martyred John the Baptist for his righteous rebuke of the king's incestuous marriage (Mark 6:17–19).

---

183. Jer 2:8; 23:1
184. Mark 7:6–7, 9 // Matt 15:3, 6–9
185. Matt 6:1–8, 16–18; Matt 23:5–8 // Mark 12:38–39
186. Matt 15:4–6 // Mark 7:10–13; Matt 23:14 // Mark 12:40
187. Mark 12:38–40 // Luke 20:46–47
188. Matt 23:34; John 8:3–7

Paul blamed the religious leadership for Christ's death and for obstructing the Word's spread to the Gentiles (1 Thess 2:14-15).

God's discipline of Israel included continued subjugation under the mighty tyranny of Rome. After the Crucifixion, Israel's history became only more tragic under Rome. Jerusalem, Capernaum, Chorazin and Bethsaida and many other cities would be judged violently for rejecting Christ.[189] But the ultimate judgment on Israel was that their kingdom would be given to another "people"[190] and that Gentile nations will someday condemn Israel. The Gentiles from Nineveh and Sheba would be the credible witnesses at the final judgment against Israel for her unbelief.[191]

When it comes to judging the church at large, the New Testament has little to say. The church was so young that patterns were hard to find to compare with the hundreds of years of Old Testament Israel's sin. Instead, the church leaders were encouraged to be shepherds unlike Israel's uncaring shepherds. Paul and Peter encouraged them to be humble servants and tenacious protectors of the sheep.

> *Shepherd* God's *flock* among you, overseeing them willingly . . . not for dishonest gain, but eagerly; not domineering them, but as examples to the *flock*. So when the chief *Shepherd* appears, you will receive the crown of glory that never fades. 1 Pet 5:2-4

> Keep watch over yourselves and all the *flock* . . . Be *shepherds* of the church of God; . . . savage wolves will come in among you and will not spare the *flock*. Acts 20:28-29

But there were leaders like Diotrephes, who was self-centered, domineering, and taught his own man-made gospel (3 John 9-10). False teaching accompanied by greedy motives of the teachers endangered the believers in the Old and New Testaments. But today, just as prevalently, believers should heed a common warning in the New Testament against false teachers and their deceptive manipulation of the truth.[192]

Peter says that God's discipline starts with the household of God.[193] This is because the Lord loves his Bride and wants to see her in all her depth and beauty. So the seven letters to the churches in Revelation reveal some problems and the Lord's assessments and threats against them (Rev 2:1—3:22). The interpretation of these letters is difficult, but they show nonetheless that God holds his church accountable and reserves the right to discipline them just as he blesses them and delivers them from their trials and dangers.

---

189. Luke 13:34-35 // Matt 23:37-38; 19:41-44; Luke 10:13-15 // Matt 11:20-24

190. Matt 21:39-43 // Mark 12:8-11 // Luke 20:15-18

191. Matt 12:41-45 // Luke 11:29-32

192. Acts 20:28-30; Rom 16:17-18; 2 Cor 11:3-4, 12-13; Eph 4:14; 5:6; Phil 3:2-3; Col 2:8, 16-23; 1 Tim 1:3-7; 4:1-3, 7; 6:3-5, 20-21; 2 Tim 2:15-18; 3:6-9, 13; 4:3-4; Titus 1:9-16; 2 Pet 2:1-3; 3:3-4, 14-17; 1 John 2:21-26; 4:1-5; 2 John 7-11; 3 John 9-10; Jude 4, 8-13, 16-19; Rev 2:2, 14-15, 20; 22:18-19

193. 1 Pet 4:17; also Paul: 1 Cor 5:5; 1 Tim 1:20

10

Shepherding the Believer

GOD SHEPHERDS US

GOD'S GRANDEUR AS KING of the entire universe, king of this planet, king of the human race, and king of his people, magnifies the wonder that he is also *my* king, *my* shepherding Lord of *my* life! The Old Testament patriarchs, judges, monarchs, poets, prophets, barren maidens, and unnamed heroes, all counted on the Lord's shepherding care of each of them, personally. All who are loyal to the king of the universe enjoy their personal assurance of his deliverance, forgiveness, and loving discipline. Melchizedek, David, Solomon, Asaph, and the sons of Korah all recognized the kingship of the Lord over each individual believer's life.[1]

Working with our king in his eternal design is our greatest honor and pleasure. To be trusted to act on his behalf as his commissioner in each of our parts of his realm is an exciting assignment with all the power of the Holy Spirit to accomplish it. To be given so many gifts and guides for success in the primary commission is relieving since I do not need to pursue it ill-equipped and alone. To be shepherded by his wonderful ways is an encouraging model that empowers me to shepherd others. His blessings, deliverance, and discipline define our relationship with him as we walk through his kingdom with him at our side.

Of course, there is a personal, royal relationship between the Lord and those who do not trust him as believers too. The Lord has a ruling relationship with each and every inhabitant of the earth. He is the king of every people and every person regardless of their belief. No one elects God king of their life or makes him king. But the Lord does not just hold the *position* as king, he acts as the king. He has been involved in the life of every lost individual from ages past and from distant lands. God is no less aware of the life circumstances and moral actions of any lost soul than he is of the believer's life circumstances and moral actions. Their alleged "independent" decisions have

---

1. Gen 14:17–20; Pss 5:2; 44.4; 68:24; 74:12; 84:3; Eccl 12:1

always and have already been included in the Lord's universal sovereign rule.[2] Each person and each of their acts are known by him, and they will be revealed and judged by him (Eccl 12:14). Though God's daily relationship with those who are undelivered from sin is nearly completely unknown and unappreciated, no one has lived who has not received God's attention and response.

Christians are not the only people whom God shepherds. We discussed this in chapter 8 in reference to all humanity, but we repeat it here while focusing on the individual person. The Lord's blessings are experienced by unregenerate societies, and each individual within any community or nation benefits from that common grace we spoke of in chapter 8. Though God's blessings to the peoples are not nearly as extravagant as they are to his believing communities, still, individuals around the world enjoy the goodness of creation.

Most people enjoy their caring and shepherding relationships with their family, friends, and strangers. God's image is present in the unrepentant heart and conscience and regularly overwhelms that heart's moral depravity so that life is at least bearable for most individuals. This is not to say that the individual is *godly* in one's priorities, morality and relationships with others. That would require one to act morally in a loving response to the Trinity, empowered by the Holy Spirit. However, there are activities, attitudes and successes that express the Trinity's indwelling image even if done to please oneself. An unbeliever's kindness and mercy to others is ultimately unacceptable for eternal salvation—yes, it benefits others, but any goodness is far less valuable if not motivated to please the loving Savior and King.

GOD BLESSES THE BELIEVER

Jacob speaks for all believers when he identifies God as the one "who has been my *shepherd* my whole life." And he prays for the same shepherding blessing to be experienced by his two grandsons, Ephraim and Manasseh (Gen 48:15–16). God had promised his shepherding care would be with Jacob always, "I am with you and will keep you wherever you go" (Gen 28:15). In Psalm 23, David echoes Jacob's appreciation for God's shepherding relationship regardless of time, place, or impending circumstances:

> The Lord is my shepherd . . .
> Though I walk through the valley of death's shadow I fear no evil because you are with me. . . .
> Goodness, love and kindness will follow me my whole life. Ps 23:1, 4, 6

The Shepherd's blessings to believers will come from various directions. Blessings come from God to us through the conduct of others, through their loyalty and generous attention to us and our needs. For instance, loyalty from friends, brother, or

---

2. Prov 16:9; 19:21; 20:24

spouse, and the obedience of our children honor us.[3] The Lord blessed Old Testament individuals while they lived in a holy Israelite community where any gift from God's to the community also benefitted the individual. During the Golden Age of David and Solomon, it is said that everyone was eating, drinking, rejoicing, and living in safety under his vine and fig tree (1 Kgs 4:25). But the reverse was also true—Israel's strength, stability, and peace depended on its individual citizens' obedience to the Mosaic laws and wisdom instructions. Of course, the individual believer was also blessed because of personal faith and obedience to God's instructions.

God's blessings come to us as wisdom, kindness, joy, honor, security, long life, prosperity, success, others' assets, and gifts and fruits of the Spirit. We will look at each of these briefly now.

Wisdom is a blessing that comes from meditating on and following God's instructions. Revering God as our personal king is the basis for all of our wisdom and righteousness.[4] Innumerable other blessings from one's Shepherd followed when an Israelite obeyed the laws of the conscience, the Mosaic law, and the wisdom instructions.

> The Lord God is a sun and shield, giving grace and honor;
> He keeps nothing good from those who do what is right.
> O Lord of hosts, truly blessed is the one who trusts in you. Ps 84:11–12

For instance, the Old Testament teaches that our *kindness* to others will bring their *kindness* back to us and will even bring kindness from others, including from our Lord, who have noticed our kindness.[5] Puah and Shiphrah were rewarded by God for showing kindness to unborn children and their mothers (Ex 1:15–21). Naomi prayed that God would bless Ruth and Orpah with kindness in return for their kindness to her. And Boaz blessed Ruth for serving Naomi. He welcomed her to his field and comforted Ruth by providing for her and Naomi's needs. Boaz respected the women by applying God's compassionate Mosaic laws for the poor. The great-grandson of Boaz, David, told Solomon to bless the children of those who were kind and had served David in crisis (1 Kgs 2:7).[6]

God's blessings to us also includes *joy* in our lives: "Who can have food and enjoyment without God?" (Eccl 2:25).[7] He blesses us with joy regardless of the tragedies that will come in life, since our personal joy does not come only from circumstances *around* us but more profoundly from the wisdom and righteousness that go out *from* us. Our delight is to do God's will, to pursue his wisdom and to act wisely.[8] Joy comes

---

3. Prov 10:1; 12:4; 17:17; 18:24; 31:23; Eccl 4:9–12
4. Job 28:28; Ps 111:10; Prov 9:10
5. Deut 24:19; Prov 3:3; 14:22; 24:11–12
6. Ruth 1:8–9; 2:8–13
7. Prov 17:22; Eccl 2:26; 3:22; 5:18–20; 8:15; 9:7–8
8. Ps 97:11–12; Prov 3:18; 10:28; 29:18; Eccl 3:12–13

from love and kindness of every sort, and from protecting the truth, peace, and justice.[9] Joy also comes through the blessings of a marriage where wisdom prevails.[10]

The righteous are blessed with *honor* for their wisdom and the successes that come from it. There are many reasons to honor the righteous. However, it is not the isolated righteous acts that bring great honor; one's reputation is staked on habitual goodness from a mature moral character.[11] Just a few reasons for honoring an Old Testament believer included humility,[12] kindness,[13] and being teachable.[14] Diligence and wisdom can lead to further honor when one is promoted to leadership.[15] This blessing of promotion in one's level of responsibility is seen in the lives of Joseph, Nehemiah, and Daniel.[16]

There are few desires that are more important to most people than *security*, whether physical, financial, emotional, spiritual or otherwise. God promises family security for those who are obedient to his commandments and wisdom.[17] Security will come from the stability of the faithful person who avoids stumbling in life.[18] Rest and peace are God's promises to his often anxious sheep.[19]

The blessing of a *longer life* is given to most who pursue godliness and wisdom.[20] Those believers who die too young are already living that longer, eternal life. Nonetheless, a high value is placed throughout the Old Testament on living long in this life—living long in the land as a nation to fill and subdue it, as well as living long personally to care for others. The message of the older testament is that even if a wicked person might live long, the righteous person's days are lengthened according to God's perfect discretion. One obvious reason for the lengthier days is the physical health and strength of the believer.[21] Physical and mental health would come from following the biblical health laws that included paths to emotional and spiritual health. The ultimate extension of life, however, is the everlasting life that the Old Testament promises for the believer who will live eternally in New Earth.[22]

9. Prov 12:20; 14:21; 21:15; 24:25; 29:2

10. Prov 5:15–19; 12:4; 31:11–12, 28–29; Eccl 9:9

11. Prov 3:35; 4:8–9; 10:7; 12:8; 16:31; 20:11; 21:21; 22:29; 31:26–29; Eccl 7:1

12. Prov 15:33; 18:12; 22:4; 29:23

13. Prov 11:16; 19:11; 31:20, 26, 28–29

14. Prov 13:18; 15:31–33

15. Prov 12:24; 17:2; Dan 2:48; 5:29

16. Prov 14:35; 16:13–15; 19:12; 22:11; Gen 39:2, 21; 41:39–43; Neh 1:11; 2:8; Dan 1:9

17. Prov 1:33; 2:8, 11; 3:23–26; 4:6; 10:9; 11:8–9, 21; 12:7; 13:6; 14:26; 15:25; 16:6; 18:10–11; 19:23

18. Pss 1:1–3; 112:6–8; Prov 3:23; 10:29–30; 12:3; 24:16

19. Ps 23:2–3; Prov 3:1–2, 17, 24; 16:7

20. Ps 92:12–14; Prov 3:1–2, 16; 4:10; 9:11; 10:2, 27; 11:4, 19; 12:28; 13:3; 14:27; 15:27; 16:17; 19:16, 23; 20:29; 28:16; Eccl 7:12

21. Ps 103:3–5; Prov 3:7–8; 4:22; 14:30; 17:22

22. Job 19:26–27; Pss 22:26; 41:12; 61:4–8; 70:20; 73:26; 75:9–10; 115:17–18; 145:1–2; Prov 10:25; 12:19; 14:32; 15:24; 21:28; Isa 25:8; 26:19; Dan 12:2, 13

Generally, God blesses the believer with *prosperity* if one routinely applies his laws and wisdom in one's life.[23] The two primary reasons for God's blessing of prosperity is one's diligence[24] and one's generous blessing of others.[25] So God's goodness blesses and rewards the faithful with prosperity.[26] It is not ungodly to seek financial security when one's material prosperity is from God. It is critical that this word "prosperity" is not misunderstood to mean opulent wealth or an end in itself.[27] The word simply means having more than enough, including adequate food.[28] Neither should the term "prosperity" be relentlessly and inappropriately spiritualized whenever it is read in the Old Testament. God's Word and his will are disrespected when interpretations of passages about God's physical blessings are forced to speak of spiritual riches. We need to be very careful not to make passages that God has clearly inspired to pertain to his physical blessings into passages that allegedly have "deeper spiritual meanings" and essentially tell God what he should have said. It obscures what is already a profound truth by our own imaginative and unnecessary embellishments. In other words, the following text should be interpreted literally, about architecture and furnishings:

> Wisdom builds a house and it is established by understanding.
>
> Knowledge fills its rooms with precious and good riches. Prov 24:3–4

Success is another blessing for those humble enough to follow God's wise instructions since "the advantage to one's wisdom is success."[29] The Lord was praised by servants, psalmists, and sages throughout the Old Testament for his personal guidance to success.[30] But a strong believer will accept the fact that success may be deferred or even withheld by unfair authorities. The wise are warned, "There is not always food for the wise, riches to the discerning, or favor to the knowledgeable" (Ecc 3:11).[31] For example, the jealousy or lies of others can keep the deserving from receiving success and acclamation.

Another source of blessing could be *another person's assets* which the Lord transfers to the believer. The Bible teaches that in God's wisdom and timing, the righteous may garner the assets of the wicked; the Lord transfers the possessions of the wicked to the righteous. The wisdom literature encourages the believer to persist in their righteousness because what belongs to another could become theirs: "The sinner's estate

---

23. Job 1:10; Pss 23:1; Prov 13:21; 14:11; 15:6; 21:20; 22:4; 28:25
24. Prov 6:6–8; 10:4–5; 13:11; 14:23–24; 27:23–27; 28:19
25. Prov 3:9–10; 11:25–26; 28:27
26. Gen 14:21–24; Deut 8:17; Ps 127:1–2; Prov 10:22
27. Prov 23:4–5; 28:20; 30:8–9
28. Prov 10:3; 12:11–12; 13:2, 25; 15:16–17; 16:8, 26; 18:20; 20:13; 28:27
29. Eccl 10:10; also, Prov 4:12, 26; 10:24; 11:5; 20:28; 21:29; Eccl 2:9–10
30. Gen 24:26–27; 39:2, 21; Pss 16:7; 18:28 (2 Sam 22:29); 23:2–4; 119:105; Prov 19:21
31. Job 7:19–21; 9:20–24

passes to the godly" (Prov 13:22).³² To covet other's assets is sin but to receive them is to acknowledge God's grace.

The *gifts of the Spirit* for Old Testament believers were as diverse as in the New Testament. The Holy Spirit was *in* the believer, not just on the believer, for leadership ability: for example, it is said that Joshua was "a man who has the Spirit *in* him" (Num 27:18). Judges says that the Spirit "clothed himself with Gideon"; in other words, the Spirit inside Gideon wore the military leader as a garment—he was *in* Gideon (6:34). The Holy Spirit comes "to" or "into" David, and an evil spirit. The Spirit indwelt the tabernacle artisans; they had the Spirit *in* them because they were "filled with the Spirit of God" and were given wisdom to be creative and skilled.³³ Peter tells us plainly that the Holy Spirit was *in* the Old Testament prophets when they prophesied about the Messiah (1 Pet 1:10–11). So Micah says he was *filled* with the Spirit—indwelt for power and courage (Mic 3:8).

The *fruit of the Spirit* listed concisely in Galatians 6:22–23 also came from the indwelling Spirit to Old Testament believers: love, joy, peace, patience, kindness, goodness, faithfulness, gentleness, and self-control. The Spirit's presence within the believer empowered the faithful person's obedience. David did not want to lose the Lord's creative power through the Spirit which purified and fortified his heart. He was fully aware that the absence of the Spirit meant he would not have a genuine love for the Lord and his righteousness.

> O God, create a pure heart in me, and renew a steadfast spirit in me.
>
> Do not cast me away from you or take your Holy Spirit away from me. Ps 51:10–11

But this Spiritual relationship was not only experienced by kings and prophets. In our last two chapters of this book, the Lord's ethical instructions on how to shepherd will rest on these fruits of the Spirit. Only by the recreating power of the Holy Spirit can one do what is right out of a pure heart for the Lord. New Testament believers were told that they could not please God without becoming a new creation, purified for righteousness. The same held true for Old Testament believers.

CHRIST AND THE BELIEVER'S BLESSINGS

Jesus Christ's good news about God's pervasive shepherding care was highly personal since he himself was God, the Good Shepherd of the individual believer. Christ spoke at some length about his shepherding in John 10:1–30. Like the Old Testament prophets, Christ distinguished between godly shepherding and selfish shepherding in these verses. The evil shepherds are lax and when they do make any effort, it is for their benefit alone. As the Good Shepherd of each sheep, his very voice encourages their trust (4, 14–16, 27); he leads them wisely to places of peace, nourishment, and blessing (9);

---
32. Also, Job 27:16–17; Prov 28:8; Eccl 2:26
33. Ex 31:3; 35:31

he gives them an abundant life (10, 28) and delivers them from evil (27–29). Psalm 23 is certainly his reference point for these reassurances.

Christ encourages us by pointing to his Father as the Father of the believer too. His exemplary prayer instructs us to pray, "Our Father . . . " This Fatherly role is the basis for the "family" identity in the New Testament which became a substitute for the earlier national identity for the Old Testament Israelites. The common identity for God's followers in both Testaments is as members of his kingdom, but the concept of "family" also became prevalent in the New. The Father fathered Jesus, his Son, through the Holy Spirit's conception in Mary. So Christ, as human, then becomes our "brother." And Christ's brothers and sisters are our brothers and sisters.[34] There are also spiritual "children" as Paul calls his converts, Timothy and Onesimus.[35]

This family theme would be expected from the God who tells us to "multiply" as he has multiplied. The Lord has multiplied himself by lodging his image within all humanity in all eras and areas. Additionally, he is our Father since we are his adopted spiritual children. But the infinite separation of the Divine Son and human sons must be understood since, though we are sons and daughters, loved by an infinite God, we are *adopted* children.[36] Though adopted, we are still blessed by receiving the inheritance that the divine and true Son inherits.[37] That inheritance is not only eternal life[38] but an eternal kingdom[39] and an eternal life of shepherding and ruling.[40]

An over-arching promise for the believer is that God works all things together for good for those who are called by him and who love him (Rom 8:28). Notice how active and pervasively God is involved. It is *God himself* who works, and he works *everything* to our favor. Our Shepherd has no limitations to his blessings. If we ask wisely, our requests will be granted in God's way and in his time.[41] God feeds us with regular food (Matt 6:11). Jesus even cares enough to cook breakfast for his disciples before he tells them to care for his sheep (John 21:13).

These encouragements are possible because God is with the believer, always. He is not a distant absentee landlord as the unbeliever prefers him to be. Matthew begins and ends his Gospel by assuring us that Jesus is with us.[42] The Spirit also abided with the apostles (John 14:17) and surely does with us. The Spirit has always lived within the believer who is the temple for him (1 Cor 6:19). The Spirit is Immanuel (meaning "God with us") too because of his intimate and powerful indwelling of each believer.

34. Matt 12:48–50 // Mark 3:33–35 // Luke 8:19–21
35. 1 Tim 1:18; 2 Tim 1:2; 2:1; Philem 1:10
36. Rom 8:15, 23; 9:4; Gal 4:5; Eph 1:5
37. Matt 5:5; Acts 20:32; 26:18; Rom 8:16–17; Eph 1:11, 14, 18; 5:5
38. Matt 19:16; Mark 10:17; Luke 10:25; 18:18; 1 Cor 15:50
39. Matt 25:34; 1 Cor 6:9–10; 15:50; Gal 5:21; Eph 5:5
40. Dan 7:18, 22, 27; Rev 5:10; 22:5
41. Luke 11:5–13; also, Matt 7:7–11
42. Matt 1:23; 28:20

God's blessings are for those who are loyal to him. Yes, even the unsaved receive the Lord's blessings in many ways, but his sheep are blessed especially. We are friends and family members with God if we are his followers and he will will even honor us for our obedience.

> You are my friends if you do what I command you. John 15:14

> Anyone who loves me will obey my words. My Father will love them and we will come to live with them. John 14:23

> The Father will honor anyone who serves me. John 12:26

> Those who hear the word of God and obey are to be blessed. Luke 11:28

He is a king who shepherds me tenderly as his lamb but powerfully too, to make me a conqueror. I do not mind having such a king, in fact I want to worship and be accountable to such a loving Father, Shepherd, Brother, and comforting friend.

> Seek first his kingdom and his righteousness and all these things will be given to you. Matt. 6:33

> The one who concentrates on the perfect Law . . . [and is] an effectual doer—whatever he does will be blessed. Jas 1:25

> Blessed are those who hear this prophecy and obey what is written in it. Rev 1:3

We find in the New Testament the same blessings from the Lord which were promised in the Old. I named a few of these Old Testament blessings already: wisdom, kindness, joy, honor, security, longer life, prosperity, success, another's assets, Spiritual gifts and fruits. Here, we will only highlight a few of those same blessings which are mentioned in the New Testament.

As in the Old Testament, the New Testament believer may be blessed with the *assets of others* who have proven unwise or wicked. Those assets of another could be transferred to us in God's justice and grace—justice against the foolish, grace to us. We remember Christ's parables about the master who distributes cash to his servants so that while he is away they can prudently invest their share and grow it. The unwise servant who invested nothing had his share given to the wisest steward.[43]

God also blesses the believer with Spiritual *gifts* to enjoy by using them for the edification of the church, not themselves. This is the eternal design at work—the Lord empowers us with abilities to shepherd others through our Spiritual gifts. The Spirit, along with Christ and the Father, gives certain abilities to each believer as privileges yet as responsibilities too (1 Cor 12:4-8, 11). In Corinthians 12, wisdom is the first Spiritual gift listed and the next chapter elevates faith, hope, and love as the greatest gifts. Love is preeminent above all as the greatest Spiritual gift (1 Cor 12:31; 13:13)

---

43. Matt 5:5; 24:45-47; 25:14-30 // Luke 19:12-27; Mark 4:23-25; Luke 8:18

because it is the summation of the entire Old and New Testament moral teaching—love God and love your neighbor.

The *fruits* of the Spirit are repeated from the older testament in Galatians 6:22–23. For example, peace is a specific gift that sheep desperately want their shepherd to provide. So Jesus says,

> All you weary and burdened souls, come to me and I will give you rest. Matt 11:28

> Do not worry about life, what you will eat, or how you will clothe yourself. Luke 12:22

> Peace to you . . . Why are you troubled and doubts arise in your hearts? Luke 24:36, 38

> Do not let your heart be troubled; believe in God and also in me. John 14:1

> Peace I leave with you; my peace I give to you . . . Do not let your heart be troubled or full of fear. John 14:27–28

> I have told you this so you can have peace in me. John 16:33

> Peace *be* with you. John 20:19

The Trinity is the source of our peace as the New Testament writers remind us in almost every letter.[44] "Grace and peace" from the Father and Son introduces each of these letters. Peter encourages us that God cares for us and wishes that we would not be so anxious (1 Pet 5:6–7).

GOD DELIVERS THE BELIEVER

God Delivers the Believer from Adversity

We look forward to the time when the Lord's shepherding deliverance and discipline will no longer be necessary because his parenthetical design will have served its purpose. Because he will have saved nature and humanity, there will be no longer be a need for his saving acts. Yet for now, we praise the Lord for his constant deliverance from life's adversities and sin.

Old Testament believers praised God as the Shepherd who delivered them. Jacob testified that "God has been my *shepherd* my whole life—the 'angel' who has *delivered* me from every evil."[45] David expressed his confidence in the Lord's shepherding, saying, "I fear no evil since you are with me; your rod and staff comfort me" (Ps 23:4).

---

44. Rom 1:7; 15:33; 2 Cor 1:2; 13:11; Gal 1:3; 6:16; Eph 1:2; 6:23; Phil 1:2; 4:7, 9; Col 1:2; 3:15; 1 Thess 1:1; 5:23; 2 Thess 1:2; 3:16; 1 Tim 1:2; 2 Tim 1:2; Titus 1:4; Philem 1:3; Heb 13:20; 1 Pet 1:2; 5:14; 2 Pet 1:2; 3:14; 2 John 3; 3 John 15; Jude 1:2; Rev 1:4

45. Gen 48:15–16; also, 49:24

Other psalmists praised God and pled for his shepherding care: "The Lord raises the afflicted above reach and cares for their families as a *flock*" (Ps 107:41); "I have strayed like a lost *sheep*. Search for me, your servant, since I do not neglect your commandments (Ps 119:176)."

Though there was an expectation that God would save the believer from sin, it was much more often that he was asked for salvation from the difficulties that surrounded the believer. There are more psalms about salvation from adversity than any other category of psalms. There are psalms asking for forgiveness but not nearly as many asking for deliverance from adversity. God in his wisdom allows tragedy into the life of the believer. But even so, he may also save the righteous from those same circumstances. God's prerogative is to reward the righteous with deliverance. But it is not his obligation; it is his love and kindness that delivers even his righteous ones.[46] Our Savior God listens to the voice of each of his sheep: "The Lord is far away from the wicked, but he hears the righteous person's prayer" (Prov 15:29). Psalm 107 lists the types of victims who cried for salvation and were saved: those lost in a wilderness, prisoners, the sick, the sea-tossed, and the afflicted.

The Lord's gracious salvation of the individual believer is praised throughout the older testament in the same terms that describe his salvation of the Israelite nation. He is praised as the believer's savior,[47] deliverer,[48] redeemer,[49] protecting refuge,[50] safety,[51] a shield,[52] fortress,[53] and rock.[54]

> I glory in the Lord, and rejoice in the God of my salvation. Hab 3:18–19
>
> The Lord is my rock, my fortress, my deliverer . . .
> my shield, the horn of my salvation, my stronghold. Ps 18:2[55]
>
> Our God is a God of deliverances. Escapes from death are of the Lord. Ps 68:20
>
> I am the faithful one who will bear you even through your old age and gray hair.
> I made you and I will *carry* you. I will *bear* you and deliver you.[56]

---

46. Pss 4:3; 7:10; 9:10; 31:23–24; 32:6–7; 34:15–22; 37:25, 39; 50:14–15, 22–23; 91:14–16; 92:10–11; Isa 33:14–16; 57:1–2; 58:6–11; Jer 15:19–21; Hos 14:1, 4–5

47. 2 Sam 22:3, 47; Pss 25:5; 27:9; 38:22; 42:5, 11; 43:1–4; 89:26; Mic 7:7; Hab 3:18

48. 2 Sam 22:2; Pss 18:2; 40:17; 70:5; 140:7; 144:2

49. Job 19:25; Ps 19:14

50. Ruth 2:12; 2 Sam 22:31; Pss 4:1–3, 8; 15:1; 18:1–2; 27:4–5; 31:19–20; 40:1–2; 55:22; 59:16–17; 91:1–4; 118:5–14; Prov 30:5; Isa 25:4; 27:5; 57:13; Jer 16:19; 17:17; Joel 3:16; Nah 1:7

51. Pss 4:8; 16:1; 27:5; Prov 28:18, 26; 29:25

52. Gen 15:1; 2 Sam 22:3, 31; Pss 3:3; 7:10; 18:2, 30; 33:20; 119:114; 144:2; Prov 2:7; 30:5

53. 2 Sam 22:2, 51; Pss 28:8; 31:2–3; 59:9, 16–17; 62:2, 6; 71:3; 91:2; 94:22; 144:2; Prov 14:26; Jer 16:19

54. Deut 32:4; 1 Sam 2:2; 2 Sam 22:3, 32, 47; Pss 19:14; 28:1; 42:9; 89:26; 92:15; Hab 1:12

55. Also, 2 Sam 22:3, 31; Pss 62:1–2, 5–8; 71:19–21; 103:2–5; 121:5–8

56. Isa 46:4, also Ps 22:4–5

God is the same Savior of the believer in the New Testament as he was in the Old Testament. The Trinity continued to save the believer in various ways as they had before. Yes, when God came in the flesh he was named "Jesus," meaning "savior," and salvation from sin was the focus of his naming. But God was the Savior in several others ways too. Jesus describes his shepherding care in his Shepherd Discourse in John 10 and we have already heard of the blessings that he mentions there. He also describes our deliverances in that passage: deliverance from those seeking to steal us away from God, or even to destroy us (1, 8, 10, 12). But he comforts us as the Good Shepherd who protects us even if it means his own death (11–12, 15, 17–18, 29). He not only *protects* our life, he extends it *eternally* by giving us everlasting life (28). He rebuked the Jewish religious shepherds for prioritizing formal religion over the heart of a true shepherd: "Which of you whose *sheep* falls into a pit on the Sabbath will not grab it and lift it out?" (Matt 12:9–12). Jesus succeeded perfectly and could report to his Father, "I have not lost one of those whom you gave me" (John 18:9).

Paul described his multiple deliverances: whipped five times; beaten with rods three times; stoned once; shipwrecked three times; overboard at sea for hours on end; floated in dangerous rivers; physically endangered by thieves and religious zealots; sleepless; starving; exposed to the elements (2 Cor 11:24–27). He was saved from a venomous viper bite (Acts 28:3–6), yet not from his thorn in the flesh (2 Cor 12:7–9). God's mercy can be mysterious.

Deliverance from Enemies

The psalmists pray repeatedly for deliverance from their enemies. But many of these psalms can be disturbing for some since they can be tough prayers for the defeat and even destruction of one's enemies. They voice a very explicit preference for God's just character and righteous purposes to be accomplished. After all, it is *his* name and honor that are at stake.

> O God, how long will you let our enemies insult you?
> Will you allow them to discredit your name forever?
> See how these enemies are insulting you, Lord.
> A foolish nation has discredited your name. Ps 74:10, 18

Prayers of this type cry for the Lord's defeat of the enemy both for God's glory and for the believer's deliverance.

These prayers are not sung from a self-centered and arrogant heart of vengeance bent on personal vendettas.[57] Rather, they are sung from a desperation that clings respectfully to God's justice and strength. The righteous person prays for deliverance, understanding that "'Vengeance and retribution are mine,' says the Lord" (Deut 32:35).

---

57. Pss 9:3–4; 38:18–22; 56:7; 59:1–5; 64:1–6

Old Testament believers expected that the Lord wanted to deliver them from their enemies.[58] But a believer's cry against one's enemies asks humbly for both God's grace and justice at the same time. The believer asks for God's grace of deliverance since no one, including the believer, deserves it. But the believer also asks for judgment on the enemy who deserves punishment for inflicting stress, misery, bodily harm, or death on the weaker, undefended, righteous believer.

Believers recognize that conflict is not merely between them and their enemy. The more profound rift is between whoever their enemy is and God! The pride of the enemy will plummet to shame when God has finished dealing with this wicked, rebellious foe.[59] This makes the believer an observer of God's victory over God's enemy. Then the believer re-enters the scene when finally delivered, praising and honoring God before Israel and all peoples.[60]

> Glory be to God my savior, the God who executes my vengeance and subdues nations under me![61]

> Many look for the attention of the ruler, but one's justice comes from the Lord.
> Prov 29:26

This is the same act and venue of praise as that of national Israel when she was delivered.[62]

David had his own personal enemies; after all, he was a king with surrounding kings as his enemies and with political foes within his own borders. But what enemies does the normal believer have? We might be tempted to spiritualize psalms which deal with enemies and drift toward applying these psalms to our battles in the heavenly places. But that is not the original intent of these psalms. There were numerous human enemies for Israelite believers just as there are for us.

Today believers have flesh-and-blood enemies where governments, terrorizing bands, and jihadists hate Christ. Our brothers and sisters are threatened with torture and death. They are regularly intimidated, imprisoned, raped, dismembered, and martyred for their faith. The persecution and hatred which the psalmists described personally are experienced daily, even now, by the Lord's people in many places of the world. The hatred for the righteous is evident, and it is reason for us to pray for God's swift and delivering justice.[63] We must pray for God's deliverance of the persecuted and justice for their persecutors.

In addition to praying for our brothers and sisters, we pray compassionately for suffering unbelievers too: women, children, and the poor are oppressed and exploited

---

58. Pss 3:1–6; 7:1–2; 13:10; 22:11–21; 23:5; 25:2;30:1; 31:8, 15; 35:1–10, 17; 40:13–17; 55:16–18; 56:1–7, 9; 69:18–19; 138:7; 142:5–6; Jer 17:17–18; Mic 7:7–8

59. Pss 6:7–10; 35:4; 40:13–15; 70:1–3; 71:12–13; 143:11–12

60. Pss 18:46–49; 22:21–22; 27:6; 57:2–9; 64:7–9; 71:13–16

61. Ps 18:46–47; also, Deut 32:41–43; Pss 3:7; 38:12–15; 54:2–5; 57:2–3; 143:10–12

62. Isa 52:10; Pss 67:1–2; 77:14–15; 98:2–3; 102:13–22; 106:7–8

63. Pss 9:13, 16; 18:17–19; 25:19–20; 41:4–11; 69:4, 14

for the worst sordid purposes in lands cursed by idolatry, despotism, corruption, and dark religions. The extreme injustice against humanity is far worse than our comfortable, sanitized reflections on the human condition have deceived us into thinking. The tragic is so often normal for those people in societies that are relatively untouched by God's Kingdom gospel. Surely, in our God-like hearts, we consider these diabolical enemies of believers and nonbelievers to be enemies of the just and compassionate Lord of all humanity.

I am not referring to only distant lands—enemies prowl our streets and neighborhoods and attack the innocent. Sadistic thugs exploit members of their own family emotionally, physically, even sexually. Unwarranted lawsuits are lodged with malice and punitive intent. Enemies who are anti-God and pro-self abound in our culture and flood the media, the educational, and even religious centers with vain and imaginative worldviews. Pornographers, atheists, profit-worshippers, abortionists, pedophiles, and Satanists are only a few examples of those whom God considers his enemies.

Though it can be hard to accept at times, we are expected to imitate the just motives of the Lord in every way; we are expected to think as he thinks. Wicked enemies cannot be trusted and it is through their deceitful words and actions that they assault their undeserving prey.[64] Should our stance be different from God's? Should we take on God's perspective of the wicked and consider them our enemies as well, just as the Old Testament believers did?[65] Do we believe in the authority of Scripture, or are we embarrassed by it and feel we need to apologize for it publicly?

David knew that we ourselves must be engaged in our deliverance. This does not make us vengeful, just responsible.

> Blessed be the Lord; he is my rock. He trains my hands for war, and my fingers for battle;
> He loves me by being my fortress, my stronghold and my deliverer.
> He is my shield and in him I take refuge; he subdues the peoples under me. Ps 144:1-2

Our praise of God for our deliverance from enemies cannot become an excuse for not taking our shepherding partnership with him seriously. He wants to defeat his enemies *with* us, not *in spite of us*. We cannot be passive when those who should be God's and our enemies drag the innocent to their death: "Deliver those being led to their death; hold them back from staggering toward their slaughter" (Prov 24:11).

However, the believer must be wise when balancing biblical responsibilities against the wicked enemies of God's kingdom with the Testaments' instruction to love and to be sensitive to one's personal enemies. What God expected from Israel as a nation and from the individual were two different scenarios. Obviously, the Lord ordered

---

64. Pss 27:11-12; 31:15-18; 35:10-11, 19-21; 41:4-7; 43:1-2; 55:20-21; 59:1, 12; 109:1-6; 116:8-11; 120:1-4; 144:7-8; Prov 2:11-12; Isa 29:21

65. Pss 10:1-2; 71:2-4; 97:10; 140:1-8; 141:8-10; Prov 2:11-19; Jer 20:10-13

his people to war against his and their enemies, but it is equally obvious there was a different standard for everyday encounters between individuals living in community.

> When your enemy stumbles and falls, don't be glad or rejoice, or the Lord, when he sees your evil response, will turn his anger away from your enemy.
>
> Give your enemy food to eat when he is hungry, and give him water when he is thirsty. You will heap glowing coals on his head and the Lord will reward you.[66]

Even an enemy's lost animal was to be cared for and returned (Ex 23:4–5). All of the Law assumed every Israelite deserved respect and justice, whether a personal enemy or not. David, a frequent pleader for God's destruction of his enemies, does not destroy an obnoxious, rebellious enemy in Shimei. In David's humility, he could not determine at that time whether Shimei was correct in rebuking David or not (2 Sam 16:5–13). Out of respect for his king, David honored his worst enemy, Saul, by not killing him twice when he could easily have done so.[67] However, in the end, though we love our enemies, when a choice is necessary between them and our commitment to God's justice, we are always to choose God.

New Testament teaching about the believer's enemies are the same as those in the Old. The older testament warned of Israel's enemies from outside the Lord's nation and warned against their wicked leaders within the nation. In the New Testament, the enemies of Christ and his followers persecuted believers from outside the Kingdom (the Romans), and evil shepherds and false teachers took advantage of the sheep from within the Kingdom. Christ and his apostles were martyred as were thousands of others in their day. The Lord and the apostles were not naïve about the dangers they were in, nor were those martyrs who are commended for their faith in Hebrews 11:37–38. Peter says, "Even if you suffer for righteousness, you will be blessed."[68] The Lord's salvation will always come eventually, since, as Jesus asks, "Will God not render justice for his elect who cry out to him day and night?" (Luke 18:7–8).

How do we pray and act for the defeat of our enemies, yet love our enemies? Well, how could the Lord pray for the forgiveness of those who crucified him but lead the battle to annihilate his enemies at Armageddon? Christ's statement in Matthew 5:44, "Love your enemies and pray for those who persecute you," was in the context of one's neighbors, the ones who are within our immediate vicinity and who are very near for our love or contempt as our friends or enemies. Believers are to show the same balance in character that God showed in dying for some of his enemies, yet destroying other enemies in his righteous indignation. We must walk by the Spirit who leads us in truth toward the appropriate response to God's enemies in various situations.

---

66. Prov 24:17–18; 25:21–22
67. 1 Sam 24:3–6, 10; 26:7–12
68. Dan 3:17–18; 1 Pet 3:14

The war between spirits became more obvious when Christ began the final defeat of Satan. This included casting out demons, which Jesus said proved that God's kingdom had come.[69] We covered Christ's subjugation of the demonic kingdom at great length earlier in this study. The tender care with which Christ delivered the victims in these exorcisms is emphasized in that no harm was done to the possessed during these miracles. His love and kindness is the opposite of Satan's intent which prefers that the possessed throw themselves into scorching fire or drowning water (Mark 9:20–22).

Thieves of the Lord's sheep are ruthless and powerful when Satan rouses them to abduct or kill a lamb from God's Kingdom. Christ asked his Father to protect his people from "the evil one," including Satan (John 17:15). And John writes in his first letter about Jesus' own protective role "the One born of God keeps them safe so the evil one cannot harm them" (1 John 5:18). Paul makes it clear that we must escape from the Enemy's snares which trap us and leash us to sin (2 Tim 2:24–26). Paul, in addition to John, encouraged the churches when he told them that believers will be safe from "the evil one" (2 Thess 3:2–3).

Deliverance through Obedience

All enemies are not the wicked violent *other* nations. One's own sin or the sin of one's own surrounding community brought suffering to Israel's individual citizens. One can be one's worst enemy or a community can fail to follow moral standards and provide a safe environment for the believer.

Deliverance was built into God's *laws and wisdom* because wisdom and righteousness deliver the faithful as often as they obey each instruction of God.[70] The obedient will need deliverance from fewer problems of their own making. Examples of ways we can be delivered in this way include avoiding the wicked, avoiding oppressive debt, and careless accidents.[71] Wisdom and righteousness will even deliver believers from death.[72]

The individual was also delivered by the responsible conduct of those around them. The Lord is a deliverer of his sheep, and he expects his believing communities and believers to deliver his sheep as well. Deliverance is a moment-to-moment experience of a society, its families, and individual members when the protective divine laws and instructions are followed.

Our Shepherd has compassion on the disadvantaged and delivers them in various ways.[73] Tragedies come especially to aliens, widows, and orphans, the sick, the emotionally distressed, and the barren. The Lord focuses on those who lack normal levels of

---

69. Matt 12:28 // Luke 11:20; also, Matt 9:35–36; 10:7–8; Acts 10:38
70. Prov 11:6, 9, 21; 27:12; 28:18, 26; 30:5
71. Prov 2:11–19; 3:25–26; 6:1–5; Ecc 10:8–10
72. Prov 10:2, 27; 11:4, 19; 13:3; 14:27; 15:27; 16:17; 19:16
73. Job 34:28; 36:15; Pss 9:18; 10:12; 22:24; 25:16–17; 34:6; 40:17; Isa 25:4; 61:1–2

subsistence and their salvation is frequently mentioned and exemplified.[74] Orphans and widows are threatened by their poverty and lack of protection, so God became their protector and deliverer.[75] So, communities with righteous leadership enforced the Lord's laws. Justice in the courts protected everyone, but particularly the disadvantaged from false witnesses, excessive sentencing, and bribery. Obeying the community health laws, food restrictions, and quarantine requirements saved lives. Safety was insured by following building codes and by honoring laws protecting the handicapped. The impoverished were saved from hunger, including the widow, the orphan, the poor, the alien and the elderly because of access to storehouses and poverty programs like gleaning. Servants were protected from any abuse at the hand of their masters. Many "cities of refuge" were identified where those only suspected of homicide, should flee and find protection until their court appearance. In chapter 12 we will see in greater detail how the Lord's commandments and wisdom instructions protect the believer.

The Christian subculture of fellowship and accountability within the local and global church should also be a pleasant environment of people filled with the fruits of the Spirit and glad to use their Spiritual gifts for all believers. Here is where the eternal design is experienced every day while Christians shepherd and deliver one another in biblically moral ways that reflect the shepherd heart of the saving Trinity. Here is where the merciful will receive mercy (Matt 5:7), where one believer saves another believer even from death by steering him to truth (Jas 5:19–20), where believers' prayers bring deliverance to other believers (Phil 1:19).

Deliverance from Ailments and Death

God will deliver the stressed and brokenhearted and will heal their debilitating illnesses of the soul.[76] Our deliverances are not only from physical dangers and troubles. God also saves us from the anxiety *about* the threat or reality of adversities. He gives many reasons for hope and trust in his perfect wisdom and timing for deliverance even if there is no evident reason for one's trials. Psalmists who were worn out emotionally because of adversaries pled for God's deliverance from their stressful circumstances.[77]

Salvation from physical ailments is frequent in the older testament too. David testifies personally,

> I cried to you for help and you healed me. Ps 30:2

> The Lord sustains the poor on his sickbed;
> You restore him from sickness to health. Ps 41:3

---

74. Gen 21:14–19; 1 Sam 2:5, 8; 1 Kgs 17:10–16; 2 Kgs 4:1–7; Pss 9:18; 12:5; 113:7; 140:12
75. Deut 10:18; 1 Kgs 17:9–24; Pss 10:17–18; 68:5–6; 69:32–33
76. Pss 6:1–7; 23:4; 30:10–11; 34:17–18; 42:6–8; 91:4–5; 94:19; 119:25, 28, 50, 92–93, 114–116; 143:1–4; 147:3, 6; Isa 28:12; 53:4; 57:15, 18–19; Lam 3:32
77. Pss 31:9–13; 102:1–11

The Lord delivered many people from all kinds of ailments in the Old Testament. Miriam and Naaman were healed of leprosy; rebellious Israelites were healed from poisonous snake bites; Job and Hezekiah's boils were healed; the Philistines were healed of some sort of tumor; Jeroboam I was healed of a withered hand.[78] Hannah, Manoah's wife, and the matriarchs were healed of their barrenness.[79] Many confessions of sin in the Old Testament not only request forgiveness but desire further deliverance from sin's impact on one's emotional and physical health.[80] But wonderfully, in New Earth all will be healed, and there will never be sickness again.[81]

Yes, the Lord may save one from various causes of death,[82] however, only in our most sober moments do we recognize with Isaiah and Solomon that our death in itself is God's salvation from an exhausting world.

> The righteous person perishes but no one cares.
> The devout are taken but no one understands why.
> For the righteous person is removed from evil and enters into peace.
> Those who walked uprightly *rest* in their graves. Isa 57:1–2

> The day of one's death is better than the day of one's birth. Eccl 7:1

For example, God told obedient Josiah that his death would save him from seeing the coming evils upon South Israel.[83]

Even death can be deliverance from the torturous experiences of the oppressed, the sexually violated, and exploited slaves; and death relieves from chronic and debilitating illness. The books of Job and Ecclesiastes are transparent about what we already believe to be true; death can be our only compassionate deliverance from the Lord.[84] After all, it is better to be with the Lord than living in this cursed earth, especially if one is experiencing life's worst. By our death we see what the prophets assure us will also be true in New Earth—no sin, only moral peace and harmony.[85] Many deny that there is any definitive teaching of eternal life in the Old Testament. But given that even the surrounding cultures believed in this truth, it is very odd to think that God would withhold this fact from the Israelites. There are many references to eternal life in the Old Testament.[86]

---

78. Num 12:10, 14–16; 21:6–9; Job 42:10; 1 Sam 5:11–12; 1 Kgs 13:3–6; 2 Kgs 5:1–14; 20:5–7

79. Gen 11:30; 15:2; 16:1; 17:15–21; 21:2; 25:21; 29:31; 30:1, 22–24; 49:25; Ex 23:26; Judg 13:2–3, 24; 1 Sam 1:2, 5–6, 19–20; 2:5, 20–21; 2 Kgs 4:12–17; Ps 113:9

80. Pss 31:10; 32:3–5; 38:1–8

81. Isa 33:24; 35:5–6; 42:6–7

82. Pss 18:4–6; 26:9–11; 27:1–2; 30:3; 33:18–20; 56:13; 91:5–7; 94:17; 116:3–9; Dan 3:13–14, 19, 24–27; 6:16–23, 27; Jonah 2:2, 6, 9–10

83. 2 Kgs 22:18–20 // 2 Chr 34:26–28

84. Job 3:3–26; 6:8–9; 7:13–15; 10:18–19; 19:25–26; Eccl 4:1–3; 6:3–6

85. 1 Chr 17:9; Ezek 37:23–24; Mic 4:5; Zeph 3:13; Zech 14:10–11

86. Gen 3:22–24; 2 Kgs 2:11; Job 14:12; 19:26–27; Pss 16:9–11; 22:26; 41:12; 49:15; 61:4–8; 73:24–26; 75:9–10; 115:17–18; 145:1–2; Prov 10:25; 12:19; 14:32; 15:24; 21:28; Isa 25:8; 26:19; Dan

Shepherding the Believer

The Good Shepherd fed the hungry, freed many from demon possession, healed the infirm, raised the dead, and comforted the tired and anxious. His ministry of deliverance was daily, including some Sabbaths.[87] Most of his miracles delivered those who were seriously afflicted physically, emotionally, or by demons, or all three! His miracles were similar to those by Elijah and Elisha showing God's heart to supply the needs of the common person. In one chapter alone, Elijah raised the Shunammite child from the dead as Jesus would; Elisha changed rancid food to fresh food similar to Jesus changing water into wine; Elijah and Elisha miraculously multiplied food for many people with much food left over just as when Jesus twice fed thousands with one basket of food and several baskets left over (2 Kgs 4:2–6, 32–44).

Christ healed the blind,[88] mute,[89] deaf,[90] lame,[91] leprous,[92] epileptic,[93] paralyzed,[94] feverish[95] as well as the hemorrhaging, the swollen, and one with a severed ear.[96] He reversed death and the natural decay of the body, reviving corpses and returning souls that had left momentarily.[97] He was so successful in his miraculous deliverances that his taunters at his crucifixion even admitted, "He saved others but he cannot save himself!"[98] Our Shepherd also tends to the emotional needs of his sheep. The Lord gives solace to mourners, rest to the tired and comfort to the humble believer.[99]

Christ fulfilled God's promise "to preach the gospel to the poor . . . to proclaim freedom to the captives and to return sight to the blind and to free the oppressed" (Luke 4:18). He then shared his own kingdom mission with his shepherding apostles, passing on his healing,[100] and exorcizing,[101] and resurrection power and authority to them.

> Go to the lost *sheep* of Israel preaching this message—"The kingdom of heaven is near." Heal the sick, raise the dead, cure leprosy, cast out demons. Give others as freely as you have received.[102]

12:2, 13; Hos 13:14

87. Matt 12:10–13 // Mark 3:1–5 // Luke 6:6–10
88. Matt 9:27, 30; 11:4–5 // Luke 7:21–22; Matt 12:22; 15:30; 20:32–34 // Mark 10:51–52 // Luke 18:41–43; Matt 21:14; Luke 7:21–22; John 9:6–7
89. Matt 9:32–33; 12:22 // Luke 11:14; Matt 15:30 // Mark 7:37
90. Matt 11:4–5 // Luke 7:21–22; Mark 7:32, 37; 9:25
91. Matt 9:2, 6–7 // Mark 2:3, 11–12; Matt 15:30; 21:14; John 5:5, 8
92. Matt 8:2–3 // Mark 1:40–41 // Luke 5:12–13; Matt 11:4–5 // Luke 7:22; Luke 17:12–14
93. Matt 17:14–15, 18 // Mark 9:17–18, 25–27 // Luke 9:38–39, 42
94. Matt 4:24; 8:5–6, 13
95. Matt 8:14–15 // Mark 1:30–31 // Luke 4:38–39
96. Matt 9:20–22; Luke 14:2–4; 22:50–51
97. Matt 9:18, 25 // Mark 5:22–23, 40–42 // Luke 8:41–42, 54–55; Luke 7:12, 15; John 11:14, 43–44
98. Matt 27:42 // Mark 15:31 // Luke 23:35
99. Matt 5:4 // Luke 6:21; Matt 11:28–30; 2 Cor 1:3–5; 7:6–7; 2 Thess 2:16–17; Phil 4:6–9
100. Acts 3:2, 6–8; 4:16; 5:14–16; 8:7; 9:17–18, 33–34; 14:8–10; 19:11–12; 28:8–9
101. Acts 5:16; 8:7; 16:16–18
102. Matt 10:6–8 // Luke 9:1–2, 6

Peter and Paul even raised the dead.[103] This is yet another way that the shepherding chain in God's eternal design continued on: from the Father sending Jesus to heal, to Jesus sending his disciples to heal, to the apostles instructing elders and those who are gifted in healing to heal as well.[104]

The ultimate salvation, however, will only come when believers are delivered into New Earth where we will rule with the Lord forever. The persecuted are encouraged that they will not perish but have eternal life because they are patient and endure their abuse (Luke 21:16–19). Yet eternal life is the salvation that we all will share. We will be saved with new bodies and appendages so we can walk and work as we continue to shepherd creation.[105]

Deliverance through Creation: Angels, Nature, and Humanity

The rest of creation, including the angels and nature play a part in God's salvation of his people, and we noted these in chapters 6 and 7. A psalmist says, "He commissions his angels concerning you, to guard all your ways. Their hands will lift you up so your feet do not hit a stone."[106] For instance, the angels are enlisted in God's salvation of Lot from Sodom and Gomorrah (Gen 19:1, 10–22), in God's deliverance from Egypt (Ps 78:49), and Elijah is awakened by a food-bearing angel (1 Kgs 19:4–8).

God delivered New Testament believers by angels as he did in the Old Testament. An angel told Joseph to escape Herod by moving to Egypt for a while and then again to move to Galilee to avoid Archelaus (Matt 2:13–15, 19–23). And angels are also interested in *our* deliverance: "Are not all angels ministering spirits sent to serve the inheritors of salvation?" (Heb 1:14). In the end, God will deliver the believer from all affliction when Christ returns with his angels (2 Thess 1:7).

God also uses nature for saving the believer. Sarah and Abraham were delivered by disasters the Lord sent against an Egyptian Pharaoh; Elijah was fed by ravens; an axe head sunk deep in water was raised miraculously to the joy of its wielder; Jonah was saved miraculously by a large fish and a large shade plant.[107] God multiplied food miraculously in the Old Testament: perpetual manna in the wilderness, perpetual flour and oil in a widow's food containers. In another case enough oil was multiplied to pay a debt, and in yet another case inadequate amounts of bread and grain were multiplied to feed a hundred people with a great deal left over.[108]

As in the Old Testament, God used his power over nature by causing an earthquake to shake open the prison doors, and then somehow he miraculously loosened the chains

---

103. Acts 9:40–41; 20:9–10
104. 1 Cor. 12:9, 28–30; Jas 5:14–15
105. 1 Cor 15:42–54; 2 Cor 5:1–8
106. Ps 91:11–12; also, Ex 23:20–23; Num 20:14–16; Ps 78:49
107. Gen 12:17–20; 1 Kgs 17:3–7; 2 Kgs 6:4–7; Jonah 1:17; 4:6
108. 1 Kgs 17:14–16; 2 Kgs 4:3–6, 42–44; also, Num 11:13, 31–32

on Paul, Silas, and others in prison (16:25–26). The Lord also opened gates and loosened chains for Peter and other apostles to walk out of their prison cells.[109] Paul and Timothy were delivered from something dire but not described (2 Cor 1:8–11).

The Old Testament recounts numerous events when the Lord delivered someone by another person exercising wisdom, discretion, position, or strength. Abraham delivered Lot from his abduction from Sodom. Moses' parents, his sister, Miriam, and Pharaoh's daughter saved him from infanticide. Moses delivered an Israelite from an assaulting Egyptian and he delivered Reuel's daughters from bullying shepherds. Rahab protected two Israelite spies. Jonathan and David's wife, Michal, rescued David from Saul's murderous plans. Abishai defended the aging David against the monstrous Ishbi-benob. Jehosheba saved Joash from death by the hand of Athaliah. Mordecai delivered the Persian king Ahaseurus from assassination. Jeremiah was rescued from a cistern by Ebed-melech and King Zedekiah. Jonah's honesty saved the sinking seamen who were endangered by him as a rebellious stowaway.[110]

We are also protected and saved by the government authorities that God appoints over us. Our obedience to civil laws and governments contributes to a culture of law and order. Certainly, there are despotic and brutal governments—New Testament Christians lived under the fist of one of the cruelest (Rom 13:3–4). Yet the alternative of living within the chaos of anarchy is far less stable and predictable.

God Delivers the Believer from Sin

Sin is hard for humanity to admit. We drown in it, breathing it in, suffocating below its physical and spiritual density. We smell its stench, feel its coarseness, see its revolting images, hear its horrid sounds, taste its bitterness. But we search for any number of ways to ignore sin, rationalize sin, glorify sin, minimize sin, and blame others for it. Nonetheless, the Testaments have one consistent comment about sin.

> There is no one who does not sin.[111]
>
> Is anyone pure before his Maker? Job 4:17
>
> How can anyone be righteous before God? Job 9:2
>
> Can anyone born of a woman be pure? Job 25:4
>
> There is no one who is righteous, not even one.[112]
>
> No living person is righteous. Ps 143:2

---

109. Acts 5:19; 12:6–10; 16:23, 38–39
110. Gen 14:12–16; Ex 2:3–12, 16–19; Josh 2:1–6; 1 Sam 19:1–7, 11–12; 20:12–15; 2 Sam 21:15–17; 2 Kgs 11:1–3 // 2 Chr 22:10–12; Esth 2:21–23; Jer 38:9–13; Jonah 1:12–16
111. 1 Kgs 8:46 // 2 Chr 6:36
112. Pss 14:3; 53:3 // Rom 3:10

> Who can say . . . 'I am pure from my sin?' Prov 20:9
>
> There is not a righteous person . . . who never sins. Eccl 7:20
>
> We all stumble in many ways. Jas 3:2
>
> If we say we are sinless we are deceiving ourselves. 1 John 1:10

Isaiah describes it in shepherding terms, "Like *sheep* we have all gone astray" (Isa 53:6).

Perfection is the Standard

Another high standard is set before us. Our loving Shepherd King starts with the assumption that when someone does what they are expected to do they have no right to demand a "thank you" for doing it. "Thank you" implies that someone has done something beyond what is expected. Often we thank others and appreciate what they do when it was a requirement in the first place. But when we do that, we are only being gracious. In this fallen world, we may say "thank you" because the person could have done less or nothing at all. We sometimes feel fortunate they did just something close to the requirement.

Christ makes it perfectly clear why we should try to be righteous. It is not because we can then demand God's appreciation and favor. It is because we are obligated to be perfect!

> Will one thank a servant because he did what he was told? So when you have done everything you are supposed to do, you should say, "As servants we are undeserving of thanks since we have only done our duty." Luke 17:9–10

Our perfect obedience is what we owe God; we deserve nothing for simply obeying; no grace can be earned even by being perfect. In New Earth, we will still live by God's grace. Though we will behave perfectly, eternally, we still will deserve nothing. What we receive will still only be unmerited. Until then, God still demands perfection from us. But since we are not perfect, we benefit from his grace and forgiveness in Christ whose perfect life is our substitute for our imperfection just as his death is our substitute for our eternal death.

It is because of God's wonderful love, however, that he does stoop to encourage us and to commend us for what are far too few acts of obedience. Both James and Peter tell us that we will be honored in the end because of our persistence and pursuit of righteousness.

> God blesses the one who perseveres under trial . . . that one will receive the crown of life promised by the Lord. Jas 1:12
>
> Your proven genuine faith . . . may it result in praise and glory and honor when Jesus Christ is revealed. 1 Pet 1:7

We are not perfect, but we are given all we need to know what perfection is in God's Law, in his wisdom instructions, and in the perfect life of obedience by the Son to his Father.

So God planned a way to deliver us from our sins and their impact on us so we can continue to achieve the eternal design unburdened by sin. He disciplines us by convicting our sensitive conscience until we confess our obvious sin and receive his grace to start a new moment in life, perfect again in his sight. The following shepherding pattern is repeated much too often, yet it is very comforting at the same time:

> God blesses => we sin =>
> > God disciplines => we confess, repent =>
> > > God delivers us => we are blessed again =>
>
> BUT, we sin again! =>
> > God disciplines => we confess, repent =>
> > > God delivers us => we are blessed again =>
>
> BUT . . .

The Lord expects us to subdue sin, not for sin to subdue us. But he expects us to ask for help too: David pleads, "Keep your servant back from deliberate sins, do not let them rule over me" (Ps 19:13). Fortunately, the Shepherd encourages us that he will assist us in our victory over sin. Shepherding God shepherds the shepherding believer. He has planned for our partnership to apply to this aspect of our lives too. Micah encouraged the Israelites that their Shepherd would assist in their victory over sin.

> *Shepherd* your people with your staff, the *flock* of your inheritance . . . You will again have compassion on us; you will *subdue* sins underfoot and hurl all our iniquities into the depths of the sea. Mic 7:14, 19

Absolutely, the Testaments preach a relentless pursuit of one's righteousness, but God reminds us over and over that it is the partnership of his eternal design that will shepherd us to victory as he forgives us and empowers us to subdue the sin that seeks to enslave us. Micah uses the very same word for this alliance against sin as the Trinity uses in the primary commission to describe the strength with which we are to shepherd creation—we are to *subdue* sin under our feet. Paul picks up on this imagery, "The God of peace soon will crush Satan under *your* feet" (Rom 16:20).

It was God's forgiveness that encouraged psalmists to return to a relationship of peace and partnership with him to battle against their common enemies and to endure other troubles.[113]

> Blessed is the one whose sins are forgiven and covered.
> Blessed is the one the Lord does not convict of iniquity.

---

113. Pss 25:18; 38:17–20; 40:11–14; 103:2–3

> As far as the east is from the west,
> is how far the Lord has separated us from our sin.[114]

God knows our weakness and propensity to sin, and he is ready, willing and quick to forgive when we confess that we have succumbed to sin.[115]

Genuine confession starts with *honesty* and *realism*. Honesty, in that we must tell the truth about our moral condition and not act as if we have not offended the Lord. Realism, in that God knows of our specific sin anyway, so not being honest is simply foolish. We are not going to surprise God or inform him of anything when we tell him we have sinned. It is not as if David had really hidden his sin from the Lord when he confesses, "I have acknowledged to you my sin and have not hidden it" (Ps 32:5). It is only a figure of speech.

When we confess our sins, we only start the cleansing process by admitting there is a moral problem standing in the way of our relationship with God and preventing his further blessing and deliverance.[116] It is not adequate simply to mouth words of confession or acknowledge one's sin as only a fact. Ethical awareness or fickle emotions are not enough. Neither is confession credible when it tries to fix some other problem than one's relational problem with God. For instance, Pharaoh confessed his sin to God through Moses but was not repentant as a true believer with a holistic commitment to the Lord (Ex 10:16–17). His motive was solely to stop the onslaught of plagues.

One can confess wrongdoing but still not be repentant. One can even be truly sorry for sin without repenting. Mere confession can be done in the formalities of sacrifices or by empty religious words. Repentance, on the other hand, is a decision and commitment to turn from the sin and obey—a decision that matters; it must and will lead to righteous acts.

> None repent of their wickedness and say, "What have I done?"
> They refuse to return . . . Everyone turns to his own course. Jer 8:6

> Repent and turn away from your idols; turn your faces away from all your detestable deeds. Ezek 14:6

> Repent and turn away from all your sins or they will destroy you. Ezek 18:30

Sincere repentance is what God requires. Though repentance can be pledged in a confession, the Lord knows the heart and whether one's commitment in spirit matches the pledge: "Forgive and deal actively with each person and *what they do* since you know the heart of each and every heart."[117] There is a genuine confession and that will prove true by the changed walk of the forgiven. Genuine repentance will lead

---

114. Pss 32:1–2; 103:12
115. Pss 32:5; 51:1–4; 79:8–9; 86:4–6; 103:8–14; 130:3–4; Isa 6:1–7
116. 1 Kgs 21:25–29; Pss 19:12–14; 25:11; 41:4; 51:2–4
117. 1 Kgs 8:39; also, vss. 31–32 // 2 Chr 6:24–25

to forgiveness and make one eligible for even further deliverances of the Lord, even from physical death![118]

One could simply confess their sins, and feel bad about them, but almost every human in all ages and eras do that. There is nothing particularly Christian about that. Nor is it exclusive to Christians to want to change their behavior. The difference? One's confession, sorrow, and commitment to change must be directed in the purity of love for the only true God. That is supplied only by the Holy Spirit. Only then are we able to respond with a heart sincerely committed to change: "The sorrow that God wants will bring repentance without reluctance, leading to salvation. But the world's sorrow brings death" (2 Cor 7:10).

The Lord's priority is his intimate connection with the sinner, over and above formalities. God's forgiveness is because of a personal, spiritual relationship. After David's egregious sin against God when he seduced Bathsheba and murdered her husband, the king made his plea in fairly radical terms:

> You would not be delighted with sacrifices like a burnt offering, or I would bring one.
>
> The sacrifice you want is a broken spirit. A broken and repentant heart you will not despise. Ps 51:16–17

Sacrifices are put in their secondary place in this passage and in many others where mere religiosity is rebuked.[119] If there was not a genuine Spirit-driven contrite and humble heart of obedience to God along with the sacrifice, the individual Israelite was no better off than those New Testament Pharisees who went through ceremonial motions but were relying solely on their works. Offering sacrifices as a claim to salvation was as repugnant to the Lord in the Old Testament as it was to him in the New.

But still, an involved sacrificial system for personal forgiveness was provided by God to emphasize the seriousness of disobeying him. Sacrifices were begun as early as Cain and Abel (Gen 4:4–5), and the requirement of sacrifices spanned from that time into the Mosaic era. Human sacrifice was not acceptable until the adequate Human appeared, which puts Abraham's near-sacrifice of his only covenantal son in suspenseful perspective (Gen 22:10–14). Human sacrifice was God's plan that was foreshadowed as early as Abraham. But it took the appropriate human, the perfect Jesus to accomplish that requirement.

Even in these sacrifices, God includes nature in his deliverance. Humanity's preeminence over nature is affirmed by the lesser creatures being substitutes for sinful, condemned humans. Israel's sacrificial ceremonies were public and bloody illustrations that the sinner deserved to perish rather than this innocent animal whose throat the sinner was about to slit at the altar. Bulls, goats, sheep, turtle doves, pigeons, flour,

---

118. Isa 38:17; Ezek 18:27–28; 33:14–16

119. Pss 40:6–8; 51:16–17; 69:30–31; 141:1–2; Prov 15:8; 16:6; 21:3, 27; Jer 7:2–24; Isa 1:10–17; 58:5–7; Hos 6:6; Amos 5:21–27; Mic 6:4–8

and olive oil were sacrificed, depending on what the sinner could afford by their socio-economic situation.[120]

Finally, as in all things, God's nature and character is our model for our relationships with others too. God is the primary one offended by our sin, and his merciful, loving approach is to forgive. He expects us to do the same to others: "Love covers every transgression" (Prov 10:12). Israel's greatest kings, David and Solomon, regardless of their power, forgave those who threatened them.[121] And when we sin against another, we owe those who have been offended an apology and should at least request their forgiveness. After all, "Whoever hides his sins does not prosper, but whoever confesses and repents finds mercy." (Prov 28:13). Whether or not the offended accepts our request for forgiveness is beyond our power—if not, well, they need to ask for ours now!

The Father and Son Deliver the Believer from Sin

Out of reverence for the Trinity we must not ignore the preeminence of the Father in the salvation of the world from sin. Christ is the Father's means of salvation for this world. The startling, yet wonderful choice for the Father was the death of his Son over humanity's eternal damnation.

> Like *sheep* we have all gone astray . . .
> But the Lord [Father] has put the sin of all of us to on him [Jesus]. Isa 53:6

Zechariah says it even more strongly. The Father ordered his Son to be struck and crucified:

> Wake up, sword! Go against my [Father's] *Shepherd* [Son],
> against my Associate . . . Strike the *Shepherd* so the *sheep* are scattered.[122]

But then again, it was the Father who delivered his Son by raising him from the dead; he raised "the great Shepherd of the sheep," the Shepherd whose blood saves us.

> May the God of peace, who . . . brought our Lord Jesus back from the dead,
> that great Shepherd of the sheep, equip you . . . Heb 13:20

The Father delivered his own Son from the grave.

Micah prophesied that when the Son was born in Bethlehem, he would accomplish his Father's shepherding plan. We know from the Bible's most famous verse and other passages that it was the Father's heart to save and to send the Second Person to

---

120. Ex 29:10–14; Lev 4:1–35; 5:7; 6:14–30; 8:14–17; 12:6–8; 14:10–20; 15:15, 30; Num 15:1–10; 24–32; 28:7–9

121. 2 Sam 19:18–23; 1 Kgs 1:50–53

122. Zech 13:7 // Matt 26:31 // Mark 14:27

save Israel and the world. So Micah, John, and Paul refer to the Father and the Son separately as the Sender and the Sent.

> From you [Bethlehem], a ruler in Israel will come forward for me [the Father];
> ... He [the Son] will stand and *shepherd* his *flock*. Mic 5:2–4

> For God [the Father] so loved the world that he gave his only Son. John 3:16

> God [the Father] reconciled us with himself through Christ... in Christ, God [the Father] was reconciling the world to himself. 2 Cor 5:18–19

> God [the Father] showed his love by sending his one and only Son among us into the world so we could live through him. 1 John 4:9–10

One might say, "God" does not necessarily mean the Father exclusively, and "God" refers to the whole Trinity. But this is not what the Son says. He says very clearly that his Father sent him.

One of Christ's vineyard parables illustrates the Father's plan for his Son and his kingdom. A father sent his son to collect the fruit from the workers who tended the vineyards that the father owned. The son is killed. It is a sad story that predicts the divine Son's murder while carrying out the Father's instructions.[123]

It is the Father who is the Savior and he delivers us from darkness and rebellion into the kingdom he had given to his Son (Col 1:12–13). The Father is the forgiver: Christ tells us to ask his Father for forgiveness just as he asks the Father to forgive his executioners.[124] The Father coordinates the saving acts of each Trinity member for our benefit. Paul says,

> The kindness of God our Savior [Father] and his love for humanity appeared.
> He saved us... through the washing of new birth and renewal by the Holy
> Spirit whom he poured out on us completely through Jesus Christ our Savior.
> So, since we have been justified by his grace, we are heirs. Titus 3:4–7

Because the Father is a savior, nearly all of Paul's letters open by naming the Father before the Son when speaking of God's grace and peace. For example: "Grace and peace to you from God our Father and the Lord Jesus Christ" (Rom 1:7).

Deliverance from Sin

Deliverance from sin has three progressive phases: justification, sanctification, and glorification. Each of these phases reduces our sinful status or condition and is the reason for our eternal hope and thankfulness.

---

123. Matt 21:33–39 // Mark 12:1–8 // Luke 20:9–15
124. Matt 6:12 // Luke 11:4; Luke 23:34

Justification = God declares us to be perfect because of Christ's perfect life and death.

Sanctification = God moves us closer to moral perfection in our life.

Glorification = God finally makes us morally perfect—we will never sin again.

Let us look at these individually and then look at how these three work together. They complement each other; like the Trinity. There is one salvation, but it consists of three interdependent parts.

We first experience our deliverance from sin when the Spirit frees us from its power so we can at least move toward the Kingdom. While moving toward the Kingdom, we experience all of the following at one time.

> Our mind is convinced by the Spirit of God's love and grace;
> > our will softens and humbly admits our need for salvation from sin;
> > > our appreciative heart trusts Christ's death as the payment for our sinful debt;
> > > > our new love for the Trinity drives us to commit to eternal obedience.

Sin's mastery over us has begun to break down!

Justification

The standard God has set for us to have a saving relationship with him is that we must be perfect. If we are perfect, we needn't be punished by death. How is that going to happen since obviously we are not perfect? The answer is simple yet the profoundest of truths: while we approach the Kingdom by the Spirit's motivation, God makes a formal, welcoming decision to declare us perfect—a legal decision by God to confer the status of "perfect" upon us.

God's declaration that we are now perfect is called our moment of "justification," and it is granted because of our willful association with Jesus Christ. And why is it, exactly, that we are associating ourselves with him? First, because it is Jesus' perfect life that we want God to accept as the substitute for our sinful life. And second, it was Jesus' torturous death as the perfect human Sacrifice that we want to pay for the necessary death penalty we deserve for our sinful life.

Behind the death of Christ was the near-sacrifice of Isaac, the wrong descendant of Abraham to be sacrificed. Human sacrifice is not wrong; in fact, it is necessary. But the human sacrifice would have to be perfect, which, of course, Isaac certainly was not. Only one Human would do, and it would be a descendant of Abraham, but it would not be his son Isaac.

> We have been made holy through the once for all offering of the body of Jesus Christ. Heb 10:10

> Jesus suffered outside the gate to make the people holy through his own blood. Heb 13:12

Christ was the Shepherd who gave his life for his sheep, and he was the Lamb who gave his life for us, his shepherds.[125]

By trusting Jesus not only as Savior but also as Christ the Lord, we are now considered perfect. We certainly could not be justified on the basis of even *perfect* obedience to God. So Paul explains clearly that we are not saved, or justified by works, but by faith alone.

> This showed his righteousness . . . in his justice he justifies the one who has faith in Jesus. Rom 3:26

> You have been saved by grace through faith, not by any of your works. It is the gift of God, not a result from works. Eph 2:8–9

We are known by the company we keep, and since we rely on our newfound Friend, God sees us now as perfect, if only legally speaking. Everyone knows we are not actually perfect. So God's pronouncement of our perfection is in response to our faith and accepting the Substitute's perfect life and sacrificial death for our own.

But we cannot only accept God's forgiveness; to be justified, we must also accept that Jesus Christ is still alive and that he is the Lord over our lives.

> If you confess with your mouth that Jesus is Lord and believe in your heart that God raised him from the dead, you will be saved. Rom 10:9

This would be discouraging to someone who merely wants to trust the Lord for forgiveness, since the Lord's arrangement requires one to trust him also as *Lord*. Paul does not give us the choice to be saved but not obedient to our lord.

However, no perfectly innocent Friend and Savior was available to Old Testament believers. How were they saved then? If there was no perfect human whose morally perfect life could substitute for a believer's imperfect life, and whose earned death only could pay for their own sinful life, how could there have been any justified souls before Christ came? If God had always required perfection, how was that standard met by anyone before Christ?

Until God's fullest plan for deliverance from sin was revealed in Jesus Christ, believing Israelites had only perfectly innocent beasts and vegetation as their substitute for their sins: sheep, goats, oxen, doves, and grain. Even though these substitutes of animals or grain were not morally pure, they at least were not morally impure. They were in a sense "innocent" substitutes for the non-innocent who brought them to the altar as sacrifices. God's grace and wisdom deemed this adequate depending on one other requirement. If the Spirit had propelled one to love and trust God as their savior

---

125. John 1:29; 10:11; Acts 8:32–35; Rom 4:25; 5:6–9, 15–17; Eph 1:7; 5:2; Col 2:12–14; Gal 1:3–4; 2:20; 1 Thess 5:9–10; 1 Tim 2:5–6; Titus 2:13–14; Heb 1:3; 2:9; 7:26–27; 9:11–15, 28; 10:11–12; 12:2–4; 1 Pet 1:18–19; 2:24; 3:18; 1 John 1:7; 3:16; Rev 1:5; 5:6, 9

and king, they were saved by their faith, and this faith was proven by their obedience to the Lord, including his instructions about sacrifices. Entering the Kingdom was not earned by an Old Testament believer's resume' of works any more than it is for us; it was by trusting God and his forgiveness. This is all the Old Testament believer knew about their forgiveness. They knew that empty religiosity and sacrifices were unacceptable to the Lord.[126]

Sanctification

God does not cease to be our savior after this initial pronouncement of justification. He continues to move us progressively toward our spiritual and moral maturation, toward our "sanctification." The Spirit who drove us toward the Kingdom where we received our justification continues to shepherds us in our spiritual growth as well. That same faith that the Spirit inspired during our first sanctifying moments continues on in our progressive, life-long sanctification. Our part then was to respond with a genuine love for the Lord, with a convinced mind, with a softened and humble will, and an appreciative and eager heart to obey diligently.

We began an adventurous and exciting life when we entered our new Kingdom of believers. Now life is an alliance with the holy angels against their sworn, wicked, angelic counterparts in Satan's kingdom. It is a profound life, dealing with the most critical matters of life. Our life is now designed by God's eternal design rather than our confused and fragmented mass of selfish, temporal and shallow goals. Life becomes truly creative and productive. Life is filled with mutual love and service to spiritual sisters and brothers. Though a believer experiences losses and even tragedy, still a glorious, infinite and eternal context surrounds these negatives and overwhelms them with the light of God's intimate, shepherding presence and constant deliverances.

After entering the Kingdom and after being pronounced justified, sanctification gradually returns us toward the moral condition God intended for us, his shepherds, before the Fall. A goal for us now is to anticipate and model how we will live in New Earth, according to God's eternal design. In our first chapter we referenced the "Re-" words which thread through our Christian conversations: Regenerate, Reconcile, Redeem, Restore, Repent, and Renew. When these renovations finally take place, only then can God and humanity continue, without resistance, their glorious pursuit of managing, enhancing, ruling, creating, enjoying, and sharing the Lord's pristine eternal creation.

Through our sanctification, God's image becomes more evident in our lives. Paul and Peter encourage us to progress in our righteousness and to mature further into God's glorious image.

---

126. 1 Sam 15:22–23; Pss 40:6–8; 51:16–17; 69:30–31; 141:1–2; Prov 15:8; 16:6; 21:3, 27; Jer 7:2–24; Isa 1:10–17; 58:5–7; Hos 6:6; Amos 5:21–27; Mic 6:4–8

> We are all . . . being transformed into his image with increasing glory, which comes from the Lord who is the Spirit. 2 Cor 3:18

> Through his precious and great promises we share his divine nature, by escaping the world's corrupting desires. 2 Pet 1:4[127]

The most encouraging fact of our sanctification is Paul's phrase above, "being transformed into his image with increasing glory, *which comes from the Lord who is the Spirit.*" The reassuring basis for our transformation is that it comes from the Spirit, who is God, and who is also called "the Lord." We do not, nor could we produce, this image on our own. It takes a re-creation.

We have just read above in 2 Peter 1:4 about the great promises of escaping corruption. One of those great promises is that God is the one who equips us with everything we need to obey his will.

> May the God of peace, who raised the great Shepherd of the sheep from the dead . . . equip you with everything to do his will, working in us what is pleasing in His sight. Heb 13:20–21

The Lord does equip us. He does not lead us into any temptation to sin or into the evil that follows; instead, he protects us from it.[128] The Lord also finishes what he starts; we are assured that the Lord will drive our righteousness to completion, ending when Christ returns to lead us to New Earth where we will live out our eternal perfection.[129]

The sanctifying Spirit leads us to freedom from sin and into freedom to obey.[130] Paul says this freedom all started "by the washing of rebirth and renewal by the Holy Spirit" (Titus 3:5). God is working right now in our body and soul, equipping us to do the things that will be pleasing to him. He is patiently waiting for us to activate the sanctification that he has already embedded within us.

> Work out your salvation with fear and trembling; for it is God who works in you so you want to work to fulfill his good purpose. Phil 2:12–13

We will prove the Spirit's sanctifying work within us by working it out in our moral behavior. We do not sanctify ourselves, nor does the Spirit do it without our faithful effort. It is, as usual, another shepherding partnership in God's eternal design. When we become more and more sanctified, we become much better at shepherding. Even now we are a renewed creation—we do not need to wait until New Earth. The Holy Spirit started changing our spiritual nature when guiding us into the Kingdom. Old

---

127. Also, Eph 2:8–10; 4:22–24; Phil 1:9–11; Col 1:10; 3:9–10
128. Matt 6:13 // Luke 11:4; 1 Cor 10:13; Heb 2:18; Jas 1:13
129. 1 Cor 1:8–9; Phil 1:6, 9–11; 1 Thess 5:23; 1 Pet 5:10
130. Rom 8:12–14; 2 Thess 2:13; 1 Pet 1:2

"things" died[131] at that time, and we were reborn[132] with a new nature that is free to respond in faith, free from Satan and sin's domination, and free to use our righteousness which God has provided through the Spirit.[133]

Glorification

Our personal salvation is perfectly completed at our death. This sometimes is called our "glorification." Not that we will ever have the full "glory" of God in his infinite and pristine moral character or boundless power and wisdom. But we will be recreated in yet one more phase—recreated to be incapable of sin. From then on we will not only be pronounced perfect, nor will we need to strive for perfection by sanctification. We will be literally perfect forever.

Let us review the big picture. God's eternal design has always been, and will always be that he shepherds his shepherding creation by his blessings. This design applies to every part of creation, the spirits, nature, and humanity.

God's Eternal Design

Creation ●———God shepherds shepherding creation by his blessings━━▶ eternity

However, after the sin of Adam and Eve, humanity needs to be delivered and disciplined in this parenthetical age of shepherding by God and us.

The Parenthetical Design within the Eternal Design

Creation ●— (fall, blessing, deliverance, discipline, cross, millennium) New Earth ━▶ eternity

After Christ's return, and at a time debated by many, there will be an eternal New Earth where all creation will be returned to its originally created perfection and glory: "I will create new heavens and a new earth" (Isa 65:17). That means something unique to humanity; we will return to our original moral perfection and glory, which mirrors the image of God—both in nature and in deed. When we look back at the history of the world from our new eternal perspective, this timeline will then look quite different, with the parenthetical age fading as an era in the far, far distant past.

A Thousand Years as One Day

Creation ●— (parenthetical age) perfect New Earth ━━━━━━━━━━━━▶ eternity

In a sense, this is the same personal experience for believers. We must suffer the conditions of a parenthetical age during our own lives when we need deliverance and discipline. But at our death we will experience a new stage of our life, that of our

---

131. Rom 6:4–7; 2 Tim 2:11–12
132. John 3:3; Col 3:9–10; 1 Pet 1:3, 23
133. 2 Cor 5:17; Gal 5:13, 16, 22, 25; 6:15

glorification—we will be perfect. Just as all creation will experience in New Earth, we will be saved from this fallen world into a new life with the Lord. It is called our glorification because it is then that we will finally mirror the glory of God's image, including his desire and deeds of communication, emotional balance, wisdom and righteousness, creativity, and sovereignty.

Paul's incentive to persevere in his ministry was his converts' salvation from sin, including their glorification: "I endure everything for the chosen ones, so they will obtain the salvation in Christ and *eternal glory* with it" (2 Tim 2:10). Peter also encouraged believers by telling them that God had called them to reflect his *eternal glory* and that he would perfect them (1 Pet 5:10). Hebrews says that one of the attributes of the righteous who have died is that their spirits are now perfect (12:23). This eternal glory will also provide us with eternally perfected bodies to contain our perfect spirits.[134] So our glory will be similar to that of Christ's; whose perfectly coordinated body and spirit will be the pattern for our glorified condition.

We are heirs of God's glory with Christ. Rom 8:17

> Just as we bear the image of a human on earth, we will also bear the image of a heavenly human . . . the dead will be raised imperishable, so we will be changed. 1 Cor 15:49, 52

Our glorification is not just in our nature—it is not a passive "state" in which we merely exist. Rather, our glory will be in our shepherding actions, just as it has always been for God. We do not merely become a shining star in the sky; we become wonderfully creative, productive, and achieving believers in assisting Christ in his kingdom that will grow and grow forever and ever (Isa 9:7). After all, we are promised that we "will reign *on the earth*" (Rev 5:10).

In New Earth we will shepherd as God always has wanted us to shepherd. However, we will continue to grow in those attributes he has shared with us. We will not have met all our creative, wise, relational, enjoyable, and productive potential, any more than creation will have met all its potential; it will still need our tending and shepherding. Look at the glory of human productivity even in this parenthetical age! What could be the wondrous extent of human achievement under God's power and guidance in New Earth where we will progress unimpeded by sin and sorrow? The only limitations would be those with which the Trinity would bless us to have.

The Unity of Sanctification, Justification, and Glorification

Being saved by entering the Kingdom is a wonderful time of God's grace, but it cannot be all that we are serious about, preach about, and thank the Lord about. "Getting in" is only the start of salvation, not the focus. "Getting in" the kingdom of believers is

---

134. Rom 8:23–24; 1 Cor 15:42–44; Phil 3:20–21

important because the saving process needs to start somewhere and sometime. God's dealing with the Israelites is a perfect example. They needed to be rescued from Egypt, but, obviously, the rescue itself was not the ultimate reason for Israel's salvation. The point was not to be rescued to the Sinai desert; it was to move on from there and grow into the mature nation God always intended them to be. Likewise, we are rescued from Satan's kingdom to prosper in Christ's kingdom. We were never expected to remain in a spiritual "Sinai desert," nor would we want to. We want to move far past our "exodus" from Satan's kingdom; we want to move forward to our shepherding responsibilities ahead.

This may seem so elementary, but the Bible message, which is sometimes called the "gospel," is reduced very often to just entering the Kingdom rather than emphasizing the reason for entering. It is discouraging how pervasively this unbalanced view is circulated within the church. It is unfortunate that this entering phase is all that many preachers and evangelists consider to be "the gospel." To consider oneself an evangelist as Christ was, one must proclaim his gospel that the kingdom of God had come, not only that Jesus died on the cross for our sins (Mark 1:14–15).

The great commission's end, or its purpose, is often neglected by concentrating on its means or strategy. The means of the great commission is to convert people from all the nations, but the purpose for the great commission is to make disciples who *obey Christ's commandments*. Again, salvation from sin and baptism is not the focus of the great commission; it includes those elements but the focus is on obedience to Christ. After all, that is how he introduces and concludes his great commission: "All authority has been given to me over heaven and earth . . . teach them to keep all that I have commanded you. Look, I am always with you to the end of the age" (Matt 28:18, 20).

We deprive ourselves and the church of the richness and vast extent of salvation if we think it is only talking about "entering salvation or justification. " We cheat ourselves, but more importantly, we disrespect God for all he does as our Savior. He saves us by justifying us, but he justifies us so we will grow continually in moral maturity—God's salvation is non-stop until our glorification. He saved us to live and walk with him within the eternal design, not to lie stagnant within the profound moment of our justification. We cannot lounge around the cross; we need to march on toward greater righteousness. The cross is at the gate of the Kingdom, not in the Kingdom's square where the living Lamb reigns from his throne.

We have seen that to honor God as our Savior is far more than giving Jesus credit for dying on the cross. What a wonderful and eternal fact that is! But that is not the Lord's focus. His focus is his eternal design—that is, how will we, once died for, become better shepherds? That is his focus now in this parenthetical age and it will be his everlasting focus when we shepherd in New Earth.

Christ, Paul, James, and the book of Hebrews teach that it will take obedience to God's instructions for us to be saved! That may sound like we are saved by our works, so it may be a jolting phrase for many. But listen to our most revered teachers . . .

Christ: "If you want to enter life, keep the commandments . . . You shall not murder, commit adultery, steal, give false testimony, but honor your father and mother and love your neighbor as yourself."[135]

Paul: "The hearers of the Law are not just before God, but the doers of the Law will be justified." Rom 2:13

Hebrews: "Pursue . . . sanctification without which no one will see the Lord." Heb 12:14

James: "Humbly receive the word planted in you which can save your souls. But be doers of the word, not hearers only." Jas 1:21–22

"One is justified by works and not by faith alone." Jas 2:24

We are not justified by our works, but we are not justified without them.

The eternal design puts these statements in perspective. Since we know that God shepherds shepherding believers, we assume that we will have a role to play in God's design for our salvation. We are not expected to be passive. The eternal design requires us to be involved—it has been and always will be a partnership. Fortunately, we hear assurances that God will accomplish our salvation to the same extent as we hear about our own responsibilities for salvation. Romans 8:29–30 provides the clearest assurance of God's resolve to shepherd our salvation deliberately from beginning to end.

> Those whom he foreknew,
> > he predestined to conform to the image of his Son . . .
> > those whom he predestined,
> > > he called, and whom he called,
> > > he justified; and whom he justified,
> > > he glorified.

In the first two lines above, Paul gives the very beginning and end to God's process of salvation. The Lord begins with his foreknowledge of those whom he will save, and he ends it with their perfect conformity to Christ's sinless image. Our conformity is only complete when we are glorified. The remaining lines fill in the steps between foreknowledge and glorification. We are predestined, called, justified, and then glorified. We might ask where sanctification is in this chain. It is implied in our "conformity to the image of Christ"—the conformity we pursue *during* our sanctification process, and the conformity God *finalizes* for us when we are perfected at our glorification.

The responsibilities we have in our sanctification are more than equaled by the certainty of the Lord's finishing what he has begun in us. Compared to Paul's salvation chain in Romans 8:29–30, Peter has an abbreviated chain: we are "chosen by God the Father's foreknowledge and by the sanctifying work of the Spirit for our obedience to

---

135. Matt 19:16–19 // Mark 10:17–19 // Luke 18:18–20; also Luke 10:25–28

Jesus Christ and to be cleansed by His blood" (1 Pet 1:1–2). Luke says it even more briefly: "As many as had been appointed to eternal life, believed" (Acts 13:48). In other words, the whole salvation process begins with God's selection. Unfortunately, how or why we are selected is a point of deep contention, a divisive argument among believers, and a point with which we will not distract ourselves now.

Peter again summarizes the salvation process from beginning to end—from our selection to our glorification.

> Be diligent to confirm your calling and election . . . This way you will be given a rich entrance into the eternal kingdom of our Lord and Savior Jesus Christ. 2 Pet 1:10–11

But Peter also encourages us with the fact of God's guaranteed shepherding blessings and deliverance throughout our journey toward that rich entrance into the eternal kingdom.

> The God of all grace, who has called you to his eternal glory in Christ, will himself restore, confirm, strengthen, and establish you. 1 Pet 5:10

Jude agrees:

> He is able to keep you from stumbling and to make you stand in his glorious presence as blameless and very joyful. Jude 24

Our salvation starts with God's initiative toward us, is nurtured by his patient strengthening of us, and ends with his absolute perfection of us.

God starts us on our path toward conformity to the image of his Son by recreating us, by renewing us. John describes this in a spiritual "genetics" way. Because God has birthed us a second time, we are reborn with his nature within us.[136] In our rebirth, God "washed, sanctified and justified [us] in the name of the Lord Jesus Christ and in the Spirit of our God" (1 Cor 6:11). So God is ultimately responsible for all of our salvation, all three phases of it: justification, sanctification, and glorification. We cannot even take credit for our obedience. Our justification is not "on the basis of righteous deeds, but by his mercy, by the washing of regeneration and renewing by the Holy Spirit . . . so being justified by his grace we would be heirs" (Titus 3:4–7).

These two passages, 1 Corinthians 6:11 and Titus 3:4–7, span the whole salvation process from our saving selection for rebirth, to our saving justification, to our saving glorification as joint heirs with Christ. Paul encourages us further that this rebirth equips us to do the good works which have been worked into us by God through the Spirit. Our obedience will come from within, where God has already planted the power and inclination: "Work out your salvation with fear and trembling; for it is God who works in you so you want to work to fulfill his good purpose."[137]

---

136. 1 John 2:29; 3:9
137. Phil 2:12–13; also, Eph 2:10

We will be considered "blameless" before God at the Judgment because our justification will pronounce us blameless. Our justification is proven only by our sanctified life that God has enabled and assured that we would achieve. So we do not earn glorification; we prove by our Spirit-empowered works that God has called us, justified us, sanctified us, and eventually will glorify us as his sinless shepherds.

GOD DISCIPLINES THE BELIEVER

Old Testament Discipline

All humanity has been afflicted with God's judgments in Eden, including believers. The Lord's disciplinary curses in Eden on humanity were intended to drive humanity back to the Creator himself. They were not vindictive—they were redemptive. But humanity continues to use God's redemptive discipline as an accusation of injustice and judgment *against him* and against his justice. The rebellion just keeps going. Satan just keeps deceiving.

The Lord's discipline is intended to deliver us; it is a blessing! And it is a sign of spiritual maturity to accept discipline and any afflictions stemming from the Eden curses, and to turn to God for strength or deliverance.

> Do not reject the Lord's discipline, or resent his correction
>
> because the Lord corrects those he loves,
>
> just as a father corrects his child in whom he delights. Prov 3:11–12

> It is good for me to be afflicted so I will learn your statutes. Ps 119:71

> I know your statutes are righteous and that you have afflicted me because of your faithfulness. Ps 119:175

Since the Lord's discipline for us entails blessing and deliverance, the same is expected of us as we shepherd the rest of creation according to the eternal design. It will require us to discipline creation as well as bless and deliver it.

Ecclesiastes compares God's wisdom instructions to the goads used by shepherds to keep animals moving along on the correct path: "The words of the wise are like goads... They are given by one Shepherd" (12:11). These rods, staffs, or sticks pricked the animal's flesh, and though they annoyed the animal, the point was to move them in the right direction and at the right pace. God's discipline has the same objective and can even save us sheep from death.[138] The Lord's discipline of believers keeps us honest to our words, motivating us to act consistently with those commitments. And our discipline of those for whom we are responsible is our shepherding role, which helps them if they are not resistant and resentful.[139]

---

138. Prov 5:23; 15:10; 19:18

139. Prov 5:12; 6:23; 12:1; 13:1, 24; 15:5; 22:15; 23:13; 29:15, 17

There were three ways God disciplined believers in the Old Testament. One way was by the common consequences they suffered by behaving contrary to the Lord's moral order. Carelessness can be harmful, lying can be a snare, and violence can end in self-destruction. Second, discipline and judgment also came through Israel's courts when one disobeyed the Law. Finally, the Lord's prerogative was to discipline the believer directly.[140]

When we looked at the specific sins of Israel earlier, we included the nation's individual leaders because of the national implications of their wise or foolish leadership. Wicked kings suffered discipline whether it was through their own disappointing failures as a leader, through an ailment sent by the Lord, or by assassination. But even wonderfully heroic leaders like Moses and Aaron were disciplined severely for their disobedience. For example, Moses was kept from entering the Promised Land because he disobeyed by striking a rock rather than speaking to it.[141]

Discipline for moral foolishness very frequently comes as the natural consequence of one's own irresponsibility. We can be humiliated and lose a good reputation for our adultery, addiction, a crime, or choosing poor friends. A believer's own sinful talk will lead them into trouble,[142] and even petty carelessness is potentially life threatening (Eccl 10:8–10). In routine life, an irresponsible believer will be dominated by those who are more responsible.

> The fool will serve the wise. Prov 11:29
>
> A wise servant will rule over a shameful son. Prov 17:2
>
> The borrower is the lender's slave. Prov 22:7

These penalties are simply built into the moral structure of most human cultures.

Simply surviving when living and thriving is possible can be the judgment one brings upon one's self.[143] One can be poor for a number of reasons beyond one's control, but greed and stinginess can also lead to poverty even though the sinner thinks these financial methods will somehow add to one's possessions.[144] Poverty can also come from laziness and merely chattering rather than working hard.[145]

Not all the Lord's discipline is felt physically or affects physical property. Fear, anxiety, and shame are intense feelings that plague the rebellious believer's heart when God is willing instead to bless with courage, peace, and confidence. Even Adam and Eve, living in a pristine paradise, feared because of their sin.[146] The believer can lose a reputation

---

140. Lev 20:4–5; Eccl 3:16–17; Ps 50:18–22
141. Num 20:8–12, 23–28; 27:12–14; 33:38; Deut 1:37; 3:25–27; 4:21–22; 32:48–52
142. Prov 12:13; 21:6
143. Prov 10:3; 11:29; 13:18, 25; 17:20; 21:20; 22:26–27
144. Prov 11:6, 24; 13:11; 15:27; 21:5, 13; 22:16, 22–23; 28:8, 22
145. Prov 10:4, 8; 12:27; 13:3–4; 19:15; 20:4, 13; 21:17; 14:23; 23:19–21; 24:33–34; 28:19; Eccl 4:5; 5:6;
146. Gen 3:8–10; 4:13–14

when the community judges their folly fairly; they may even be hated.[147] This is also true for those who are so concerned about their reputation that they feel their own self-promotion is needed rather than letting their accomplishments speak for themselves.[148]

New Testament Discipline

One of Jesus' responsibilities as the Messiah is to judge humanity. We mentioned this when focusing on God's judgment of the peoples, but it is true for individuals as well. So he says about himself,

> When the Son of Man comes in his glory with all the angels, he will sit on his glorious throne. All nations will be gathered to him, and he will separate the people as a *shepherd* separates the *sheep* from the goats . . . He will say to those on his left, 'Leave me, you cursed; go into the eternal fire prepared for the devil and his demons . . . These will go into eternal punishment, but the righteous into eternal life.[149]

Jesus Christ's shepherding actions certainly included his blessings and deliverances, but they also included his loving discipline and severe judgments. Whether he condemns the Pharisees, wields the whip in the temple or withers the unproductive fig tree, as the Good Shepherd he will discipline the wicked as extremely as he delivers their victims. He will also discipline his own sheep as tenderly as he delivered them.

The eternal design has chains of shepherding as we have seen a number of times already. In the case of discipline and judgment, another chain is in God's judgment on his Son, the Son's judgment of humanity, humanity's judgment of its individuals, and the individual's judgment of themselves and others. Jesus himself received the severe judgment by his Father, even to the point of torture and death on a cross. Zechariah had recorded God's promise that he would have the "Shepherd" struck down since he became sin for us.[150] Our savior, Christ, experienced the worst for us, taking our sins on himself so we would be seen as pure and justified. He took the Father's judgment on himself as our substitute.

The Lord disciplines his believers like an earthly father disciplines his children. We quoted Proverbs 3:11–12 above and heard that the Lord's discipline of his children is a sign of his love for us. Hebrews 12:4–11 is a commentary on those two verses from Proverbs.

> Do not reject the discipline of the Lord, or resent his correction because the Lord corrects those he loves, just as a father corrects his child in whom he delights. . . . If you are not disciplined, since God disciplines all his children,

---

147. Prov 10:5, 7; 14:17; 18:3; 24:8, 23–24; 25:17; 26:1
148. Prov 11:2; 25:6–7, 27; 29:23
149. Matt 25:31–32, 41, 46; also, Matt 3:12 // Luke 3:17; Luke 19:26–27
150. Zech 13:7; also, Matt 26:31–32 // Mark 14:27–28; 2 Cor 5:21

> you are not legitimate, true children.... For the moment, all discipline seems painful, not pleasant. But eventually, those who receive discipline's training will yield the peaceful fruit of righteousness. Heb 12:5, 8, 10–11

The same point is made twice in John. He tells us in his Gospel and in Revelation that our discipline from God is for our further growth and perfection: "I rebuke and discipline those I love" (Rev 3:19); "He prunes every branch that does bear fruit so it will be even more fruitful" (John 15:2). Paul tells Timothy that the Old Testament was good for him in its rebukes and correction (2 Tim 3:16).

Another shepherding chain link is certainly a significant one. God disciplines us, but then we must discipline ourselves. Paul says,

> You who teach others, do you teach yourself first? Rom 2:21
>
> I discipline my body, making it my slave. 1 Cor 9:27
>
> Train yourself to be godly. 1 Tim 4:7

Hebrews also emphasizes the need for initiative and diligence to maintain our own spiritual life and health: "Strengthen your frail arms and feeble knees. Level out the path for your feet" (Heb 12:12–13). The alternative is moral frailty and death.[151]

Only when we discipline ourselves are we qualified to shepherd others under our care, disciplining them for greater godliness and effectiveness in their Kingdom life. This can be in the very literal sense of disciplining our children as their fathers and mothers (Eph 6:4). Church leaders also must discipline their sheep in orderly and redemptive ways, including public actions against the wayward.[152]

But even in our discipline of others, we are to be like the Lord who wants us to grow, not to be devastated. Our judgment on other believers is to be humble and fair.[153] Instructions from Christ and Paul tell us not to judge another believer in cases when our own hypocrisy disqualifies us.[154] Elsewhere Christ says we must judge, but we must do so in an orderly and dignified way (Matt 18:15–17). A habit of judgment, excessive judgment, or petty criticisms are what destroy the body of Christ. One last qualification: "Vengeance is the Lord's," so our discipline of others should never be retaliatory (Rom 12:19).

As believers we will be declared righteous in the Final Judgment because God has already justified us in Christ. Still, everybody's thoughts and actions will be revealed at the Throne. Both Testaments attest to this.

> God will bring every action to judgment beyond all secrecy, whether good or evil. Eccl 12:14

---

151. Jas 1:14–15; 1 John 5:17

152. Rom 16:17–18; 1 Cor 4:21; 5:5, 9–13; 6:2–3; 2 Cor 13:2, 10; 2 Thess 3:6, 13–15; 1 Tim 5:20; 2 Tim 2:24–25; Titus 3:9–11

153. 2 Cor 2:5–11; Gal 6:1; Jas 5:19–20

154. Matt 7:1–2 // Luke 6:37; Rom 14:10–12

We will all stand before God's judgment seat. Rom 14:10

Each of us will give an account of ourselves to God. Rom 14:12

We must all appear before Christ's judgment seat so that each may receive what is due for what was done in the body, good or evil. 2 Cor 5:10

We may be relaxed that our justification will end in our glorification. But we will have to suffer while our personal failures are brought to light since our sins will be made public. We will be assessed thoroughly, even our secret sins, known only to God and the believer.[155]

One might ask why we would need to go through this exposure and recounting of all our sins as well as our godly deeds. It is necessary because it will show us individually and all peoples just how generously gracious God is. As far as our godly deeds, they will be announced publicly to prove to us and all peoples that the Holy Spirit was enormously successful in equipping us to follow the Lord. It will finally be proven to all that our justification was the beginning of God's eternal glorification of us.[156] As horrific as the Judgment will be for the unsaved, for believers it will be a time when the angels and peoples will praise the Lord for his grace and justice to all creation.

---

155. 1 Cor 4:5; Luke 8:17; Rom 2:16

156. Ps 62:12; Matt 16:27 // Mark 8:38 // Luke 9:26; Rom 2:5–8; 1 Cor 3:13; Jas 2:12–13; Rev 2:23; 20:12; 22:12

11

Shepherding Essentials

WHAT DOES IT TAKE TO BE A GODLY SHEPHERD?

SO FAR WE HAVE focused on how God shepherds his creation: spirits, nature, and humanity. We have reviewed his loving shepherding ways as the foundation for his eternal design. However, we could not help but see along the way how humanity is to shepherd by specific ethical principles. We have looked closely at the shepherding roles that spirits and nature have played throughout history in the chapters "Shepherding Spirits" and "Shepherding Nature." But details on humanity's role as shepherds in the eternal design have been deferred until these final three chapters. We have introduced the primary commission and its shepherding responsibilities for humanity, and we have accentuated human links in the eternal design's chains of shepherding. Now, for the rest of this outline of theology we will survey how we shepherd on a day-to-day, even hour-to-hour basis.

God has designed creation to shepherd itself under his authority for eternity. Spirits, nature, and humanity were created for productive shepherding of one another in his eternal design. But, of course, humanity's role in shepherding is most prominent, and we are the most equipped to do so in godly ways. To repeat the Testaments' statements dealing with human authority, we distill the list of examples given in chapter 3.

> Subdue the earth and rule. Gen 1:28
>
> You have created humanity to rule over your works. Ps 8:6
>
> The expansion of [Christ's] government and peace will be endless. Isa 9:7
>
> The holy ones . . . will receive and possess the Kingdom forever. Dan 7:18
>
> The time arrived when the holy ones took possession of the Kingdom. Dan 7:22
>
> All kingdoms will be given to the holy people. Dan 7:27
>
> The meek will inherit the earth. Matt 5:5

We will reign with him [Christ]. 2 Tim 2:12

I give authority over the nations to the victorious and obedient. Rev 2:26

The one who overcomes I will allow to sit with me on my throne. Rev 3:21

You have made them to be a kingdom . . . and they will reign on earth. Rev 5:10

[His servants] will reign forever and ever. Rev 22:5

The grand panorama of shepherding within God's eternal design narrows down from God, to humanity, to the believing community, to you, to me and our individual responsibility. The eternal design is actively modeled by God and is variously interpreted and followed by the peoples, yet mostly in error. To the Lord's credit, the design is much better activated by the believing community and its individual believers.

But first, let us discuss a few elements of the Christian life that are essential for day-to-day shepherding. We could not have come this far in our study without already using these basic truths of Christian living as shepherds, but now we go deeper to explain them. They are a combination of who we are and what we do, and without these elements, we are not equipped to be successful shepherds. These basic truths are about (1) God's image, (2) our love, (3) our faith, (4) our self-shepherding, and (5) our righteousness. They are not separate elements—they are completely integrated. They are so integrated that separate pages about each of them is bound to be somewhat artificial. Furthermore, we do not claim these are the only basic elements, but at least any such list should include these five.

GOD'S IMAGE

All humans are created in the Trinity's image, regardless of era and area, social status, economic means, race, age, or gender. The Lord is the most inclusive, equal opportunity employer because everyone carries his image to the extent it has not been marred by sin. So everyone shepherds because that is the nature of God, and his shepherding attributes equip humanity for God's primary commission.[1]

Though all humans carry God's image within them, the Spirit progressively recasts believers into God's glorious image in a more substantial way. We are being

---

1. Gen 1:26–28; Acts 17:29; Jas 3:9

transformed in a way that our nature will reflect his glory but, of course, it will not shine nearly as brightly since we are not infinite.[2] God's procreative act was to produce sons and daughters like him, and he did that most literally in the birth of his Son. Jesus Christ is the perfect image of his Father; like Father, like Son.[3] So when we are promised that we have been "predestined to be conformed his Son's image," we are promised that we will conform to the image of God (Rom 8:29). "We know when Christ appears that we will see him as he really is and we will be like him" (1 John 3:2). Even our bodies will be like Christ's so that we can walk, work, and act like he did—not just feel, or think like him (Phil 3:21). What is God's image then, and what are his glorious attributes that we reflect more and more as we become more sanctified? I would suggest these basic godly attributes include emotion, righteousness, creativity, power, complexity, and sovereignty.

God's *emotions* are a standard for ours. Some feel that we should deny or discount what the Bible says about the Lord's emotions. From this wooden opinion is carved an idolatrous image of God. After all, God is love (1 John 4:8). Love is the foundational emotional attribute for human righteousness since love for God and others motivates us to do what is right. Should we redefine the love of God and the weeping of Christ as emotionless acts? To shepherd as God shepherds requires us to love as he does: from the heart and through our actions. Joy is also a common emotion to God and humanity; it can be a reward for those who see fruit from their shepherding. Bringing delight to God and others brings us joy too. But, like God, we can be grieved when the curses of the Fall make their way into our lives and the lives of those we know. Our grief may lead to correcting the circumstances and even those who caused the grief. The Lord's anger was felt by Israel's enemies and the self-righteous Pharisees. When controlled, anger can be a tool for righteousness as it flames against irresponsibility and injustice. And when anger is justified, it can stem from an emotional hatred for the sinful causes of that anger.

God's perfect *righteousness* is an attribute he expects humanity to copy as well. His righteousness is the standard by which he blesses, delivers, and judges his creation. Our obedience to his laws and wisdom will do the same. He declares us righteous when we are justified, and we prove ourselves righteous by our faithful submission to his standards. It is this capacity for righteousness that equips us to restore the rest of the fallen world. Eventually, in recreated New Earth our nature will be perfectly righteous again. But until then, we struggle, yet progress in imaging God's righteousness.

Human *creativity* also mirrors the nature of God. His invention and maintenance of the world started and continues as a protracted series of creative acts. The beauty of his creation is just the face of his deeper, broader, innovative and elaborate management of all the mathematical, chemical, physical, and biological components of

---

2. 2 Cor 3:18; Col 3:9–10
3. John 10:30; 14:7–9; Heb 1:3

creation. Since humanity carries God's amazing nature, we too are to creatively manage all components of reality by wisdom and discernment.

Creativity is instinctive to us. Whatever our gifting might be, our God-given skills include the ability to use them in creative ways. This routine but creative management of our daily lives in inventive ways is far more frequent and more profound than artistic pieces that make their way into museums, onto stages or into concert halls. Of course, the gift of artistry that produces plays, poetry, music, sculptures, paintings, novels, and dances is a marvelous expression of the human imagination. But how we survive or thrive through life requires that everyone craft responses to ominous and complicated circumstances. Serving others demands that we innovate and improvise specialized solutions to meet their unique needs as individuals or groups.

Though only the Lord is *all*-powerful, we are expected to apply our limited power to his purposes when fulfilling our primary commission. Using that power appropriately requires the emotion of love and the compass of righteousness to copy God's loving shepherding of his creation. Otherwise, power becomes oppressive and abusive. Using our physical, emotional, intellectual, and spiritual strengths to impose God's order on the earth is not just our opportunity, it is our daily and life-long responsibility as stewards of God's world.

Transcending space and time is not an attribute we share with God as closely as his other attributes. The Lord has put the sense of eternity within us (Eccl 3:11), and we do have eternal life. But we do not and will not exist outside of time as God does. But it is satisfying to conceive of eternity in some way—but better to experience it eventually in New Earth. Only in our minds can we escape the restraints of space and time, as we apply our memories to the past and our imaginations to the future. We cannot travel outside time apart from that, and travel is also limited through space.

However, we are still tasked to manage time and space; we manage them from within these dimensions while God manages them from without. Time management is a critical part of our entire life management, and we cannot succeed in the primary commission without "timing" our plans, efforts and results. Managing life is always done some*place*: in the home, at work, in the countryside, on the sea. Managing those spaces themselves and managing what happens in those spaces is our regular moral duty.

The Lord's *complexity* is shown by his knowledge of absolutely everything. "Everything" includes the relationships between every object, thought and action, even their potential relationships. His complexity is not due to his knowledge alone, however. He *acts* wisely, responding to everything he knows, which again, is everything. Humanity does not have any such breadth and depth of knowledge, much less wise and errorless responses and management of what little we do know. Yet, we are responsible to be as informed as possible about the most profound and urgent realities in our world so that we are able to pray and act effectively as God's partner in blessing, delivering, and disciplining this world. Though we do not know everything, we are to learn more and to act increasingly more wisely. This is a necessary part of our righteousness so we can restore ourselves and our surroundings to God's standards in practical ways.

The *sovereignty* of God and humanity is his attribute that combines and applies his other attributes when shepherding his creation. So, our sovereignty as shepherds also depends on our godly attributes. Human emotion, righteousness, creativity, power, and complexity, as well as our ability to manage space and time, all prepare and empower us to be faithful followers in the Lord's reclaiming of this earth. Since we are created in his image to shepherd the way he shepherds, his personal attributes are the pattern for achieving the primary commission.

God's *holiness* and *glory* are the whole of all of his attributes together. His attributes make up the total nature of God which is incomprehensible and overwhelming in its infiniteness. Nonetheless, since we are God's children, we have the Father's "DNA" and should act like our Father acts: "Be imitators of God as his loved children" (Eph 5:1). Peter refers to Leviticus 11:44–45, 19:2, and 20:26 for the most general of all moral commands in both Testaments,

> Be holy in all you do, like him who called you is holy, since it is written: "Be holy, because I am holy." 1 Pet 1:15–16

That completeness found in the perfect combination of all of God's attributes is the completeness that we have always been called to copy.

But how can we be so optimistic that we can even start toward this completeness, this holiness and glory? When the Holy Spirit recreates us as new believers, he uses God's nature as the cast to recast us. So we have the fruits of the Spirit within us that need to be activated in daily life. These fruits from God the Holy Spirit become evident because they are his fruit from his holy nature: love, joy, peace, patience, kindness, goodness, faithfulness, gentleness, and self-control (Gal 5:22–23). James adds another list to Paul's: God's wisdom which we should copy is pure, peaceable, gentle, reasonable, merciful, steadfast, and not hypocritical (3:17).

LOVE

There is something just as profound and foundational as the eternal design and its primary commission—love! Love is the basis for the Trinity's unity, it is the basis for the Trinity's relationship with creation, it is the basis of our relationship with the Trinity, it is the basis for relationships with others. Yes, God created humanity to manage his creation, but the reason he wants creation managed well is that he loves it so much. The Father made his Son king of creation because he loves his Son and he loves his creation. God made us kings and queens in his kingdom because he loves us too. This is why Jesus reduced the Law to one principle with two parts: love your God and love your neighbor.

God has developed meaningful and very active relationships with all nations, peoples, and individuals. Not by simply loving emotionally, but by *enacting* his emotional love through his blessing, delivering, and disciplining us all. The Lord's eternal design expects a *productive* relationship of love shown through the whole person—through emotions and actions. We would not have needed a physical body to simply love God and "have a relationship with him." We were given a powerful body and mind to empower and equip us for the daunting task to lovingly shepherd his very physical and very powerful creation.

Love and actions cannot be separated. We are commanded to love God, but we cannot say we love him if we are not obedient. Christ says, "If you love me, keep my commandments" (John 14:15). Love determines whether what we do is out of appreciation and worship of God or for only ourselves. Mere compliance is not acceptable to God. Never has been, never will be. Ask the Pharisees. This is sin's deceit—to separate our acts from our nature and excuse ourselves because we have one and not the other. We must follow God's example—he does who he is. We do who we are.

It is in the Old Testament law where we first hear the main directions of our love: "Love the Lord your God with all your heart, soul and might" and "Love your neighbor as yourself."[4] Loving God is an Old Testament theme behind all of its teaching, reprimands, correction, and training for our righteousness. It is commanded frequently in the Law itself and referenced again often in the rest of the Testament."[5] Half of these commands link loving God with obedience and service.[6] That is the way we prove our love; that is the way God proves his love—by powerful, faithful actions.

The second love commandment, "Love your neighbor as yourself," covers anything we do where another person is involved. The command to love one's neighbor requires our ethical awareness just as often as keeping the command to love God. Loving God and obeying *all* his commandments includes this second command to love others, so by loving others we are loving God. The Israelites were expected to be merciful to others since God was merciful to them in so many ways.[7] So even public punishment for a crime was properly humbling but not humiliating (Deut 25:3). God's justice and mercy are delicately balanced on the fulcrum of love.

We are to love others *as ourselves*; this implies then that we are expected to love ourselves in appropriate ways too. For example, Proverbs 19:8 says, "Whoever gets wisdom loves his own soul." That is an appropriate incentive to be wise—to satisfy oneself. There are benefits for ourselves in taking care of our mental health and to pursue joy. So it is not self-centered to compare our love for others with love for ourselves; instead love for ourselves becomes a pattern for us to treat others as we would want to be treated. We will at look at this point more deeply from New Testament passage in a moment.

---

4. Deut 6:5; Lev 19:18

5. Deut 7:9; 10:12; 11:1, 13, 22; 13:3; 19:9; 30:6, 16; Josh 22:5; 23:11; Judg 5:31; Neh 1:5; Pss 5:11; 18:1; 31:23; 69:36; 97:10; 116:1; 145:20; Isa 56:6; Dan 9:4

6. Deut 7:9; 10:12; 11:1, 13, 22; 30:16; Josh 22:5; Neh 1:5; Pss 69:36; 145:20; Dan 9:4

7. Ex 22:26–27; Lev 25:38, 42–43, 53; Deut 15:15; 24:17–18

As shepherds in God's image, our love will bless others with forgiveness rather than hateful revenge in thought or deed: "Hatred stirs up conflict, but love covers all offenses" (Prov 10:12). But our shepherding love will also discipline others:

> Whoever spares the rod hates their child, but one shows his caring love by disciplining their child. Prov 13:24

> Open rebuke is better than hidden love. Prov 27:5

How the Israelites were to love their neighbor as themselves is explained through the hundreds of laws and wisdom instructions which we will examine in the last two chapters of this study. Commandments, wisdom instruction, and other biblical instructions describe in detail our orderly, loving and fair ways to shepherd the world. The same fruits mentioned in the New Testament that come through the Spirit were just as necessary for the Old Testament Israelites to genuinely love their neighbors with patience, kindness, goodness, loyalty, and gentleness.[8] The Law added foreigners as objects of neighborly love too, and Christ echoes these passages in his Good Samaritan parable (Luke 10:30–37).

> You must not hate your brother . . . Do not look for revenge or bear a grudge against the sons of your people, but love your neighbor as yourself. Lev 19:17–18

> Treat the foreigner living among you as an Israelite. Love them as yourself. Lev 19:34

> Show your love to foreigners. Deut 10:19

Fortunately, in his powerful grace, God has promised to change our hearts to want to love and serve him and others. So the Spirit empowers us for change. God knows our sinful nature and our weaknesses, so he promised to do the necessary heart-changing himself so that his people could love him. He wrote his commandments on the Israelites' hearts so they could obey more easily.

> The Lord your God will circumcise your heart and the heart of your children, to love the Lord your God with all your heart and with all your soul. My commandment today is not too difficult or out of your reach . . . The word is very near you; it is in your mouth and *in your heart* so that you can obey it. Deut 30:6, 11, 14

The Lord has blessed us by making us capable of loving him and following his commandments. It takes *his* doing to empower us to work against our sinful nature and to love and obey him. Praise him for understanding us and loving us to bring us to this point.

Jesus Christ summed up righteousness by the same two Old Testament love commandments.

---

8. Gal 5:22–23; Jas 3:17

> All that is in the Law and Prophets depends on these two commandments: "Love the Lord your God with all your heart and with all your soul and with all your mind." This is the primary and greatest commandment. And the second is like it: 'Love your neighbor as yourself.'[9]

It is clear that this summary of Old Testament morality was known already before the New Testament times since a religious leader recited it to Christ (Luke 10:27–28). Christ repeats this Old Testament teaching when warning the Pharisees of their misguided emphasis on traditions rather than these two summary laws of love for others and for God: "You tithe your miniscule mint, rue, and other herbs, yet you ignore justice [for others] and love for God" (Luke 11:42).

Christ's summary of Christian morality is reaffirmed by John and Paul. John records the breakfast conversation between Christ and Peter when Christ asks whether Peter loves him. Peter's response of love to the Master is then met with "Then shepherd my sheep." Our love for the Lord leads to our actions of shepherding love to others. Later, John reaffirmed these inseparable commands, merging the two into just one: "And the commandment from him is this: the one who loves God should love his fellow believer too" (1 John 4:21). Paul, Peter, and John continue to repeat the Old Testament law and Christ's summary of it, making it a central topic for the entire New Testament.[10]

There are three ways one uses oneself as a reference point for what shepherding in love would look like. We know we are to love others *as ourselves*. This is not a selfish comment since the Trinity loves itself as the core relationship between the Father, Son, and Spirit. Another way of saying "Love your neighbor as yourself" is to say what Christ says: "Whatever you would want done for you, do for others."[11] The Lord's "Golden Rule" is a restatement of Christ's second summary law of loving others as ourselves. Husbands are to exemplify this in their family: "Let each husband love his wife as himself" (Eph 5:33). A second way we use ourselves as a reference point is when we use the example of Christ's love for us; just as Christ loves us, we are to love others. We love others in the way we are loved by the Lord. Christ says, "Love one another as I have loved you."[12] We are the benchmark for loving others in a third way: we are to give preference to others. We are to love others *more than ourselves*.[13] Do we prioritize our wants or the more pressing needs of others? Self-sacrifice is implicit in many acts of love. There are loving acts that cost us virtually nothing or are only a minor inconvenience. But love is shown when at the risk of sleep, health, recreation, or even life, the shepherd goes out to look for that one lost sheep.

---

9. Matt 22:40, 37–39; also, Mark 12:29–33; John 15:17; 1 Cor 13:1–13; 16:22

10. Rom 13:8–10; 1 John 3:23; also, 1 Cor 16:14; Col 3:14; 1 Thess 4:9; 2 Thess 1:3; Titus 3:3; Philem 7; Heb 13:1; 1 Pet 1:22; 4:8; 2 Pet 1:7; 1 John 2:10; 3:10–19; 4:7

11. Matt 7:12 // Luke 6:31

12. John 13:34–35; 15:12–13, 17; also, Eph 5:25

13. Rom 12:10; 1 Cor 10:24, 33; Phil 2:3–4; 2 Cor 12:14–15; also, John 15:13

We cherish and praise Jesus for proving that there is no greater love than giving up one's life for another person (John 15:13), but very seldom is that literally necessary. Our love that prefers others over ourselves is the pinnacle of ethical living. The "Love Chapter," 1 Corinthians 13, tells us that love will show the other fruits of the Spirit: patience, kindness, humility, generosity, forgiveness, and joy (4–7). There is joy in giving our Spiritual fruit to please and build up our neighbors so that they will profit, not ourselves.[14]

A significant self-sacrifice on the believer's part is to restrict one's own moral freedom for the sake of another person who might mishandle that freedom out of spiritual weakness. Freedom is very important to us since God's truth does set us free. But we must defer to others when what we know is our moral freedom is not healthy for other Christians. The important consideration here is that the other may be a weak, possibly new Christian, with little understanding of their freedom. It does not refer to another person who is arrogant and judgmental with an unteachable spirit. The simple, unwise Christian has a conscience that is too sensitive for some freedoms. They are the ones who need protection from contradicting their beliefs and being hypocrites in their own eyes, self-judging and stumbling in their faith.[15]

On the other hand, another believer's background, experiences, current circumstances, or unhealthy propensities make it very hard, even harmful for them to share in some behavior. One's specific behavior itself may not be morally wrong, yet it can conjure up thoughts and emotions in other believers, triggering actions which for them are then uncontrollable, even devastating. Those from abusive families, addictive pasts or presents, incarceration, or any traumatic situation do not need "liberated souls" to dangle their liberties irresponsibly for all to see. A sensitive, shepherding Christian will not flaunt their freedom in front of those who will always be fragile about certain actions.

FAITH

Our relationship with our Lord God is based on our love and our "faith" or "trust" in him. In this sense, we take "faith" and "trust" to mean the same thing. When we "have faith" in something, we are trusting it.

Faith has one significant basis—the revealed character of God who is perfect and cannot contradict himself. If God was able to make mistakes or if he was inconsistent, we could only guess about his relationship with us. If God was capable of deception, we could not love him; we could only be terrorized by him. He models honesty, dependability, and loving shepherding. The Lord leaves no reasonable alternative for us than to trust his all-knowing, all-powerful capacity to do only what is just, wise, and gracious. Any distrust of the Lord ignores his blessing and deliverance. Our relationship

---

14. Rom 15:2; 1 Cor 10:33
15. Rom 14:1–6, 21–23; 1 Cor 8:9–13; 10:28–29

with God is only as deep as our trust in his moral character. Faith is not based on the dread of an unpredictable God whose compassion is only occasionally evident. Faith is not a starry-eyed, mystified obsession with an unknowable "Totally Other."

Faith is not in spite of reason, but because of it. God is not so pitiless that he would ask us to cast aside such a critical component of our nature and ability as reason, to only "feel" like we should trust him. His nature is to know, and to act intelligently on that knowledge. He created us to live the same way. He designed us to function by using all of our godly attributes simultaneously, and he is disappointed when in our shepherding we do not reflect his balanced character of feeling, knowledge, reason, and intuition. This is the description of faith in Hebrews 11:1: "Faith is the *confidence* in what we hope for and the *assurance* of what we cannot see." Faith is not the same as hope; faith is the basis for intelligent hope.

There are at least three ways we trust our Lord. First, there is the foundational trust that pervades our whole approach to our life, a trust that is implicit within our conscious and unconscious resignation to God's loving will and goals for our lives:

> I eternally trust in God's unfailing love. Ps 52:8[16]

> Trust in Him at all times. Ps 62:8

This type of faith is the primary consideration in our concerns, priorities, and decisions as we look for the reasons, direction, and results of our experiences on a daily basis. This faith is behind our drive to live and act for the Lord even when we are not praying, worshipping, studying his Word, or consciously thinking about him at the moment. This confidence that "God has made everything beautiful in its time" informs and forms our perception of reality from the Trinity's viewpoint even if we do not know what that might be specifically (Eccl 3:11). The believer naturally trusts God without knowing the exact decision that will come from that perfect council between the Father, Son, and Spirit.

Second, our trust is shown when coming to God with *specific concerns* and requests for deliverance for ourselves or others: "The Lord is my strength and shield; I trust him and he helps me."[17] This faith is founded on the first level: that pervasive sense of God's total trustworthiness. But this second level of faith applies the first level by a purposeful voicing of one's vulnerability and inadequacy. So the act of humbling oneself to ask for the Lord's shepherding blessings or deliverance is an act of faith that God will listen to our request. Then there is the confidence that his all-powerful, all-knowing love will resolve the matter in his best time and way. An opposite relationship with the Lord is presumption—the "faith" we often have in ourselves and assumes we know what God must do and expects his obedience to our solution. We expect him

---

16. Also, Pss 31:14; 33:21; 78:32; Prov 3:5; 28:25; Isa 43:10
17. Ps 28:7; also, 2 Chr 14:11; 20:20; Pss 13:5; 22:4–5; 37:5; 56:11; 91:2; Isa 12:2; Jer. 17:7; 39:18

to do more than just consider our recommendations for his response, we assume he will act as we recommended.

A third demonstration of our faith in the Lord is our active, *genuine obedience* to him and his Word: "Trust in the Lord, and do good things."[18] When we obey a specific instruction of God out of devotion and humility, we have committed ourselves to God's will and we accept the consequences that will come from it. We are trusting regardless of the results. We trust that God's wisdom is revealed in his instructions in the first place, and we trust his wisdom will be proven in his response to our obedience. Obedience, then, is not just what we *have to do* to be considered a person after God's own heart, but what we *thirst to do* because of God's dependable, perfect love for us. This third expression of our trust for God, though it is inseparable from the other two, is what the remainder of our study is about.

We see the same three ways of trusting the Lord in the New Testament. First, trust is that foundational belief upon which our very being depends in all of our thinking and doing. It is the framework within which all of life is understood and lived: "God causes all things to work together for good for those who *love* God" (Rom 8:28). Peter expresses the inexpressibility of this trust and joy:

> You love him without ever having seen him, and you believe in him without seeing him even now, and you rejoice with indescribable joy. 1 Pet 1:8

Faith is based on our inexpressible love for God and faith *is* our confidence that he loves us. It is like the complete faith of a child in a parent's love—that trust provides the comprehensive life context in which to grow up.[19]

Second, there is the faith shown at critical times when we come to the Lord with specific requests. We would not do this without faith in the Lord's wisdom and ability, so we approach him, walking in steps of faith toward his throne. Approaching the throne is the first act of faith, believing he will hear us. Then we trust him for his answer. Peter commended the lame man for his trust in the Lord: "His faith that has come through Jesus has given him this complete health" (Acts 3:16). Jesus compliments the centurion for his unparalleled faith in requesting that Jesus heal the centurion's servant from a distance.[20] And a Gentile woman showed her confidence in Jesus by even jousting with him verbally about her nationality, and then the Lord responded to her faith by healing her possessed daughter.[21]

The third expression of our trust is our obedient actions from our whole heart, soul, mind, and strength. This is the faith that proves us to be successful shepherds in the Kingdom. Yes, it proceeds from the faith that is behind all our attitudes and priorities. But these *actions* prove that we are driven by that foundational faith and love for

---

18. Ps 37:3; also, Pss 4:5; 119:66; 143:8; Prov 16:20; Isa 50:10
19. Matt 19:14–15 // Mark 10:14–16 // Luke 18:16–17
20. Matt 8:9–13 // Luke 7:8–9
21. Matt 15:22–28 // Mark 7:24–30

the Lord. This is the whole point of the "Faith Chapter," Hebrews 11. The following saints, because of their faith, *did* things; they did not just believe or feel things.

Abel	Offered an acceptable sacrifice
Enoch	Pleased God
Noah	Built an ark
Abraham	Left home, nearly offered Isaac as sacrifice
Sarah	Gave birth
Isaac	Blessed Jacob and Esau
Jacob	Blessed his grandsons
Joseph	Ordered his bones be carried from Egypt
Moses' Parents	Hid baby Moses
Moses	Left Egypt after obeying Passover command
Israelites	Crossed Red Sea and destroyed Jericho
Rahab	Welcomed the spies
Others	Conquered nations, were righteous, etc.

This popular passage is not about faith in general; it is about how faith motivates hopeful endurance in doing the right things. Although these saints did not see everything for which they had hoped come to fruition in their lifetime, they had every confidence and assurance that what they hoped for would come, eventually.

Our trust in the Lord and his Word are the beginning of shepherding morality. By faith we act obediently to God's perfect instructions which lead us to serve him and to serve others by blessing, delivering, and disciplining them. This is James' point: we cannot shepherd the poor by simply believing facts about God. The actions from faith impress God, not just the believing.

> Faith by itself, without works, is dead . . . I show you my faith by my works. Was not Abraham our father justified by works when he offered his son Isaac on the altar? You see then that his faith worked with his works and was completed by his works. Jas 2:17–18, 21–22

This puts our moral behavior up front in the eternal design. Shepherding means we *do* loving things in obedience to God, we can not just believe, talk about, preach about, share about, sing about doctrinal truth.

SELF-SHEPHERDING

Our privilege to shepherd starts with our own selves. We cannot grow in our faith after becoming Christians by our own efforts alone, but neither can we grow in righteousness without personal effort. Though we do not *enter* the Kingdom because of our works, we do *walk* in the Kingdom by our works by faith and obedience. We are told numerous times that our works must be righteous; our works are to be pleasing to

God. However, our caring, understanding Trinity, Father, Son, and Spirit, have promised to give us all the strength and wisdom we need to do so. To start with, we have his nature within us in the Spirit's fruit and gifts.

The Lord's conversation with Cain was one of the most critical discussions in the entire Bible. It brought shepherding one's self into the very center of the primary commission. God told Cain,

> If you do what is right, you are acceptable. But if you do not do the right things, sin crouches at the door desiring you. So, you must *rule over* sin. Gen 4:7

God's eternal design can only be attained when one subdues one's own spiritual and moral life. Before this conversation with Cain, Adam and Eve had already failed to rule over their personal sinful lust for the forbidden tree's fruit and for the greater "wisdom" that they desired. The Lord's challenge to Cain exposed clearly the spiritual warfare in which we are constantly engaged. Sin waits to pounce on us and consume us. The Serpent still waits for an open door to slither through and to have his way with us. But to be free from the power of sin and its mastery over us is what God has always intended for humanity, even now.

Can you see how the primary commission's word "subdue" is not too strong? We must be in charge of sin! Ezekiel relays God's message that the alternative is our own destruction: "Turn away from all your sins or they will destroy you" (18:30). All creation is fallen; humanity, dark spiritual forces, and even at times the physical world all vie to control whatever is within reach for its own purposes. "Subdue the earth" is not too strong a phrase when one must either control one's environment or be controlled by it.

This is exactly David's own concern when he asks for the Lord's assistance in not letting sin control him: "Restrain your servant from deliberate sins, do not let them *rule over* me" (Ps 19:13). It is this assistance that he does not want God to withhold by removing the Spirit from him (Ps 51:10–11). However, when David proved less vigilant and did not work with the Spirit within him, he had to confess defeat by sin: "My iniquities have *overtaken* me" (Ps 40:12). Life against sin is "subdue or be subdued." Paul reminds us of this same urgent requirement just as forcefully as Cain heard it in Genesis and David confessed it in Psalms.

> Do not let sin reign in your mortal body so that you obey its evil desires. Sin is no longer your master. Rom 6:12, 14

Sin crouches at our door, but then it rears up to tempt us. The natural self, or "flesh" as it is sometimes referred to in the New Testament, is sin's best friend; it opens the door and invites sin in. Sin looks for an opportunity, and our flesh looks for an excuse. Sin is always there and willing to offer one.[22] It was the Couple's flesh that desired

---

22. Matt 26:41 // Mark 14:38 // Luke 22:40; Rom 13:14; 1 Cor 6:12; Eph 2:1–3; Jas 1:14

the fruit, and sin has reigned over humanity ever since.[23] "Do not be conquered by evil; conquer evil with good" (Rom 12:21).

Sin not only crouches and wins a battle, it moves into the house and then goes on to subject the weak to slavery and harsh bondage.[24] Jesus Christ says, "Everyone who sins is the slave of sin" (John 8:34). Paul calls it captivity by Satan to do his will (2 Tim 2:26). Paul devotes three long chapters in Romans 6–8 to the subject of sin's enslavement, so they are an extended commentary on that very short conversation between the Lord and Cain. The declaration of our independence from sin started with our Spirit-driven walk toward the Kingdom. But until New Earth we will be plagued by the weakness of our flesh.

> Our old [natural] self was crucified with him . . . so we would no longer be enslaved to sin. 6:6
>
> Do not let sin reign in your body so that you obey its lusts. 6:12
>
> Sin will no longer be your master. 6:14
>
> Though you were sin's slave you became sincerely obedient. 6:17
>
> You once presented your body as slaves to impurity. 6:19
>
> I am fleshly, sold as a slave to sin. 7:14
>
> I see a different law in my body . . . making me a prisoner of the law of sin. 7:23

Satan and sin do not play—they do horrendous harm (1 Thess 3:5). For Satan and his minions temptation is not a hobby, it is a 24/7 career—no weekends, holidays, vacations, or retirement. Satan is extremely wise, well-practiced, and passionately devoted. He never misses an opportunity to succeed. We who are progressing in our sanctification are also becoming extremely wise, well-practiced, passionately devoted, and will not miss an opportunity to succeed. It is a war. Spiritual warfare is not only in the "heavenly places"; it is in every room of our house, every office, every Sunday School classroom, everywhere. Satan thrives on any disbelief that one is in a massive power struggle with him. Yet the Spirit's overpowering alliance with us, and in us, will strengthen us for victory.

Our aggressive righteousness is not just hanging on, not just persevering. It is an offensive war against sin and the dark kingdom's Leader and soldiers: "Fight the good fight!"[25] We mentioned this when we focused on our role in fighting evil spirits in chapter 6. Of course, we would not stand a chance except for our Leader, Equipper, and Encourager, but we are enlisted to fight with him in this conflict of enormous proportions. The war started in Eden and will end at Armageddon. It is a war with

---

23. Rom 5:21; Jas 1:15
24. Acts 8:23; Rom 16:18; 5:1; Titus 3:3; Heb 2:15; 2 Pet 2:19
25. 1 Tim 1:18; 6:12

sin, our natural self, demons, and temptation and is fought as closely as hand-to-hand, one-on-one combat. It is battled by the church in its local and wider surroundings in community and national public policies. It is fought between persecuting regimes and their vulnerable Christian citizens. The fight is physical; it is spiritual, but we fight with fellow-soldiers[26] and with spiritual armor and weapons.[27]

On the other hand, praise the Lord that he does not allow the believer to be overly tempted, and he is always gracious to equip and empower us to shepherd ourselves, our lives, and our surroundings.

> God is faithful and will not let you be tempted beyond your ability. When you are tempted, he will also provide an escape so you can endure it.[28]

We have the strength and righteousness already within us through the Holy Spirit who provides all that we need to walk morally, uprightly and righteously. It is our responsibility to work with that strength and righteousness regardless of the strength of this struggle. Paul encourages us many times with the assurance that God has provided his strength, power, and hope so that we are able to be righteous in our conduct. Peter and the book of Hebrews reinforce our assurance.

> Work out your salvation with fear and trembling since God has worked in you to want to work for his good purposes. Phil 2:12–13

> His power has given us everything we need for life and godliness. 2 Pet 1:3

> May our Lord Jesus Christ himself and God our Father . . . strengthen you in everything you do and say. 2 Thess 2:16–17[29]

> May the God of peace . . . that great *Shepherd* of the *sheep*, equip you with everything good to do his will. Heb 13:20–21

These verses identify the Father and Son in this strengthening process, but Paul also attributes our success over sin to the Holy Spirit: "I pray that he will strengthen you from his glorious riches with power through his Spirit in your inner being" (Eph 3:16). The fruit of the Spirit which we have had recreated within us includes self-control (Gal 5:22–23). John attributes the believer's success in self-control to our indwelling God.

> No one who is born of God practices sin because God's nature abides in him. So he cannot sin, because he is born of God. 1 John 3:9

Of all the profound things Paul could have discussed with Judea's governor and his wife, Paul discusses self-control, along with faith, righteousness, and judgment (Acts 24:24–25). Self-control is that important. Timothy is told to discipline himself as a

---

26. Phil 2:25; 2 Tim 2:3–4; Philem 2
27. Rom 13:12; 2 Cor 6:7; 10:3–4; Eph 6:11–17; 1 Pet 2:11
28. 1 Cor 10:13; also, 2 Pet 2:9
29. Also, Eph 3:20; 6:10; 2 Thess 1:11; 1 Tim 1:12; 2 Tim 1:7; 1 Pet 4:11

formal leader of his church, and other leaders especially are required to control themselves.[30] But we are all shepherds and are expected to discipline ourselves, exercising self-control in everything.[31]

Just one example of the struggle with self-control is dealing with the highly resistant tongue. Jesus says, "What comes out of the mouth comes from the heart, and this is what defiles a person."[32] How and when we speak reveals volumes about our self-control. Proverbs, Solomon, and James dwell significantly on the matter.[33] James narrows down the greatest challenge to accomplishing the primary commission to this one test of self-control: "All kinds of beast, bird, reptile and sea creature can be, and have been tamed by humanity, but no one can tame the tongue" (Jas 3:7, 8). Humanity has made great strides in subduing the beasts, but little has been accomplished as far as the tongue is concerned.

Diligence follows our self-control; we override any physical or spiritual laziness of the flesh and assert our dominance over sin.[34] Diligence and perseverance are allies in the pursuit of righteousness. Our moral endurance proves our justification and defines our sanctification. Peter lists the characteristics of diligent righteousness by a chain of attributes, and the result is to love others, one of the two greatest commandments.

> *Diligently* add to your faith virtue, and
> by virtue, knowledge and
> by knowledge, *self-control* and
> by *self-control*, perseverance and
> by *perseverance*, godliness and
> by godliness, brotherly affection and
> by brotherly affection, *love*. 2 Pet 1:5–7

Personal effort, diligence, self-control, and perseverance are our primary commission responsibilities. Yes, it takes work and perseverance, but the New Testament alone has more than forty passages referring explicitly to our perseverance and endurance in fighting and subduing sin, even in the midst of persecution.[35]

---

30. 1 Tim 4:7–8; Titus 1:8
31. 1 Cor 7:37; 9:25; 10:6; Gal 5:23; 2 Tim 1:7; 3:3
32. Matt 15:11, 18 // Luke 6:45
33. E.g. Prov 10:19; 11:12; 12:23; 17:28; Eccl 3:7; 5:3, 7; 10:11–14; Jas 3:2–10
34. Col 3:5, 8, 12, 23; Heb 6:10–12; 12:4, 14; 2 Pet 1:6–7, 10; 3:14
35. Matt 10:22; Luke 21:16–19, 36; Rom 2:6–7, 10; 1 Cor 10:13; 15:1–2; 2 Cor 1:24; 4:11; 6:4; Gal 5:1; 6:9–10; Eph 6:10–18; Phil 3:6, 9–14; 4:1; Col 1:10–11, 21–23; 2:5–7; 1 Thess 1:3; 3:8; 5:6, 8, 14, 21–22; 1 Tim 4:16; 6:11; 2 Tim 2:1, 4–6, 10–12; 3:2–3, 10; 4:5–8; Heb 3:6, 12; 6:1, 11–12; 10:23, 35–39; 11:1; 12:1–2, 14; Jas 1:2–4; 3:17; 1 Pet 1:6–9; 4:7–8; 5:12; 2 Pet 1:9–11; 3:14–15, 17; Rev 2:7, 10, 17, 26; 3:4–5, 10–11

RIGHTEOUSNESS

Trust and obey; faith and work: they are inseparable. Though we say without qualification that one is not justified by one's works, we say just as strongly that one is not justified unless there are works to follow that prove that justification. Most of the Bible is about God's works as the Shepherd and our works as his vice-shepherds. Scripture is not primarily about the Lord's attributes, his being, or even his plans; it is about his actions, all which are righteous, and about our actions, all which are supposed to be righteous.

God's "righteousness" refers to his perfect attitudes and actions within the Trinity and toward his creation. It is primarily a moral description, but like everything concerning God, to separate righteousness with precision from his wisdom, creativity, and his emotional and relational attributes would compose a nice theological dictionary, but not an adequate theology.

The Lord challenged Israel to find any other legal code as morally pure as his Law: "What great nation has statutes and judgments as righteous as this entire law which I present to you today?" (Deut 4:8). They would not be able to answer this question since the Law reflects the moral perfection of the only God, while all other nations had to rely solely on the laws of conscience and their own relatively uninformed moral estimations. And keeping the Law defined who a righteous person was: "It will be our righteousness when we carefully observe all these commandments" (Deut 6:25). Like the error of the Pharisees in the New Testament, keeping the Law did not mean that Israelites who kept the Law were justified. Justification could come only through a genuine spiritual faith.

The wisdom teachings in Job, Proverbs, and Ecclesiastes also demand personal righteousness. Nearly a hundred times Proverbs and Ecclesiastes emphasize that one's righteousness will prove wisdom's superiority over sin. Ecclesiastes 7:20 repeats what is said elsewhere in the Old Testament about the universality of unrighteousness: "There is not a righteous person on earth who does only good and does not sin."[36] But further, Ecclesiastes and Proverbs equate righteousness with wisdom.

> The righteous, the wise and their deeds are in God's hand. Eccl 9:1

> I have taught you wisdom's way; I have led you in upright paths. Prov 4:11

The wisdom instructions provide hundreds of guideposts toward righteous living.[37]

The complicated weaving of our daily decisions is achieved best when the wisdom instructions are contemplated, balanced, and aptly applied. Hundreds of moral instructions are given in the wisdom books, but deciding which to apply, and when, requires the wisdom of the Spirit. So we are told to seek wisdom and knowledge.[38] For example, Solomon studied wisdom to determine how best to shepherd the people

---

36. Also, 1 Kgs 8:46; 2 Chr 6:36; Ps 143:2; Prov 20:9
37. E.g., Prov 8:8; 11:30; 12:6
38. Prov 2:4; 8:17; 15:14; 18:15

(Eccl 12:9). When one finds wisdom, Proverbs urges the believer to diligently pursue goodness and righteousness: "The Lord loves the one who pursues righteousness."[39]

Contrary to what we might be led to believe, we are partly responsible for our own moral cleansing. It is not all up to God. It is up to us to participate in our sanctification: "Let us complete our holiness and cleanse ourselves from all that defiles body and spirit" (2 Cor 7:1).[40] We are assured, however, that fellowship with other believers helps us resist the crouching, slinking Satan (1 Cor 7:5), and even greater protection comes from the Lord himself: "God is faithful and will not let you be tempted beyond your ability. When tempted, he will also provide an escape so you can endure it."[41] Peter gives a strong message about the believer's own responsibilities.

> Be diligent to confirm your calling and election. For if you do these things [vss. 5–7], you will never stumble but will be given a rich entrance into the eternal kingdom of our Lord and Savior Jesus Christ. 2 Pet 1:10–11

Not only do we love God, we love his commandments too. Passion for the Old Testament law is the subject of the longest single passage in all of Scripture, Psalm 119. This psalm is summarized by verse 97, "I really love your Law!" The model is the same; if we love the commandments we will obey them just as we obey God because we love him.[42] Every biblical covenant and every age is full of God's grace, instruction, and the expectation of obedience. We would not want it any other way. God loves us and knows what is best for us and for our conduct. So how could we not love his commandments and strive hard to follow them?

Righteousness and goodness are goals that require deep thought and strong action to defeat the flesh and its natural tendency toward shallow and lazy morality. Our life of devotion and obedience requires a focused mind and deliberate actions consistent with that mind. Using the most general biblical descriptions of righteousness, Paul encourages the Philippians to "Ponder what is true, honorable, right, pure, lovely, and commendable" (4:8). Meditation on God's standards for moral conduct is a first step to acting wisely. Leaning only on the preaching, teaching, or insights of other Christians cannot substitute for our own immersion in God's Testaments as we hear directly from him what he expects and how he will generously bless those who love to meditate on his Word. The meditator is promised great things.

> His delight is in the Law of the Lord; he meditates on it day and night.
> He is like as a tree planted near a stream, yielding its seasonal fruit.
> As its leaf does not wither, in whatever he does he prospers too. Ps 1:2–3

---

39. Prov 15:9; also, Prov 11:19, 27; 21:21
40. Also, 2 Tim 2:21–22; Rev 7:14
41. 1 Cor 10:13; also, 2 Pet 2:9
42. Pss 119:97, 113, 119, 127, 159, 163, 165, 167; Prov 4:4–6; 8:21; 29:3; Amos 5:15; Mic 6:8; Zech 8:19

This is the primary commission at work in our lives at the rudimentary level—our self-control, our self-management, our self-subduing, that is, shepherding ourselves toward wisdom and righteousness. We cannot take up our cross with our index finger. Following Jesus is not walking for one city block or reserved for Sundays alone. It is an hour-by-hour walk under a cross the size our Lord believes each of us is capable of carrying.[43] Accomplishing the primary commission in our life means persevering in righteousness with the strength and endurance that the Spirit gives.

> We pray you will be filled with the knowledge of His will in complete spiritual wisdom and understanding... bearing fruit in every good work... strengthened by all his glorious power so you have all the needed endurance and patience.[44]

Often this perseverance is not just a matter of pressing on morally against our natural selves, but it is a matter of taking on the dark kingdom and its evil forces while persisting in righteousness despite serious and torturous opposition and oppression.[45] Today's persecuted brothers and sisters, and hundreds if not thousands of murdered martyrs around this world, have known what this level of perseverance in moral living means. Moral surrender would be more convenient and less painful, if not lifesaving. They are daily throwing themselves upon their cross for the truth and glory of Jesus Christ our Lord.

---

43. Matt 16:24 // Mark 8:34 // Luke 9:23; 14:27
44. Col 1:9–11; also, 1 Cor 15:10; 1 Tim 6:11, 15–16; Heb 12:7–11; Jas 1:2–5; 5:11
45. Rom 5:3–5; 12:9–12; 2 Cor 6:4–6; 2 Thess 1:4; Heb 10:32–34; 11:24–25; Jas 1:12; Rev 1:9; 13:10

12

God's Commandments for Shepherding

HOW SHOULD WE SHEPHERD?

WE NOW COME TO our final two chapters which outline precisely how the believer and the believing community contribute to God's eternal design. Most generally, the eternal design is that *God shepherds shepherding creation*, and we have looked at how God shepherds the spirits and nature. We also discussed how spirits, nature, and humanity mutually shepherd one another, including how we join with God in shepherding the spirits and nature. But we did not go into much depth in those middle chapters in explaining how we shepherd unsaved humanity, the Lord's people, and other individuals. We have waited until now, in these next couple of chapters to do this.

The primary commission was given in the strongest terms for how we are to shepherd God's creation. It is tempting even to apologize for the strength of the term "subdue" which can offend a world and church who underestimate the power of the world gone awry. But we are convinced that the powers and principalities need to be defeated not only in the end times but now. Spirits, nature, and humanity are all very complex as well, and to shepherd the Lord's creation requires the Lord's wisdom on very specific situations in a vast and complicated world.

So, if we want to contribute to God's eternal design by shepherding through blessing, delivering, and disciplining, what are God's specific moral standards to guide us in this? How are we to fulfill our primary commission morally? Well, most of what we read in the Testaments is about exactly that. The contents of the Old Testament and New Testament encourage us to shepherd as God shepherds. The Testaments certainly reveal the character and actions of our Shepherding Lord, but we are not satisfied with only knowing what God has done, is doing and will do. The Bible is equally clear about how we are to shepherd as it is about how God does.

We have noticed that to separate the shepherding roles of blessing, deliverance and discipline into three unrelated roles is impossible since most of the time they intersect and overlap in different combinations. For example, the Lord's deliverances are blessings. He also delivers us at times, and by doing so judges others who intimidate us. The Lord blesses and delivers by disciplining us toward our greater righteousness. This does not mean they are all the same thing, but it does mean that shepherding often involves two of them if not all three and they usually need a judicious balance.

So, as we look at the Lord's instructions for our shepherding, we will not separate the hundreds of teachings between these three roles of blessing, deliverance, and discipline and discuss the numberless combinations of the three for each teaching. As you can imagine, that would take several books, not several paragraphs. Though we may not know God's ways in detail, we are held accountable for our own ways, and we are expected to balance blessing, deliverance, and discipline in our daily life as we contribute to God's eternal design. Fortunately, the Holy Spirit guides us when looking intently at the Lord's shepherding instructions. It is exciting to see how the wisdom that the Lord has already worked into us through the Spirit can be worked out within our own lives and surroundings.

The Trinity's own moral nature has never changed, so God's moral expectations from us never will either. We were created in his image to reflect his glory in his moral attitudes and actions regardless of which historical phase of his eternal design we examine. His moral expectations will change in *how* we meet them specifically but never *whether* we meet them. For example, we are to ask for forgiveness of our sins; that's an absolute. But we no longer meet that expectation by sacrificing animals.

The Trinity's own moral nature is reflected in both the Mosaic law and the wisdom instructions, but the wisdom literature has broader interests than the Law. I consider the wisdom literature to include all of Job, Proverbs, Ecclesiastes, and Song of Solomon. These wisdom books have hundreds of instructions for personal and inter-personal success and repeat many moral maxims from the Mosaic law. The Law was a product of direct revelation to Moses, and wisdom instruction also had as its source the divinely inspired conclusions drawn from routine human experience. In other words, still guided by the Holy Spirit, wisdom instruction includes descriptions of what its authors found to be the best approaches to human interaction *in addition* to the Law.

The wisdom literature affirms the Mosaic law and subsumes it within its catalog of moral behavior. Proverbs alone includes around one hundred twenty sayings which support specific Mosaic laws: for example, stealing, moving boundary stones, withholding wages, false commodity measurements, lending, collateral, treatment of servants, animal care, adultery, respecting parents and elders, gluttony, drunkenness, lying, impartial courts, false testimony, bribery, compassion for the disadvantaged, care for the handicapped, loving one's neighbors, murder, and limitations to royal prerogatives. The wisdom literature addresses how to live a godly, routine daily life in community, whereas the Mosaic law addressed most frequently the enforcement of ceremonial and legal, even criminal offenses, that could end up in court. Examples that we will use in this admittedly pragmatic distinction would be the following.

Mosaic Law	Wisdom Instruction
Marketplace standards	Communication
Land ownership	Companions
Stealing	Prayer
Liability	Humility
Loans	Patience
Indentured servitude	Kindness
Social programs	Mercy
Fornication	Forgiveness
Court justice	Diligence
Murder and assault	Joyfulness
Sacrifices and feasts	Being peaceable

In surveying New Testament ethics we will follow the same ethical categories as the Old Testament Law and wisdom instructions since the believer and the believing community's righteousness is an extension of the Old Testament moral principles in nearly every category. So we will continue a helpful distinction between legal and wisdom instructions. Not that there is any longer an extensive legal and penal code in the New Testament as in the older testament, but simply because the New Testament pervasively affirms Old Testament Mosaic moral standards. In other words, when New Testament ethics conform to the moral nature of God as first expressed in the Mosaic law, we will consider these moral teachings as "shepherding *commandments*" simply because "commandments" are associated with Sinai.

We will also survey New Testament ethics along the lines of the Old Testament wisdom instructions. Again, these ethical teachings are broader and more concerned with the attitudes and behavior within the fabric of daily existence and within one's surroundings within and outside the believing community. This same approach is taken by Christ and the New Testament writers as we see in their teaching, parables, preaching, letter writing, encouragement, and moral challenges which they delivered for everyday living.

Admittedly, the distinction between whether a New Testament moral principle is an extension of the legal code or of the wisdom instruction can be blurry because of the significant overlap between these two Old Testament ethics sources in the first place. At the end of the day, Old and New Testament "commandments" are "instructions" and the wisdom literature's "instructions" are "commandments"; neither carries any more weight than the other. What is distinguishing in a general sense is which moral guides are first promoted as legal guidelines for righteousness (Law), and which moral guides fathom one's underlying attitudes and subsequent righteousness within the ordinary moral conduct of one's morning, afternoon, and evening.

THE OLD TESTAMENT AND ITS LAW

The laws and wisdom literature served as a basis for the Lord's assessment of Israel's success in managing their lives and land. If obeyed, they would ensure the formation of their nation into the model of how their sovereign God shepherded in conjunction with them, his vice-shepherds (Deut 4:5–8). In this chapter, the legal code is the foundation for the moral summaries. The rest of the Old Testament repeats, reinforces, and assesses obedience to these legal and moral principles.

Few other words in the Testaments are more complex than "law" in its many meanings and contexts. There are at least four different uses of the term "law" in the Bible.

God's law of conscience
God's Law of Moses
God's ceremonial laws
The Messiah's new royal law

Yet, there is a single view in the Testaments on God's commandments: they instruct us about righteousness but they have never been a substitute for the Lord's grace and forgiveness as we trust him from a heart transformed by the Holy Spirit.

The Law's Grace

Israel's laws were part of God's wonderful grace to her. The nation did not deserve God's laws, but they were his gift of wisdom to them. Unfortunately, many see a clash between law and grace as if God loves law and only grudgingly grants grace while we love grace and loathe the law. God's commandments *are* grace, giving order to one's life and providing many other benefits to those who are wise enough to keep them. And they are grace for the members of a community that lives by the rule of his Law and the security and stability that come from doing so (Prov 21:15). This was God's purpose for the Mosaic law—to bless his people with a safe and prosperous structure within which to live and enjoy their partnership with God in managing their life and world together. The Israelites were responsible for developing and maintaining a civil community where they were routinely kind, cared for one another's property, told one another the truth, and took care of their clergy.[1]

Paul directs Timothy to the Old Testament for his own sanctification. He tells Timothy the Old Testament has the wisdom that will lead to salvation by faith. That is, not only salvation to get into the Kingdom, but also perpetual salvation through sanctification while in the Kingdom. Paul describes the Old Testament to be a source of deliverance since it teaches, reproves, and corrects us so we are equipped for good works (2 Tim 3:15–16).

---

1. Ex 23:4, 5; Lev 19:11; Deut 12:19; 22:1–3

Sins of the Heart

The believers in Old Testament times had already been given good news about God's kingdom, and they were expected to respond with faith and repentance. For Old Testament believers, trusting the Lord was a commitment of one's heart, soul, and bodily might, not just one's will power to obey the rules (Deut 6:5). It meant changing the way one thought and setting new priorities that were pre-eminently honoring to God rather than to others or oneself. It meant changing the habits of the individual and any customs of the believing community which did not please God.

God's perfect actions conform to his nature, not merely to a set of moral standards. Being like God, and as new creatures, our righteous actions conform to our godly nature too. A truly moral act is done with the right motivation. For the Lord, acceptable moral conduct comes from our transformed heart motivated by a Spiritual impetus to love and please the Trinity. Consequently, kingdom living requires more than obedience to a moral *behavioral* code. This was Christ's message to the Pharisees who were good at "the list" but not good at the loving motives to obey the list. Moral living then cannot be described as merely obedience. Obedience without a heart that exudes a love for God and that trusts him to recreate our nature to be like his is as filthy rags (Isa 64:6). Believers and faithful leaders of the Old Testament would have had the same problem with the Pharisees as Jesus had.

The Ten Commandments have the distinction between the motive that leads to acts of sin and the sinful act itself. Both are equally sin, but one is an attitude, an inclination of a sinful heart. For example, the tenth commandment, "You shall not covet," condemns the attitude that can lead to breaking other commandments like the seventh and eighth, adultery and stealing. A coveting, greedy heart can lead to murder, working on the Sabbath, or worshipping a god which is assumed to give greater crop fertility and wealth. The Law addresses the heart as well as the will and actions that the heart affects.

This was not a new moral perspective for those who heard Christ's teaching on the importance of righteous thoughts and attitudes in his Sermon on the Mount (Matt 5:21–22, 27–28, 38–39). For instance, when Christ Jesus reflected on the sinful equivalence of lustful thoughts and actual adultery, he reminded his hearers of what the Old Testament had already warned about. He repeats the moral teaching of Job and Proverbs which had described lust itself as sinful, even without committing physical adultery.

> Anyone who looks at a woman lustfully already has committed adultery with her in his heart. Matt 5:28

> I covenanted with my eyes, so how could I look at a young woman lustfully . . . If my heart has been enticed by a woman, or if I have stalked my neighbor's wife . . . that lust would be a punishable, criminal sin. Job 31:1, 9, 11

> Do not let your heart lust the beauty of an adulteress. Prov 6:25

Like the tenth commandment, the wisdom books of Job and Proverbs underscore the condition of the heart as sinful, not just an external act.

The Old Testament does not portray God as being primarily interested in the ceremonial formalities of the Law. He preferred the believer's sincere heart of love for him and others. He established these formalities, but they were never a substitute for obedience to the weightier command to all Israelites to shepherd one another. Hosea and Micah convey the same message on this subject:

> I want steadfast love, not sacrifice. Hos 6:6

> Does the Lord delight in thousands of sacrificed rams?
> The Lord requires your justice, love and kindness, and humble walk with your God. Mic 6:7–8

These are only a couple of examples of the many passages where the Lord made his preference clear.[2] Shepherding is the Lord's primary concern, not religious ceremony.

Jesus makes the same point when chastising the scribes and Pharisees, referring to the statement in Micah 6:8.

> You tithe mint, dill and cumin, but neglect the weightier matters of the Law: justice, mercy and faithfulness. You should do all these without neglecting any. Matt 23:23

Twice, Jesus quotes Hosea 6:6 as well. He was adamant about God's preference for shepherding compassion over sacrifice alone.[3]

The Holy Spirit and the Law

God says as early as Deuteronomy that his Law was written on the Israelites' hearts so that it would be easier to honor the Lord in word and deed. David and Isaiah repeat the fact:

> This commandment that I command today is not too hard for you, nor is it far off... Instead, the word is very near you—in your mouth and in your heart. Deut 30:11, 14

> The Law of his God is in the heart of the righteous. Ps 37:31

> I delight to do your will, O my God; your Law is in my heart. Ps 40:8

> You who know righteousness, you people in whose heart is my Law. Isa 51:7

---

2. 1 Sam 15:22–23; 2 Chr 30:18–20; Pss 40:6; 51:16–19; 69:30–31; 141:1–2; Prov 15:8; 16:6; 21:3, 27; Jer 7:2–24; Isa 1:10–17; 58:5–7; Hos 6:6; Amos 5:21–27; Mic 6:6–8

3. Matt 9:13; 12:7

So when God promised he would make a new covenant with his people and that his Law would be written on their hearts, he promised that the covenant would be changed, thus new, but that his standards would again be written on his believers' hearts. This confirms the Lord's consistency in how he deals with his people and guides them toward willing righteousness. So Jeremiah 31:33 extends the Lord's promise to always put his law on the heart of the believer, including when he extends a new covenant to his people.

> This is the covenant which I will make with the house of Israel after those days
> ... I will put My law within them, I will write it on their heart; I will be their
> God, and they will be My people.

This law certainly would be different from the Law of Moses since it will not include many Mosaic laws such as the ceremonial laws.

In chapter 10 we considered the role of the Spirit in righteous living. We saw how concerned David was about the Spirit's role in his moral living. He was so concerned that he pled with God not to withdraw the Holy Spirit from him as a penalty for his adultery with Bathsheba. What he wanted from the Spirit was for his own spirit to be cleansed so he could continue to be righteous and willing to obey.

Some believe that David feared that the Spirit would leave him and would only remove his specific spiritual anointing as king of Israel. But that is not the context of David's comments in Psalm 51. David is not praying as a king wishing to keep his special anointing; rather he is praying as a king who is a sad sinner and wants the Spirit's moral cleansing and refreshment, "the washing of regeneration and renewing by the Holy Spirit" (Titus 3:5). We must read the full context of David's concern:

> Create a clean heart in me, O God. Renew a right spirit in me.
>
> Do not throw me away from you and do not take your Holy Spirit from me.
>
> Restore my joy in your salvation and sustain my willingness to obey you. Ps 51:10–12

David says in a later psalm that he desired the Spirit to lead him to righteousness:

> Since you are my God, teach me to do your will.
>
> Let your good Spirit lead me on level ground! Ps 143:10

For David, that the Spirit might leave him was a profound moral issue, not a career issue. We would expect this perspective from one who the Lord had said was "a man after his own heart" (1 Sam 13:14).

We noted in chapter 10 as well that the Spirit was not only "on" believers in the Old Testament, he was "in" them. The indwelling Spirit was necessary for the Spiritual gifts as well as Spiritual fruits. Joshua, Gideon, David, the tabernacle artisans, and the prophets were simply examples of those individuals who were indwelt by the Holy Spirit.[4]

---

4. Ex 31:3; 35:31; Num 27:18; Judg 6:34; 1 Sam 16:13–14; Mic 3:8; 1 Pet 1:10–11;

THE NEW TESTAMENT AND LAW

God's Law of Conscience

The relevance of the Old Testament for shepherding ethics is clearly reaffirmed by the New Testament. Christ Jesus and the apostles frequently used the Old Testament to instruct us on many things, including what we should believe about God and what we should do in loving obedience to him.

There are grounds for moral assessment of any culture and any individual even without God having revealed oral or written instruction to them. The moral law found in the individual's conscience and in the collective conscience of a society is enough to vindicate or condemn. For instance, before the Mosaic law is revealed in Exodus through Deuteronomy, peoples and individuals of Genesis were held accountable for their actions. And throughout history since the Bible, peoples have been judged for their immorality in lands where the Lord's Law and wisdom instruction has never been revealed.

Most generally, the law of God often refers to these moral standards known through the laws of conscience. Fortunately for the human race, and so for the rest of creation, God has written his law into the hearts of all individuals, believers and non-believers. As depraved as humanity is, the image of God which all persons have includes an innate knowledge of right and wrong. Everyone has a conscience, one that does not make them basically good, but one which betrays their intentional disobedience to a moral law within them. This meaning of law is not the Mosaic law since it is not written on every heart in its entirety. The specific ceremonial laws are not known apart from God's revelation of those religious practice expectations.

Both Testaments attest to the reality and force of the law of the conscience. We have looked at this in some detail in chapter 8 in the section "The Sins of the Peoples." There we cited many passages proving the power of God's image within all humanity, an image that contains God's moral standards within the individual's conscience. We gave examples in that section as to what extent and in what detail the conscience carries God's moral expectations. God's law, written on the human heart, reflects his shepherding care for believers and non-believers alike. The conscience with which all have been created maintains some semblance of moral and civil order in our world, while the ravaging Enemy is only intent on dismembering and destroying it.

God's Law of Moses

A second use of "law" refers to the commandments given by God to Moses at Sinai and repeated in Deuteronomy. We have capitalized this word when it stands alone and is used for "the Law of Moses." Many of these commandments are continued into the New Testament either because they reflect the laws of conscience or because what was good for God's people then is still good for God's people now.

The Mosaic Law includes the law of conscience, so one could say that much of the Law of God is written on the hearts of all people—all have the Mosaic Law written on their heart, even if not in its entirety, because their conscience confirms much that is written in the Law. This is why Paul says that even the Gentiles have God's Law written into their conscience, into their heart.

> Even Gentiles who have not had God's written Law prove that they know what his Law is when they obey it instinctively . . . They show that God's law is written in their hearts when their conscience and thoughts accuse them of doing wrong or confirm them doing right. Rom 2:14–15

> They know God's decree that those who do such [evil] things deserve to die. Rom 1:32

On the other hand, Paul says later in Romans that the Law informed him of sin of which he would not have been aware.

> I would not have known what sin was apart from the Law since I would not have known what coveting was if the Law had not said, 'You shall not covet.'" Rom 7:7

Either Paul is contradicting himself or he is saying that as a Jew, presumably as a child, he learned what sin was from the Mosaic law when he was first instructed by it. He would not have known it otherwise at that point as a child, but as even Gentiles do, he eventually would have. His point in this passage is that God's Law leads one to know what sin is.

Jesus and the New Testament writers spoke frequently of the goodness of the Mosaic laws. They are "holy, righteous and good" (Rom 7:12) though it was considered a relief not to have to continue the elaborate ceremonial laws into New Testament times. Jesus taught that one must teach others to fulfill the Law too (Matt 5:19). Paul demands the believer to keep God's commandments: "Keeping God's commandments is what counts" (1 Cor 7:19).

Old Testament laws are affirmed repeatedly in the New Testament, but their limitations are also emphasized. An error would be made in moving too far to either side of this continuum. It is wrong to reaffirm imprecisely every one of the Old Testament laws. At the other extreme, not to extend the relevance of any Old Testament laws into the New Testament, nor to see their value for guiding Christian living leads to an equally unbiblical position. The New Testament gives all the guidance we need to stay clear of these extremes and please our Lord with our obedience.

The gospels and letters give three reasons why the Mosaic law is good. The first and third are very similar, but they apply at different times.

1. It makes all people aware of what righteousness and sin is—it explains why we are guilty.

2. So, it drives us to seek a solution to our guilt, to the acceptable Sacrifice.

3. And again, after our justification, the Law guides us in righteous living as believers.

Paul writes to Timothy, "The Law is good if used properly. It is for the lawless, not the perfectly righteous" (1 Tim 1:8–9). So the Law shows us our sin and is used by the Spirit to drive us away from disobedience and toward kingdom obedience.

But as good as the Law is, it cannot bring justification—God's pronouncement that we are innocent by our association with the perfect life and death of Christ: "No mortal is justified by the works of the Law" (Gal 2:16). The Law can lead us toward justification by showing us our sin and the need for a solution, but it cannot save us.

The Law condemns the sinner. It exposes the sin and sentences the sinner to death. We experience the wonderful grace of God when we are justified in Christ and are no longer under the Law's condemnation as our accuser, prosecutor, judge, and sentencer. The Law is no longer our master; we are now outside its jurisdiction; we have died as far as the Law's condemning authority over us.[5]

After our justification, we continue the next phase of our salvation which is a moral life powered by the Holy Spirit within us. This is called "sanctification," and this phase pits our "new person" against the weakness and habits of the "old person" we were. Justification-salvation does not come through the Law, but the Spirit enables us to live in obedience to the Law as we are progressively sanctified. The Law of God written on our heart is used by the Holy Spirit to convict, equip and motivate us to follow God's Law.

Paul says that when we love God and neighbor we fulfill the Law.

> The one who loves another, fulfills the Law. The words "You shall love your neighbor as yourself" sum up the commandments, "You shall not commit adultery, You shall not murder, You shall not steal, You shall not covet" . . . Love fulfills the Law. Rom 13:8–10

Jesus says he came to fulfill the Law (Matt 5:17–18), and we fulfill the Law when we act in love toward others just as the Old Testament had taught. Jesus says reconciliation with another person is what legitimized one's sacrifice. Both reconciliation and sacrifice were good, but the meaningfulness of the sacrifice depended on the loving obedience of the one offering the sacrifice (Matt 5:23–26).

We should not be surprised then that the commandments from Jesus and the New Testament writers sound similar to the Old Testament commandments. After all, Paul endorses Old Testament teaching:

> All Scripture is from God's own breath and is valuable for teaching, reprimands, correction and training for our righteousness so that we will be thoroughly equipped for every good work to serve him. 2 Tim 3:16–17

---

5. Rom 6:14; 7:4–6; 1 Cor 9:20–21; Gal 2:19; 5:18

God's Ceremonial Laws

Religious practice in the New Testament sees a significant change from the Old Testament because the whole sacrificial system was no longer needed, and the many accompanying ceremonial laws were now allowed to be changed. This is a third and more specific New Testament use of "law," namely the Old Testament's commandments about *ceremonial* or *religious* practices. Christ is the new high priest now, but he is from the tribe of Judah. Since he was not a descendant of Levi and Aaron, a foundational stone of the ceremonial laws was removed, and the Old Testament religious structure toppled: "When the priesthood changes, the law must be changed . . . since clearly our Lord descended from Judah" (Heb 7:12, 14). This complete change in the true high priesthood led Paul to a sarcastic moment. When under abusive court questioning, he challenged the high priesthood of Ananias: "Brothers, I did not know that he was the high priest," implying of course that Ananias was not the high priest any longer. Of course Paul would have known who Ananias was and his official position.

A new priesthood under Christ was a blessing for all the nations because now the flood of Gentiles entering the Kingdom could come without the burden of complicated ceremonial expectations. After all, even Peter admitted publicly to all the apostles at an assembly in Jerusalem that the radical change in the ceremonial laws was a relief: "Why are you testing God by putting on the neck of the disciples a yoke that even our ancestors and we have not been able to bear?" (Acts 15:10). Peter was speaking of the intricate ceremonial laws of Moses, not the whole Law since all the apostles reaffirmed many details of the Old Testament Law in their letters and ministry to Jews and Gentiles. James agreed with Peter's comments during the assembly and concluded himself that the Gentile believers should not be "troubled" with the minutia of the ceremonial laws (Acts 15:19).

In New Earth, the ceremonial laws will not even be missed. For example, the Lord told Jeremiah,

> I will give you *shepherds* after My own heart . . . When you have multiplied and been fruitful in the land . . . no one will even mention the ark of the covenant of the Lord. It will not come to mind, be remembered, or missed . . . In that day, Jerusalem will be called the throne of the Lord, where all nations gather.
> Jer 3:15–17

Besides, some of the Law was geographically irrelevant in a new global kingdom of believers that permeates all peoples. For example the laws pertaining to refuge cities, war camp sewage systems, military deferments, etc.

Speaking of the ceremonial laws, and the sacrifices specifically, Hebrews warns against ever overestimating their value. They served only as a reminder of the individual's and nation's sin and had no saving power in themselves, and were now unneeded after the cross.

> The [ceremonial] law was but a shadow of the good things yet to come—not the good things themselves. Those sacrifices are only a reminder of sins year after

> year since it is impossible for the blood of bulls and goats to take away sins. . . . We have been made holy through the offering of the body of Jesus Christ once for all. But every priest stands day after day serving and offering the same sacrifices again and again—sacrifices that can never take away sins. 10:3–4, 10–11

The Old Testament sacrifices were only temporary signs that sin must be dealt with and were never designed to make people perfect. We covered how Old Testament believers were "saved" in chapter 10 when discussing justification.

John tells us, "The Law was given through Moses; grace and truth came through Jesus Christ" (John 1:17). Unfortunately some translations add to the verse a word that is not there, misleading us by saying, "The Law was given through Moses; [but] grace and truth came through Jesus Christ." This additional word could be considered dismissive of the Old Testament Law by implying it possessed no grace or truth when it was full of both. What the verse means is that as truthful as the Law was, it could not justify sinners—that was the result of Christ's sacrifice. And we are now blessed by that justification and the truth of Christ's teachings and commandments.

Another cherished ceremonial law was circumcision, but Paul discounts this rite in comparison with faith and love: "In Christ Jesus it does not matter whether one is circumcised or not; what does matter is faith working through love" (Gal 5:6). Paul also says something that sounds like a contradiction: "Circumcision is nothing and uncircumcision is nothing. What counts is keeping God's commandments" (1 Cor 7:19). But, if one of God's commandments is circumcision, how can it not matter? What appears to be a contradiction is really Paul's way to prioritize God's legal expectations. This priority of love for God and neighbor was common knowledge to the New Testament religious community. It was not a new revelation from Christ Jesus or his apostles. An enlightened scribe proved this was the common understanding of the role of sacrifices when he told Christ that the two summary commands to love God and neighbor were worth "much more than all burnt offerings and sacrifices" (Mark 12:33).

Paul believed that there are commandments that affirm loving God and one's neighbor but others that are merely ceremonial. If it were not Paul saying it, we might find it hard to come to the conclusion that these ceremonial laws were weak and worthless:

> How can you turn back to those weak and worthless elements? . . . You observe religious days, months, seasons and years. Gal 4:9–10

> Do not let anyone judge you for what you eat or drink, or whether you celebrate feasts, the new moon, or the Sabbath. Col 2:16

The Messiah's New Royal Law

There is a fourth reference to "law" that encompasses God's Old Testament Law and Christ's New Testament law. Not only did Jesus say the Old Testament Law was summed up in loving God and one's neighbor, but he and his apostles continued that summation of ethical living throughout their New Testament teachings. We saw this in chapter eleven when looking at love as one of the shepherding essentials. This law may have a few different expressions at times, but it is the same law.

But Jesus said he had a *new* commandment for us and John picks up on that *new* commandment in one of his letters. If it is new, we surely want to know what it is. Here it is:

> I am giving you a new commandment: love one another: *just as I have loved you*, you also must love one another. John 13:34-35

How is this a new commandment if it was given to the Israelites way back in Leviticus 19:18? One way in which it is new is that it has a much fuller meaning now because we have seen it exemplified by Jesus himself. The words are not brand new, but the meaning is much clearer.

What John records Jesus saying in his Gospel in John 13, he repeats as a new commandment in his first letter, 1 John.

> I am not writing you a new command, it is an old one which you have had since the beginning . . . On the other hand, I am writing you a new command; *its truth is seen in his life and yours* . . . Anyone saying he is in the light but hates his brother is still in darkness. Anyone who loves his brother lives in the light. 1 John 2:7-10

Again, though Christ's commandment is the same commandment as in Leviticus, it is new because we see it exemplified in Christ and realize it in our own lives.

Another way in which this is a new commandment is that it is given by a new human king who is also God. Israel had many kings before who reconfirmed God's authority at every inauguration. Now, under the new Messiah's authority, all laws, commandments, and expectations are reconfirmed yet again. Christ equates himself with God in a way that the New Testament Jews understood when he says, "If you love me, keep my commandments" (John 14:15, 21). God had said the same thing to the Israelites in Deuteronomy 5:10: "I show loyal love to thousands who love me and keep my commandments."[6] John is especially concerned about the importance of *lovingly* obeying the commandments of God and Christ, again quoting Christ in his Gospel and adding his own comments in 1 John.[7] "Keeping his commandments is love for God, and they are not any burden" (1 John 5:3).

The difference now in God's law and commandments is that the Old Testament moral principles extend into the Messiah's new kingdom moral system. Paul speaks of being under the "law of Christ" but not as if Christ's law was distinct from God's Law; rather it is included in it. Christ the King's commandments and laws reflect the Trinity's

---

6. Also, Ex 20:6; Dan 9:4
7. John 15:14; 1 John 2:5-6; 5:1-3

very moral fiber. He is the Second Person, his nature is the same as in the Old Testament, and he expects his image-bearers to reflect the moral principles of the Old Testament.

> I am not outside God's Law since I am under the law of Christ [Messiah]. 1 Cor 9:21

> Carry each other's burdens and you will fulfill the law of Christ [Messiah]. Gal 6:2

James more subtly refers to the "*royal* law" which includes the command to love one another. It is royal because it is the law of the king, the law of Jesus the anointed, the Messiah: "You are doing well when you truly keep Scripture's royal law, 'Love your neighbor as yourself'" (Jas 2:8). This specific command is not exclusively the royal law since the other part of this law is to "Love the Lord your God with all your heart and with all your soul and with all your strength."

Mosaic Law Outlines God's Shepherding Commandments

In this chapter 12, the Mosaic law forms our outline for Old Testament moral principles and we will see that the rest of the Old Testament repeats and reinforces these legal and moral principles. So, in our footnotes, these later passages that confirm God's Law are in italics. This includes references where the moral principles are reinforced by the wisdom literature and by the moral *assessments* of Israel and individuals in the rest of the Old Testament literature. In other words, the Old Testament Law was affirmed by the wisdom books, Psalms, and the prophets, and it was an ethical foundation for shepherding by the Israelites in their blessing, delivering, and disciplining of each other and those in the world around them. For instance, the king was required to obey God's Law just as his subjects were. Deuteronomy 17:18–20 required such obedience. Subsequent Old Testament passages confirmed the Lord's equal expectations from king and subject, so we italicize these confirming passages in the footnotes: *Ps 40:7–8; Prov 16:12; 28:15; 29:2, 14; Isa 10:1.*

The New Testament confirms the Old Testament moral principles as well. The following table lists examples of shepherding instructions that are found in the Mosaic law and are reaffirmed by any combination of the wisdom literature, prophets, Christ and his apostles. These examples are a few of the means of godly shepherding that consistently proceed from the heart of God and ensure the eternal design's success in our lives as believers within a believing community and within a fallen world during this parenthetical age. We have restricted our biblical references to only one or two examples when in most cases many more texts could have been cited. The pages that follow this table will provide other examples of righteous shepherding and numerous additional passages that prove the Testaments' wide and deep ranging passion for guiding us in our moral behavior.

Standard	Law	Wisdom	Prophets	Christ	Apostles
Adultery	Ex 20:14; Lev 18:20	Prov 22:14; 23:26–28	Jer 23:10; Ezek 33:26	Matt 5:27–28; Mark 7:21	Heb 13:4; Jas 2:11
Prostitution	Lev 19:29; 21:9	Prov 6:26; 23:27	Isa 57:3–4; Hos 4:11	Luke 15:29–30	1 Cor 6:15–16
Homosexuality	Lev 18:22; 20:13				1 Cor 6:9–10; 1 Tim 1:10
Incest	Lev 18:10; Deut 27:20–23		Ezek 22:10–11		1 Cor 5:1
Gluttony	Deut 21:20	Prov 23:19–21; 28:7		Matt 11:19	Titus 1:12
Drunkenness	Deut 21:20	Prov 20:1; 23:29–35	Isa 5:22; 28:1–3	Luke 12:45–46; 21:34	Rom. 13:13; Eph 5:18
Impartial courts	Ex 23:6; Deut 24:17; 27:19	Job 29:12–17; Prov 13:23	Isa 1:23; Lam 3:35–36	Matt 23:23 // Luke 11:42	1 Cor 6:2–5; 1 Tim 5:19
False testimony	Ex 20:16; 23:1–2, 7	Prov 19:5, 9; 21:28	Ezek 22:9	Matt 15:19; Mark 10:19	Acts 5:4–10; 1 Tim 1:10
Bribery	Ex 23:8; Deut 16:19	Prov 17:23; 29:4	Isa 5:23; Amos 5:12;		
Care for widows	Ex 22:22–24; Deut 14:29	Job 24:21;	Isa 1:17; Mal 3:5	Mark 12:38–40	Acts 6:1; 1 Tim 5:3
Care for orphans	Deut 16:11, 14; 24:19–21	Job 24:9; Prov 23:10	Jer 22:3; Ezek 22:7		Jas 1:27
Care for the alien	Ex 23:9; Lev 19:33–34	Job 31:32	Jer 22:3; Ezek 22:29		
Care for handicapped	Lev 19:14; Deut 27:18	Job 29:15		Matt 4:24; 8:5; Luke 13:11	Acts 3:6–8; 14:8–10
Care for the poor	Deut 15:7, 11; 24:14	Job 30:25; Prov 14:21, 31	Isa 3:15; Amos 4:1	Luke 14:13; 18:22	Acts 4:34–35; Jam 2:15–16
Care for servants	Lev 25:39–40; Deut 15:12–14	Prov 31:15; Eccl 7:21–22	Jer 34:8–10		Eph 6:9; Col 4:1;
Withholding wages	Lev 19:13; Deut 24:15	Job 24:10–11	Jer 22:13; Mal 3:5	Matt 20:8–9	1 Tim 6:18; Jas 5:4
Lending	Ex 22:25–26; Deut 23:19	Prov 19:17; 28:8	Ezek 18:8–9; 22:12	Matt 5:42; Luke 6:34–35	
Collateral	Ex 22:26–27; Deut 24:10–13	Job 24:3, 9–10	Ezek 18:7; Amos 2:8;		
Care for animals	Ex 23:12; Deut 22:6–7	Prov 12:10; 27:23			1 Cor 9:9; 1 Tim 5:18
Respect parents	Lev 19:3; Deut 27:16	Prov 19:26; 28:24		Matt 15:4–6; Mark 7:10	Col 3:20; 2 Tim 3:2
Divorce	Ex 21:10–11; Deut 24:1–4		Jer 3:1; Mal 2:16	Matt 5:31–32; 19:3–8	1 Cor 7:7–8, 15, 39–40
Idolatry	Lev 26:1; Deut 27:15	Job 31:26–28	Hos 8:4–6; Zeph 1:4		1 John 5:21; 1 Pet 4:3

Sorcery	Deut 18:10			Gal 5:20; Rev 21:8
Lying	Lev 19:11	Prov 4:24; 12:22; 19:22	Jer 27:9; Mal 3:5	Col 3:9; 1 Tim 1:10
Coveting	Ex 20:17; Deut 5:21	Job 31:1, 9, 11	Isa 59:12–13; Jer 9:5	Acts 20:33; 1 Cor 5:10–11;
Murder	Lev 24:17; Num 35:30	Job 24:14; Prov 29:10	Mic 2:2	1 Tim 1:9–10; 1 Pet 4:15
Slave dealing	Ex 21:16; Deut 24:7		Jer 22:17; Hos 4:2	1 Tim 1:10
False measures	Lev 19:35–36; Deut 25:13–15	Prov 11:1; 16:11	Hos 12:7; Amos 8:5	
Stealing	Ex 20:15; Deut 5:19	Job 20:19; 24:2–3	Mic 2:2; Mal 3:8–9	Eph 4:28; Titus 2:10
Moving boundaries	Deut 19:14; 27:17;	Job 24:2; Prov 22:28		Luke 3:14
Limit royal privilege	Deut 17:14–20	Prov 16:12; 29:4	Jer 22:14–15; Isa 10:1	Matt 23:25–35	1 Pet 5:1–3; 2 Pet 2:2–3

God's Commandments for Shepherding

A significant reason why we will see how closely New Testament ethics parallel Old Testament Mosaic and wisdom moral principles is that both Testaments are consistent with the laws of the conscience. The laws of conscience and God's biblical instructions confirm the moral validity of the other regardless of which Testament we are considering. The same (and only) God created both the human conscience and the moral standards revealed in the Testaments. Both the conscience and biblical ethical standards stem from God's unchangeable character.

LEADERSHIP

The ineffective sequence of Israel's military judges led God's people to prefer the appearance of greater stability under a monarchy. In God's perfect foresight, he had already anticipated Israel's anxiety about not having a *king* and had set in place the expectations and spirit of a humble royalty within the Mosaic law which predated Israel's call for a king by hundreds of years. But the Lord's grace is that he wants as close a relationship with us as possible. This extra shepherding chain link was an unnecessary administrative layer. Proverbs 30:27 claims that even insects can follow God without a king, "The locusts, without a king, still all go out in ranks."

Since the Lord was Israel's absolute sovereign king, he was the one to appoint Israel's shepherds to serve his purposes, including Moses, Joshua, David, and the coming Messiah.[8] And as the divine king, God constrained Israel's kings with the same Mosaic laws written for all other Israelites, yet added other limitations and promises.[9] These shepherding kings "sat on the throne" with the Lord.[10] This shepherding chain of God shepherding the kings as they shepherded the Lord's sheep included his blessings, deliverance and discipline of the monarchs, just as he expected them to bless, deliver, and discipline their subjects. The king was a co-shepherd with God, a sovereign but subordinate partner with God to manage his people compassionately. The ultimate human King, personified in the Messiah, exemplifies this shepherding role of a godly monarch.

> I will appoint shepherds over them who will truly shepherd them so my sheep will not be afraid, terrified or go missing any more. Days are coming when I will appoint for David a righteous Branch [Christ] who will reign as king, wisely and fairly in the land. Jer 23:4–5

Even though this position was most often abused, God did not abandon the model of the shepherding king which is ultimately fulfilled by his Son.

Deuteronomy 17:14–20 humbled any king along with his subjects beneath the Law. The king personally wrote out by hand all the Mosaic law. He kept it with him at all times and read from it daily. He was to be saturated with God's Law lest he begin

---

8. Num 27:16; Deut 17:14–15; Josh 1:6–9; 2 Chr 9:8; 17.5; Ps 2:4–6; Dan 7:13–14; Hag 2:23; Mic 5:2
9. Deut 17:15–20; 1 Kgs 2:2–4; 9:3–5
10. 1 Chr 29:23; 2 Chr 9:8

to compromise his personal life or leadership of Israel with standards contrary to that Law in word and spirit.[11] These daily "devotions" would remind him that he was like the rest of the Israelites—in total subjection to God's Law.

The conventional luxuries to which royalty believe themselves entitled are anathema to God. Such indulgences only serve to artificially elevate a king when he is a mere servant of the Lord equal under the law to the king's subjects. So, a sensible frugality was another sign that the king was simply an administrative servant of the Lord, not one to lord it over God's great people.[12] Ostentatious herds of horses for military showcasing, or worse, for military dependence, sent the wrong message to the people. God's message was that he would still go before them in battle, so a huge cavalry was an act of unbelief.[13] David complies with this instruction by hamstringing horses won in battle so they could not be used for military purposes.[14] Harems of many wives were to be avoided since the king's and Israel's spiritual commitments would suffer since the harem would include foreign wives with compromising beliefs and customs. Hoarding money and accumulating wealth and its purchases were also signs of misplaced priorities.

Local government was led by *elders*, or *judges*, and apparently there was an abundance of these; Succoth alone had seventy seven (Judg 8:14). Elders had already been a part of God's deliverance of the Israelites from Egypt and a part of receiving and administering divine law and justice in the wilderness.[15] This assembly was presumed to be wise and committed to God's Law and was entrusted with the law's application to the various legal issues arising within their vicinity. Their judgments would be determined after testimonies and other proceedings were held in their court within the city's gate area. Some judges were both legal and military leaders, and the military role is the predominant use of the term "judge" in the book of Judges.

Elders were to administer justice purely, with no other motivation than to bring God's justice into the court (Deut 16:18–20). Appeals were made to a higher level of elders and priests in the most difficult or ambiguous scenarios. Implicit in this appeal was the need for more experienced counsel or the mediatory role of a higher authority, such as Moses or a priest, in determining God's wisdom, perhaps through casting the Urim and Thumim as lots.[16] Nearly all legal decisions were made by these elders; for example, cases about rebellious sons, questions of virginity, levirate marriage, and extradition.[17] Sentencing was also part of the proceedings, e.g. Deut 25:1–3.

---

11. Deut 17:18–20; Ps 40:7–8; Prov 16:12; 28:15; 29:2, 14; Isa 10:1
12. Deut 17:17; Prov 28:16; 29:4; Jer 22:13–15;
13. Deut 17:16; Pss 20:7; 33:16–17; 44:3–8; 147:10; Prov 21:31
14. 2 Sam 8:4 // 1 Chr 18:4
15. Ex 3:16–18; 4:29; 12:21; 18:21; 24:1, 9–11; Num 11:16–17; 25:4–5
16. Deut 1:17; 17:8–13; 21:1–5; *also*, Prov 16:33; 18:18; 2 Chr 19:8
17. Num 35:12; Deut 19:11–13; 21:18–21; 22:13–21; 25:7–10

The *priests'* responsibilities appear to be the most varied in Israel. They served as stewards of formal worship and the sacrifices,[18] teachers of the Mosaic law,[19] God's spokesmen on various occasions for blessings and encouragements,[20] and overseers in certain judicial proceedings. Their role in formal worship and the numerous (for some priests, daily) bloody sacrificial tasks required a practical and ceremonial cleanliness that surpassed the normal cleanliness laws of the lay person.

Certain priests were called upon in particularly challenging cases when evidence was either ambiguous or non-existent because as mediators for God, they could ascertain his wisdom directly. When thorny questions about the motive, legal degree, or perpetrator of a homicide stymied the local elders, or when it was too subtle to determine whether there was false testimony and what its penalties should be, an appeal to priests helped conclude the cases.[21] If there was a lack of evidence for adultery, a priest oversaw a unique test of the accused that God used to reveal the truth (Num 5:12–31).

Prophets arose by God's appointment and empowerment, and no formal process or responsibilities are defined in the Mosaic law other than that the prophets must speak the truths that God had revealed to them. Self-appointed or otherwise appointed prophets who appeared in Israel who did not speak for God were to be executed. False prophecy included promoting false religion and predicting inaccurately.[22] Forbidden methods to determine the future were called "divination," which was the foolish hope of reading the future from natural, physical signs.[23]

It is so disheartening to hear the constant rebuke of Israel's leaders. Since they were the ones responsible for the nation and its smaller communities, they came under the most frequent and severe complaints of the Lord. His disappointment in their shepherding participation in the eternal design was profound.

> They are *shepherds* with no understanding, doing only what they want to do.
> They are unjust in their dealings, every last one of them. Isa 56:11

> Woe to the *shepherds* destroying and scattering the *sheep* in my *pasture*. Jer 23:1

> You drink the milk, wear the wool, and butcher the best animals, but you let your flocks starve. You do not take care of the weak, the sick or the crippled. You have not sought the *sheep* who have wandered and are lost. Instead, your rule is harsh and cruel. So my *sheep* have been scattered without a *shepherd*, easy prey for wild beasts. Ezek 34:3–4

18. Ex 29:35–46; Lev 1:7—7:36; 16:5—17:9; 23:10–21; *Jer* 32:32–35; *Ezek* 22:26; *Zeph* 3:4
19. Lev 10:9–11; Deut 31:9–12; 33:10; 2 *Chr* 17:7–9; *Ezek* 22:26; *Mal* 2:8
20. Num 6:22–26; Deut 20:1–4
21. Deut 17:8–12; 19:15–19; 21:1–5
22. Deut 13:1–5; 18:14–22; *Isa* 9:15; 30:10–11; *Jer* 2:8;5:13; 6:13–14; 14:14–16; 23:13, 16–21, 25–38; 27:14–22; 28:1–4, 15; 29:22–23; 32:32–35; *Lam* 2:14; *Ezek* 12:22–24; 13:1–23; 22:28; *Zech* 10:2
23. Lev 19:26; Deut 18:10–11, 14; *Isa* 2:6; 44:24–25; *Jer* 14:14; 27:9; 29:8–9; *Ezek* 12:23–24; 13:6; 22:28; *Hos* 4:12; *Mic* 3:6, 11; 5:12; *Zech* 10:2

In both Testaments God uses his prerogative as the King to appoint his Kingdom leaders. So, as God, Jesus called his twelve disciples. The Lord determined Judas Iscariot's successor (Acts 1:26). Paul was appointed by the Lord in a dramatic way.[24] And elders were appointed by Paul, Barnabas, Timothy, and others.[25] There is always a shepherding chain.

Christ's assessment of the religious leaders sounds similar to God's indictments of Old Testament leaders. They were "the blind leading the blind" (Matt 15:13–14). They were all about the rituals but not about the heart of God which values more highly "justice, mercy and faithfulness."[26] It was sometimes worse than foolish guidance of the sheep; it was robbery! Many New Testament leaders were guilty of extortion and leading the people only for personal and financial indulgence. They falsely ministered for the money demanded from their vulnerable sheep.[27]

Christ showed that leadership entails service, not oppression. He came "to serve, not to be served."[28] Whereas the Old Testament leaders scattered the sheep (Jer 23:1), he came to seek the scattered sheep, and he expects us to shepherd them back together too: "Whoever does not gather with me scatters" (Matt 12:30). The Old Testament shepherds did not feed the sheep, but the Good Shepherd, through his disciples, fed thousands on the hillsides.

In the Old Testament, Jeremiah conveyed God's promise that better shepherds were coming.

> I will give you *shepherds* with hearts like mine who will feed you with knowledge and understanding. Jer 3:15

> I will appoint *shepherds* over them who will care for them, and they will not be afraid again or be dismayed or lost. Jer 23:4

So the Lord spent much of his ministry shepherding his future shepherds of his flock, culminating in his breakfast discussion with Peter. Three times Jesus told Peter that if he really loved him as Lord, then he would feed and care for his sheep: "Do you love me? . . . Then tend my *lambs* . . . Do you love me? . . . Then *shepherd my sheep* . . . Do you love me? Then tend my *sheep*" (John 21:15–17).

And this stuck with Peter since he later writes to those he was shepherding himself,

> *Shepherd* God's *flock* among you, overseeing them willingly . . . not domineering them, but as examples to the *flock*. So when the chief *Shepherd* appears, you will receive the crown of glory that never fades. 1 Pet 5:2–4

---

24. Acts 9:3–9; 22:6–11; 26:12–18; 1 Cor 15:8
25. Acts 14:23; Titus 1:5
26. Matt 23:23 // Luke 11:42; *Mic* 6:8
27. Matt 23:25–35; Acts 20:33–35; Rom 16:18; 1 Tim 3:3; 6:3–5; 1 Pet 5:1–3; 2 Pet 2:2–3
28. Matt 20:28 // Mark 10:45

Paul instructs his Ephesian shepherd/elders to so the same, to shepherd against the wolves.

> Keep watch over yourselves and all the *flock* . . . Be *shepherds* of the church of God . . . savage wolves will come in among you and will not spare the *flock*.
> Acts 20:28–29

We mentioned in an earlier chapter that Paul uses the word *"shepherds"* when listing those Spiritually gifted for the edification of the church. It is the Greek word for the most often translated "pastors" (Eph 4:11).

Several leadership roles in the church are mentioned in the New Testament; unfortunately, specific duties are not described for many of them. More is mentioned about the moral character, qualifications and style of loving shepherds rather than their official responsibilities. Surely, gifted teachers were to teach, gifted administrators were to lead and manage,[29] shepherd-pastors shepherded, elders ruled and taught, and deacons served in other ways.

Even though we get a better idea about the elders' role, again, the emphasis is on the moral character of the elder with only general reference to responsibilities. Elders are the Lord's house managers (stewards, Titus 1:7), so it was important that they show an ability to manage their own literal household, including children (1 Tim 3:4). As with Old Testament elders, the New Testament elders were to be honored and obeyed as the top "shepherds" since they had authority "over" their local congregations.[30] Elders were to teach and monitor teaching of others. They visited the sick, anointing them with oil, and praying for them (Jas 5:14).

By far, most concerns about church leadership are about the teaching-leader roles. New Testament writers intensely cautioned both the teachers and the lay person that teaching had to be monitored for its consistency with the Truth.[31] We know elders were to teach, but we assume administrators, deacons, and others could teach as well, including faithful men and older women.[32] But James warns against too many teachers (Jas 3:1–2).

We mentioned in chapter 3 that Paul does not list "pastors" as having a Spiritual gift, contrary to most translations (Eph 4:11). Paul's word is "shepherd." So his list is, literally, "apostles, prophets, evangelists, *shepherds,* and teachers." If one is honored as a great "pastor," then they should be doing routine shepherding in the church. If they are good preachers or teachers, that is good, but different from having the gift of shepherding, or pastoring.

29. Rom 12:7; 1 Cor 12:28; Eph. 4:11
30. Acts 20:28–29; 1 Tim 5:17; 1 Pet 5:1–5
31. Acts 20:28–30; Rom 16:17–18; 2 Cor 11:3–4, 12–13; Eph 4:14; 5:6; Phil 3:2–3; Col 2:8, 16–23; 1 Thess 2:3–5; 1 Tim 1:3–7; 4:1–3, 7; 6:3–5, 20–21; 2 Tim 2:15–18; 3:6–9, 13; 4:3–4; Titus 1:9–16; Heb 13:9; 2 Pet 2:1–3; 3:3–4, 14–17; 1 John. 2:21–26; 4:1–5; 2 John 7–11; 3 John 9–10; Jude 4, 8–13, 16–19; Rev 2:2, 14–15, 20; 22:18–19
32. 2 Tim 2:2; Titus 2:3

The primary and great commissions' command to fill the earth with God's followers has been very successful. Fortunately, it has led to several regional and local believing communities, even denominations that have diverse cultural expressions across the world. Paul had his churches. Others had theirs. Denominations are preferable to a single terrestrial kingdom with a multi-layered hierarchy with all the excesses and extravagance that squander the Lord's resources. A centralized monarchy where local discretion would be compromised by a remote and artificially standardized and fallible authority was not the Lord's preference in the Old Testament, and fortunately, the Lord has not allowed it to come to that in more recent church history.

ECONOMIC AND BUSINESS POLICY

Historically, primarily the family has produced and exchanged the community's goods and services. Biblical ethics determines proper material priorities as well as fair and godly management of employees, contracts, and resources such as animals, crops, ores, and money. Business is an important concern throughout the Mosaic code, wisdom literature, Christ's parables and other teachings, and in the apostles' letters.

Land Ownership

God owns the entire cosmos—world, seas, continents, and any territories within them.[33] So, in Israel's agrarian culture it was basic economic policy that God owned the land and his people only leased it: "The land must not be sold permanently for it is mine, you are only aliens and tenants living with me" (Lev 25:23).

The Law did not allow land speculation, but if the land had to be sold because of poverty, the land was returned to the original owner in the Jubilee year. Since no one owned the land but God, it was his prerogative to keep the land filled by assuring its re-distribution according to his original allocation revealed to Moses.[34] This year of Jubilee, the added capstone year to seven cycles of seven years, made it the fiftieth year (Lev 25:10, 13). Then, all land, regardless of how it was acquired, was returned to the family of the original inhabitants after the Conquest. Even before the Jubilee year, if possible, the closest relative stepped in to buy the lease that the poor relative was forced to sell—to keep the land as close to the family as possible. But the ultimate goal was for the original owner to buy the land back himself as soon as financially stable. But Jubilee marked more than simply a repossession of the land; it was also a wonderful re-unification of families as they came back closer to their original proximity before the land was sold to non-family individuals. Getting the land back affirmed

---

33. Gen 14:19, 22; Ex 9:29; 19:5; Deut 10:14; 1 Kgs 20:23, 28; Job 41:11; Pss 24:1; 50:10–12; 82:8; 89:11; 95:3–5; 108:7–9; Isa 43:1

34. Num 34:1–15; Deut 4:47–49; 11:24–25; 34:1–4; Josh 1:3–4; 12:1–8; 13:1–7; 1 Sam 7:12–14; 1 Kgs 4:25; Isa 5:8; Ezek 45:8; Mic 2:2

the value of working one's own land to subdue one's own inheritance according to the Lord's blessings. There were similar laws for selling and buying city houses as well as specific exemptions for Levites (Lev 25:14–16, 25–34).

The sabbatical year, every seventh year, had many economic implications. One was that the land was given rest that year from production, allowing it to refortify itself for future productivity.[35] Of course, edible produce would still come up without intentional sowing, and the landowner's family, indentured servants, employees, resident aliens were allowed to eat what came straight from the fields. But this fallow produce could not be stored up and hoarded since the food from the fields, groves, and vineyards belonged to the poor as well as domesticated and wild animals.[36] God's miraculous sovereignty over nature ensured his promise that each sixth year would produce threefold. Its abundance would be sufficient for the fallow year, the following planting year, and the subsequent reaping year (Lev 25:20–22).

Stealing

Coveting, even if not acted on was at least an *attitude* of theft and so, immoral.[37] Stealing is an act of ingratitude to God for what he has already given. Outright stealing of another's animal was restituted at least one to five times the animal's value.[38] If the thief was unable to pay, he became the servant of the victim. But if the owner killed the thief in the act, the owner was exonerated completely (Ex 22:1–4). Taking produce from someone's land was considered stealing as was allowing one's animals to graze on a neighbor's property.[39]

Stealing land included moving the boundary stones between plots of land from their initially assayed spot.[40] It was considered robbery to withhold wages due an employee at an agreed upon time.[41] Deception in commodity measurements in the marketplace such as false weights or any other unit of measurement was theft, as was lying about the quality of the goods.[42] When someone entrusted another with their property for safe keeping, for collateral, or as a loan, and the other kept it, or lied

---

35. Ex 23:10–11; Lev 25:2–5; 26:34–35
36. Ex 23:11; Lev 25:6–7
37. Ex 20:17; Deut 5:21
38. Ex 22:1, 4, 7; Lev 6:5
39. Deut 23:24–25; Ex 22:5
40. Deut 19:14; 27:17; *Job* 24:2; *Prov* 22:28; 23:10, 11
41. Lev 19:13; Deut 24:14–15; *Prov* 3:27–28; *Jer* 22:13; *Mal* 3:5
42. Lev 19:35–36; Deut 25:13–16; *Prov* 11:1; 16:11; 20:10, 14, 23; *Hos* 12:7; *Amos* 8:5–6; *Mic* 6:10–11

about whether it was lost or stolen while under their watch, it was considered theft.[43] Extortion was also criminal.[44]

New Testament teaching ascribes the source of stealing to the coveting heart just as the Old Testament had.[45] Christ and Paul affirmed the Ten Commandments by condemning stealing.[46] Outright robbery or thievery, whether by soldiers, thieves, or pilfering employees is also immoral.[47] Just as sinful is the theft by cheating others as a swindler or an over-charging tax collector.[48] We already mentioned that false teachers in the local church when they taught for money amounted to stealing from the naïve believers.[49]

Property and Liability

Mosaic law echoed Noah's primary commission by requiring one to subdue domesticated animals.[50] The animal was to be stoned if it killed someone, and a servant was compensated for lost labor time if injured. If the owner's animal had injured people often enough, the inattentive owner would be executed or redeemed by some other form of restitution. When one was responsible for another person's animal and it died due to his own recklessness, he needed to pay for the lost animal. And restitution was expected when a domesticated animal injured another person's animal.[51]

Other liability laws dealt with property and safety. When one found anyone else's property, for example, clothing or a stray animal, it was one's responsibility to care for it until it could be returned to its owner. In the spirit of loving one's enemies, this was equally true for their property.[52] Other liabilities included keeping a brush fire from consuming another's produce or property (Ex 22:6) or ensuring a safe home for anyone to enjoy without injury or death by securing a roof with a surrounding railing, for instance (Deut 22:8).

Loans

Debt was to be handled with love and respect for the debtor. In fact being a creditor was an obligation since, if there were any poor in the vicinity, they were to be

---

43. Ex 22:7–8, 10–11; Lev 6:2–3
44. Lev 6:2; Isa 33:15
45. Acts 20:33; Rom 7:7; 13:9; 1 Cor 5:11; 6:9–10; Eph 5:5; Jas 1.14; 4.2
46. Matt 19:18 // Mark 10:19 // Luke 18:20; Rom 13:9
47. Matt. 15:19 // Mark 7:22; Luke 3:14; Rom 2:21–22; 1 Cor 6:9–10; Eph 4:28; Titus 2:10; 1 Pet 4:15
48. Luke 3:12–13; 1 Cor 5:10–11
49. Matt 23:25; Acts 20:33–35; Rom 16:18; 1 Tim 3:3; 6:3–5; 1 Pet 5:1–3; 2 Pet 2:2–3
50. Gen 9:5; Ex 21:28–32
51. Ex 21:33–36; Lev 24:21
52. Ex 23:4–5; Deut 22:1–4

generously credited—and at no interest. The assumption was that if a fellow Israelite was poor enough to be in debt in the first place, to add to that debt with interest was not an act of grace.[53] The issue was not that interest in itself was morally wrong since nothing was said of loans made for investment purposes, and one could extract interest from a foreigner. Furthermore, any debt by an Israelite was to be cancelled at least by the sabbatical year, and one was not to withhold a loan in anticipation of an imminent sabbatical year when the debt would expire (Deut 15:1–3, 9–10).

Collateral could be demanded but in civil and compassionate ways only. For instance, one could not storm into the debtor's house to extract collateral but was to wait outside the debtor's door where it would be brought to him (Deut 24:10–13). Objects necessary for anyone's subsistence such as food implements and garments from widows were off limits.[54] If one secured the poor person's garment, it was to be returned each night—a requirement which in itself was a deterrent against requiring a pledge from one so destitute in the first place.[55]

Debt was to be avoided according to the New Testament too (Rom. 13:8), but when it came to lending to others or when someone owed anything to another believer, generosity was expected, perhaps even paying someone's debt for them! Jesus says,

> Give to those who ask, and do not refuse those who want to borrow. Matt 5:42

> Love your enemies and do good; lend to others, expecting nothing back. Luke 6:35

Paul expected this generosity from Philemon, or Paul would take care of the debt himself.

> If Onesimus has defrauded you or owes you anything, charge that to me. Philem 18

Indentured Servitude

"Slavery" in Israel was primarily indentured servitude, a relationship in which a debtor was under an extended contract with the one to whom he was indebted.[56] However, the servant's contract could be bought out earlier by a generous relative or by the servant himself who might otherwise pay the contract debt and be freed (Lev 25:48–53). The indentured servant was to be treated with grace, as a regular employee, not with the harshness the Israelites experienced themselves as slaves in Egypt.[57] If the servant

---

53. Ex 22:25–26; Lev 25:35–37; Deut 15:7–11; 23:19–21; *Pss* 15:5; 37:21, 26; 112:5–6, 9; *Prov* 19:17; 28:8; *Ezek* 18:8–10, 17; 22:12

54. Deut 24:6, 17; *Job* 24:3, 9–10; *Prov* 25:20; *Ezek* 18:7; 33:14–15; *Amos* 2:8

55. Ex 22:26–27; Deut 24:10–13; *Ezek* 18:7; 33:15

56. Prov 11:29; 22:7

57. Lev 25:39–46; *Prov* 31:15; *Eccl* 7:21–22

was injured by their master, they were immediately freed from their contract. If a master caused a servant's immediate death he was sentenced for murder and executed. A servant was granted asylum in another city as a fugitive from the master's physical abuse.[58] Servants were given the same Sabbath rest every seventh day as everyone else was.[59] Israelite law encouraged one to gain economic and contractual freedom before the required emancipation at the sabbatical year. Even then, the master was to grant the contractual freedom and to supply the newly freed person with enough to get started without being destitute again from the start.[60] On the other hand, if one found the working conditions as a servant to be pleasant enough one could choose to remain with the master permanently.[61] This was added reason for the master to treat the servant and his family well.

For whatever reason one might be a servant or slave to another during the New Testament, the master is to treat the servant as a peer in God's kingdom. The servant is not to be intimidated, is to be paid appropriately, and is to be treated as an equal before the Savior who delivered them.[62] Servants were to respect their master as well, looking past those who were unreasonable, seeing that it is the Lord they were truly serving, not an abusive overseer.[63] Those called to the ministry of the message of God were to be fairly supported by those they served just as the Levites and priests had been compensated in the Old Testament.[64]

Social Care

The Trinity's concern for the poor, orphan, widow, handicapped, and alien is deep and passionate. God's ownership of all the land, and his compassion for the disadvantaged, assured that the needy were provided for if they had no land of their own to grow food for eating or bartering. However, in most cases it required their effort to collect the food. On a day-to-day basis there was freedom to eat a meal's worth from someone's field (Deut 23:24–25). Also, any fruit that had fallen naturally from a vine or tree belonged to the needy, not the land owner. On a seasonal basis land owners were to leave the produce from the corners of their fields untouched so that the poor could harvest it themselves. And the owner could not clearcut a field or vineyard when harvesting by going over it a second time to collect what was missed.[65] On a three-year cycle, a special contribution was made by land owners to the community food bank for the

---

58. Ex 21:20–21, 26–27; Deut 23:15–16
59. Ex 20:10; 23:12; Deut 5:14
60. Ex 21:2–4; Deut 15:12–15, 18; Jer 34:8–16
61. Ex 21:5–6; Deut 15:16–17
62. 1 Cor 12:13; Gal 3:28; Eph 6:9; Col 4:1; Philem 15–17; Jas 5:4
63. Eph 6:5–8; Col 3:22–25; 1 Tim 6:1–2; Titus 2:9; 1 Pet 2:18–19
64. Matt 10:9–10 // Luke 10:7–8; 1 Cor 9:6–14; Gal 6:6; 1 Tim 5:17–18
65. Lev 19:9–10; 23:22; Deut 24:19–21

poor as well as the Levites.[66] These resources were stored for the needy to withdraw over the span of the three years.

Animal Care

God's shepherding heart led to moral standards for subduing the earth and its animals of every sort. It made good business and ecological sense to care for one's animals, even the wild ones, according to the primary commission and the Mosaic law derived from it. Domesticated and wild beasts were to benefit from the same Sabbath day and sabbatical year rest as the Israelites did.[67] Animals were fed while they worked, not driven to exhaustion and emaciation.[68] We know human moral conscience before the Law required care for animals since Levi and Simeon were rebuked by their father and lost their favored status partly because of their cruelty to animals (Gen 49:6). It was mentioned above that it was a neighborly responsibility to return a stray animal to its owner, but at the same time it was a humane deliverance of the animal itself.

As an example of how to avoid regional extinction of the natural habitat, it was required to leave the wild hen when taking her eggs so she could still lay eggs again (Deut 22:6–7). Finally, there were intuitive sentiments expressed about respecting the mother-child bond in laws that forbade offering animal sacrifices which were less than eight days old, or offering the mother and young on the same day, or boiling the young one's flesh for food in the otherwise nurturing milk of its mother.[69]

FAMILY STRENGTH

God's Law focused significantly on the strength of the Israelite family. The family unit served many purposes. It was a center of love, learning, commerce, worship, and protection. For example, the Lord demanded one-year military deferments for those who needed first to put their marriage and economic house in order before soldiering. The year was to be spent stabilizing one's critical spousal and marketplace responsibilities (Deut 20:5–7; 24:5).

Spousal Arrangements

Surprisingly, given the detail of spousal relationships in Mosaic law, there is no definitive statement against polygamy related to either literal wives or "half-wives," namely, concubines. In fact, Mosaic law assumed polygamy in some laws. On the other hand,

---

66. Deut 14:28–29; 26:12–13
67. Ex 20:10; 23:12; Lev 25:7; Deut 5:14
68. Deut 25:4; *Prov* 12:10; 27:23–27
69. Ex 22:30; 34:26; Lev 22:27, 28; Deut 14:21

it is difficult to find even one polygamous arrangement in the Old Testament that was harmonious and not fraught with bitterness. Besides, we cannot know to what extent polygamy and concubinage was even practiced by the common Israelite. It is clear that God commands against *many* wives for kings, but that is not in itself a command for monogamy (Deut 17:17). We assume that God preferred monogamy even though he did not condemn nor institute sentences against polygamists. Priests were to marry only a virgin—widows, divorcees, or former prostitutes were not eligible spouses for them (Lev 21:7, 14).

God's Law focused on avoiding possible abuses in polygamous and concubinous arrangements. For example, a second wife or a concubine could walk out of the relationship if her subsistence or conjugal rights were neglected, and she was not treated equally as the first wife in these regards. There were three inalienable rights of the wife or the concubine, and if they were not satisfied, she was free to leave.

> [Her husband] may not neglect her right to food, clothing, or her conjugal rights.
>
> If he will not give these three rights to her, then she shall go out owing nothing. Ex 21:10–11

This implies, of course, that the first wife could do the same. A husband was to publicly file for divorce from an adulterous wife and could not remarry her if she married someone else and was separated from the second husband by divorce or his death (Deut 24:1–4).

Apparently many if not all the apostles were married except Paul. Though he was not married, he affirms marriage, believing it to be good, even a "right" and a "gift."[70] He called those who disapproved of marriage "liars" who followed the doctrine of demons (1 Tim 4:3–5). But, obviously, he did not believe marriage was for everyone. Celibacy could deliver one from the inevitable trials of being married; it could be a gift and blessing as well.[71] So Paul does challenge those wanting to be married or remarried to reconsider the advantages they might have by remaining single (1 Cor 7:7–8, 15, 39–40). Paul does feel more strongly that younger widows who had already been called to marriage should remarry since there is plenty of constructive kingdom work a wife and mother could continue to accomplish.[72] Caring for children as a widow would seem to deserve the help of a new husband.

Considering the issue of divorce must start by understanding the shepherding heart of God for those victimized by a poor marriage. In the Old Testament, the Lord allowed a woman to leave her husband if he was unfaithful or did not provide for her at least three inalienable rights: to food, clothing and sexual fulfillment. These were just examples of physical and psychological shepherding care for the spouse. One cannot imagine physical violence not being added to the list, especially if life threatening.

---

70. 1 Cor 7:7; 9:5
71. 1 Cor 7:28–34; also, Matt 19:12
72. 1 Cor. 7:9; 1 Tim 5:14

Harm to merely a servant ended in release from a contract. Surely a wife would be given at least that freedom as well. Abandoning the woman altogether would of course result in not providing her any of these rights.

Paul opens 1 Corinthians 7 with comments on fidelity and sexual fulfillment in order to frame the discussion of divorce. He repeats the expectation of both the Old Testament and Jesus about sexual fidelity in 7:1–2. He then repeats the Old Testament moral obligations for a spouse to fulfill the other sexually in 7:3–4. This could not be done if one abandoned or left the other (7:11, 15). Again, this is only an example of depriving the spouse of certain rights. So, abandonment was not grounds for divorce just because the person was no longer there; grounds for divorce was that they were no longer providing the needs of the spouse. If a person had not left physically, but their behavior amounted to the same dereliction of responsibility, reason would conclude that the victim was free to leave, owing nothing. So there are two grounds for divorce in the Old and New Testaments: adultery and abandonment of critical responsibilities. One cannot conceive of Christ's and Paul's standards being punitive to the victim when Old Testament standards were not. Surely Christ and Paul would not have prescribed more restrictive divorce rules than the Old Testament!

One reason to not allow remarriage in some situations is that an irresponsible spouse (rather than the victimized spouse) had already failed profoundly in the exclusive sexual relationship of marriage. This is how we read Romans 7:3, "She will be called an adulteress if she marries another man while her husband is alive." This statement is true in some cases, but not in the cases where the woman's husband is an adulterer himself or he abandoned her, or abused her. The widow or widower is also free to remarry.[73]

The daily relationship between husband and wife was to have a more intense love and wisdom than is expected between only friends, and even enemies. "Love your neighbor as yourself" is the second summary command and Paul applies it specifically to marriage as well.

> Husbands must love their wives as their own bodies. He who loves his wife loves himself. For no one hates his own flesh, but nourishes and cherishes it.
> Eph 5:28–29

So husbands must love, honor, and cherish their wives which always implies being humble and treating one's wife as even more important than one's self rather than looking for opportunities to be the authoritarian husband or any other self-seeking behavior.[74] Referring to all relationships between believers, Paul says,

> Do nothing from selfishness or conceit, but humbly consider others more important than yourselves. Phil 2:3

---

73. Rom 7:2–3; 1 Cor 7:39
74. Eph 5:25, 28–29, 33; Col 3:19

Since wives are equal and fellow heirs to the Kingdom of God, there is no place for a hierarchy of the male's personal value or personal priorities in the marriage (1 Pet 3:7).

It is only within this context of extreme deference to the wife from the heart of a loving, shepherding husband that we can understand the expectation that women subject themselves to their husbands. It is infrequent when 'subjection' is necessary in a healthy marriage where there is mutual respect and deference. It is a rare and last resort when a decision is necessary and the husband's view is different from his wife's. While the husband defers to the wife out of love and devotion, the wife does the same.[75] It is the same attitude that Christ Jesus had with his Father when facing death, "My Father, if possible, take this cup from me; yet not as I will, but as you will."[76] Surely, subjecting oneself to the will of another will scarcely rise even to this level of self-sacrifice, so mutual submission in much lesser situations should be with love and ease.

Fornication

The primary commission's command to multiply assumes there are proper moral ways to procreate. It does not mean multiply in every conceivable way. Fornication, that is, any illegal sexual act, including adultery, was addressed in Mosaic law to provide the safest and most productive structure for family strength. Multiplying and filling the earth were profound and enjoyable steps toward managing the earth. But the devastating results of lacking control and boundaries for sexual expression were a serious consideration when God prescribed sexual morality. Multiplication was a foundational element in the primary commission, but it was to be accomplished only between husband and wife. Intercourse outside of marriage was a misuse of the wonderful means to procreate and multiply participants in God's eternal design.

Fornication, including adultery was a capital crime for both parties.[77] If it was rape, only the man was executed. If there were no witnesses to a woman's alleged adultery, and even if she failed a test of her innocence, she was not executed (Num 5:12–31). Consensual premarital sex with a virgin was overlooked if the woman's father approved their marriage. If he did not approve, the man paid the dowry anyway. Virginity was a virtue to be protected, so a false accusation against a woman was dealt with harshly.[78]

The ominous threat from incest to family stability was identified very specifically and was considered to be a capital crime in most cases: between a son or daughter and their parent or grandparent; with one's sibling, daughter-in-law or son-in-law, aunt

---

75. Eph 5:22–24, 33; Col 3:18; Titus 2:4; 1 Pet 3:1–2

76. Matt 26:42 // Mark 14:36 // Luke 22:42

77. Ex 20:14; Lev 18:20; 20:10–11, 14; Deut 5:18; 22:23–27; *Job* 24:15; 31:1, 9–12; *Ps* 50:18; *Prov* 2:16–19; 5:3–23; 6:23–35; 7:5–27; 22:14; 23:26–28; 29:3; 30:20; 31:3; *Eccl* 7:26; *Jer* 5:7–9; 7:9; 23:10, 14; 29:22–23; *Ezek* 18:6; 33:26; *Hos* 4:2, 13–14; *Mal* 3:5

78. Ex 22:16–17; Deut 22:13–21, 28–29

or uncle, brother's wife (unless one is taking responsibility for his brother's surviving wife). If a person married someone who already had children, he was not to lie with the stepchildren or step-grandchildren.[79]

Fruitless simulations of the procreative act which were committed outside the family were a travesty of natural and divine law and were capital crimes. Unproductive intercourse between two or more men or two or more women was as repulsive as intercourse with an animal. The costuming of the transvestite was forbidden as well. Homosexuality, prostitution, and bestiality were equally abominable with death as their penalty.[80]

Paul acknowledges the pleasure from sexual intimacy as an important element of a marriage, even to the extent that it is sin not to engage one's spouse sexually (1 Cor 7:3-5). The teaching that sexual pleasure is a blessing did not change between the times of the Song of Solomon and the New Testament. But this pleasure was still to be experienced only between spouses.

What was unlawful sexually in the Old Testament remains immoral in the New Testament. The Tenth Commandment says one could not covet another's spouse, and Jesus repeats the same standard (Matt 5:27-28). Fornication, that is, any illicit sexual activity is just as strongly forbidden.

> The sexually immoral, idolaters, adulterers, practicing homosexuals, thieves, the greedy, drunkards, revilers, swindlers will not inherit the Kingdom of God.[81]

Adultery is forbidden in many passages,[82] as are incest and prostitution.[83]

The humiliating and fruitless practice of homosexuality is explicitly condemned in no vague terms. We have already looked at Romans 1:20-27 where Paul explains homosexuality as a self-denigrating result of denying God's existence, power and divine attributes. We meet clear passages in 1 Corinthians 6:9-10, 1 Timothy 1:10, and Jude 7 where the Lord conveys that homosexuality is a perversion of the sexual intimacy reserved for a husband and wife of the opposite sex.

Respecting Elders

Family strength was fortified through clear lines of authority and respect. Parents were responsible for teaching their children the Mosaic law and wisdom instructions, and the children were responsible to listen and obey.[84] The authority of the husband and

---

79. Lev 18:6-18; 20:11-21; Deut 22:30; 27:20, 22, 23; *Ezek* 22:10

80. Ex 22:19; Lev 18:22-23; 19:29; 20:13, 15-16; 21:9; Deut 22:5; 23:17-18; 27:21; *Isa* 57:3-4; *Hos* 4:11-14; *Amos* 2:7-8

81. 1 Cor 6:9-10; also, Acts 21:25; Rom 13:13; 1 Cor 6:18; 2 Cor 12:21; Gal 5:19; Eph 5:3; Col 3:5; 1 Thess 4:3-7; 1 Tim 1:10; Heb 13:4; Rev 2:14, 20

82. Matt 5:27-28; 15:19 // Mark 7:21; Matt 19:18 // Mark 10:19 // Luke 18:20; Rom 2:22; 7:3; 13:9; Jas 2:11; 2 Pet 2:14

83. 1 Cor 5:1; 6:15-16

84. Deut 4:10; 6:5-7; *Prov* 1:8-9; 4:1-4; 6:20-23; 10:1; 13:1, 24; 15:5, 20; 17:21, 25; 19:13; 22:6;

father could negate a vow made by a wife or child (Num 30:3–15). The aged were to be respected out of respect for God.[85] Honoring one's parents was a gravely guarded expectation with drastic results for the offending child.[86] If a son was found to be incurably rebellious, including cursing or hitting a parent, he could be executed.[87]

Family roles for parents and children remained unchanged from one Testament to the other. Children were still to honor their parents, even into their later years.[88] And parents were to love and shepherd their children with good things physically and emotionally as well as to discipline them accordingly.[89]

HEALTH PRECAUTIONS

Many laws ensured that illness and disease were prevented in the first place or that their spread was minimized. Proper management of public and personal health through correct diet, precautionary customs, and reducing contact with possibly contagious (or actually contagious) people, animals, and objects was a significant blessing to the community. The Sabbath rest was intended to refresh and strengthen the body of both people and their work animals.[90] Eating the fat of animals is not a good idea from a cardiovascular perspective (Lev 7:23). Gluttony and drunkenness are known to be unhealthy excesses.[91] Injury was to be prevented too, and laws guided the Israelites toward safety in their communities. God does not explain the pathology of illness or health in either of the Testaments; he simply instructs the people how to stay healthy with prohibitions that reduced the risk of infection. What one might consider now to be a simple infection could be life threatening in the medically primitive world.

Laws about acceptable meats demonstrated the application of the responsibilities of the primary commission. By naming, ordering, and subduing the creatures, as Adam did, the dietary laws were possible. Prevention of infection seems to be one critical consideration. Land animals with paws or those which do not have split hooves *and* which chew their cud were forbidden. This eliminated among other animals, carnivores and scavengers.[92] Various other mammals and reptiles like mice and lizards were also barred from human consumption (Lev 11:29–30, 41–44). Aquatic animals

---

15; 23:13–16; 22–25; 27:11; 28:7; 29:15, 17; *Ezek* 22:7; *Mic* 7:6

85. Lev 19:32; *Prov* 16:31; 17:6; 20:29

86. Ex 20:12; Lev 19:3; Deut 5:16; 27:16; *Prov* 19:18, 26; 28:24

87. Ex 21:15, 17; Lev 20:9; Deut 21:18–21; *Prov* 20:20; 30:11, 17

88. Matt 15:4-6; 19:19 // Mark 7:10 // Luke 18:20; Eph 6:1–3; Col 3:20; 1 Tim 1:9; 5:4; 2 Tim 3:2; Heb 12:8–10

89. Matt 7:9–11 // Luke 11:11–13; Eph 6:4; Col 3:21; Titus 2:4; Heb 12:9–10

90. Ex 16:22–23; 20:8–11; 23:12; 31:14–15; 34:21; 35:2–3; Deut 5:13–15

91. Deut 21:20; *Prov* 20:1; 21:17; 23:19–21, 29–35; 25:16, 27; 28:7; 31:4–7; *Eccl* 10:16–17; *Isa* 5:22; 28:1–3, 7; 56:10–12; *Hos* 4:11, 17–18; 7:5, 14; *Amos* 4:1; *Mic* 2:11

92. Lev 11:2–8, 26–27; Deut 14:4–8; *Isa* 65:4; 66:17

could be eaten only if they had fins and scales, again precluding scavengers and many bottom feeders.[93] Many scavenging birds were forbidden, and only insects on a very short list were legally edible.[94] Carcasses of any animals not intentionally killed were to be avoided as well as anything they may have touched.[95] Eating blood, a main carrier of infection, was anathema.[96]

Several laws sought to prevent or suppress disease contracted by infection. Any contact with a dead animal or human flesh required both isolation for some period of time and participation in a purification ritual.[97] Body fluids are also carriers of contagious elements, and there was great care in isolating the contaminated. Again, people were to distance themselves from blood from childbirth and menstruation because of its tendency to become impure and infectious.[98] One's vulnerability to infection indirectly from others in these cases also needed to be considered. Ejaculation was to be followed by washing (Lev 15:16–18, 31–33). Caution and purification were prescribed for other unidentified discharges which presumably would have included urine, feces, saliva, vomit, mucous, puss, and amniotic fluid, and secretions from wounds and skin diseases.[99] Circumcision served as a hygienic aid to cleanliness.[100] The instructions for disposing fecal material during a military encampment imply sewage laws were probably given for routine life as well (Deut 23:12–14). Venereal disease was contracted by someone having had illicit sex or passing it on to an innocent partner.[101]

Public safety and liability laws about dangerous domesticated animals and houses have already been discussed.[102] Public safety and health were also addressed through laws which deterred crimes which injured victims intentionally or because of carelessness. Violence of this sort will be discussed later, including homicide, physical assault, and rape.

COURT JUSTICE

Telling the truth was the foundation for judicial process in Mosaic law. Lying in general is addressed in only one passage of the Mosaic law, but numerous laws protecting the innocent and punishing the guilty relied on truth telling.[103] The disadvantaged,

---

93. Lev 11:9–12; Deut 14:9–10
94. Lev 11:13–23; 20:25; Deut 14:11–20
95. Ex 22:31; Lev 7:24; 11:24–28, 31–38; Deut 14:21
96. Gen 9:4; Lev 7:6–27; 19:26; *Ezek* 33:25
97. Lev 5:2; Num 5:2–3; 19:2–22
98. Lev 12:2–7; 18:19; 15:19–24, 33; 20:18; *Ezek* 18:6; 22:10
99. Lev 13:2–59; 14:33–57; 15:1–13, 25–30; Num 5:2–3; Deut 23:9–11
100. Gen 17:10–14; Ex 12:48
101. Prov 5:3–11; 7:25–27
102. Gen 9:5; Ex 21:28–36; Lev 24:21; Deut 22:8
103. Lev 19:11; but also, *Pss* 5:6, 9; 12:2–4; 31:18; 34:13; 36:3; 50:19–20; 52:1–4; 58:2; 59:12; 62:4;

the poor, aliens, orphans, and widows who are weak, alone, and perhaps without the resources to mount a strong defense, were supposed to be protected by impartial witnesses and judges.[104] On the other hand impartiality was to be just that: no sentimentality for the poor was to prejudice judges against those who were better off. There was to be equal justice to everyone based on truth alone.[105]

One's testimony was to be truthful.[106] There were to be two or three witnesses to triangulate the truth and assure fairness. If they committed perjury they would be punished to the same severity that the defendant's penalty would have been if convicted (Deut 19:15–21). Bribery of witnesses or judges was treachery.[107]

The same fairness and justice was expected within the New Testament believing community. Christ rebuked the Pharisees, scribes, and lawyers for their injustice and unmerciful treatment of the disadvantaged.[108] Some leaders stole from widows and virtually killed the poor with their selfish decisions.[109]

Paul expected wise decisions in legal cases within the church because believers would someday judge the angels (1 Cor 6:2–3). If we will have that responsibility then, we should now be able to handle the legal matters between two believers in the church. Rather than go to the civil authorities and embarrass the church by airing dirty laundry, wise people within the church should be able to mediate instead.

As in the Old Testament Law, there was to be equal justice to everyone based on the truth alone; perjury was still immoral.[110] Perjury was a tragic practice in the New Testament which surfaced in the testimony of false witnesses at the trials of Christ and Stephen.[111] Two or three witnesses were required when there were accusations against an elder, but that probably was not the only occasion for such a precaution (1 Tim 5:19). Ananias and Sapphira were struck dead for lying, not withholding their assets (Acts 5:4–10).

101:5–7; 116:9–11; 119:69, 78, 86; 120:2–4; *Prov* 4:24, 31; 6:12–13, 17; 12:19; 22; 15:4; 17:4, 7, 20; 19:22; 20:14; 22:16; 24:26; 30:8; *Isa* 59:13–15; *Jer* 9:3–5; *Hos* 7:3; *Mic* 6:12; *Zeph* 3:13

104. Ex 23:6; Lev 5:1; Num 35:30; Deut 5:20; 17:6; 24:17; 27:19; Ps 82:1–4; *Job* 29:7–17; *Prov* 6:19; 12:17; 13:23; 14:5, 25; 22:22–23; 25:18; 29:7; 31:8–9; *Isa* 1:23; 10:1–2; *Amos* 5:12

105. Ex 23:3, 7; Lev 19:15; Deut 1:16–17; 16:18–20; *Ps* 94:20–22; *Prov* 17:15, 26; 18:5, 17; 24:11–12, 23–25; 25:18; 29:14; *Jer* 21:12; 22:3; *Lam* 3:35–36

106. Ex 20:16; 22:9; 23:1–2, 7; Lev 5:4; 6:2–5; 19:16; Deut 22:13–19; *Pss* 27:12; *Prov* 19:5, 9, 28; 21:28; 24:28–29; *Ezek* 22:9

107. Ex 23:8; Deut 16:19; *Ps* 15:5; *Prov* 17:23; 28:21; 29:4; *Eccl* 4:1; *Isa* 1:23; 5:23; *Amos* 5:12

108. Matt 23:23 // Luke 11:42

109. Matt 23:14 // Mark 12:38–40 // Luke 20:47; Jas 5:6

110. Matt 15:19; 19:18 // Mark 10:19 // Luke 18:20; Luke 3:14; 1 Tim 1:10

111. Matt 26:59–61; Acts 6:11–14

DISADVANTAGED PROTECTED

A fallen world is hardest on those least able to protect themselves because of their vulnerability to stronger forces from many directions. God leveraged the Israelites' own torturous destitution and vulnerability while slaves in Egypt to punctuate his expectations of them in their care for the disadvantaged.[112] Israelites with greater resources and stronger networks were to love and care for those who were destitute, alone, subservient, old, handicapped, employed by God (Levites), or strangers in their land.

The Lord assured the Israelites that there would be no poor in the land if they were obedient. That would have been true because of the abundant blessings of his grace and rewards for their obedience and because their obedience would have led to their generosity to all those who were in need of resources and companionship. However, since God is a realist, he made provision for the disadvantaged who would inevitably be present in great number due to Israel's unfaithfulness to them and to God (Deut 15:4–5, 11). Ruling with God according to his standards of management and leadership would lead to a satisfying life even in the midst of the Fall's curses.

We have already highlighted protecting the poor, widows, orphans, and aliens in court, and the care due to the indentured servant. We have surveyed the laws for social welfare to balance the excesses of a free market economy. Since the land was shared by the Lord with the owner, the community was obligated to foster gleaning and food banks for the disadvantaged. The elderly were to be honored, not dismissed (Lev 19:32). The handicapped were to be respected and not ridiculed.[113] Anything leading to the further affliction of the widow, orphan, or alien was sorely hypocritical given the Lord's care in response to Israel's cry for deliverance and justice while oppressed in Egypt.[114]

The New Testament charges the church to be just as concerned for the disadvantaged, but does not develop an elaborate legal system to ensure it since believers had the Old Testament as their tutor. Deacons were appointed initially to care for the disadvantaged, specifically the widows, and Paul gives guidelines to Timothy for their care as well.[115] The responsibility fell primarily on families to care for widows. But if they failed to so or none were able, widows sixty years and older were to be cared for by the church if they had been righteous and had shown themselves to be strong caregivers themselves during their younger life.

Orchestrated efforts for serving the disadvantaged included pooling assets of the believers in Jerusalem so that none would be destitute (Acts 4:32–35). However, this

---

112. Ex 23:9; Lev 19:34; Deut 24:18; *Prov* 3:28–29; 14:21; 17:5; 22:2, 9;28:3, 27; 31:20

113. Lev 19:14; Deut 27:18; *Job* 29:15

114. Ex 22:21–24; 23:9; Lev 19:33–34; Deut 25:5–10; 27:19; *Job* 20:5, 19; 24:3–14, 21; 30:25; 31:16–22, 31–32; 34:24–28; *Pss* 9:9, 12, 18; 10:2, 12–18; 12:5; 37:14; 41:1–3; 68:5–6; 72:1–4; 12–14; 94:3–7; 102:17, 20; 107:40–41; 109:9–16; 140:12; 146:7–9; *Isa* 1:17; 3:14–15; 10:1–2; 32:6–7; 58:6–7, 10; *Jer* 2:34; 5:28; 7:5–7; 19:4; 22:3, 15–16; *Ezek* 16:49; 18:7; 22:7, 29; *Hos* 14:3; *Amos* 2:6–8; 8:6; 4:1; 5:11; *Mic* 2:9; *Zech* 7:10; *Mal* 3:5

115. Acts 6:1–3; 1 Tim 5:3–4, 9, 16

appears to be a spontaneous effort at that specific time of starting the church in very difficult times. Yet giving our tithes and offerings is an extension of this pooling of resources (2 Cor 8:1–4, 10–15).

VIOLENT ATTITUDES AND ACTS

God knows that the pit of vengeance is lined with grudges and hatred. We allow God to avenge us because his motives, wisdom, and means are perfect, whereas ours can be selfish and reactionary, even impulsive. So his laws include specific commands to control not only one's actions but one's heart and emotions as well. "You must not hate your Israelite brother . . . or take vengeance or bear a grudge . . . you must love your neighbor as yourself."[116] The essence of keeping the laws was to do so in love for God and love of those around us. Passive aggression is also a destructive form of violence since intentional neglect keeps others from physical and emotional safety (Prov 24:11–12). Words can also be violent in the slander that destroys reputations and careers. False testimony could bring lashing or even execution to an innocent person.[117] Mockery of the handicapped, even if only in words, or misleading them in any way was cruel, and detestable. If the mockery ended in bodily harm, then it would have been considered a physical assault.[118]

Premeditated murder was a capital offense but required at least two witnesses for a conviction.[119] Child sacrifice was, of course, murder as well.[120] Unintentional homicide or manslaughter was not a capital crime. But to keep the suspect safe until a trial was arranged, six "cities of refuge" were safe zones where suspects could flee to avoid fatal retribution from avenging family members.[121]

All other assaults were forbidden, and the attacker was sentenced depending on the circumstances (Deut. 27:24). Rape of an engaged or married woman was a capital crime. If the woman was not engaged and there was a question concerning force, the two were required to be married after a fine was paid to the father (Deut 22:26–29). If an indentured servant was assaulted but lived at least two days after an assault, the assault was assumed not to be premeditated, so the attacker was found liable for the lost time of the servant. But if the servant lost a body part or its use, the servant was freed permanently (Ex 21:20–21, 26–27). Merely striking one's parent was a capital

---

116. Lev 19:17–18; *also,* Prov 20:22; 24:17–18; 25:21–22

117. Lev 19:16; *Ps* 15:3; *Prov* 10:11, 18; 11:9; 12:6; 26:18–19, 24–26, 28; 30:10; *Isa* 32:6–7; 59:4; Ezek 22:9–12

118. Lev 19:14; Deut 27:18

119. Gen 9:5–6; Ex 20:13; 21:12–14, 20; Lev 24:17, 21; Num 35:16–21, 30; Deut 5:17; 19:11–13; 27:25; *Job* 24:14; *Pss* 5:6; 10:8–10; 37:32; 55:23; 62:3; 94:3–7; 109:16; *Prov* 1:10–19; 6:16–17; 29:10; *Isa* 5:7; 33:15; 59:3–7; *Jer* 2:34; 7:5–9; 22:3, 17; *Lam* 4:13; *Ezek* 11:6; 13:19; 22:4–6, 25–27; *Hos* 4:2; 6:9; *Mic* 3:2–3

120. Lev 18:21; 20:1–5; Deut 18:10; *Jer* 32:35

121. Ex 21:12–13; Num 35:6, 10–15, 22–28; Deut 19:1–6; *Prov* 28:17

crime (Ex 21:15). Injury from brawling rather than from an attack was to be compensated on the basis of income lost from work by the victim and any rehabilitation was financed by the inflictor (Ex 21:18–19). If a fight caused a premature birth due to a woman being struck inadvertently, a fine was imposed. But if anything more physically traumatic occurred, the penalty was an eye for an eye, life for life, etc. This was an ominous deterrent to fighting in the first place (Ex 21:22–25). Kidnapping for any reason was a capital crime even if there were no physical injury.[122]

Of course Old Testament condemnation of murder and cruelty is continued into the New Testament. Murder is mentioned usually in the context of a partial list of the Ten Commandments, reaffirming them individually and as a whole.[123] Still, in the New Testament the Ten Commandments represent a core of the heart of God and his moral character. To murder an image of him, an innocent person, including the unborn child is too profound of an act of God-defiance to let stand. Kidnapping is condemned again (1 Tim 1:10) as well as cruel beatings of one's subordinates.[124] Jesus reaffirmed the Old Testament's disapproval of anger and its destructive effects when he equates anger with premeditated murder in his sermon on the mount.[125]

RELIGIOUS PRACTICE

Most Mosaic law dealt with what would be the routine life of the community. Nonetheless, there were religious events that stood out as particularly expressive of the direct relationship of the believer and the Lord. The subordination of the Israelites to the gracious but sovereign Lord was to be evident not only in obedience to social standards, but also to ceremonial practices that lifted one's personal, sometimes private devotion, to a substantially public and formal level.

Israelite religious practices were expressions of humility, relief, fellowship, sharing, thankfulness, joy, and praise. Detailed descriptions of the sacrifices, feasts, and the priests' specific qualifications and procedures could distract one from appreciating the pure enjoyment and celebration in these events. There was satisfaction in relying on religious procedures that graphically and experientially represented the loving relationship and forgiveness between the Lord and his subjects.

Various "times" and festivals regularly celebrated the individual, family and national blessings from God. The Sabbath day of rest poetically parallels God's rest after creation. This obligation was a blessing but required trusting God for his provisions by taking a day off every week.[126] Breaking the Sabbath was no less than a capital crime. On

---

122. Ex 21:16; Deut 24:7

123. Matt 15:19 // Mark 7:21; Matt 19:18–20 // Mark 10:18–19 // Luke 18:19–20; Rom 13:9; 1 Tim 1:9–10; Jas 2:11; 4:2; 1 Pet 4:15; 1 John 3:15

124. Matt 24:48–50 // Luke 12:43–46

125. Lev 19:17–18; Matt 5:21–22

126. Ex 20:8–11; 31:12–17; 34:21; 35:2–3; Lev 19:3; 23:1–4; Deut 5:12–15

a monthly basis, the New Moon sacrificial rites were observed (Num 28:11–15). The annual "dancing" festivals required all men to attend in Jerusalem. These festivals were Passover, Weeks, and Tents. For a week, Passover celebrated Israel's independence from Egypt and dependence on their saving Lord.[127] The festival of Weeks, or Pentecost, was a day-long event that was seven *weeks* after the Passover events and celebrated God's provision from the grain harvests that season.[128] The festival of Tents celebrated God's agricultural provisions again as well as his protection of the Israelites while they lived in simple tents in the Sinai wilderness after leaving Egypt.[129] The Day of Atonement was five days before the festival of Tents and marked the annual remission of Israel's sin as a nation.[130] Here, two goats were involved: the slaughtered goat to die for Israel's sin, and the live goat (scapegoat) which carried Israel's sin as it walked into the void of the wilderness. It was released into the wilderness, and Israel's sins were "released."

There were five categories of sacrifices with complicated combinations of their purposes, animals, or grains, and proportions of the sacrifice to be burnt on the altar. Certain people could eat certain portions of the remaining sacrifice. The instructions were quite elaborate, but were very meaningful to the one bringing the sacrifice. The one sacrificing would bring a sacrifice that reflected their level of affluence, from an expensive bull down to an inexpensive pigeon, the latter which could even be gathered free from nature. Grain could even be acceptable from the poorest citizens.

The whole *Burnt* Offering was offered every day at the Jerusalem Temple to reconcile God and Israel, but it could be offered voluntarily by anyone wanting to reconcile with God. It was consumed totally by the altar's fire.[131] The *Grain* Offering was for expressing one's love and thanksgiving to God through a gift of a grain loaf that was partially burnt—the rest was reserved for the priests' own subsistence. This was a voluntary offering as well.[132] The voluntary *Peace* Offering symbolized fellowship with God and the community as the sacrificed grilled meat was shared between the one sacrificing, the priests, and God.[133] The *Sin* Offering was required for forgiveness from primarily unintentional sins and was burnt in part on the altar, the rest going to the priests for food.[134] Finally, the *Guilt* Offering was also for unintentional sin and was sometimes accompanied by a monetary or in-kind restitution.[135] Parts were burnt and, again, the rest was given to the priests.

---

127. Num 9:1–14; Ex 23:14–15; 34:18–19, 25; Lev 23:4–8; Num 28:16–25; Deut 16:1–8, 16
128. Ex 23:16; 34:22–23; Lev 23:15–21; Num 28:26–31; Deut 16:9–12, 16
129. Ex 23:16–17; 34:22–23; Lev 23:34–43; Deut 16:13–17; 31:10–13
130. Lev 16:3–34; 23:27–32; Num 29:7–11
131. Lev 1:3–17; 6:8–13; 7:8; 8:18–21; 16:24
132. Lev 2:1–16; 6:14–23; 7:9–10
133. Lev 3:1–17; 7:11–34
134. Lev 4:1—5:13; 6:24–30; 7:7; 8:14–17; 16:3–22; Num 15:22–31
135. Lev 5:14—6:7; 7:1–6

The offerings would have had solemn moments, but the Lord required rejoicing and celebrating by the participants at the feasts.[136] In fact, God was generous on how one could celebrate if unable to attend a tithing ceremony in Jerusalem. They could use the tithe money at home in a way that would aid their rejoicing in the Lord's annual provision of their needs.

> Spend the money for whatever you want to eat or drink: oxen, sheep, wine or stronger drink—whatever your heart desires. Eat it there before the Lord your God and rejoice, you and your household. Deut 14:26

Improper ceremonial worship was clearly itemized and was the most basic and frequently mentioned sin of the Israelites.[137] Human sacrifice was not allowed until the right Man appeared.[138] Contacting the spiritual world directly or through a medium, or sorcery was apostasy.[139] Contact with spirits of the dead was forbidden as when Saul requested a prophecy from deceased Samuel (1 Sam 28:8–19). Engaging in temple prostitution as either the prostitute or the "worshipper" was a step toward execution (Deut 23:17–18). Worshipping celestial bodies or aquatic creatures or anything in between the skies and waters through idolatry was subject to ridicule and, more severely, to execution. Since everything was created by God, worshipping created life or objects was a total misdirection of one's attention and devotion.[140] Other religious practices were forbidden too, such as tattooing, cutting oneself, or rounding one's beard.[141]

Cursing God publicly was either calling for his harm, death or failure, or it was compromising his name in false or sinful oaths. This was so disrespectful that one could be executed for it depending on its severity.[142] If one promised to devote a child for religious service to God, or promised an animal or land property in return for God's specific blessing, the requirement to fulfill that contract was very serious.[143]

But God and the people were not fooled by mere external compliance with these sacrificial, festive, and ceremonial occasions. Israel's heart and the individual's heart, soul, and mind were what God desired, not mechanical conformity to mere religious rites. The sacrifices and feasts were meters of hypocrisy as much as obedience. If one were obedient out of love for God and trust in his wisdom and grace for the rest of

---

136. Lev 23:40; Deut 12:7, 12, 18; 14:26; 16:11, 14; 26:11; 27:7

137. Ex 20:2–7; Deut 5:6–10; *Pss* 81:8–10; 96:4–5; 97:7–9; *Jer* 7:9

138. Gen 22:2, 11–14; Lev 18:21; 20:2–5; Deut.12:31; 18:10; *Ps* 106:37; *Isa* 53

139. Ex 22:18; Lev 19:31; 20:6–7, 27; Deut 18:9–14; 32:15–17; *Isa* 8:19; 57:3; 65:4; *Jer* 27:9–10; *Mic* 5:12; *Mal* 3:5

140. Ex 20:4; Lev 19:4; 26:1; Deut 4:15–19, 25–26; 5:8; 17:2–7; 27:15; 32:21; *Job* 31:26–28; *Pss* 16:4; 31:6; 78:58–60; 106:34–39; 115:4–8; 135:15–18; *Isa* 40:18–20; 41:27–29; 44:9–20; *Jer.* 2:8, 26–28; 32:32–34; *Hos* 8:4–6; 10:5; 13:2; 14:3; *Amos* 5:26; *Zeph* 1:4

141. Lev 19:28; 21:5; Deut 14:1

142. Ex 20:7; 22:28; Lev 5:4–6; 19:12; 24:10–16, 23; Deut 5:11; 6:13; *Pss* 24:4; 109:17–19; 28; 139:20; *Prov* 20:25; *Eccl* 5:4–6;*Jer* 5:1–3, 7; 7:9; *Hos* 4:15–16; 10:4; *Mal* 3:5; *Zeph* 1:5

143. Num 30:2–15; Deut 23:21–23; *Pss* 22:25; 56:12; 61:8; 65:1–2; 66:13–15; 76:11; *Prov* 20:25

their life, then their formal worship was not hypocritical. Old Testament historians, poets, sages, and prophets expressed this in their assessments of empty ceremonial religiosity.[144] For example,

> Obedience is better than sacrifice. 1 Sam 15:22
>
> I want steadfast love, not sacrifice. Hos 6:6
>
> Does the Lord delight in thousands of sacrificed rams?
>
> The Lord requires your justice, love and kindness, and humble walk with your God. Mic 6:7–8

The Lord told the Samaritan woman that worshipping the Lord was not adequate even if done with doctrinal and procedural purity; it was to be done with the right spirit of humility (John 4:23–24). James also could not congratulate anyone for having the right theology—the demons know more theology than we do (2:19–20). Religion is worthless, James says, unless the tongue is bridled and widows and orphans are cared for (1:26–27).

On the other hand, it is a blessing to others not to offend them unnecessarily and to meet their expectations of us if we do not sin in the process. For instance, on one occasion Paul kept the purification laws publicly in Jerusalem to appease the Jews. It did not work since there was a riot anyway, but it was courteous at least to try (Acts 21:26). It then became a practice for Paul to be a Jew when Jews were around, and at other times to show the Gentiles their freedom by not following the ceremonial laws when around them. He was free not to offend either group.[145]

When it came to the center of the Pharisees' world, the Sabbath, Christ Jesus was perceived to be irreverent as far as they were concerned. Apart from implying that he was God, Christ's view of the Sabbath was the most infuriating for the religious leaders. There were no Old Testament laws against Christ's conduct which the leaders declared unlawful. All the leaders had were traditions that Judaism had added to God's Old Testament revelation. Christ chided the religious leaders for their hypocrisy.

> You invalidated God's Word by preferring your tradition. You hypocrites, Isaiah was right when he prophesied about you, "These people honor me with their lips but their hearts are far from me. They worship me uselessly while teaching human ideas as if they were God's doctrine."[146] Matt 15:6–9

Christ turned their mistaken ethical system into an indictment of God the Father! He says their charge against him was also against the Father: "My Father is working until now [the seventh day of the week], so I am working too" (John 5:17).

---

144. 1 Sam 15:22–23; 2 Chr 30:18–20; Pss 40:6; 51:16–19; 69:30–31; 141:1–2; Prov 15:8; 16:6; 21:3, 27; Jer 7:2–24; Isa 1:10–17; 58:5–7; Hos 6:6; Amos 5:21–27; Mic 6:6–8

145. 1 Cor 9:20; 10:32–33

146. Matt 15:6–9 // Mark 7:6–9

Of course it was not "work" at all, really. His conclusion about the Sabbath applied to all of God's religious laws, whether sacrifices, the Sabbath, or ceremonial food: "The Sabbath was for people's needs. People were not made for the Sabbath."[147] So it was lawful and moral to care for human and even animals' needs on the Sabbath, including healing and exorcisms.[148]

Some religious practices were left to the personal preference of the believer: foods, fasting,[149] circumcision,[150] and "holy days."[151] Deciding which foods could or could not be eaten could become an obsession for the believer who might forget that the Creator provides innumerable sources of nutrition and pleasure.[152] But strong warnings are given to believers to be careful not to flaunt freedom but to show sensitivity to the moral scruples of other believers. Those weaker believers may not be as aware of their freedoms as they should be; nonetheless, wiser believers are to use their wisdom and restraint not to offend these "weaker" spiritual siblings.[153]

Flaunting one's freedoms is discouraged, but the most severe words were saved for those flaunting their religiosity. Jesus Christ's "Lord's Prayer" was part of his warnings *against* showy religiosity. Yet, strangely enough, the "Lord's Prayer" itself has become a new liturgical formality. Jesus mentioned other pretentious acts of holiness: public benevolence so all could notice, showy prayers, or fasting dramatized to be great suffering (Matt 6:1–8, 16–18). Ecclesiastes 5:2 advises, "God is in heaven and you are on the earth so keep your words to a minimum." Jesus affirms Ecclesiastes' wisdom about brevity in our prayers: "Gentiles assume they will be heard better for their many words" (Matt 6:7).

Idolatry is mocked in the New Testament as it is in the older testament.[154] The psalmist says, "Idols are made of silver and gold, they are man-made. They have mouths that cannot speak, eyes that cannot see, ears that cannot hear."[155] Paul calls idols "speechless" too, and John repeats the ridicule.[156] The Thessalonians are encouraged that they now serve a "living God," not a motionless man-made image (1 Thess 1:9).

But there is a demonic reality behind idols. When humanity refuses to worship God for his glorious existence and perfect attributes, they are compelled to worship something. They do not worship the Creator, so they worship what he created: humans,

---

147. Mark 2:27; also, Matt 12:1–8 // Luke 6:1–5
148. Matt 12:10–13 // Mark 3:1–5 // Luke 6:6–10; 13:14–16; 14:2–5; John 7:23–24
149. Matt 6:16–17; Matt 9:14–15 // Mark 2:18–20 // Luke 5:33–35
150. Rom 2:26–29; 1 Cor 7:19
151. Rom 14:5–6; Col 2:16–17
152. 1 Tim 4:3–5; Rom 14:2, 14, 20
153. Rom 14:1, 15–17, 21–23; 15:1–2; 1 Cor 8:9–13
154. Acts 19:24–28; 1 Cor 5:10–11; 6:9–10; 10:14; Rom 2:22; Gal 5:19–20; Eph 5:5; 1 John 5:21; 1 Pet 4:3; Rev 21:8; 22:15
155. Ps 115:4–7; also, 135:15–17; Dan 5:23
156. 1 Cor 12:2; Rev 9:20

birds, and other animals (Rom 1:23, 25). Further, when these or their images are worshipped, the worship is received by demons: "The pagans sacrifice to demons, not to God. I do not want you to partner with demons" (1 Cor 10:20–21). Perhaps this is the reason why eating meat that had been offered to idols was still on the short list of forbidden religious practices, not because idols have any power or even life in themselves, but because the unseen demons associated with the food are alive and powerful.[157]

For Paul, idolatry is more than the foolish worshipping of inanimate raw materials and the demons behind them. Evil passions also are idols since they distract us from the worship of God: "Fornication, impurity, lust, evil desire, and greed are idolatry."[158] (Col 3:5). Preoccupations with these fleshy sins will detract from focusing on the Lord.

The New Testament saints were required to fellowship with one another, but no prescribed order of worship was suggested (Heb 10:25). What happened during these times of fellowship and how frequently a specific practice was to be followed is not stipulated. Paul does encourage believers to teach and sing, but he does not say anything more specific about when or how often.

> Let Christ's Word dwell richly in you while teaching and admonishing one another with all wisdom, and while singing psalms, hymns, and spiritual songs to God with thankful hearts.[159]

There is no written requirement that the meetings be weekly, though the church in Troas met at least one Sunday to break bread (Acts 20:7). This lack of detail was true in the Old Testament too. Given the lack of a model for a worship service and the freedoms Paul explains at length regarding religious practices, it is impossible to prescribe exactly what should be done at any given assembly of believers.

There is no recorded baptism during a New Testament service, no call to an altar, no list of biblical verses that should be read and re-read, no prescribed prayers or creeds, no job descriptions or position requirements to serve communion. No length of a worship service is recommended, and no recorded sermon was longer than five to ten minutes. Paul frequently requested that money be collected from the saints to distribute to other churches, but it is never said to be during any service; it was to be set aside and saved by each person, not necessarily placed in a collection plate (1 Cor 16:2). Of course, none of these actions would be inappropriate for a worship service, but there is no biblical precedent that requires any of them to be regularly practiced, much less in any particular order. If a church decides to do it in a certain way, that is fine. However, there is no prescribed way for it to be done. There have been many man-made traditions that have developed in the history of the church which Paul would have been the first to warn against their becoming routine requirements or a new unbearable yoke of ceremonial burdens.

---

157. Acts 15:20, 29; 21:25; 1 Cor 8:7–10; Rev 2:14, 20
158. Col 3:5; also, 1 Cor 10:7
159. Col 3:16; also, Eph 5:19

Surely there was praise and thanksgiving given to the Lord when Christians met. Yes, they probably sang, taught, preached, prophesied, spoke in tongues, interpreted tongues, and evangelized when they assembled just as 1 Corinthians 14:26, 39–40 says. And all this was to be done in an edifying, and orderly way, but that does not mean that each were always done in the same order, or that they were done every week.

Baptism is a religious practice to exemplify (1) the union of the believer with Christ through his death and resurrection[160] and (2) our personal cleansing from sin.[161] This religious practice has many different interpreters and traditions, and these varying interpretations are an unfortunate cause for division within the church. As we have seen already, Paul's attitude was one of disdain and sorrow toward similar types of differences in religious practice that were held so arrogantly by different believers and churches. Believers today are not welcome to fellowship as members in an astounding percentage of churches if they disagree with a church on this religious practice. All sorts of proud defenses for divisiveness have been offered through the millennia.

Participating in Communion is directly commanded so that believers would be reminded of the Lord's death.[162] But the strength of the views of the various denominations surrounding this religious practice today is equal to that of baptism. This time it is the proud certainty about the spiritual nature of the bread and wine. Are they literally his body and blood? Do they contain his body and blood? Are they symbols of his body and blood? However, Paul's main concern when discussing this celebration is that when believers participate in this meal that they will have eaten enough at home rather than gorge themselves at the event.

Certain New Testament church leaders were to be supported financially by the rest of the believing community, consistent with the Old Testament's expectation that the priests and other religious teachers and workers be supported. This parallel "Levitic" right is explained by Paul:

> Those serving in the temple eat the food from the temple, and those serving at the altar are entitled to a part of the offerings. So, for the same reason the Lord demands that those who proclaim the gospel get their living by the gospel.[163]

It is no surprise that blasphemy, sorcery, and worshipping angels were forbidden in the New Testament as they were in the Old.[164]

Christ's anger over merchandizing in the Temple stands out in our memory since it is the only record of him becoming physically violent.[165]

---

160. Rom 6:3–6; 1 Cor 12:13; Gal 3:27–28; Col 2:11–12
161. Acts 2:38; 22:16; 1 Pet 3:21
162. Matt 26:26–28 // Mark 14:22–24 // Luke 22:19–20; 1 Cor 11:20–26
163. 1 Cor 9:6–14; also, Matt 10:9–10 // Luke 10:7–8; Gal 6:6; 1 Tim 5:17–18
164. Matt 12:31–32; mark 3:29; Luke 12:10; Gal 5:20; Col 2:18; 1 Tim 1:20; Jas 2:7; Rev 21:8
165. Matt 21:12–13 // Mark 11:15–17 // Luke 19:45–46; John 2:14–16

The conclusion to this section on the reaffirmation of many Old Testament Mosaic laws by the New Testament is that they still stand as moral standards for believers as we pursue our primary commission within God's eternal design. That is the non-debatable position of Jesus Christ and his apostles. One is not justified by keeping these moral laws, but one cannot claim to be justified without living a life of obedience to them. These reaffirmed standards are about honoring, supporting, and obeying official elders, coveting, thieving, swindling, debt, care for servants, payment to workers, respect for masters, legitimate divorce, fornication, adultery, homosexuality, honoring and obeying one's parents, merciful treatment of the poor and widows, perjury, witnesses in legal proceedings, murder, kidnapping, anger, love over ritual, Sabbath, bloody food, idolatry, blasphemy, sorcery and worshipping angels.

13

God's Wisdom for Shepherding

WISDOM AND LAW

As WE DRAW NEAR to the end of our study we continue our outline of how the believer and the believing community are to pursue God's eternal design. We began our study by describing God's eternal design of shepherding, a design that models his shepherding heart to his shepherding creation. And we are concluding our study by looking at the specifics of how to shepherd. Chapter 12 reviewed shepherding from the perspective of the Old Testament Law and the New Testament's confirmation of it. This chapter will close our study by reviewing the Old Testament wisdom instructions and, again, the New Testament's confirmation of those moral standards.

When we surveyed the moral categories of Law in the last chapter, I italicized the portion of the footnotes showing the wisdom instructions and other Old Testament texts that referred to Mosaic legal obligations. As I said then, around one hundred and twenty wisdom instructions refer to the Law's moral standards: for example, stealing, moving boundary stones, withholding wages, false commodity measurements, lending, collateral, treatment of servants, animal care, adultery, respecting parents and elders, gluttony, drunkenness, lying, impartial courts, false testimony, bribery, compassion for the disadvantaged, care for the handicapped, loving one's neighbors, slander, murder, manslaughter, and limitations to royal prerogatives.

The wisdom literature has the highest respect for the Law. For example, Proverbs and Ecclesiastes make it a center-piece for righteousness and goodness.[1] Speaking clearly of God's revelation of the Law and the civil order it ensures, Proverbs observes, "If there is no revelation, the people reject restraints, but the one who keeps the Law is blessed."[2] Ecclesiastes endorses the Law in the most general terms, "Fear God and keep his commandments" (12:13). So, reverence for God and his revelation is behind the

---

1. Prov 13:13; 19:16; 28:7, 9; Eccl 12:13–14
2. Prov 29:18; also, 28:4

wisdom instructions,[3] and obeying Mosaic law was a substantial part of Israel's and the individual's wisdom. After all the Law says, "Carefully obey the statutes and judgments because that is your wisdom" (Deut 4:6). Of course the opposite was true as well. If one was disobedient to the Law, one was not only sinful but foolish and unwise.

The Law was directly revealed to Moses by God, but biblical wisdom instruction was inspired in a less direct way. It had as its source the divinely inspired and written conclusions drawn from routine human experience about what is loving, prudent, and effective while reigning with God in his kingdom. In other words, still guided by the Holy Spirit, wisdom instruction includes descriptions of what its authors found to be the best approaches to human interaction in addition to the Law. The wisdom literature includes Job, Proverbs, Ecclesiastes, and Song of Solomon. These wisdom books have nearly seven hundred instructions. But we will look at wisdom instruction in different categories than Mosaic law since wisdom instructions address broader and deeper subjects than issues that are simply legal ones.

THE NATURE OF WISDOM INSTRUCTION

As much as the wisdom literature includes requirements to keep the Mosaic law, it goes far beyond law-keeping in defining true righteousness and wisdom. Its ethical reach is far broader and deeper than the Law since wisdom literature reveals in greater detail the spirit of community, individual civility, and the means to personal, even professional success. This is not to say that the Mosaic law did not highlight very general motivations for keeping the Law, such as love and respect for God and one's neighbor, and the resulting humility and mercy shown by godly believers. But success in one's daily physical and spiritual life did not come from keeping only the Law but, to an equal if not greater extent, by following the instructions of wisdom in addition to the Law. Mosaic law does not address how loudly one should speak early in the morning, the frequency of one's visits to a neighbor's house, or how to retain mental balance. The Law does not with the same specificity address the value of responsible speech, diligence, friends, or being teachable. Though there is much implied in the Law, God was gracious to give many more explicit details in the wisdom literature about how to live routine life more smoothly, profitably, and righteously.

Biblical ethics can barely be explained by an alphabetic dictionary of conduct with clean separations between attitudes and behaviors. This is where the wisdom literature becomes most valuable. It blends attitudes and behavior much more thoroughly than the Law was designed to do. Our conduct crosses many categories within one single action. Self-control, anger, patience, wise speech, gentleness, humility, peacefulness, and forgiveness could all be involved in a single word reply or outburst. This is not surprising since the two summary laws of God's ethics are described in one

---

3. Prov 1:7, 28–29; 8:13; 9:10; 14:26–27; 23:17; 31:30; Job 1:1, 8–9; 2:3; 28:28; Eccl 3:14; 5:7; 7:18; 8:12–13; 12:13–14

word—love (for God and neighbor). These two laws are behind every moral standard in a most direct way. Yet, as a summary, these two commands are too broad to help us see the specific responsibilities we have to God and neighbor. So, fortunately, the Lord has supplied us with hundreds of specific moral passages which we will now survey.

Wisdom will need to be contemplated, sorted out, balanced, aptly applied, compared, etc. because it deals with the complex structure of our daily decisions. Yes, nearly seven hundred moral instructions are given in the wisdom books, but *which* to apply *when* requires the wisdom of the Spirit in our lives to do what is good. We are told, then, to seek wisdom and knowledge, not merely absorb it if it happens to float by.[4] So Ecclesiastes says, "There is a suitable time for everything, a suitable time for every choice under the skies" (3:1). How do we know the suitable time? By having been immersed in the wisdom literature and its guiding principles. And then, just as the Mosaic law required, we are to diligently pursue goodness and righteousness: "The Lord loves the one who pursues righteousness."[5]

Those who do not see these wisdom instructions as equally authoritative over the Christian's life impoverish themselves from the innumerable benefits that are promised by the wisdom instructions. Ecclesiastes defines the preferred life of the believer, "I know there is nothing better for humanity than to be happy and to do good in one's life" (3:12). The benefits to doing good are generalized in Proverbs 14:22: "Kindness and truth will come to those who plan what is good."

Ecclesiastes 7:20 repeats what is said elsewhere in the Old Testament about the universality of sin: "There is not a righteous person on earth who does only good and does not sin."[6] And the wisdom instructions have a person's righteousness as its goal. Nearly 100 times in Proverbs and Ecclesiastes "righteousness" and "the righteous" are held up as proof of wisdom's superiority to wicked foolishness. The wisdom instructions go on to equate righteousness, uprightness, and wisdom. The wisdom instructions provide critical teaching toward "righteous" living.[7] Wisdom instruction focuses on "goodness" too. Where the general term "good" is mentioned in Proverbs, for example, it is often aligned with very specific wise acts of righteousness.[8]

We see another reason for the similarity between New Testament ethics and wisdom instruction since now there are no geographical boundaries to the Kingdom of the believing community as there were to a great extent in the Old Testament. So, the New Testament emphasizes the normal individual person in everyday community rather than the national kingdom law regulating civil obedience and any legal penalties seen in the Law.

---

4. Prov 2:4; 8:17; 15:14; 18:15; Eccl 7:25
5. Prov 15:9; also, 11:19, 27; 21:21
6. Also, 1 Kgs 8:46; 2 Chr 6:36; Ps 143:2; Prov 20:9
7. E.g., Prov 8:8, 32, 35; 12:6
8. Prov 3:27; 12:25; 13:22; 17:13;18:5; 20:23; 24:23 // 28:21; 31:12

While surveying New Testament ethics in the last chapter, we followed essentially the same ethical categories as the Old Testament Law. Again, in this chapter, we will survey New Testament moral instructions which are not literally linked to the Law and are more reminiscent of the Old Testament wisdom instructions. Just as the Old Testament wisdom instructions went broader and deeper than the Mosaic law, the New Testament follows the same pattern. We are about to see how the New Testament moral instructions delve into the believer's heart and into the routine expressions of wisdom in our daily life. After all, speaking wisely is first in the list of the Spiritual gifts mentioned in 1 Cor 12:7–10.

WISDOM INSTRUCTION AND THE NEW TESTAMENT

There is a surprising amount of New Testament ethics that is based more on wisdom instruction than the Law. The apostle's meeting in Jerusalem showed that the laws of conscience and wisdom instruction could be trusted since the apostles felt it unnecessary to list the moral standards that the conscience and wisdom instruction requires the believer to obey. They believed fornication needed to be warned against, but they continued considering loose and irresponsible talk, greed, arrogance, to be sin too (Acts 15:19–20, 28–29). Later, in proverbial fashion, Paul quotes an adage which all cultures appreciate and Old Testament wisdom supports, "Bad company corrupts good morals" (1 Cor 15:33). However, the Jerusalem council did not feel it important to list this principle because everybody knows that companions affect one's conduct.

The Messiah's nature was *predicted* to be wise and understanding, and his wisdom would be *proven* by his care for the poor and afflicted and by a deep interest in the Law and wisdom books (Is 11:1–4). Becoming wiser was not only Jesus Christ's challenge to us—it was his own personal experience as he matured into a young man. He grew up as a boy in many ways, including in his wisdom (Luke 2:40, 52), to the point where he was easily wiser than any model of wisdom, including King Solomon.[9] His wisdom was recognized when he spoke and amazed his listening public.[10]

The first principle of Old Testament wisdom was to be obedient to the Lord's commandments.

> Respect for the Lord is the beginning of wisdom. Everyone who obeys his precepts has a good understanding. Ps 111:10[11]

Later, Jesus implies his own divinity when he equates himself with the Lord who expects the same response from his followers, echoing Psalm 111:10. Jesus says about himself,

---

9. Matt 12:42 // Luke 11:31
10. Matt 13:54 // Mark 6:2; Luke 2:47
11. Also, Prov 1:7; 9:10; 15:32; Job 28:28

Everyone who hears my words and does them will be like a wise man.[12]

The Old Testament is endorsed by Jesus when he spoke of *true* wisdom: "Wisdom is proven by its resulting works."[13] James repeats Jesus' principle: "Who is wise and understanding among you? Show it by a good life and by works from humility that comes from wisdom" (Jas 3:13). Wisdom also guides the believer in how they prove their love for God and neighbor. Using words that had the same thrust as "wisdom," Paul prays that the Philippians' "love will increase steadily through real *knowledge* and all *discernment*" (Phil 1:9). We are to be wise or prudent as serpents (since once a serpent out-witted us in Eden), but that wisdom is to be dove-like in its gentleness (Matt 10:16).

We would go a long way to begin a list of specific moral responsibilities if we repeated only two passages from James and Paul. James calls ethical behavior "wisdom from heaven" and Paul calls ethical behavior "the fruit of the Spirit." We are about to survey the Old Testament wisdom instructions to see the New Testament repetitions of those moral attitudes and actions:

> The fruit of the Spirit is love, joy, peace, patience, kindness, goodness, faithfulness, gentleness, and self-control. Gal 5:22–23

> The wisdom from heaven is first pure, then it is peaceful, gentle, reasonable, full of mercy and good fruit, impartial and without hypocrisy. Jas 3:17

Paul and James also list characteristics and behaviors that are opposite of wisdom and contrary-to-conscience and demonic-inspired folly: sexual immorality, impurity, lust, idolatry, sorcery, hostility, strife, jealousy, outbursts of rage, rivalries, dissensions, divisiveness, envy, drunkenness, orgies, jealousy and selfishness and arrogance.[14] However, neither James nor Paul intended these to be complete lists of wise or foolish behavior. For instance, we might add the apostles' own teaching on forgiveness, encouragement, obedience, contentment, diligence and honesty.

Wisdom is a key attribute of the believer while shepherding in godly ways and conforming to the eternal design. The primary commission is achieved by biblical wisdom, understanding, and discernment which are informed by our dear indwelling Spirit. Paul instructs believers to be "wise" in their conversations (Col 4:5–6) and in their diligence and time management (Eph 5:15–16). Peter encourages believers to excel in "knowledge" (2 Pet 1:5–6). Certain disciples who were "wise" were commissioned to care for the practical needs of the church (Acts 6:2–3). Peter and Paul use the term "sober" to encourage their readers to be focused, resolute, attentive to their morality and in their expectation of the Lord's return.[15] Jesus, Paul, Peter and James quote directly from the wisdom of Proverbs to encourage righteousness.

---

12. Matt 7:24–27 // Luke 6:47–49
13. Matt 11:19; Luke 7:35
14. Gal 5:19–21; Jas 3:14–16; 1 Cor 1:21
15. Matt 25:2–8; 1 Thess 5:6, 8; 1 Tim 3:2, 11; 2 Tim 4:5; 1 Pet 1:13; 4:7; 5:8

Feed your enemy if he is hungry. Give him a drink if he is thirsty.[16]

A dog returns to eat its own vomit.[17]

The Master of both the slave and you is in heaven.[18]

God opposes the proud but is gracious to the humble.[19]

The New Testament, then, continues to teach the moral wisdom of God found in the wisdom books of the Old Testament.

LEADERSHIP

Since the Fall, God's discipline has been a necessary part of his shepherding care of creation and humanity. His discipline is always pure and right and has as its ultimate goal to make individuals and humanity as a whole pure and right; his judgments are restorative. His Final Judgment will leave only his believers who will no longer need deliverance or discipline since New Earth will be perfect just as he had created it to be from the outset.

Everyone is in the role of a leader or manager at some time. The primary commission is the basis for our responsibility to subdue the earth by God's standards—to lead others in proper stewardship of their time and other resources—to lead them toward greater self-control. So, by the effective and compassionate correction of others, we achieve one of the most important aspects of the primary commission. Of course, God's sovereignty ultimately determines the course of leaders at even the highest level: "The heart of the king is in the Lord's hand. He turns it wherever he wants, like a swerving river."[20] Yet, as sub-shepherds in God's eternal design, we lead along with our lead Shepherd.

The overwhelming message of the wisdom instructions about leadership is that one must be fair—more interested in what is right than what is in the interest of the leader. Avoiding the abuse of power is the greatest concern for wise leadership. Whether the power is political, familial, administrative, or ecclesiastical, leaders have the responsibility to reflect God's leadership qualities. Fairness requires punishment for the guilty. This is true in the family where disciplining children is necessary[21] as well as for irresponsible adults in the marketplace and judicial courts.[22]

---

16. Rom 12:20 // Prov 25:21f, also Matt 5:44 // Luke 6:27
17. 2 Pet 2:22 // Prov 26:11
18. Eph 6:9; Prov 22:2
19. 1 Pet 5:5; Jas 4:6; Prov 3:34
20. Prov 21:1; also 29:26
21. Prov 13:24; 19:18; 22:6, 15; 23:13–14; 29:15, 17
22. Prov 10:13; 14:3; 17:11; 18:6; 19:25, 29; 20:30; 21:11; 22:10; 26:3; 29:19

The leader's justice, discernment, and graciousness are necessary components for effective leadership according to the wisdom instructions: "A king's justice ensures a land's stability."[23] The security and safety from a righteous leader's unfailing commitment to honesty and impartiality lengthens one's tenure in a position and provides a comfortable environment for stability and progress. But when the unrighteous rule, the ruled are anxious and fearful whether they are a nation, a workplace or a family.[24] Wisdom requires perpetual vigilance by a leader to discern who the unfair and abusive people are and to remove them so that they do no more harm or discredit the leader further, or even usurp the leader's position.[25]

Proverbs 21:15 affirms *judgment's* critical role in maintaining the moral order and at the same time affirms it as a *blessing*: "It is a joy to the righteous to see justice done, but it terrifies evildoers." The innocent will be exonerated if the authorities are diligent to pursue truth and expect honesty from those who report to them.[26] Bribes that distort judgments and disciplinary action are not to find their way into the hands of the wise leader.[27]

New Testament shepherds could rely on the Old Testament's perspective on leadership. Humble leaders who acknowledged their place before the Creator did not see themselves as superior beings, only as equals with their subjects. Paul echoes the words of Proverbs.

> The poor man and the oppressor are alike: the Lord gives light to the eyes of both. Prov 29:13

> Masters . . . stop threatening; you know both your servant's Master and yours is in heaven and he is not partial. Eph 6:9

> Masters, be just and fair with your slaves, you know you too have a Master in heaven. Col 4:1

The chain of shepherding in God's eternal design requires human leaders to remember that they are under God's ultimate shepherding authority. And it is not as if God himself did not humble himself even to the point of death. The practice of humility reflects the heart of the Lord to make the ultimate sacrifice.

> He was willing to be born as a creature who had human limitations
> He tolerated being human under the authority of his creatures
> His soul breathed the morally toxic human condition
> He lived within the means of a blue collar family

---

23. Prov 29:4; also, 20:28; 28:2; 29:14
24. Prov 11:10; 14:19; 16:12; 17:7; 28:2–3, 12, 15–16, 28; 29:2
25. Eccl 5:8–9; 8:11; Prov 20:8, 26; 25:2–5; 29:12
26. Prov 17:15, 26; 18:5, 17; 24:23–25; 28:3; 29:14
27. Prov 17:8, 23; 29:4

> He labored as a blue collar tradesman himself
> He submitted wholly to his divine Father
> He stooped to argue with foolish minds
> He was humiliated by public disrobing
> He was mocked for his elegant, sober truth
> He was demeaned by physically harsh whipping
> He was spat on though he was the spitter's only hope
> He stood as an accused defendant rather than as the Judge

The New Testament emphasizes humility when instructing leaders how to shepherd the Lord's sheep. Church leaders are not to "lord it over" the sheep but to love them.[28] The leaders are servants themselves, to the Lord[29] so they are not to pull rank or presume on those they lead.[30] True shepherds lead by exemplifying the moral standards they teach.[31] They see themselves as fellow soldiers and fellow workers in God's Kingdom—peers and equals in the eyes of God and his people.[32]

For Christ, leadership meant service not domination: "Whoever wants to be great among you must be your servant . . . the Son of Man did not come to be served, but to serve."[33] The Lord equates a poor leader to a servant who beats innocent subordinates while he himself is a glutton and drunk.[34] John named Diotrephes as the exact opposite of who the Lord wanted to shepherd his flock. He was self-centered, authoritative, and taught his own version of the gospel (3 John 9–10).

OBEYING AUTHORITY

Wisdom instructs one to respect leaders because of their position and because of their potential effect on one's future. "Do not curse a king in your bedroom, a little bird will reveal it" (Eccl 10:20). There should be a healthy concern about the authorities since their power, which is necessary to keep order, can be turned toward the individual for blessing or injustice.[35] This should always be in mind when acting for or against the leader. The leader's anger may not be a simple annoyance—it could be an alarm of an imminent threat to one's livelihood or life.[36] However, though the wise can find themselves at risk, they will know how to avoid the worst consequences. The leader

---

28. Luke 22:25–26; 2 Cor 1:24; 1 Pet 5:3; 2 John 1; 3 John 1–2
29. Rom 1:1; Phil 1:1; Titus 1:1; Jas 1:1; 2 Pet 1:1; Jude 1; Rev 1:1
30. 1 Thess 2:6–11; Philem 14
31. 2 Thess 3:7–10; Phil 4:9; 1 Pet 5:2–3
32. Rom 16:3, 9, 21; 2 Cor 8:23; Phil 2:25; Col 4:11; 1 Thess 3:2; Philem 2
33. Matt 20:26–28 // Mark 10:42–45; also, Matt 23:2–4; Luke 11:46; Luke 22:25–27; 1 Pet 5:1–3
34. Matt 24:45–49 // Luke 12:45–46
35. Prov 14:35; 16:13, 15; 19:12; 20:2; 25:6–7
36. Eccl 10:4; Prov 16:14; 25:15

is not always right, but the wise are patient and wait for the right time, words, and actions to respond.[37] The goal is to have the leader as your "friend."[38]

What are a Christian's moral responsibilities to the national or imperial government leadership? Since our "citizenship is in heaven," we might expect to be free of any secular authority (Phil 3:20). But just as we are subject to the shepherding physical laws of inanimate nature, we are also to subject ourselves to the laws of those shepherds who are not obedient to all of God's laws. Even wicked governments follow the laws of conscience to an extent, but the alternative, anarchy, would certainly be even more brutal.

Paul makes it clear that Christians were not only to submit to the same regime of murderous Roman dictators, including paying taxes,[39] but to pray for them and for order to be sustained so that Christians could live in peace (1 Tim 2:1–2). Christ had also affirmed the right of the government to demand tax payments.[40] Since chaos and anarchy lead only to further and worse injustices, we are instructed to trust the level of shepherding that governments provide in blessing, delivering, and judging their constituents. Since believers' prayers for authorities matter, God can and does determine who the rulers are and what their actions will be. Regardless of evil shepherds, we submit ourselves to them because we want to contribute to the social order; it ensures the stability within which we can experience and appreciate God's gift of life. Our trust is in the Shepherd who is sovereign over all leaders—who restrains the evil that Satan strives to maximize to the point of total destruction.

Submission to governing authorities resulted in the ultimate travesty of judgment in all history, the crucifixion of a completely pure and perfect God. God himself did not respond with violence or vengeance. Instead, he used that evil for good. In the midst of Christ's arrest and Peter's understandable attempt to defend his savior, Jesus asks Peter, "Do you think that I could not call on my Father and right now he would send for me more than twelve legions of angels?" (Matt 26:53). From his arrest to his death, he restrained himself from what would have been a just resistance; rather, he surrendered himself to the Roman and Jewish leaders in order to save the world.

However, when priorities are required, when it becomes a matter of obeying God or human leaders, then one reaffirms one's heavenly citizenship in the supreme Kingdom of God as their primary allegiance. So, Paul could boldly challenge Governor Festus and King Agrippa (Acts 26:24–29), and Peter and John with humble confidence could defy the instructions of High Priest Caiaphas and other religious leaders (Acts 4:18–20).

On the local church level, believers were instructed to subject themselves to the authority of the elders out of appreciation for their diligence and for their teaching the message of God.[41] Having too many leaders and teachers in the local church inevitably

---

37. Eccl 8:2–6; 10:4–7; Prov 16:14; 24:21–22; 25:15
38. Prov 22:11; also, 27:18
39. Rom 13:1–7; also, Titus 3:1; 1 Pet 2:13–17
40. Matt 22:17–21 // Mark 12:14–17 // Luke 20:22–25
41. 1 Cor 16:15–16; 1 Thess 5:12–13; Heb 13:17; 1 Pet 5:5

confuses the sheep and can be divisive, so they are to be minimized (Jas 3:1). Believers are not only to respect their elders' leadership but to imitate their elder's conduct (Heb 13:7). We have discussed the moral godliness that was required for one to become an elder, and that godliness is to be an example to all, including those who aspire to become elders (1 Tim 3:1).

There are divinely ordained authority structures for maintaining order in a fallen world. But unfortunately sinners are in charge within these structures and their subordinates suffer: men, women, children, and servants. However, this is not a reason to dismantle the divinely designed structures; instead, it is a reason for passionate pursuits of justice against abusive excesses within these structures. Women are to quietly receive instruction in the church meetings (1 Tim 2:11–12) as should all who are being taught under the authority of a spiritually gifted teacher. Younger women are to submit to the teaching of older women (Titus 2:3–5). And women are to submit to their husbands in the exceptional and infrequent case when there is a fundamental difference on a matter, remembering the rule was for mutual submission and deference to the other person whenever possible (Eph 5:20).

Servants and slaves were to obey their masters and without disrespectful backtalk,[42] even if mistreated (1 Pet 2:18–20). But the reason for this goes well beyond bald obedience. Paul raises the servant's career to a level of service to the Lord, not just service to an earthly master; any daily work is a spiritual activity for the believer, it is not simply an economic activity! This expands believers' godliness into the details of their profession, making every endeavor a living sacrifice to God as an act of worship. "Work at whatever you do with all your heart, working for the Lord, not for human masters."[43]

DILIGENCE IN ONE'S LIVELIHOOD

One cannot expect that simply praying, reading the Bible, and waiting on the Holy Spirit will bring spiritual or material prosperity. These proper disciplines do show one's humility and trust, but true righteousness includes one's diligence in all areas of life. Ecclesiastes encourages us in this all-out effort in everything: "*All* that your hand finds to do, do it with all your strength" (9:10). We have already highlighted the need for our diligence to subdue sin in our life and in the world around us. It is a critical part of our sanctification.

Yes, life is a partnership with God; everything is a partnership with him in his eternal design. So, diligence is not just for "Spiritual" things, but everything, because as new creatures, everything we do is empowered by the indwelling Spirit. It is God's desire that we work diligently with him. Though we are thankful for God's generous provisions, rarely do they come in abundance or are they kept in abundance without wise and vigorous planning and work.

42. Titus 2:9–10; Eph 6:5–8; Col 3:22–25
43. Col 3:23; also, Eph 6:5–7

It is fulfilling to work. Not only is diligence considered righteous, but the enjoyment of diligent work in itself is even commanded. Our work not only bears fruit to be enjoyed, but the work itself that produces that fruit is to be a delight as well (Eccl 2:24–25)! "It is good and beautiful to eat and to drink and to enjoy one's labor . . . since it is one's reward" (Eccl 5:18). When Ecclesiastes asks, "What advantage is there to all my hard, toiling labor?" the answer is given repeatedly in that book that in spite of the rigor of labor, one should enjoy life, work, and the fruits of wise, diligent work—all that makes up one's livelihood.

The simple pleasures of life available to the righteous and diligent are extolled as more than adequate.[44] Adequate food, drink, pleasant sleep, wine, clean clothing, body oil, a loving, stable marriage, and peace in the family are components of the life that the righteous and wise find satisfying.[45] Being poor, though not starving, can be a better condition than that of being affluent. If the choice is between being poor, wise, and just, rather than rich and wicked, righteousness trumps wickedness.[46] If the choice is a "higher" standard of living where there is strife and hatred in the house rather than peace and simple foods, then it is a gift to be simple.[47]

If by wisdom one wants to build up an estate, then there should be diligent preparations for it and vigilant maintenance of it. Proverbs and Ecclesiastes are key sources for the value of work and the means to be successful. For example, on planning . . .

> Complete your work in the fields, only then build a house for yourself. Prov 24:27

Those who farm know that observing nature determines the apt time for planting and harvesting.

> The one who observes the wind may not sow, and the one who watches the clouds may not reap. Eccl 11:4

On the other hand, when the wind is not so strong as to blow sown seeds all over the place . . .

> In the morning sow your seed, and until the evening do not relax your hand. Eccl 11:6

Wisdom will guide our work from moment to moment, including our attentive maintenance of what we have planned and built.

> Know well the condition of your flocks, and give attention to your herds, for riches do not last forever. Prov 27:23–24

---

44. Eccl 2:24–26; 3:12–13, 22; 5:17–18; 8:15; 9:7
45. Eccl 5:12; 9:7–9; Prov 31:22
46. Prov 15:16; 16:8, 19; 19:1; 28:6, 11
47. Prov 15:17; 17:1

> If the axe is blunt but one does not sharpen its edge, then one has to exert more strength. So the advantage of wisdom is success. Eccl 10:10

Wise effort, and plenty of it, provides plenty of fruit, but only poverty comes from laziness; that is, not working at all or just not working enough.[48] The primary commission is the context to all human activity since we are to rule and shepherd creation. Speaking in terms of ruling or being ruled, we are told: "Diligent hands will rule, but slack hands will do forced labor" (12:24). Laziness and its partner, sleepiness, are the opposite of taking God's primary commission seriously, and they inevitably and rightfully will bring a person to poverty. They are sins which bring their judgment soon enough.[49] The lazy always impress themselves with their wisdom in developing excuses for not working at all or hard enough.[50] Furthermore, any attempt to be rich without hard work or to be rich by pursuing the quick buck, is strongly discouraged in the wisdom instructions.[51]

Spiritualizing the wisdom instructions to redefine prosperity and riches to no longer pertain to literal prosperity and wealth is an irresponsible way to interpret the Bible. So one should be encouraged that wisdom and hard work will provide the believer with all that is needed.

> One builds a house by wisdom, and it is established by understanding.
> Knowledge fills its rooms with desirable and valuable riches. Prov 24:3–4

> Do not give me poverty or riches; feed me with what is enough for me.
> Otherwise, if I have more than enough I say, "Who needs God?"
> Or if I am poor, I might steal. Prov 30:8–9

Notice that prosperity, wealth, and riches are possessed by all who simply have *more than enough* materially and have peace in their life. Just enough, is enough. To demand that God give to us some arbitrary monetary amount beyond what is simply enough exposes a heart that serves two masters: money and God. There is no command for someone to be a millionaire. If so, Jesus would have been a very guilty man.

Wisdom instruction assumes that the righteous are hardworking and reap the rewards from their diligence, and that indolence brings disaster in one's life.[52] However, it is illogical to conclude that all who are wealthy are righteous; wealth can come from sin, oppression, greed and abuse. Another error in logic assumes that those who are poor or suffer disaster are unrighteous.

---

48. Prov 10:4–5; 12:27; 13:4; 14:23; 15:19; 18:9; 20:4; 21:25–26
49. Eccl 4:5; Prov 10:5, 26; 19:15, 24; 20:13; 24:30–34; 26:14–15
50. Prov 22:13; 26:13, 16
51. Prov 13:11; 20:21; 28:20
52. Prov 8:18–21; 10:3; 12:12,14; 13:21, 25; 14:11, 24; 15:6; 21:20; 22:4; 28:25

Wisdom instruction has a very realistic view of money. Money can provide a certain amount of protection.[53] For better or worse, it can also increase the number of one's friends, but obviously this can quickly reduce one's funds too.[54] Wisdom's overwhelming attitude toward wealth, however, is that it is limited in what it can promise. Money is a false security since it cannot deliver one from the time of death that God ordains, nor is it enjoyed after death.[55] Actually, one should always be prepared to lose their money at any time according to God's sovereign prerogatives. An abundance of money is not God's promise; it can be gone in little time. But the Lord will bless generously those who give proper and proportionate offerings to him (Prov 3:9–10).

The Lord will bless those who engage the marketplace with honesty and compassion, not self-interest and greed. Commerce is something that all people must participate in, and commerce is where one's righteousness can show in a public and accountable way. Mosaic law provided many business and economic principles and wisdom instruction confirms many of them literally. Any profit from lying during a transaction puts one at legal risk, including using false weights on a scale or any other deceptive measurement.[56] Moving boundary stones to steal a stretch of land nullified God's distribution of his land and definition of family and tribal boundaries.[57] Mercy is to be the preference over greed in the marketplace. It is a marketplace travesty to charge interest, to hoard one's assets by not selling them when other people are in grievous need, or refusing to share one's assets with the disadvantaged.[58] Righteousness will allow one's estate to last as an inheritance for one's grandchildren (Prov 13:22).

A few other instructions round out the practicality of wisdom and its effect on one's livelihood. One's livelihood can be jeopardized by debt, whether it is one's own debt or somebody else's for which one co-signs—it is risky business. One could lose what one has if the person being helped does not come through on their own.[59] Lending to strangers prompts the wise to get enough collateral in return. Diversifying one's assets is also wise so all is not lost at one time (Eccl 11:1–2). Righteous wisdom is evident when one takes care of oneself, avoids occupational dangers, and keeps equipment in good condition (Eccl 10:8–10). Humans and animals can be great partners in our work for a pleasant, rewarding life, but hiring just anyone can be a business disaster.[60]

Righteousness is improved by diligence in doing what is right and one becomes godlier with diligent effort. Peter says, "Diligently add to your faith virtue, and by virtue, knowledge and by knowledge, self-control and by self-control, perseverance

---

53. Eccl 7:11–12; Prov 10:15; 13:8
54. Eccl 5:11; Prov 14:20; 19:4, 7
55. Eccl 5:15–16; Prov 10:15; 11:4, 28; 18:11; 30:8–9;
56. Prov 11:1, 18; 13:11; 15:27; 16:11; 20:14, 17, 10, 23; 21:6
57. Prov 22:28; 23:10–11
58. Prov 11:26; 18:23; 21:25–26; 22:9; 28:8
59. Prov 6:1–5; 11:15; 17:18; 22:7
60. Eccl 4:9–12; Prov 12:10; 26:10

and by perseverance, godliness and by godliness, brotherly affection and by brotherly affection, love" (2 Pet 1:5–7). "Let us not get tired of doing good" (Gal 6:9).[61]

Before significant work starts, diligent planning is needed. Jesus gives examples of counting the financial costs before laying a foundation for a building construction site (Luke 14:28–30); he emphasizes planning before building on the firmest base (not sand);[62] he commends those who plan in advance and are prepared with adequate lighting at night (Matt 25:3–4). It is the diligence of the shepherd that drives him out to look for the one lost sheep.[63] It is the persistent effort of the woman who lost one of her ten coins that finally results in finding the coin (Luke 15:8–9).

We are to make the most of our time as wise believers, Paul says: "Walk not like the unwise walk but as the wise. Make the best use of your time because the days are evil" (Eph 5:15–16). One way to walk wisely is to work urgently so we can meet the pressing needs of others.[64] That is, we work hard for our income so we can share it with the disadvantaged! "Whoever sows generously will reap generously" (2 Cor 9:6). "Use your hands for good, hard work, and then give generously to others in need" (Eph 4:28). But to work this hard means we need to tend to our own business,[65] earning more than enough for our own food without expecting others to provide it (2 Thess 3:6–12).

The New Testament values money just as the Old Testament does. Money has value, but it cannot be allowed to become a slave master. It does not have eternal value since we leave it behind, having no need for it where we are going.[66] So greed is a miserable distraction to the contentment that comes to the believer regardless of financial circumstances.[67] The desire to be rich only invites temptation to walk along with us toward destruction. Money has all kinds of trouble in store for those who are attracted to it (1 Tim 6:9–10).

We should hurry to negotiate a financial suit, not hang on to every penny only to lose every dollar. In fact, out of love for our enemy, we should give more than what is fair in the suit (Matt 5:25–26, 40). After all, while we were yet sinners, enemies of God, he was generous in eternal ways; we can afford to be generous in mere material ways.

Of course, those writing about diligence were speaking from their own experience as gospel ministers. Paul says, "This is why I work and struggle so hard while depending on Christ's mighty power that works within me" (Col 1:29). Though persecuted, Paul and the apostles toiled with their own hands as humble guests who did

---

61. Also, 2 Thess 3:13; Heb 12:3; Rev 2:3
62. Matt 7:24–27; Luke 6:47–49
63. Matt 18:12–14 // Luke 15:4–7
64. Acts 20:35; Titus 3:14
65. 1 Thess 4:11–12; 1 Pet 4:15
66. Job 1:21; 1 Tim 6:7; Jam 1:11; Luke 12:15–21
67. Matt 6:19–34; Phil 4:11–12; 1 Tim 6:8; Heb 13:5

not expect to be served,[68] though they deserved to be.[69] And those who worked hard at their ministry are commended: only some of their names have been recorded as diligent fellow-workers; for example: Phoebe, Priscilla, Aquila, Mary, Urbanus, Tryphena, Tryphosa, Persis, Epaphroditus, Justus, Epaphras, and even an unnamed, very eager worker who represents all those who have gone before us as diligent ministers for our Lord.[70] Yet whether we are in "the ministry" or not, our occupational duties are to be done for the Lord, so they must be pursued diligently.[71]

COMMUNICATION

It has been said that the hardest thing to control in this whole world is the tongue. So, as sovereign shepherds in God's creation, managing our life and surroundings starts with managing our mouth. There are more wisdom instructions about wise speech than any other wisdom subject in Proverbs. Ecclesiastes also contributes frequently to the topic. One's speech can be as valuable as a sincere kiss, rubies, gold, silver, and elegant jewelry, or as invaluable as charred rubble.[72] There is no quicker way to show oneself to be wise or foolish than by one's use or restraint of the tongue. So wisdom, righteousness, and discernment are necessary before one can speak wisely. Wise speech comes from the heart and mind, so wicked fools can rarely speak it.[73]

One cannot allow the lips to move before the mind has prepared an appropriate statement, command, question or answer. Even speaking while thinking can lead to trouble since once spoken, words cannot be retrieved. For example, when making a vow, one should consider deeply what one was about to do before speaking.[74]

One of the greatest challenges is thinking carefully before responding to a foolish comment—that can take some time. A riddle of sorts lies between two apparently contradictory proverbs about responding to a fool.

> Do not answer a fool according to his folly or you will act just like him.
> Do answer a fool according to his folly or else he will think he is wise. Prov 26:4–5

Which response, whether to speak or not to speak, depends on the probable results of what we say or do not say. If one calculates that speaking will not demean oneself in the process, then correcting a fool might be best. But one should consider whether a corrective word will even bring the fool around.[75]

68. Acts 20:33–35; 1 Cor 4:11–12; 1 Thess 2:9; 2 Thess 3:7–9
69. Luke 10:7–8; 2 Thess 3:9–10
70. Rom 16:1–12; 2 Cor 8:22; Phil 2:25–25, 30; Col 4:11–12
71. Col 3:23; also, Eph 6:5–7
72. Prov 10:20; 16:27; 20:15; 24:26; 25:11; 26:7
73. Prov 10:13, 32; 14:7; 15:2; 16:23; 18:2
74. Eccl 5:2–3, 7; Prov 15:23, 28; 18:13; 20:25; 25:8; 29:20;
75. Prov 9:7–9; 12:23; 23:9; 29:9

Thoughtful speech will also be restrained in how long and how frequent one talks. Uttering long statements and speaking too many times is the sign of the fool.[76] There are times when silence is far better than words: "There is a time to speak, but a time not to speak."[77]

The proof of whether one's speech is godly is whether it spreads wisdom or not. So much can be said that is certainly the opposite of wisdom, but also too much is said that is neither wise nor foolish—it is just nothing. Solomon taught the people knowledge and searched for satisfying words, which is the goal of any leader—to direct others through their words toward wisdom.[78] These words can actually heal another's body, soul, and mind by bringing a divine perspective of consolation. Wise words bring understanding, peace and joy if they are sincere and fitting.[79]

However, the words of the fool can destroy others, including whole communities.[80] Gossip and betrayal of trust are the routine nature of many conversations.[81] Rather than peace and joy, the fool's words lead to arguments and fights because of their uncontrolled anger or divisiveness.[82] A spouse whose nature is to be quarrelsome can especially make life absolutely miserable.[83] Guarding one's mouth will keep one from public utterances of anger and vengeance, from revealing secrets, offending the authorities, speaking too loudly in the morning and presumptuous additions to what God has said already.[84] Flattery is nothing less than a trap set by the flatterer for a future profit from the one flattered.[85]

The benefits from wise words are self-preservation and prosperity, whereas the fool's mouth brings trouble and threats. Apt words will deliver one from trouble and painful correction, maybe even death.[86] The habit of speaking the right words will bring greater influence and personal satisfaction.[87] And wise speech will lead to the acquisition and retention of material blessings.[88] On the other hand, the loose-lipped do not prosper, and their foolish words can bring trouble, anger, and severe correction.[89]

---

76. Eccl 5:3, 7; 10:11–14
77. Eccl 3:7; also, Prov 10:19; 11:12; 12:23; 17:28
78. Eccl 12:9–10; also Prov 15:7; 16:21, 23; 31:26
79. Eccl 10:12; Prov 10:11;, 21;12:18, 25; 13:14, 17; 15:4, 30; 16:24; 25:13, 25;
80. Prov 11:9, 11; 29:5
81. Prov 11:13; 16:28; 18:8; 20:19; 26:20, 22
82. Prov 15:1; 16:28; 17:14; 20:3; 26:20–21; 30:32–33
83. Prov 19:13; 21:9, 19; 25:24; 27:15–16
84. Eccl 10:20; Prov 11:13; 13:3; 21:23; 25:15; 27:14; 30:5–6;
85. Prov 26:28; 28:23; 29:5
86. Prov 11:9; 12:6, 13, 19; 14:3; 18:21; 21:23
87. Prov 12:14; 13:2; 16:13, 21; 18:20; 22:11
88. Prov 12:14; 13:2; 18:20
89. Eccl 5:6; 10:12; Prov 13:3; 17:20; 18:6–7; 25:23; 25:9–10; 30:10

Honest speech is a particularly hard standard to apply to every situation, but an honest person is a blessing and receives God's delight and protection.[90] Deceptive comments, answers, and even misleading body language do not lead to long-lasting prosperity, only trouble.[91] Wisdom instructions support the Ten Commandments' warnings about lying in court as a false witness. It is a most serious sin since it can have life and death implications for the perjurer.[92]

The Trinity's loving nature extended the intimate communication among the Three Persons to the rest of creation. God speaks to creation through creation: "The skies speak about God's glory . . . Day to day their 'speech' is poured out" (Ps 19:1–2). Revelation from God can be non-verbal—if a picture speaks a thousand words, how much does a three-dimensional cosmos speak? It is our blessing that he has spoken verbally too. So the ethics of speaking are a sizeable issue in the Testaments. And in the newest testament, Christ is the royal reference point for speaking and other works: "And whatever you say or do, do it in the name of the Lord Jesus" (Col 3:17).

That is why there is so much said in the Bible about how we talk. What we say can be powerfully descriptive of our heart's condition. An action may not come with any comment to reveal its purpose or to describe an attitude or to specify to whom the act is directed. But one's speech is the clearest way to reflect one's heart, even a deceptive heart. This is why Paul defines the Christian as one whose heart and mouth are in unison about two central truths of the faith.

> If you confess with your mouth that Jesus is Lord and you believe in your heart that God raised him from the dead, you will be saved. For with the heart one believes and is justified, and with the mouth one confesses and is saved. Rom 10:9–10

Christ had already emphasized the close connection between heart and mouth; the mouth is the channel through which we reveal what is really in our heart.

> The mouth speaks out what fills the heart . . . Your words will justify you or your words will condemn you. Matt 12:34, 37[93]

> The things that come out of the mouth come from the heart. Matt 15:18

So, the New Testament encourages us to control our mouths in order to deliver us from too frequently and too deeply exposing our sinful heart, and to deliver others from the destruction that can come from our words.[94] Timothy is told that as a shepherding leader, his speech is to be exemplary (1 Tim 4:10–12). We are told to speak

---

90. Prov 4:24; 12:22, 19; 24:26; 28:13
91. Prov 6:12–17; 10:10, 18; 16:30; 17:20; 25:14
92. Prov 6:19; 12:17; 14:5, 25; 19:5, 9, 28; 25:18; 21:28; 24:28–29; 26:24–26
93. Also, Luke 6:45
94. Jas 1:26; 2:12; 3:2–8

"good words" and to speak only the truth in love[95] so we will not return "evil for evil or insult for insult, but give a blessing instead" (1 Pet 3:9). James is disappointed, as should we be that "blessing and cursing come out of the same mouth." We bless God in one breath and even in the same prayer can accuse and condemn others (3:9–10).

Without drawing a line between formal worship and everyday practice, Paul instructs believers to teach and communicate with one another in a way that is beautiful, such as making music and using songs that inspire the lives of others and that bless the Lord.

> Speak to one another with psalms, hymns, and spiritual songs. Sing and make music from your heart to the Lord, *always* giving thanks to God the Father for everything.[96]

Paul commends the Corinthians for their faith, wisdom, and conversation and encourages all believers to be gracious, edifying, and encouraging in how they speak to one another.[97] In other words, the New Testament expects the same gracious and healing words from believers as the Old Testament does.

On the other hand, harmful talk often comes even from believers' mouths. We will give an account for our words to Christ as the Judge, including empty words like, "Go in peace; be warm and well fed" when these words are not accompanied by gifts of food and clothing.[98] We can be like the despicable Snake with our biting and poisonous words of bitterness and cursing.[99] Gossip and slander are the opposite of blessing and delivering, injuring those whose reputation we are undermining.[100] Obscene language and jokes that are just stupid, depraved, or coarse are not to be on the lips of the believer.[101] They do not raise the dignity of relationships and do not reflect the glory of God that we have been created to show the world through our godly words and acts.

Sins of the tongue convey an arrogant heart. We are introduced to them in one verse: "I fear that there may be quarreling, jealousy, anger, selfishness, slander, gossip, arrogance and disorder" (2 Cor 12:20). Bragging reveals a heart of pride in one's wisdom, position, faith, doctrinal knowledge and life plans.[102] Being argumentative can come from an arrogant heart that is unteachable and is too foolish to decide what points are worth arguing. Jesus could have won any argument while standing for his life in court, but he patiently let the plan of the Trinity unfold.[103] On the other hand,

---

95. Eph 4:15; 25; 2 Thess 2:17; Titus 2:8
96. Eph 5:19–20; Col 3:16
97. 2 Cor 8:7; Eph 4:29; 1 Thess 4:18; 5:14
98. Matt 12:36; Jas 2:15–16
99. Rom 3:13–14; Col. 3:8; 2 Tim 3:2; Jas 3:6–8
100. 2 Cor 12:20; 1 Tim 3:11; 5:13; 2 Tim 3:3; Titus 2:3
101. Eph 5:3–4, 11–12; 2 Tim 2:16
102. 1 Cor 1:29–31; 4:7, 19–20; 5:6; 13:4; 2 Cor 10:17; 12:9; Gal 5:26; Eph 2:8–9; 1 Tim 6:4; 2 Tim 3:2; Jas 3:5; 4:16; 2 Pet 2:18; 1 John 2:16
103. Acts 8:32; 1 Pet 2:21–23

the contentious heart partners with loose, flapping lips to divide believers rather than to promote unity and harmony.[104]

Since Christ is the truth, anything that is false is not of Christ. Quoting from Zechariah, Ephesians reaffirms the Lord's requirement for believers not to lie and to "lay aside falsehood and speak the truth."[105] False communication is of Satan who is a liar himself and the father of all lies.[106] Lies that amount to slander against the reputations and integrity of others prove one to be under the Enemy's sway.[107] False teachers were intentional deceivers of the church for their own greed and desire to have a following.[108] Flattery, even if the words are truthful, can be deceptive in intent since the apparent compliment cloaks the ulterior motive behind it (1 Thess 2:4–5). We should have reputations which do not require oaths to assure others that we are telling the truth. Christ says, "Do not make oaths at all . . . let your words be, 'Yes, yes' *or* 'No, no'; anything beyond these is evil."[109]

COMPANIONS

The importance of having righteous *friends* is accentuated in Proverbs. One should be cautious in choosing companions, and of course the right ones are those who are wise.[110] They can be of great help when one person is not enough for successful commerce or any challenging task or danger. We encourage others and they encourage us in our challenging times. Ecclesiastes says, "If one falls, the other person can lift up his companion. But it is too bad for the one who falls and there is no one to lift him up" (4:10). Furthermore, faithful friends are hard to find, and one who has many probably has some who are not totally trustworthy.[111] Those companions especially to be avoided are those engaged in or are prone to stealing and violence, those who are easily angered, and those who are sexually loose, or are gluttons and drunks.[112] We know the damage done by gossips whose only delight is to have other gossips as friends. Associating with grumblers about authority or who openly rebel against it can put one in jeopardy of losing one's job or wellbeing.[113]

---

104. 1 Cor 1:10–11; 11:16; 2 Cor 12:20; Gal 5:20; Phil 2:14; 1 Tim 6:3–4; 2 Tim 2:14, 23–25; Titus 3:2, 9–11
105. Zech 8:16; Eph 4:15; also, Rom 3:13–14; Col 3:9; 1 Tim 1:10; 1 Pet 3:10; Rev 14:5
106. John 8:44; Acts 13:10
107. 2 Cor 12:20; Eph 4:31; Col 3:8; 1 Pet 2:1
108. Rom 16:18; Eph 4:14; 1 Tim 1:3–7; Titus 1:10, 12; 2 Pet 2:1–3
109. Matt 5:34, 37; also, Jas 5:12, cf. Eccl 5:4–5
110. Prov 13:20; 14:7; 27:9
111. Prov 17:17; 18:24; 20:6; 25:19; 27:10
112. Prov 1:10–16; 2:12–16; 4:14–19; 16:19, 29; 22:24–25; 23:19–21; 24:1–2, 19–20; 29:3, 24
113. Eccl 8:2–3; Prov 24:21–22

Associating with the right people is an important part of our walk and maturity in Christ. We are not to be bound unequally with unbelievers since their approach to life is the opposite of ours. The weight of their priorities should not be allowed to topple ours. Paul describes the opposite priorities of those who follow God and those who contribute to the Enemy's cause. Those priorities are as distant as righteousness and lawlessness, light and dark, Christ and Satan, the temple and idols (2 Cor 6:14-16). It is not wrong to have unbelieving friends, but if a believer's approach to life is not significantly and noticeably different from theirs, then believers should question their depth of commitment to God's kingdom.

But when it comes to believers in the local church, fellowship is not just an option, it is a requirement: "Let us meet together as some neglect to do so we can encourage each other" (Heb 10:25). Christian fellowship was not just a series of scheduled, weekly formal meetings. It was a way of life. "Day by day" believers were with one another sharing, praying, eating, learning and praising the Lord (Acts 2:42–47). These meetings were intended to be times of encouragement in times of distress since it is not healthy for a believer to be alone in those times.[114]

Encouragement comes from our surrounding "family" of "sisters" and "brothers"—the fellowship is that intimate: Jesus said, "Whoever does my heavenly Father's will is my brother, sister or mother."[115] So we comfort one another, rejoicing or mourning, and bearing one another's burdens.[116] We encourage one another out of love and concern, and to strengthen one another to continue living morally.[117]

On the other hand, we are to avoid the disobedient "brother" who disregards sound teaching and behaves immorally to a significant degree.[118] No one is perfect, but those who become a distraction from the moral focus of the church which is being watched by the world must be avoided. And if the situation is severe enough, they must be dismissed from the community of believers.[119]

HEALTH

Mental and physical health is addressed often in wisdom instruction. Physical health was a significant concern also in the Mosaic law. Gluttony and heavy drinking were discouraged in the Law as in wisdom instruction since these excesses lead to poverty, injury, and sickness.[120] They also lead to further irresponsibility like mismanagement

---

114. Rom 1:12; Phil 2:1; Col 2:2; 1 Thess 3:2; 5:11, 14; Heb 3:13
115. Matt 12:50; Mark 3:35; Luke 8:21
116. Matt 18:15; Rom 12:15; 2 Cor 2:6–8; Eph 6:22; Gal 6:1–2
117. Heb 10:24–25; also, Luke 22:31–32; 1 Thess 3:2
118. Rom 16:17; 1 Cor 5:9, 11, 13; 2 Thess 3:6
119. Matt 18:16–17; 1 Cor 5:1–2, 7; Titus 3:9–11
120. Prov 20:1; 21:17; 23:1–3, 6–8, 19–21, 29–35

and poor judgment in critical decisions, including defending the disadvantaged.[121] As far as mental health goes, Proverbs tells us that a healthy spirit will contribute to a healthy body.[122] One's wise attitudes of peace and hope lead to internal health too.[123] This is where we can bless others since words wisely spoken can bring joy and healing to the anxious.

There are not nearly the number of instructions about our health in the New Testament as there are in the Old. Of course there are the numerous occasions when the Lord healed the afflicted and the apostles followed with comparable power. Even elders are channels of God's salvation from illness as they anoint with oil and pray for the sick (Jas 5:14-15). A little wine is prescribed for an upset stomach (1 Tim 5:23), and evidently the Lord took the health away from those who were not respecting the communion meal (1 Cor 11:27-30).

The health instructions of the New Testament center on instructions to avoid personal gluttony, substance addictions, and drunkenness.[124] We are also told not associate with those who are drunkards (1 Cor 5:11). In particular, those entrusted with leadership roles in the church are to be sober, just as the rest of the believers whom they shepherd are expected to be.[125]

PRAYER

Prayer is how we communicate with God. You will find many definitions that limit prayer to particular content. But prayer is simply a biblical religious word for communing with God. There are no definitions beyond that in Scripture. There are no techniques that pique God's interest or cajole him into submission to our recommendations to him about how he should manage certain affairs. Prayer is talking to God and listening for his Spirit to speak within the temple, the temple of our body and mind.

One new to the faith can be confused about what prayer is. It sounds so high and eloquent, so deep and profound. It may seem to be at an unreachable standard for anyone not fluent in the Christian subculture's dialect and vocabulary. But, in spite of our traditional forms, idioms and cliché's, any communication with God from a sincere heart is prayer. Prayer can be one word, silent, or shouted. Prayer can praise; prayer can complain. It can be "thank you"; it can be "I want." It can be "your will be done"; it can be "I want to share my heart." Prayer can be sung and danced; prayer can be signed by the deaf and mute. It is all prayer.

---

121. Eccl 10:16-18; Prov 31:2-9

122. Prov 14:30; 17:22; 18:14; 15:30

123. Prov 12:25; 13:12; 15:13

124. Luke 12:42-45; 21:34; Matt 24:48-50; Rom 13:13; 1 Cor 6:9-10; 11:20-21; Gal 5:21; Eph 5:18; 1 Pet 4:3; 2 Pet 2:13-14

125. 1 Tim 3:2-3, 8; Titus 1:6-7; 2:3

We praise God for who he is and what he does. And we are to pray continually and into eternity.[126] We praise him for his glory,[127] justice,[128] wisdom,[129] and righteousness.[130] We thank God for what he has chosen to do for us. We thank him as our shepherd who blesses, delivers, and disciplines us. We thank him for his patience,[131] faithfulness,[132] and kindness.[133] We confess our weaknesses and sins to him.[134]

The New Testament teaches that we are to pray about anything persistently and without ceasing.[135] It becomes a way of life because we realize God is always right there, available to hear, and to respond through his Spirit. He will advise with wisdom and will not criticize us if we do not know everything (Jas 1:5). But we need to pray with the right motives (Jas 4:2–3), with brevity and simplicity (Matt 6:7), and with a balanced mind (1 Pet 4:7). But since we are all inadequate in ourselves in our prayers because we cannot know the full plans of God for any of our circumstances, if we are sincere and trusting, the Spirit and Christ will speak for us, interceding for us to the Father (Rom 8:26–27, 34).

HUMILITY

Humanity and the rest of creation has been cursed with imperfection because of the lack of humility by Adam and Eve. Pride continues to be the basic impediment to human success as it substitutes inferior human wisdom for that of God's. Humility may appear to be counter-productive to success since it is a voluntary subjection of oneself, but this is an unfortunate misconception that fails to see humility as a sign of strength and a means to strength. "The fear of the Lord instructs our wisdom since humility precedes honor."[136] Humility in our relationship with the Shepherd is required for our success in God's eternal design. To move out from under his sovereign instructions because of our audacity to go it alone or submit to another authority will only end in our humiliation. It can be humbling when our plans fail or are altered or delayed

---

126. 1 Chr 16:36; Pss 34:1; 35:28; 61:4, 7–8; 71:6–8, 15; 92:2; 113:3; 119:62; Dan 6:10–11

127. Deut 32:3; Pss 8:1, 9; 19:1; 24:7–10; 26:7; 29:1; 40:5; 75:1; 96:3, 6–8; 145:3–5

128. Deut 32:4; Job 37:23; Pss 33:5; 36:5; 89:8, 14; 98:9; 99:4; 109:30–31; 119:90; Isa 25:1

129. 1 Sam 2:3; Dan 2:20–23

130. Judg 5:11; 2 Sam 22:31; Job 37:23; Pss 7:17; 11:7; 33:4–5; 92:15

131. Neh 9:30–31; Pss 103:8; 145:8

132. Deut 32:4; 1 Sam 2:2; 2 Sam 22:2–3; Neh 9:33; Pss 40:10; 89:1–2; 100:5

133. 1 Chr 16:34; 2 Chr 5:12–13; 20:21; Neh 9:17; Pss 13:5; 18:50; 33:5; 89:1–2; 100:5; 103:11–14; 118:1–4; 136; Jer 30:11; Dan 9:4

134. Lev 26:40; Ezra 10:1, 11; Neh 9:2; Pss 32:5; 38:18; Dan 9:20

135. Matt 7:7 // Luke 11:9–13; Luke 18:1–8; Eph 6:18; Phil 4:6, Col 4:2; 1 Thess 5:17, 25; 1 Tim 2:8; Heb 4:16; Jas 5:13–16

136. Prov 15:33; also, 18:12

because of God's ultimate sovereign plans for us.[137] The choice to be humble or to be humiliated is the only choice since God will sort things out now and in the future.

A sage named Agur epitomizes humility in his description of his lack of wisdom compared to God's all-knowing and all-powerful glory.

> I have not learned complete wisdom nor do I have the knowledge the Holy One has.
>
> Who but God has gone up to heaven and down? Who gathered the winds in his palms?
>
> Who wrapped the seas under his garment? Who created the whole earth?
>
> What is his name or his son's name? Of course you know! Prov 30:3–4

This reminds us of Job's spiritual journey from his initial humility to momentary arrogance and then back to humility because of the wisdom of Elihu and the Lord. He finally admits to the Lord,

> I know you can do anything, nothing can stop your plans.
>
> You asked, 'Who questions my wisdom without knowledge themselves?'
>
> I spoke about things I knew nothing about, things too magnificent for me. Job 42:2–3

Humility was necessary for the Israelites to obey God and to act lovingly and legally toward others. All were humbled by God's Law; none were above it. Even the king was humbled under it, being equally responsible to keep it as the other citizens of God's kingdom. Israelites had all been humbled while enslaved in Egypt, so their servants and the disadvantaged were to be dealt with graciously. So humility is not a new concept to wisdom instruction, but it is revealed in more explicit and thorough terms in Job, Ecclesiastes, and Proverbs.

A humble believer is driven to seek wisdom wherever it can be found, whereas the proud believes he already has it: "See someone who is wise in their own eyes? A fool has more hope than that one."[138] Ecclesiastes admits that the search for wisdom is an extensive and painful endeavor because wisdom will reveal the tragic as well as wonderful truths of this world.[139] Wisdom has to be diligently sought within the Testaments and in the counsel of other believers.[140] Wisdom is found easier in solitude or somber places like funerals rather than trivial places of entertainment and frivolous pleasures (Eccl 7:2–5). The fool may say he is searching for wisdom, but he will not find it because he does not know where to look.[141]

One source of wisdom is God's Word and specifically his Law.[142] To ask for God's wisdom without meditating on his Word is irresponsible since it dismisses the depth of understanding the Word conveys to address the routine and extraordinary challenges

---

137. Prov 16:3; 19:21; 20:24; 21:30; 29:23
138. Prov 26:12; also, 1:25–32; 3:5–7; 12:15; 14:12; 16:25; 28:26
139. Eccl 1:3—2:3; 2:12–13 .
140. Prov 2:1–3; 3:1, 13–15; 7:1–4; 10:14; 14:6; 15:14; 16:16; 17:24; 18:15; 19:8; 23:12; 24:13–14
141. Prov 14:6, 15; 17:16
142. Eccl 12:13–14; Prov 2:6–7; 13:13; 19:16; 28:4, 7, 9; 29:18;

in life. He expects us to seek wisdom where it already is, not order it from him directly to eliminate the time and effort to take his Word seriously.

In addition to submitting to the Testaments, humility will submit to the wise teaching and example of others. Whether by asking for wisdom or whether it comes unsolicited, the humble will appreciate growing in wisdom from instruction and advice.[143] Advice from others can help make critical decisions before potential conflict[144] as well as for mundane decisions. Wisdom can come from others' commands, not simply from advice. It can come in the forms of rebuke and correction. No one is so wise as never to deserve correction, so rather than resent it, the rebuke should be welcomed humbly for its challenge to live even more wisely.[145]

Humility is shown by children to their parents regardless of age. Just as the Mosaic law assumed, parents are a primary source of instruction and wisdom according to Proverbs. The mother is to be just as highly esteemed for her wisdom as the father.[146] And it is important for children to know and care that their wise or foolish behavior profoundly affects both mother and father emotionally. In fact, this is the very first point of the Proverbs after its introductory nine chapters: "A wise son brings joy to his father, but a foolish son brings grief to his mother."[147] The extreme opposite of respect for parents' instruction is a child's mocking and cursing.[148]

One's humility can be heard even in one's silence about personal success. Greater honor comes from another's praise. And when one is praised, one's humility while receiving that praise will confirm its validity.[149] Pride is a sin that God utterly abhors,[150] and the punishment of the proud is certain and could come by destruction of one's property, one's reputation, or even one's life.[151]

We hold high the perfect example of Jesus while he counted himself among the lowly: "Learn from me for I am gentle and humble in my heart" (Matt 11:29). This is a jolting statement coming from the ruler of the universe. Who can truly comprehend that statement? So, we are to be humble to the point of not only loving others *as* we love ourselves but even loving them more than ourselves.

> Do nothing from selfish ambition or conceit, but in humility count others more significant than yourselves... Appearing as a human, [Christ] humbled himself by obeying even to the point of death on a cross. Phil 2:3, 8

---

143. Eccl 9:17; Prov 1:5–7; 5:10–14; 12:15; 13:10, 20; 15:22; 16:20; 19:20, 27; 27:17;

144. Prov 20:18; 24:5

145. Prov 6:23; 10:17; 12:1; 13:18; 15:10, 12; 19:25; 21:11; 25:12; 27:6; 28:23

146. Prov 1:8–9; 4:1–5; 6:20–23; 13:1; 15:5; 23:22–25; 31:1–2

147. Prov 10:1; also, 15:20; 17:21, 25; 19:26; 23:15–16, 22–25; 27:11; 29:3

148. Prov 19:26; 20:20; 28:24; 30:17

149. Prov 12:9; 25:27; 27:2, 21; 30:32

150. Eccl 7:8; Prov 6:16–17; 21:4, 24; 30:13;

151. Prov 11:2; 15:25; 16:5, 18; 18:12; 29:23

If we are going to be God's shepherds, we must have his gentle, humble heart and submit first and foremost to the Trinity. John the Baptist's attitude when Jesus replaced him on the prophetic center stage was expressed in the simplest and clearest terms: "He must become ever greater, and I must become ever less. He comes from above and is above everything" (John 3:30–31).

Contrary to the attitudes of the dark kingdom which has taught that humility is a weakness, humility is our honorable strength. It is what will exalt us in the end and along the way. The Old Testament says, "A humble spirit will be honored" (Prov 29:23) and, "The Lord detests the proud in heart" (Prov 16:5). Jesus confirms that truth: "Anybody who exalts himself will be humbled, but anybody who humbles himself will be exalted."[152] And James makes it clear that our exaltation will not only come from others but from the Lord himself: "Humble yourselves in the Lord's presence and He will exalt you" (Jas 4:10).

Humility to one another stems from a heart of love and respect, and it is a necessary building block for the church.[153] Comparable to Christ's statement about the second summary commandment, loving others as oneself, Paul tells us not to think any more highly than we ought to think. Again, in other words, we can think of ourselves highly but only so high (Rom 12:3). The self-esteem of a believer should be high since we are the image bearers of the Shepherd, but not so high that we do not defer to others as more important than we are while we shepherd them.

Christ encourages us to deal with our own sin and blindness before we start helping others to see theirs more clearly.[154] We are not only to recognize our sin, but we are also to do one of the most difficult of all tasks—confess our sins to the very people whom we prefer would believe that we are always right (Jas 5:16).

We know that God opposes and hates arrogance.[155] When James speaks pride, it reminds us of the initial sin in Eden where the pride of the first Couple embraced Satan rather than resisting him.

> God opposes the proud, but is gracious to the humble. So submit your selves to God. Resist the devil, and he will flee from you.[156] You are in Christ Jesus, who became to us wisdom from God, righteousness, sanctification and redemption ... So let the one who boasts, boast in the Lord. 1 Cor 1:30–31

> By grace you have been saved, through faith that is not from yourselves. It is the gift of God, not through works, so no one can boast. Eph 2:8–9

Since we are saved only by God's grace, no one can boast about saving themselves by their faith. This is a self-righteousness that condemns rather than delivers. Habitual

---

152. Luke 14:11; also, 18:14; Matt 23:12
153. 1 Cor 4:6–7; Eph 4:2; Col 3:12; Jas 1:21; 1 Pet 2:21–23; 3:4, 15; 5:5–6
154. Matt 7:1–5 // Luke 6:41–42
155. Rom 12:16; 1 Cor 4:6, 18–19; 13:4; 2 Cor 12:20; 2 Tim 3:2–4
156. Jas 4:6–7; also, 1 Pet 5:5

pride is a severe sin which if misdirected might prove that an alleged salvation never really occurred.[157]

Christ says that it is from the sinful heart that arrogance comes, at least equating pride with other seriously damaging sins such as fornication, theft, and murder (Mark 7:22). There are many reasons for conceit. Some are proud of their intelligence or knowledge and mislead those who respect and follow them because of their alleged "wisdom."[158] The pride of some causes them to trust in their own planning, believing their self-determination will be the ultimate cause of their success and forgetting that all success is the Lord's blessing.[159] Others are proud of their wealth so trust in it completely (1 Tim 6:17).

We are to submit to one another, being willing to yield and not insist on our own way.[160] Even when we know what we are about to do is not sinful in itself, we need to avoid doing it if it will tempt others to do what they consider to be sin. Paul devotes at least an entire chapter on this aspect of self-sacrifice, ending with the ultimate example: "Each of us should please our neighbors for their benefit and edification since even Christ did not please himself" (Rom 14:1—15:3).

We should not only *accept* a lower position to others, we should *seek* that lowest place—it should be our aspiration to be there. Our own eternal Savior and God was born a commoner's baby and died the cruel, humiliating death of a common thief. Yet he mocked the pretentions of the religious leaders who would stride with pride toward the seats of honor at banquets, synagogues, and the marketplace.[161] Instead, the Lord says that at a banquet we should take the lowest position at the table since he promises that the humble will eventually be exalted (Luke 14:10–11).

Serving God is the obvious response to accepting Jesus our savior as Christ our king.[162] We accept his deliverance, but that cannot be done genuinely without accepting the responsibility to serve our Deliverer by serving his sheep. Shepherding others is the essence of the ethics of both Testaments. These ethical principles for service range from offering a small cup of water to a child (Matt 10:42) to offering one's life for a friend (John 15:13).

Just as the Old Testament commended a person for seeking further wisdom, the earliest church believers devoted themselves to others' teaching, seeking to mature by their increased understanding (Acts 2:42). They understood James' plea, "accept humbly the word planted in you—it is able to save you" (Jas 1:21).

---

157. Rom 3:27; 11:20–21
158. 1 Cor 8:1; Col 2:18; 2 Pet 2:18
159. Luke 12:16–20; Jas 4:13–16
160. Rom 12:10; 1 Cor 13:4–5; Eph 5:21; Jas 3:17; Titus 1:7; 2 Pet 2:10
161. Matt 23:1–7 // Mark 12:38–39 // Luke 11:43; 20:46
162. Matt 6:24; John 12:26; Rom 1:9; 14:18; Heb 9:14

PATIENCE

The Lord is patient with humanity, with his believing community, and with individual believers; his patience inspires us to praise and thankfulness. He has revealed his glorious moral character, his love, and his power to tolerate an ungrateful, unresponsive, even rebellious race for so long. He lived with us and has experienced human limitations as a finite being. He has personally experienced the effect of the curses he instituted in Eden and the challenges they present to all humanity. So his heart is patient, longsuffering, and forgiving.

Like our Shepherd, our patience is the appropriate response to challenges from circumstances or from other people when they respond impulsively or with uncontrolled irritation. It takes a planned approach to solutions since haste keeps one from considering all the options and implications of an action: "The plans of the diligent bring profit as sure as haste brings poverty" (Prov 21:5). Self-control is a fruit of the Spirit that helps one to avoid hasty responses that leave a person as defenseless as a vulnerable city: "Someone with no self-control is like a city with demolished walls" (Prov 25:28). Literally, haste makes waste as the more modern proverb says.

Ecclesiastes prescribes applying the moral standard of patience when dealing with anger, whether it is a superior's anger or one's own anger. When facing the poor decisions or the ire of one's superior it is best to stay calm, not to panic, but wait for the right moment.

> Whoever keeps a command will not experience evil since a wise heart knows a suitable time and judgment—yes, for every choice there is a suitable time and judgment. 8:5–6

> If the temper of the ruler rises against you, don't leave, since composure soothes great offenses. 10:4

Proverbs 25:15 chimes in with a strategy alongside one's loyalty to a superior—speak patiently and softly: "A ruler can be persuaded by patience, and gentle words can break bones." On the other hand, Ecclesiastes also emphasizes the benefits of patience over one's own uncontrolled outburst: "The patient spirit is better than the proud spirit. Do not rush your spirit toward anger" (Eccl 7:8–9).[163] We will return to the virtue of patience later when we discuss peace as a moral attribute.

Our patience is another fruit of the Holy Spirit, and it is a practice and habit of those who wish to shepherd others as God has shepherded us.[164] It takes the Spiritual fruit of self-control to contain our impatience with others.[165] Like our other ethical responsibilities, patience is motivated by love: "Love is patient and kind" (1 Cor 13:4). So, patience preserves unity in the body by outlasting and overpowering any turmoil

---

163. Also, Prov 12:16; 14:29; 16:32; 29:11
164. Gal 5:22; Phil 4:5; Col 1:11; 3:12; 1 Thess 5:14; 2 Tim 3:10; Jas 5:10
165. Jas 5:7–8; 1 Pet 2:20

that can come from distressed, frantic, impulsive, or unforgiving hearts.[166] We are to be patient when wronged, waiting for the Lord's vengeance, or better, forgiving the offender in love.[167] Our shepherding discipline of the sinners in our believing communities is also to be done "patiently" through instruction, not just pointing out the error (2 Tim 4:2). After all, we certainly should appreciate the patience of others with us.

Christ Jesus accents the severity of sinful anger, comparing it, but not quite equating it with murder (Matt 5:21–22). Paul and James follow Christ and the Old Testament teachings about anger and the destruction it leaves behind. Though Paul admits there is a place for anger, still, it is not to be sustained because it makes one vulnerable to Satan who uses anger for his evil purposes.[168] Controlling one's anger shows respect to everyone just as if they were immediate family (Titus 1:7) and is a necessary trait for those who wish to be church leaders (1 Tim 5:1–2). Grumbling and complaining are also verbal proof of an angry, disturbed heart.[169]

KINDNESS BY BLESSING OTHERS

God's love is active; it is not merely an emotion, attitude, or a relational status. Love has no meaning apart from actions that proceed from it. It is like faith—faith is dead unless there is an active trust in the Lord by *doing something* in faith. Many of the traits of the wise believer are not only derivatives of love but *are* love in action. God's kindness is one of these. As God shepherds, his kindness is shown to the believer by his blessing, deliverance, and discipline. His kindness is also shown to non-believers as we have discussed already. We quote an entire psalm here (though it is the shortest of all psalms) to prove God's point.

> Praise the Lord all you nations, exalt him *all peoples*!
>
> For his kindness overwhelms us and his truth is eternal. Praise the Lord! Ps 117:1-2

We have looked in detail at God's kindness when summarizing his shepherding of the peoples, the believing community, and the individual, including believers especially in chapters 8–10.

As expected, we are to bless others with kindness as our Lord does. Kindness is a jewel to be treasured for oneself and for others.

> Do not let kindness and truth escape you; bind them around your neck and write them on the tablet of your heart. Prov 3:3
>
> A man who is kind benefits himself. Prov 11:17

---

166. 2 Cor 6:6; Eph 4:2
167. Rom 12:19; Col 3:12–13; 2 Tim 2:24; 1 Pet 2:20
168. Eph 4:26; also, Gal 5:20; Eph 4:31; Col 3:8; Jas 1:19–20
169. Phil 2:14; 1 Cor 10:10; Heb 12:14–15; Jas 5:9; Jude 16

> Whoever blesses others will be well fed himself. Prov 11:25

> She opens her mouth in wisdom; her tongue teaches kindness. Prov 31:26

The one who shows kindness is as blessed as the one who is shown kindness.

Since the beginning of human history, God's has been gracious to humanity and he will continue to be gracious throughout eternity: "God raised us up with Christ and seated us with himself . . . to show the incomparable riches of his grace, expressed in his kindness to us in Christ Jesus" (Eph 2:6–7). Christ says it is God's kindness that is the model for ours: "Love your enemies, and do good . . . for the Most High is kind to the ungrateful and evil."[170] So we also are to "do good to everyone," but of course, especially to our brothers and sisters in Christ (Gal 6:10).

Kindness is a general term, like blessing, and it is a part of each of the shepherding functions of blessing, deliverance, and discipline. It can be simply a blessing from a loving heart: a smile, an embrace, compliment, encouragement, dessert, or any ordinary gift. Of course, love is the energy behind kindness, as it is for other fruits of the Spirit.[171] Tabitha is remembered for having been raised from the dead and her frequent and continual kindness (Acts 9:36–37, 40). Timothy is also encouraged to "be kind to everyone" (2 Tim 2:24). Kindness will bend a heart toward forgiving others.[172] It is gentle.[173] The opposite characteristics of kindness are listed at length by Paul: he mentions those who love only themselves, and those who are money lovers, braggarts, arrogant, revilers, unholy, cruel, proud, reckless, unloving, ungrateful, slanderous, treacherous, unforgiving, haters of good, no self-control, disobeying parents (2 Tim 3:2–3).

MERCY BY DELIVERING OTHERS

The eternal design requires our active involvement with the Trinity in the deliverance of creation. In particular, love and kindness will lead us to merciful deliverance of other people. We have reserved the word "mercy" for the type of kindness which *delivers* others who are distressed in some way. Much has been written in this study already about God's merciful deliverances in chapters 8–10. And again, the Lord's actions set the standard for the extent one should go to show grace, mercy, salvation, and deliverance. The biblical portrayal of God as Savior is vastly larger than saving his people and believers from sin. So, in turn, our mercy is what the Lord expects from us: "What does the Lord require? To act justly, love mercy, and to walk humbly with your God" (Mic 6:8).

The focus of mercy in the wisdom instructions is primarily on providing for the poor and afflicted.[174] The poor would include the destitute because of being handi-

---

170. Luke 6:35; also, Matt 5:45
171. Gal 5:22; 1 Cor 13:4–5; 2 Cor 6:6; Titus 2:4–5; 1 Pet 3:8–9; 2 Pet 1:7
172. Eph 4:32; Col 3:12–13
173. Gal 5:22; Eph 4:32
174. Prov 11:25; 14:21, 31; 19:17; 22:9; 22–23; 28:8, 27

capped, a widow, an orphan, or a foreigner, just as we saw them provided for in the Mosaic laws. Contrary to a scarcity mentality that believes hoarding brings gain, wisdom says the opposite—giving brings one more blessings in the end, including honor and material blessings.[175] In fact, the unmerciful are promised to be unblessed.[176] One's treatment of the disadvantaged reflects an attitude of love or contempt for God. Kindness or abuse honors God or disrespects him since those affected carry his image.[177] Mercy is shown by delivering the poor from any corrupt or unfair justice, and mercy should be of great concern to everyone, not merely to judicial leaders.[178]

One might be merciful to those who are friends, relatives or genuinely deserving pity, but the standard in the Old Testament is for the wise is to show mercy even to one's enemies![179] The Law had said to care for an enemy's property by saving his domesticated animal.[180] Proverbs goes on to say,

> Do not rejoice when your enemy falls, nor should your heart be happy when he stumbles. 24:17

> When your enemy is hungry, give him food to eat, and when he is thirsty, give him water to drink. 25:21

Loving, shepherding, and practical care even for one's enemies is expected of the Israelites in their daily living.

When Jesus explains the importance of loving one's enemies, it may appear that he is quoting an Old Testament passage; actually, he is paraphrasing a saying that is not totally correct so he can correct it: "You have heard that it was said, 'Love your neighbor *and hate your enemy*.' But I say, love your enemy" (Matt 5:43–44). We have already discussed the biblical command to love one's enemies as it is first found in the Old Testament in Leviticus 19:18. However, there is no Old Testament instruction to hate one's enemy. So Jesus is quoting both a biblical truth and a non-biblical saying that was current in his time. To hate one's enemies was contrary to Mosaic law, so Jesus confirms the Old Testament positive attitude to love one's enemies.

It is the Trinity's saving kindness that saves us from sin, and that kindness is more his mercy because we never deserve it.

> The kindness of God leads you to repentance. Rom 2:4

> Pay attention to the kindness and severity of God; to the fallen—his severity, but to you—his kindness if you continue in his kindness; otherwise you will be cut off too. Rom 11:22

---

175. Prov 11:16, 24–25; 14:21; 22:9; 28:27; 31:20
176. Prov 11:24; 21:13; 22:16; 28:8, 22
177. Prov 14:31; 17:5; 19:17; 22:2; 24:11–12; 29:13
178. Prov 22:22–23; 24:11–12; 28:5, 21
179. Prov 24:17–18; 25:21–22
180. Ex 23:4–5; Deut 22:1–4

> God our Savior saved us when his kindness and love for humanity appeared.
> Titus 3:4

> So you will grow in salvation if you have experienced that the Lord is kind. 1 Pet 2:3

We will see in our fuller discussion of forgiveness below that of course we are to be merciful by forgiving too, since we should mirror the merciful Shepherd in everything he does.[181]

The mercy found in God's forgiveness is also seen in his other kindnesses. It starts with a loving heart that is attentive to and convinced of the affliction people are suffering. The Lord's heart sympathized with the disadvantaged, leading him to heal and feed thousands of his sheep: "He felt sympathy for them since they were like sheep without a shepherd."[182] Our shepherding also will be motivated by a sympathetic heart for those in need; our mercy will be similar to the Good Shepherd's loving care.[183] It is one of the signs that our wisdom is from the Lord (Jas 3:17). So we are to imitate him in our shepherding: "Be merciful, just as your Father is merciful" (Luke 6:36). This includes mercy shown to those who are spiritually or emotionally weak.[184]

When Jesus was asked about the command to "love your neighbor as yourself," he did not answer by giving an ethereal definition of love. He gave a specific action of deliverance flowing from a sympathetic heart. The Good Samaritan delivered the victim of crime to a safe location, personally bandaged and cared for the man, and then paid for the victim's bills until he was better (Luke 10:33–37). Love and service is like that, humbly putting the needs of others before our own. Jesus said he had come to serve, not to be served and showed what that meant by washing the disciples' feet with water (John 13:14–16) and washing our hearts with his blood.

> Whoever wants to be first among you must become your slave, just as the Son of Man came not to be served but to serve and give his life as a ransom for many.[185]

When showing mercy, most often we are giving something tangible. Having a sympathetic heart is of no value without offering real relief to others if we are at all able to do so (Jas 2:15–16).

Delivering others by sharing with them is expected[186] because they are immediate family (1 Tim 5:4, 16), or they are spending their time ministering to others,[187] or

---

181. Matt 6:12 // Luke 11:4; also, Luke 6:36–38; 17:3–4

182. Matt 9:36; Mark 6:34; also, Matt 15:32 // Mark 8:2; Matt 14:14; 20:34; Mark 1:41; Luke 7:13; Jas 5:11

183. Rom 12:8; Phil 2:1; Col 3:12; 1 Pet 3:8

184. 1 Thess 5:14; Jude 22–23

185. Matt 20:26–28 // Mark 10:43–45 // Luke 22:26–27; also, Matt 23:11; Mark 9:35

186. Acts 2:11:27–30; Rom 12:13; 2 Cor 8:10–11; 1 Tim 6:18; Heb 13:16

187. Luke 8:1–3; Acts 18:3, 5; 2 Cor 11:8; Gal 6:6; Phil 2:25–30; 4:14–18; Heb 13:3; 3 John 5–8; 3 John 7–8

they are needy for any number of other reasons.[188] We must be cheerful givers who give a lot![189] The return from our giving increases the more we give since the Lord says, "It is more of a blessing to give than to receive" (Acts 20:35). Christ the king addressed some of these in the most personal way:

> When I was hungry you gave me food; I was thirsty and you gave me a drink; I was a stranger and you invited me in; I was naked and you clothed me; I was sick and you cared for me; I was in prison and you came to visit me ... Whatever you did for one of the least of my brothers and sisters, you did for me.[190]

The King promises that the person who gives in this way will inherit the Kingdom: "He will not lose his reward."[191]

God is owed everything we have because it belongs to him anyway, so he deserves it all to be "gifted" back to him. A way to give back to the Lord is to give to his choice of receivers, not to him directly. Giving to the poor is giving to him. So Christ tells us that we should be ready, if called to do so, to sell all we have to give to the poor.[192] But if we are not called to give everything, then still, we are to give generously for the needs of the less fortunate.[193] The world's foolishness tells us that if you give things away, you will have less. However, Proverbs teaches, "Whoever is generous to the poor lends to the Lord and will be repaid by him for it" (19:17). Christ identifies that repayment as nothing less than being made an inheritor of his kingdom.[194]

There are some further inconveniences that come from being merciful. We are reminded of the Old Testament laws instructing to give to those who ask without expecting interest, and this is true even toward our enemies![195] Even if something is stolen, we are not to demand it back (Luke 6:30). Rather than inviting to dinner those who have the luxury to come or not, we are to invite those who have the need to come: the poor, crippled, and blind (Luke 14:12–14, 21–24). The handicapped were certainly in the Lord's view when he was with us, healing many of them. Not only the handicapped but prisoners[196] and the oppressed were to find his coming a relief to their challenges. Christ says he was the fulfillment of the Old Testament's anticipation of the One:

> The Spirit of the Lord ... has anointed me to preach good news to the poor. He has sent me to preach freedom for prisoners and sight for the blind, to set the oppressed free. Luke 4:18

---

188. Acts 2:44–45; 4:34–35; 11:29–30; 1 John 3:17
189. Matt 5:42; Rom 12:8; 2 Cor 8:3, 12; 9:6–8
190. Matt 25:35–36, 40; also, Matt 18:5 // Mark 9:37 // Luke 9:48
191. Matt 25:34; also, 10:42 // Mark 9:41; Luke 6:38; 2 Cor 9:6–11
192. Matt 19:21; Mark 10:21; Luke 12:15, 33; 14:33
193. Acts 20:35; Eph 4:28; Luke 3:11; 11:41; 19:8–9; Rom 12:13; 15:26–27; Gal 2:10; 1 Tim 5:9–10
194. Matt 19:29 // Mark 10:17, 21 // Luke 10:25, 28; Luke 18:18; Titus 3:7; Jas 2:5
195. Luke 6:30, 35 // Matt 5:42
196. Heb 10:34; 13:3

And we too are to be the channels for relief through our direct participation in their deliverance.

Widows and children were the vulnerable ones in both Testaments, and their care has always been a great concern to the Lord. The church was told to care for widows meeting certain criteria.[197] These were the pitiable women who certain Jewish leaders abused and stole homes from.[198] Jesus wanted the children as near to him as the adults, and he blessed them when they came to him.[199] He also gave grave warnings to those who might mistreat them.[200] Our mercy is so important that the Lord prefers it over religious compliance with sacrificial and festal laws.[201]

The believer is called to meet the needs of the afflicted, even those who are not deserving of our mercy, such as our enemies.[202] This is what "grace" is—giving to others what they do not deserve. We have to remember that "while we were enemies, we were reconciled to God through His Son's death" (Rom 5:10).

FORGIVING OTHERS

The Lord's forgiveness is the most relieving of all his acts of deliverance. He not only forgives us permanently when we are justified, but he forgives us when we humbly and routinely confess our sins committed after our justification. This too was discussed at length in the section on God's deliverance of his people and the believer in chapters 9 and 10.

The patience and love of those who forgive those who have sinned against them prove one to be humble and righteous. They do not stir up strife, even between friends; they tolerate petty slander; they do not prove a vindictive spirit publicly. Rather, they attract honor and respect.[203] The wise understand that they should be forgiving of others' sins as God forgives them; "Whoever hides his sins does not prosper, but whoever confesses and repents finds mercy" (Prov 28:13).

God's forgiveness of our sins is beyond our understanding. His depth and wholeness of moral holiness is beyond our comprehension, so we have no idea how distant we are from that infinite righteousness. His forgiving heart sets such a high and unreachable level that there can be no exaggeration in how richly he forgives us. Consequently, there is no case when we should not forgive others, it can never be given too often.[204] At one point Jesus says the frequency should be seven times, a measurement

---

197. Acts 6:1; 1 Tim 5:3–16; Jas 1:27
198. Mark 12:38–40 // Matt 23:14 // Luke 20:46–47
199. Matt 19:14–15 // Mark 10:14–16 // Luke 18:16–17; also, Jas 1:27
200. Matt 18:5–6, 10 // Luke 9:47–48; 17:2
201. Matt 9:13; 12:7
202. Matt 5:44; Luke 6:27, 30, 35; Rom 12:20
203. Prov 10:12; 12:16; 17:9; 18:19; 19:11; 24:28–29
204. Eph. 4:32; 2 Tim 2:24

in itself that should have been adequate (Luke 17:3–4). But when Peter wants to make sure this is the standard, Christ tells him that setting the bar literally at seven misses the whole point. Christ then increases the exaggeration to 490 times of forgiveness (Matt 18:21–22).

Forgiving others is part of our shepherding and delivering responsibilities. Forgiveness means that there has been an offense that justice alone would not warrant being forgiven. But the Lord's grace is our model for delivering others mercifully by our forgiveness. Christ told his disciples that whomever they forgave, he would forgive (John 20:23). That is our shepherding blessing that he allows us to do with him. That is the eternal design: God shepherds shepherding humanity. So God shepherds others through our forgiveness of them. And Paul adds another link in the shepherding chain by following the example of Christ: "Whoever you forgive for anything I will forgive too" (2 Cor 2:10): Christ forgives whom we forgive, and we should forgive those whom others have forgiven as well.

Christ emphasizes forgiveness in the Lord's Prayer, commenting on it a bit more than other parts of the prayer, and it is an ominous comment. The words of the prayer foreshadow the Father's conditions for forgiveness: "Forgive our debts, as we have forgiven our debtors."[205] But the subtle word, "as" in the prayer introduces a critical condition when the Lord says only a couple sentences later, "If you forgive others their sins, your heavenly Father will forgive you. But if you do not forgive others, your Father will not forgive your sins (Matt 6:14–15)[206]

In fact, Christ devotes an entire parable to this condition for our forgiveness. A king forgave the debt of a lord who mercilessly did not forgive the inconsiderable debt of his slave. For withholding forgiveness, the lord was given over to torturers until he paid back the king in full. The parable then concludes: "This is what my heavenly Father will do to each of you if you do not sincerely forgive your brother" (Matt 18:23–35).

Our forgiveness of others does something for the forgiven. It delivers them from anxiety and embarrassment. God's forgiveness of us leads us to relief and peace, and that is the same result for those whom we forgive. Love must be extended to an offending brother or sister so they do not end up depressed (2 Cor 2:6–8). Also, if someone has sinned against us, we are to go to them privately to discuss the matter, not broadcast the offense to everyone. Give the offender a chance to make it right and avoid public scrutiny.[207]

Another extreme application of forgiveness is that we are to love our enemies. Though they might deserve hatred and vengeance, they are to be loved and forgiven. We not only forgive them, but we also bless them with good things like food, drink, and our prayers. Those persons could be our enemies for any number of reasons. They

---

205. Matt 6:12 // Luke 11:4
206. Also, Luke 6:36–37; Mark 11:25–26; Col 3:12–13
207. Matt 5:23–24; 18:15–16; Jas 5:19–20

may hit us, sue us, pull rank on us, cheat us, curse us, hate us, exploit, or persecute us. Nonetheless, we lovingly forgive them.[208] We have the best of models in Jesus and Stephen while they were dying cruel deaths by their enemies' hands:

> Stephen: "Lord, do not hold this sin against them." Acts 7:60

> Our Savior: "Forgive them Father; for they do not know what they are doing." Luke 23:34

It is important however to emphasize that forgiveness does not mean remaining the target of the abuser. We have a responsibility to minimize future violations against us.

JOY

To be joyful is a moral requirement, not just a benefit that comes from righteousness. "There is a time for weeping, but a time for laughing; a time for mourning, but a time for dancing" (Eccl 3:4). There were required celebrations where singing, dancing and festive fellowship were enjoyed.[209]

Joy was also to be pursued in the ordinary experiences of life: "The righteous sing and rejoice" (Prov 29:6). Proverbs and Ecclesiastes encourage happiness with one's wife.

> Rejoice in the wife of your youth. Prov 5:18

> Enjoy life with the woman whom you love. Eccl 9:9

Ecclesiastes is especially demanding that one enjoy life's basic activities.

> I know there is nothing better for humanity than to be happy and to do good in one's life . . . nothing is better than that one enjoys his activities. 3:12, 22

> In the pleasant days, be pleased. 7:14

> Eat your food with pleasure and drink your wine with joy since God has already approved your works. 9:7

> Certainly, if one lives many years, one should be pleased in all of them. 11:8

Enjoyment has its limitations however; happiness must be experienced responsibly and within moral boundaries since God does discipline his sheep as Ecclesiastes warns in the midst of encouraging a joyful life.

> Enjoy your youth, young man, and let your heart be pleased with your young days . . . *Yet know that God will bring you to account on these things.* So avoid grieving your heart and direct tragedy away from your body. 11:9–10

---

208. Matt 5:39–44 // Luke 6:27–37; Rom 12:14, 20; 2 Cor 11:19–20
209. 1 Chr 15:16; 2 Chr 29:30; Pss 33:3; 67:4; 81:1; 98:4

There is the joy that comes as a fruit of the Spirit and surfaces in our lives spontaneously. Yet, like other fruits, we are as morally responsible for being joyful as we are for being loving, kind, good, and self-controlled. The Old Testament commanded joy and so do Christ and the apostles. There are times when we are not joyful but the Bible does not expect us to remain permanently in sorrow or any consternation. We are to do something about it and to choose gladness.

> Always rejoice in the Lord; again, I say rejoice! Phil 4:4
>
> Rejoice. 2 Cor 13:11
>
> Be glad and rejoice with me. Phil 2:18
>
> Rejoice in the Lord! Phil 3:1
>
> Always rejoice. 1 Thess 5:16

To rejoice is a choice at times. Sometimes it is a natural reaction with no intention involved. At other times it is expected to be our reaction, even if it takes effort.

There are many things we are to rejoice about. We are joyful about our salvation; we rejoice when others rejoice—we share in their happiness; we rejoice in what is morally good; we are glad about Christ's victory and his marriage to the church; we celebrate God's judgment.[210] We call others to rejoice with us when we have found whatever was lost (Luke 15:6, 9, 32). Christ, James, and Peter call us to choose rejoicing rather than sorrow or despair when we are being persecuted or are experiencing severe trials.[211] We are obligated not only to do the right thing, but to be happy while doing it. We have seen that the Lord loves a cheerful, not a grudging giver (2 Cor 9:7). Our praise and thanksgiving to the Lord was discussed earlier as clear evidence of our joy for who the Lord is in all his glory and what he has done for us and for the rest of creation.

PEACE

We are also responsible for peace within our souls and in our surrounding relationships: "Seek peace, pursue it" (Ps 34:14). The Lord went a long way in the Old Testament toward making peace available and real for those who believed. The sacrifices, his perpetual love, and material provisions proved he wanted peace with his people and the believer. For instance, the "peace" offering involved a Communion-like fellowship over food with God and the community.[212]

"Those who promote peace have joy" (Prov 12:20), and peace as a moral attribute can be shown in one's ability to control one's anger: "Do not be quick to get angry for

---

210. Luke 10:20; Rom 12:15; 1 Cor 13:6; Rev 12:12; 18:20; 19:7
211. Matt 5:11–12 // Luke 6:22–23; 2 Cor 11:19–20; Heb 10:34; Jas 1:2; 1 Pet 1:6; 4:12–13
212. Lev 3:1–17; 7:11–34

anger rests in the belly of fools" (Eccl 7:9). The primary commission—our management of God's world around us—cannot be accomplished by individuals who cannot control themselves. Self-control and patience are more subtle, but more effective powers than tantrums or resentful remarks. During the parenthetical age, battles and contentions must occur for no other reason than to fight injustice, to curb territorial incursions, or to protect oneself, but "There is a time for battle, but a time for peace" (Eccl 3:8). Peace must be sought.

Wisdom instructions describe how peace is destroyed by the unwise, by their lack of restraint and impatience. Pride raises its head in outbursts of self-vindication and ugly demeaning of others: "Wrath and anger are cruel and overwhelming" (Prov 27:4). Anger's harm is not just the disruption it brings to others, but the debilitating arguments, strife, and divisions that it generates in relationships, and it can fester for years, even for life.[213] It is just better not to associate with those who cannot control their anger.[214]

Christ Jesus our Lord is the Prince of Peace who says, "Peace I leave you; my peace I give you."[215] He is the one through whom we have peace *with* the Trinity and peace *from* the Trinity.[216] As the Good Shepherd, he became the lamb himself to make this peace possible.

> The God of peace . . . brought back from the dead the great shepherd of the sheep, our Lord Jesus. Heb 13:20

Our source of peace is the Father, Son, and Spirit as the New Testament writers attested by enhancing the common ancient greeting, "grace and peace." Their letters' salutations and closings refer consistently to the Father and Son's peace.[217]

Peace is one of the fruits of the Spirit, an attribute of our delivered soul.[218] We learn to be content with whatever circumstances we encounter.[219] Peace is what God gives us when we have been relieved from the penalty of sin and are continually refreshed by the Spirit. However, again, we are not simply at peace; we are responsible to pursue peace. Our soul is to be overwhelmed and ruled by peace.[220] David, Paul, Peter, James, and the writer of Hebrews knew that peace must be pursued aggressively while we grow in righteousness.

> Seek peace, pursue it. Ps 34:14

---

213. Prov 10:12; 27:3; 29:8–9, 22; 30:32–33

214. Prov 22:24–25; 26:17

215. Isa 9:6; John 14:27

216. Acts 10:36; Rom 5:1; Eph 2:13–14; Phil 4:7, 9; Col 1:19–20; 1 Thess 5:23

217. Rom 1:7; 15:33; 2 Cor 1:2; 13:11; Gal 1:3; 6:16; Eph 1:2; 6:23; Phil 1:2; 4:7; Col 1:2; 3:15; 1 Thess 1:1; 5:23; 2 Thess 1:2; 3:16; 1 Tim 1:2; 2 Tim 1:2; Titus 1:4; Philem 1:3; Heb 13:20; 1 Pet 1:2; 5:14; 2 Pet 1:2; 3:14; 2 John 3; 3 John 15; Jude 1:2; Rev 1:4

218. Gal 5:22; Heb 12:11; Jas 3:17–18

219. Phil 4:11; 2 Thess 3:16

220. Rom 8:6; Col 3:15

> Pursue what makes peace. Rom 14:19
>
> Pursue righteousness, faith, love and peace. 2 Tim 2:22
>
> Pursue peace with everyone. Heb 12:14
>
> Seek peace, pursue it. 1 Pet 3:11
>
> Peacemakers who sow peace reap righteousness. Jas 3:18

We pursue peace for ourselves, and we are particularly encouraged to promote peace with others and among others. We remember from Proverbs that "Those who promote peace are joyful" (Prov 12:20), and again, the New Testament follows with its own blessings on peacemakers: "Blessed are the peacemakers for they will be called the 'sons of God.'"[221]

Christians must live in peaceful subjection to all authorities, as we discussed under "Leadership," including the government.[222] Really, we are to be at peace with everyone possible,[223] and living morally in God's kingdom will add to the peace of the church and the world around us. However, Christ did make one major exception to his rule of peace: "I did not come to bring peace, but a sword"—Christ did not come to make peace with Satan's kingdom.[224] The Lord is returning with a sword to decimate his enemies: "Out of His mouth came a sharp two-edged sword" (Rev 1:16). Our promotion of peace is not with the dark kingdom. We must resist that kingdom and subvert it as often as possible. Too many moral battles are lost in spiritual warfare by a foolish pursuit of peace in our life which amounts to spiritual apathy and laziness. Rather, the victorious words for engaging Satan and his minions are, "The God of peace will swiftly crush Satan under your feet!" (Rom 16:20). Christ assured us, "I have told you this so you will have peace in me . . . I have overcome the world" (John 16:33).

Uncontrolled and foolish anger brings a certain end to our peace and the peace of others around us. We will not repeat here what was described earlier when speaking of moral "Communication" in the New Testament. The same peaceful harmony among the Trinity is what believers should pursue, for the Body of Christ is a witness to the world of the emotional and spiritual health that comes from accepting Christ as Savior and King.[225]

Furthermore, quarrels and divisions also destroy the Lord's peace in our hearts and within our believing community.[226] Divisions may not be driven by anger, but they often are. The main reason for strife and quarrels in the New Testament com-

---

221. Matt 5:9; also, 23–26; Rom 14:19; Jas 3:18
222. Rom 13:1–3, 1 Tim 2:1–2; 1 Pet 2:13–17
223. Rom 12:18; Titus 3:2; Heb 12:14
224. Matt 10:34 // Luke 12:51
225. Mark 9:50; John 17:20–23; Rom 14:19; 1 Cor 7:15; 2 Cor 13:11; Eph 4:1–3; Phil 4:2; 1 Thess 5:13
226. 1 Cor 1:10–11; 12:25

munity was jealousy. Though we might camouflage our jealousies with sophisticated words and conversation, what is hidden is a heart competing for the attention or status that others have.[227]

Another subtle excuse for divisions and quarrels is to maintain the "doctrinal purity" of the church. Foolish theological disputes can be given the grandest rationale. But that rationale, will not excuse any vicious and hurtful results arising from doctrinal controversies. Such arguments do not edify, but rather stultify the believing community's spiritual and numerical growth. One is to fight and even die for Christ and the Truth, but far too many arguments fall into the following categories.

> Controversial questions and arguments about words. 1 Tim 6:4
>
> Foolish, ignorant speculations. 2 Tim 2:23–24
>
> Foolish controversies, genealogies, conflicts, and fights about the Law. Titus 3:9

---

227. Rom 13:13; 1 Cor 3:2–3; 2 Cor 12:20; Gal 5:15, 19–21; Jas 4:1–2

14

Conclusion

WE STARTED THIS STUDY by asking what unifies all of our activities in any day. What single design contains the meaning to our life and our relationship with God and his creation, including our human relationships with family, friends, fellow believers, and foreign peoples whom we have never met? We have suggested that our daily experiences are not mere fragments in a chaotic world. Rather, there is a design which God initiated from the beginning, a design to which we contribute every day in substantial ways. We experience the blessings, deliverances, and discipline from God and others as we walk through our mornings, afternoons, and evening. And we bless, deliver, and discipline others on that same daily walk. Our lives become more and more unified and meaningful when we understand that it consists of shepherding others and others shepherding us.

God's eternal design, *God shepherds shepherding creation*, has been introduced as the pattern by which God has constructed and maintains his creation. His eternal design is the structure within which all creation operates and by which each created component fulfills its purpose. Initially, creation was to shepherd by blessing itself as God had blessed it. Yet, the interruption of the eternal design by Satan and humanity's Eden rebellion now requires a temporary "parenthetical design." In this parenthetical age, shepherding by God and by his creation is now more complicated since deliverance and discipline are now added to blessing as shepherding responsibilities.

We have seen that the pervasive biblical teaching that God and Christ Jesus are creation's shepherds goes far beyond Psalm 23 and John 10. We have referenced the thousands of passages that elaborate the eternal design in all its depth and breadth, showing how pervasive God's eternal design is in all reality.

The biblical model for creation's shepherding role, particularly humanity's role, is first revealed in the "primary commission" of Genesis 1:26–28 and reaffirmed throughout the Testaments, particularly in Genesis, Psalms, Isaiah, Daniel, Matthew, Paul, Hebrews and Revelation. The forceful word, "subdue," in the primary commission is qualified by Scripture's thorough description of subduing as wise and loving shepherding by blessing, delivering, and disciplining creation, yet with conviction and strength.

Conclusion

God in the Old Testament and the God/man Christ Jesus in the New Testament, model the primary commission for humanity. God multiplies himself by creating humans who carry his image and who, in turn, reproduce themselves in their children and subsequent generations. In this way God fills the earth with his images just as he expects humans to fill the earth with their descendants. Furthermore, Christ commanded his disciples to reproduce other disciples and fill the earth with believers from every nation. But this was not the ultimate goal. The goal is that these believers will submit to the shepherding Savior and King and obey all that he had commanded. By doing so, together, they constitute a global believing kingdom. Kingdoms are not made up of minds that believe theological truths. Kingdoms are populated by active residents and citizens who enjoy and comply with the cultural and moral standards that brings the peace and order God intended in Eden.

By restating the primary commission, the great commission, under Christ, continues the shepherding role of humanity which was started in Genesis. The primary commission is confirmed from the Bible's first chapter to its last chapter, from Genesis to David to Jesus to Paul to John's Revelation. But on a grander scale, the eternal design extends into New Earth as well, *forever*.

> Fill the earth and subdue the *earth* and rule. Gen 1:28

> You have created humanity to rule over your works. Ps 8:6

> He has given the *earth* to the humanity. Ps 115:16

> The meek will inherit the *earth*. Matt 5:5

> If we endure, we will also reign with God. 2 Tim 2:12

> You made them a kingdom and priests . . . they will reign on the *earth*. Rev 5:10

> They will reign *forever* and ever. Rev 22:5

Christ was commissioned as were Adam and Eve and their descendants, but his personal commission from the Father was to be the preeminent human Messiah. Since humanity has inadequately blessed God's creation, Christ was commissioned as the anointed human king to accomplish the primary commission on behalf of humanity. The eternal design has never faded. Christ inherited the Kingdom for humanity, but he shares that authority with us; we have inherited the Kingdom with all the accompanying rights, privileges and *responsibilities*. It is by Jesus Christ's divine and human authority, and the Holy Spirit's power that the Father will accomplish his plan of eternal perfection for his world just as the Trinity intended from the outset.

God's eternal design governs all non-human parts of reality as well. He shepherds the angelic spirits, both holy and fallen, and he shepherds the spirits of deceased believers by granting them residence in his presence. The dark kingdom is distressed and defeated, yet is still a powerful enemy of God's kingdom. But God keeps this sub-kingdom in check, holding it accountable yet using it to discipline and judge humanity according to his perfect justice. The holy angels bless, deliver, and discipline humanity as well, but the fallen angels are only anti-shepherds bent on abusing us and the rest of creation. Humanity's role as shepherds of the angels is restricted to fallen angels by resisting, judging, and crushing Satan and his minions.

God shepherds nature by blessing, delivering, and disciplining it too. Nature blesses, delivers, and disciplines itself through natural physical laws and the instincts of its flora and fauna; nature blesses, delivers, and disciplines humanity; and humanity blesses, delivers, and disciplines nature. For example, nature is implicated and cursed in Eden, but it is finally delivered from its groaning in New Earth when it will continue to be blessed by God and humanity.

Though the spirits and nature are immense parts of God's eternal design, God's interest in all peoples is the ultimate vision of both Testaments. That has been his interest all along. So he has continued to bless the nations lavishly: they carry his image, they are guided by conscience, and they have been appointed lands that are highly productive. The Lord also has delivered the peoples from adversity and has maintained social equilibrium through his appointed leaders and the common conscience. He also disciplines and judges all peoples.

Humanity shepherds itself as well. The interrelationships between all human social units are complex. For example, the individual, spouses, other family members, the believing community, larger people groups, and global humanity, all interact in ways that make our experiences harmonious and meaningful or contentious and nearly unbearable. Those relationships are successes or failures to the extent their cultures comply with God's moral guidelines inherent in his image and in the conscience of the society. The shepherding roles never change, however, they are always blessing, delivering, or disciplining unless the anti-shepherding roles of abusing, ignoring, or acing unjustly prevail to a lesser or greater degree.

The Lord shepherds his shepherding people in especially generous and loving ways, whether Israel or the church. They were formed as a people to model to the world how amazing God's relationship can be and will be with all peoples someday. Again, God's shepherding relationship is seen in great detail in the Bible's review of his blessings, deliverances, and acts of discipline for his people specifically. God is the Savior of all humanity by delivering it from adversity, but he is the Savior from sin only for his eternal people.

God's shepherding realm has been surveyed in this study by starting with the spirits and continuing through the concentric realms of the rest of creation: nature, humanity, the Lord's people, and the individual believer. As expected, blessing, deliverance, and discipline characterize the Lord's loving and intimate relationship with the believer. This is where our part in the eternal design becomes exciting because it becomes personal. We experience the Lord's blessing every new day; we live by his deliverance from sin and from adversity on a continual basis; we willingly subject ourselves to his discipline so that we will mature in righteousness and mirror his character even more closely.

How we mature in our shepherding role in the eternal design is the point of the Testaments. The teachings of the Law and wisdom instructions, the assessments of the prophets and meditations of the poets consist primarily of giving moral wisdom and following up with evaluations of human performance. Encouragements, promises, rewards, and blessings for obedience are God's preference, though too often the opposite reports are given to the Old Testament individual, Israel, and the peoples at large. The teachings of Christ and his apostles also consist primarily of giving moral wisdom and following up with evaluations. Again, encouragements, promises, rewards, and blessings for obedience are also offered, though rebukes are necessary for individuals and the churches.

Both Testaments are consistent in their ethical expectations. God's own righteousness has not changed so neither have his standards of righteousness. The New Testament ethics reaffirm the Old Testament commandments apart from the ceremonial laws which Christ, the new high priest, has made obsolete. So commands pertaining to leadership, economics and business, family, judicial fairness, protection of the disadvantaged, violence, and religious practice continue into the New Testament. Wisdom instructions affirm many Mosaic laws but cover additional ethical categories which emphasize attitudes and routine ethics for which there are no legal implications. Again, there is a clear consistency of ethical expectations between the Testaments in their wisdom teachings on leadership, obeying authority, diligence, communication, companions, health, prayer, humility, patience, kindness, mercy, forgiveness, joy, and peace.

We have come to the conclusion of our outline for a theology for believers and the church. A large share of single sentences in this book, especially those with footnoted biblical references, still remain incomplete in detailing the substance and implications of the Testaments' message about the Lord's relationship with his creation. But this is a start on framing a comprehensive theology that connects these wonderfully complex components of God's creation. He has designed them to work together to reveal his glorious nature and actions, and he honors us by offering us this partnership with him to shepherd his creation for eternity.

I remind you of these images from earlier in our study. They reflect the network of shepherding relationships which if kept in mind will help the believer see the complicated but manageable life that is committed to the eternal design and is committed to shepherd in the ways which the Lord has instructed.

SHEPHERDS: THE BELIEVER'S OUTLINE OF THEOLOGY

Basic Shepherding Realms

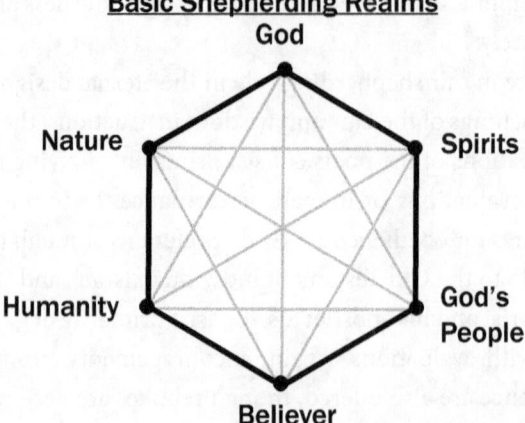

The Human Realms Bless, Deliver, and Discipline One Another

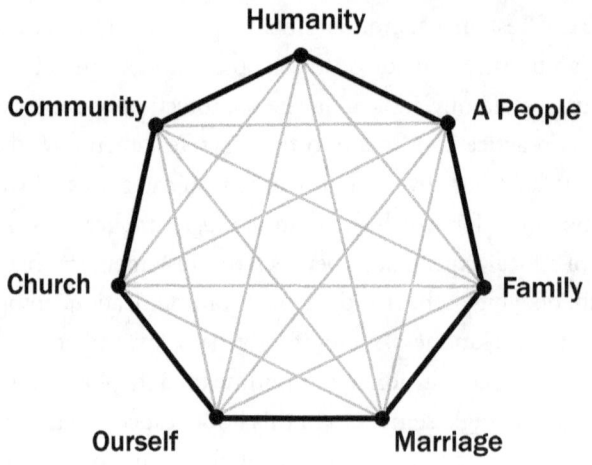

God and Creation Shepherds

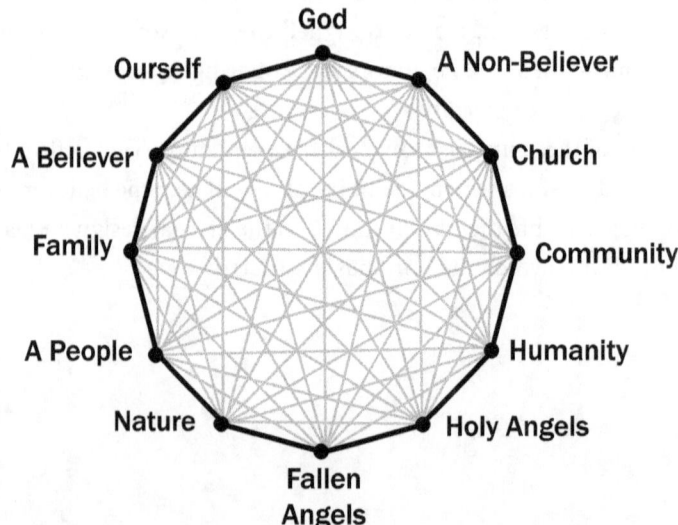

Conclusion

God's expansive and all-encompassing Kingdom is where we are blessed to live. But way beyond mere residence, God has designed us to assist in managing it. He has created us to shepherd instinctively and routinely. But it is always a matter of how godly our shepherding is, and whether we obey all that he has commanded us, just as Christ intended in his great commission.